Your Guide to the Art of Prediction

Wouldn't it be nice to know what the universe has in store for you, your family, and your friends?

- Will December bring romance?
- Is this a good year to start a family?
- Is April the best month to start a new business venture?
- Will June signal the start of a family problem?
- Is now the best time to ask your boss for a raise?
- Should you consider a career change in the coming year?

Let *The Instant Horoscope Predictor*—and the study of transits—be your guide to predicting the future! An invaluable aid for timing your actions and making decisions, transits define the relationship between where the planets are on any given day and where they were when you were born. With a look at your transits, you can discover what's in store for today, next month, or even a year from now.

The Instant Horoscope Predictor is an easy-to-use guide that will teach you to decipher the symbols in an ephemeris into clear, usable predictions. In addition, real-life studies of the lives and transits of Ted Bundy, Grace Kelly, Mata Hari, and Theodore Roosevelt will help you understand and master the art of astrological prediction.

About the Author

Julia Lupton Skalka has been a professional astrologer, writer, and teacher in the Washington, D.C., area since 1974. For over eighteen years, she has been a contributor to *Horoscope Magazine*, the leading astrology publication in the United States. Articles about her have appeared in the *Washington Post* and *USA Today*, and she has appeared on radio and television talk shows. Julia's text is used in two astrology software programs from Time Cycles Research, Inc.

To Write to the Author

If you wish to contact the author, please write to her in care of Llewellyn Worldwide, and we will forward your request. Both the author and the publisher appreciate hearing from you and learning of your enjoyment of this book and how it has helped you. Llewellyn Worldwide cannot guarantee that every letter written to the author can be answered, but all will be forwarded. Please write to:

Julia Lupton Skalka
c/o Llewellyn Worldwide
P.O. Box 64383, Dept. K668-8, St. Paul, MN 55164-0383, U.S.A.
email: lupton@mindspring.com

Please enclose a self-addressed, stamped envelope or $1.00 to cover costs.
If outside the U.S.A., enclose international postal reply coupon.

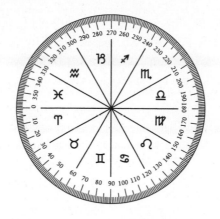

The Instant Horoscope Predictor

Find Your Future Fast

JULIA LUPTON SKALKA

1998
Llewellyn Publications
St. Paul, Minnesota, U.S.A. 55164-0383

FIRST EDITION
Second Printing 1998
Cover design by Llewellyn Art Department
Book design by Susan Van Sant
Editing and layout by Ken Schubert
Astrology charts generated through *Io Horoscope* by Time Cycles Research,
    27 Dimmock Road, Waterford, CT 06385
Ephemeris pages courtesy of Time Cycles Research

Library of Congress Cataloging-in-Publication Data
Skalka, Julia Lupton
    Instant horoscope predictor : find your future fast / Julia Lupton Skalka
        p.   cm.
    Includes bibliographical references.
    ISBN 1–56718–668–8 (trade paper)
        1. Horoscopes. 2. Transits—Miscellanea. I. Title.
BF1728.A2S537   1997
133.5'4—dc21

Llewellyn Publications
A Division of Llewellyn Worldwide, Ltd.
P.O. 64383, Dept. K668-8 St. Paul, MN 55164-0383

Printed in the United States of America

DEDICATION

For Malvina, a gentle Leo of great dignity and courage.
Her heart failed to sustain her life, but she lives on in
the hearts of those who loved her.

ACKNOWLEDGEMENTS

The Instant Horoscope Predictor is the companion to *The Instant Horoscope Reader*, and I am in debt to some of the same people for this book who assisted me in the process of writing the first one. The valuable associates and friends that I must thank once again are Julia Wagner, former Editor-in-Chief of *Horoscope Magazine*, and Dennis Haskell and his staff at Time Cycles Research. Julia Wagner is every writer's dream of an editor who patiently imposes standards of good writing on endless pages of text. She is and continues to be a constant inspiration for my astrological outpourings. Mr. Haskell's Io series of astrology programs contains the report writer on which *The Instant Horoscope Predictor* is based. The Io Forecast program is a miracle of efficiency, allowing me to quickly calculate and print the many years of transits that were necessary to examine the lives and events of the four famous personalities presented in Chapter Twelve. Without Io Forecast, these transits would have taken me many months to compute by hand.

Grateful thanks must go to Lauren Crasco, who, having helped me complete the first book, was brave enough to accept the same tasks with the second. I also want to give special thanks to Susan Borden, who added her editorial skills to my writing efforts. The laughter and good humor that Lauren and Susan brought to our sessions kept discouragement and fatigue safely at bay. Andrew Suthers uncomplainingly accepted his role of checking the many tables, and he deserves my thanks for his kind attention. Finally, I would like to thank my family—Stan, Aaron, David, and Karen—who patiently read various portions of the manuscript, listened to my complaints, and provided me with the love and encouragement that are indispensable to every writer.

CONTENTS

ILLUSTRATIONS VIII

TABLES X

PREFACE XIII

Chapter One: BASIC CONCEPTS 1

Chapter Two: TRANSIT SUN ASPECTS TO THE NATAL PLANETS 39

Chapter Three: TRANSIT MERCURY ASPECTS TO THE NATAL PLANETS . . . 59

Chapter Four: TRANSIT VENUS ASPECTS TO THE NATAL PLANETS 79

Chapter Five: TRANSIT MARS ASPECTS TO THE NATAL PLANETS 101

Chapter Six: TRANSIT JUPITER ASPECTS TO THE NATAL PLANETS 123

Chapter Seven: TRANSIT SATURN ASPECTS TO THE NATAL PLANETS 143

Chapter Eight: TRANSIT URANUS ASPECTS TO THE NATAL PLANETS 167

Chapter Nine: TRANSIT NEPTUNE ASPECTS TO THE NATAL PLANETS 197

Chapter Ten: TRANSIT PLUTO ASPECTS TO THE NATAL PLANETS 223

Chapter Eleven: TRANSIT PLANETS THROUGH THE NATAL HOUSES 249

Chapter Twelve: TRANSITS IN THE NATAL CHART: THE ART OF PREDICTION 319

Appendix A: EPHEMERIS 397

Appendix B: ASTROLOGICAL SOFTWARE AND CHART SERVICES 427

Appendix C: BIRTH DATA SOURCES 428

BIBLIOGRAPHY 429

ENDNOTES 433

PERMISSIONS 439

ILLUSTRATIONS

Figure 1.1: Zodiacal Map showing the Twelve Signs 2

Figure 1.2: Sun's Entry into the Signs 16

Figure 1.3: Zodiacal Circle 29

Figure 1.4: Opposing Signs 31

Figure 1.5: Signs that trine 32

Figure 1.6: Signs that Square 33

Figure 1.7: Signs that Sextile 34

Figure 12.1: Transit Examples 321

Figure 12.2: Ted Bundy's Natal Chart 323

Figure 12.3: Ted Bundy's 1961–1965 Transits 325

Figure 12.4: Ted Bundy's 1965–1970 Transits 327

Figure 12.5: Ted Bundy's 1971–1973 Transits 330

Figure 12.6: Ted Bundy's 1973–1978 Transits 332

Figure 12.7: Grace Kelly's Natal Chart 335

Figure 12.8: Grace Kelly's 1946–1949 Transits 337

Figure 12.9: Grace Kelly's 1950–1955 Transits 339

Figure 12.10: Grace Kelly's 1956–1965 Transits 343

Figure 12.11: Grace Kelly's 1966–1976 Transits 345

Figure 12.12: Grace Kelly's 1976–1982 Transits 348

Figure 12.13: Mata Hari's Natal Chart 352

Figure 12.14: Mata Hari's 1889–1896 transits 354

Figure 12.15: Mata Hari's 1897–1904 transits 358

ILLUSTRATIONS

Figure 12.16: MATA HARI'S 1905–1914 TRANSITS 364

Figure 12.17: MATA HARI'S 1914–1917 TRANSITS 368

Figure 12.18: THEODORE ROOSEVELT'S NATAL CHART 373

Figure 12.19: THEODORE ROOSEVELT'S 1878–1885 TRANSITS 376

Figure 12.20: THEODORE ROOSEVELT'S 1886–1896 TRANSITS 382

Figure 12.21: THEODORE ROOSEVELT'S 1897–1900 TRANSITS 390

Figure 12.22: THEODORE ROOSEVELT'S 1901–1909 TRANSITS 394

TABLES

Table 1: Signs and their Symbols 12

Table 2: Planets and their Symbols................................. 12

Table 3: Signs and their Planetary Rulers 13

Table 4: The Elements.. 14

Table 5: The Qualities 14

Table 6: Transit Cycles of the Planets............................ 15

Table 7: Saturn's transit through Taurus: 1969–1972 19

Table 8: Mercury Retrograde Periods: 1990 through 1999 21

Table 9: Venus Retrograde Periods: 1980 through 1999 22

Table 10: Mars Retrograde Periods: 1969 through 1999........... 23

Table 11: Jupiter Retrograde Periods: 1980 through 1999 24

Table 12: Saturn Retrograde Periods: 1980 through 1999........ 25

Table 13: Uranus Retrograde Periods: 1980 through 1999 26

Table 14: Neptune Retrograde Periods: 1980 through 1999 27

Table 15: Pluto Retrograde Periods: 1980 through 1999......... 28

Table 16: Planetary Aspects and their Symbols.................... 30

Table 17: Transit Uranus Conjunctions to Natal Neptune 171

Table 18: Transit Uranus Conjunctions to Natal Pluto........ 172

Table 19: Transit Uranus Sextiles to Natal Uranus............. 176

Table 20: Transit Uranus Sextiles to Natal Neptune 177

Table 21: Transit Uranus Sextiles to Natal Pluto 178

Table 22: Transit Uranus Squares to Natal Uranus 183

TABLES

Table 23: TRANSIT URANUS SQUARES TO NATAL NEPTUNE 184

Table 24: TRANSIT URANUS SQUARES TO NATAL PLUTO 185

Table 25: TRANSIT URANUS TRINES TO NATAL URANUS 189

Table 26: TRANSIT URANUS TRINES TO NATAL NEPTUNE 190

Table 27: TRANSIT URANUS TRINES TO NATAL PLUTO 191

Table 28: TRANSIT URANUS OPPOSITIONS TO NATAL NEPTUNE 195

Table 29: TRANSIT URANUS OPPOSITIONS TO NATAL PLUTO 196

Table 30: TRANSIT NEPTUNE CONJUNCTIONS TO NATAL URANUS 201

Table 31: TRANSIT NEPTUNE CONJUNCTIONS TO NATAL PLUTO 203

Table 32: TRANSIT NEPTUNE SEXTILES TO NATAL URANUS 206

Table 33: TRANSIT NEPTUNE SQUARES TO NATAL URANUS 210

Table 34: TRANSIT NEPTUNE SQUARES TO NATAL PLUTO 211

Table 35: TRANSIT NEPTUNE TRINES TO NATAL URANUS 215

Table 36: TRANSIT NEPTUNE TRINES TO NATAL PLUTO 216

Table 37: TRANSIT NEPTUNE OPPOSITIONS TO NATAL URANUS 220

Table 38: TRANSIT NEPTUNE OPPOSITIONS TO NATAL PLUTO 221

Table 39: TRANSIT PLUTO CONJUNCTIONS TO NATAL URANUS 227

Table 40: TRANSIT PLUTO CONJUNCTIONS TO NATAL NEPTUNE 228

Table 41: TRANSIT PLUTO SEXTILES TO NATAL URANUS 231

Table 42: TRANSIT PLUTO SEXTILES TO NATAL NEPTUNE 232

Table 43: TRANSIT PLUTO SEXTILES TO NATAL PLUTO 233

Table 44: TRANSIT PLUTO SQUARES TO NATAL URANUS 236

TABLES

Table 45: Transit Pluto Squares to Natal Neptune 237

Table 46: Transit Pluto Squares to Natal Pluto 237

Table 47: Transit Pluto Trines to Natal Uranus 241

Table 48: Transit Pluto Trines to Natal Neptune 242

Table 49: Transit Pluto Trines to Natal Pluto 243

Table 50: Transit Pluto Oppositions to Natal Uranus 247

Table 51: Transit Pluto Oppositions to Natal Neptune 247

Table 52: Transit Pluto Oppositions to Natal Pluto 248

Preface

From origins long buried with the ancient civilizations of Sumer, Akkad, and Babylonia, astrology and those who labored in its service have followed more than one path. Observing the cycles of the Sun, Moon, and planets, early astrologers began to correlate these celestial cycles with such natural phenomena as weather, deluge, fire, earthquake, and plague. Eventually they discovered relationships between celestial cycles and the earthly reigns of monarchs and governments and the endless battles they waged. Astrologers observed the array of human behavior and personality traits and learned to identify them in the planetary patterns of a chart cast for an individual's birth. Astrology that focused solely on planetary movements evolved into the science of astronomy. The study of correlations between celestial cycles and terrestrial activities evolved into different branches of astrology. For example, the celestial cycles associated with war, politics, economics, business, and social movements are the focus of mundane astrology. Natural astrology involves the study of weather and other natural phenomena. Interpreting the answer to a specific question from a chart cast for the moment the question is asked or making a judgment of a specific situation from a chart cast for the moment it occurs is the practice of horary astrology. Determining the best time to take certain actions is the function of electional astrology. In spite of the trivial nature often accorded it by those who are ignorant of its merit, astrology provides valuable insights and information to meteorologists, farmers, animal breeders, politicians, economists, stock and commodity brokers, and other professionals. The study of human traits and behavior associated with planetary positions has evolved into a personalized astrology that gives each of us an accurate, in-depth profile of ourselves and provides modern psychologists and sociologists with an amazingly comprehensive diagnostic tool.

In ancient times as the cycles of the Sun, Moon, and planets gradually became known and therefore predictable, it seemed reasonable to assume that weather and other phenomena that coincided with these cycles could be studied and consequently predicted. Surely it would be helpful to the farmer ready to plant crops and the traveler about to begin a journey if an astrologer informed them of potential weather conditions. Indeed, might not any action be as predictable as the planetary pattern with which it was associated? All branches of astrology engage in predictions. Astronomers calculate the course of each planet for years in advance and astrologers are as busy now as they were in antiquity figuring out weather forecasts; charting the course of monetary trends, stock market prices, and political changes; and giving clients advice about which situations to avoid and which ones to pursue or discussing the strengths and weaknesses of their relationships.

Predictions are derived by professional astrologers who have attained a high level of proficiency and understanding. However, the lack of such necessary expertise has never been a deterrent to some people. Enter the fortune-teller. As much a bane to legitimate astrologers in modern times as they were in centuries past, crystal-ball gazers and tea-leaf prognosticators continue to advertise themselves as "astrologers" and offer "astrology" as part of their repertoire. It continues to be a struggle to convince the public that *the professional astrologer is not a fortune-teller*. Nor are astrological predictions based in any way on psychic ability. There are astrologers who may possess psychic skills, but they would be (or should be) the first ones to admit that it is never wise to confuse astrological predictions with psychic impressions.

If astrology held the formula for accurately and consistently predicting the outcome of every event, astrologers would no doubt rule the earth. Obviously there are limitations to what astrology can tell us about the future. Essentially astrology is the art of recognizing and assessing potentials. On the basis of current movements of the planets as they relate to a person's natal chart, it is possible to determine the potential situations that person is likely to encounter within a given time period. It is then up to the individual to ascertain which possibilities are relevant to his or her particular circumstances. Suppose, for example, that planetary aspects indicating difficulties with speculative ventures, children, pregnancy, creative projects, or vacation plans turn up in the natal chart of a bed-ridden, eighty-five-year old woman who never bore children. Obviously the possibility of misfortune regarding children, pregnancy, or vacation plans is irrelevant, but she is warned against wasting money on lottery tickets or risky investments. If she is a writer or artist, she should also heed the possibility of negative situations involving creative endeavors.

There is no mystery and nothing so complicated in the following chapters as to prevent readers from learning the planetary patterns that form the basis of all astrological predictions, including the one described above. What is important to remember is that human beings are not creatures in a maze to be led along the corridors of life by a piece of cheese. We do not make decisions based on a set of potential circumstances as though they were items on a dinner menu. That is not what astrology is about. It is about learning to use our experiences to grow intellectually and emotionally throughout life so that our actions are tempered by wisdom, love, and decency instead of desperation, hatred, and greed.

I have had many years to practice the art of teaching—as a science teacher in elementary school, as a chemistry and physics teacher in high school, and as a teacher of astrology in many places. The only thing I enjoy more than teaching is learning. I like to savor knowledge—to take it apart and put it back together again, to take my time and let it filter down through the layers of my consciousness. This is a luxury I like to give my students and my readers. *The Instant Horoscope Reader* and *The Instant Horoscope Predictor* are books that take their time. The basic nature of the contents may be some justification for their titles. Although the loss of a more creative approach is lamentable, writers and teachers of astrology are constrained to take one aspect at a time in cookbook fashion. One cannot, after all, understand a sentence without knowing the meaning of each word. This book is not meant to be an all-encompassing, comprehensive work. There are gaps. I have not, for example, discussed the transits of the Moon because her monthly flight is of such a rapid and recurring nature. I have not explained the process of chart calculations simply because experience convinces me that most students require a teacher on hand to calm the fear that invariably arises when they are confronted with the rigors of universal time, interpolation, and logarithms. Nor have I addressed any pages to the lunar nodes, declinations, parallels, aspects to the angles, and progressions. I do not wish to minimize the importance of any of these subjects. Indeed, these and a wealth of other information can be added to what I have presented here. Nevertheless, I believe that what I have chosen to include is more than enough material for beginning and even intermediate students to investigate and understand. Of course, the descriptions in astrology books are only a beginning. Students should continually add to their understanding by reading biographical accounts of famous people and by keeping notebooks of their personal observations and experiences.

Chapter One

Basic Concepts

Who has not looked up at night and admired the silver Moon caught in a tapestry of stars? Tonight, after the Sun has set and the Moon has risen high enough to become bright, go out and marvel at the celestial drama. Take a child or two along to share the experience. Here and there among the stars you might catch sight of Mercury's tiny spark, the radiance of Venus, the reddish fire of Mars, the splendid light of Jupiter, or the glimmer of far-off Saturn. Observe the sky at different times of the year and at different hours of the night, and you will soon learn to recognize the planets as they trace their paths on the sky's darkened tableau. Eventually each planet's course ventures into the daytime reaches of the Sun, whose brilliance obscures it from our view. Though we cannot see the planets at such times, we know exactly where they are and when we can expect them to once again emerge as starlight companions of the Moon.

In astrology the sky is our celestial blackboard, a panoramic map of the heavens as it is seen from the earth and on which we follow the cycles of the Sun, Moon, and planets. On our map, the broad realm of the sky is divided into twelve sections, each section represented by one of the signs of the zodiac. The signs, which always appear in the same order, start with Aries, followed by Taurus, Gemini, Cancer, Leo, Virgo, Libra, Scorpio, Sagittarius, Capricorn, Aquarius, and

Pisces. The paths of the planets are circular, so our map is also a circle, as shown in Figure 1.1. Every circle has 360 degrees, so each of the twelve signs contains thirty degrees. It is important to note that, for the sake of convenience, when astrologers refer to the "planets" and their movements through the zodiac, they include the Sun and Moon.

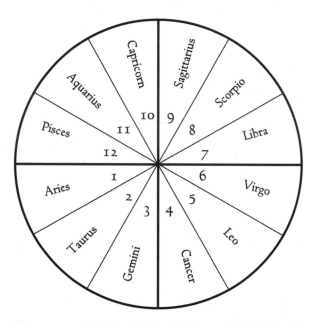

Figure 1.1: Zodiacal Map Showing the Twelve Signs

The meanings of the planets and the signs are basic concepts in learning to interpret natal charts and they are equally important in making predictions. We all want to know what kind of circumstances lie ahead. Will it be a favorable atmosphere in which much can be accomplished or an environment in which ill-timed acts can lead to disaster? To know this, we have to understand the nature of the signs.

THE ASTROLOGICAL SIGNS

Delineating the signs was covered in *The Instant Horoscope Reader* and it is appropriate to reintroduce that material in the following paragraphs. The twelve signs of the zodiac are unique fields of energy, energy that is descriptive of the cycle of life but that also represents the here and now. As you will see, the zodiacal energy is characterized in a different way for each sign.

ARIES

Aries is the first sign. The environment in this part of the zodiac is raw, undifferentiated energy. Action that feeds on itself—action for action's sake. Think of New York, Hong Kong, and other places where there is constant activity. Everywhere there is change, one building is going up while another is being torn down. Everything is available on the spot—instant gratification, no questions asked. Everyone is in motion, and work or play is attacked with equal enthusiasm. Imagine a crowded sports arena where there is so much commotion it is hard to tell the players from the spectators. Think of the courage, energy, and sometimes foolhardiness of those who are the first to venture into wild and hostile territory. Their actions allow others to come and settle the land that has been conquered. There is great passion here, a spontaneous outpouring of feelings and ideas turned into actions. As the first stage in the cycle of existence, Aries is the energy of the life force at the moment of its inception. It is the initial impulse through which the potential becomes actual, and it is therefore associated with the beginning of any cycle.

TAURUS

Unlike the pulsating, primal energy of the Aries environment, the second sign is a quiet atmosphere of focused energy. The fire of life that was generated in Aries is given opportunity to grow in Taurus, the second astrological sign. It is the energy of green pastures and fields of growing wheat or corn. It is the energy of heavy trucks carrying dirt out of great holes in the earth where buildings and homes will rise. Taurus is development and growth; its activity and energy are never random. There is also possession. Material goods are counted, weighed, and measured. Imagine storehouses of food and goods, Fort Knox and other stockpiles of gold and silver. Think of the bank-lined Bahnhofstrasse where the "gnomes of Zurich" guard the secret bank accounts of the world's wealthiest people. Feel the comfort of goosedown, the warmth of wool, and the softness of fine leather. As a stage in the cycle of existence, Taurus is the energy of physical contact, of form and structure.

GEMINI

As the third stage in the cycle of existence, Gemini is the mental energy of ideas, understanding, and communication. Borrowing from Descartes, the environment in Gemini might be described as, *Cogito Ergo Sum*, (I think, therefore I am). The life force arises in Aries, develops physically in Taurus, and is focused on awareness in Gemini. Language is learned, communication takes place. Information is acquired, processed, and traded. It is not the mental energy that creates libraries or universities. It does not seek wisdom. It wants to inform. It is energy turned to cleverness and imitation. It is the education of elementary school, and the trade school where basic skills are developed into arts or crafts. It is newspapers, magazines, and record-keeping. Think of community activities, neighbors, and gossip. Think of the postal system, business offices, meetings, and sales. It is local transportation: bicycles, taxicabs, and buses. It is physical and mental energy in a constant state of busyness—traffic in the streets, people running errands. Think of the energy of the wind that ripples the water and carries aloft the seeds of plants, the seeds of ideas, and the seeds of change from place to place in short bursts.

CANCER

The fourth astrological sign is Cancer, an environment totally dominated by emotional energy. The life force of Aries adapts to the physical world in Taurus, attains awareness in Gemini, and is focused on need and desire in the environment of Cancer. As a stage in the cycle of existence, the emotional energy introduced in Cancer is, after the creation of life itself, the strongest force of all. However, it is energy that requires nurturing before it can function and, therefore, constantly seeks to feed itself. It is immature and uncontrolled, bouncing back and forth between extremes. Protective, self-serving, and intolerant, it is strong enough to destroy whatever threatens it. It is also the positive energy of putting down roots, building strong foundations, raising families, bringing together those who share similar beliefs and common goals. It is sentimental, grasping, and amazingly successful. Because it does not exist outside the human spirit, it is the energy of all that is good and all that is evil. Emotional energy is, in fact, what gives us our unique place in the cosmos.

Leo

The environment of Leo, the fifth sign of the zodiac, is akin to the atmosphere of Aries. There is great stimulation and vitality in this energy, but it does not promote action for its own sake as it does in Aries. Leo is sustained and motivated activity. As part of the cycle of existence, Leo is energy that seeks to experience itself through re-creation. Beginning in Aries, the life force develops on a physical, mental, and emotional level. What was once the Aries spark has become a flame in Leo that adds new dimensions to the stages that preceded it. Leo's energy seeks to achieve great physical accomplishment and physical pleasure, to add humor and imagination to mental awareness, and to increase emotional capacity for enjoyment and inspiration. The energy in Leo requires recognition—it demands an audience. Uncontrolled, it is capable of consuming everything in its path. It is the energy of adventure and amusement, of noble gestures and grandiose schemes. It seeks freedom from the mundane in order to pursue the fantastic.

Virgo

The environment in Virgo, sixth sign of the zodiac, is much more subdued than Leo, though no less active in its own way. As part of the cycle of existence, Virgo is energy focused on gathering what has been gained and putting it to some higher purpose. Crops are harvested, skills are developed, information is organized, and desire is sacrificed in the line of duty. In this segment of the zodiac, virtue is its own reward. It is energy directed to the ordinary, to the carrying out of tasks, to weaving the fabric of life. It is the energy of household gods dedicated to the glory of the lint trap and the clean bathroom. It is the overseer of goods and provider of services. It is the necessary, that which is taken for granted and immediately missed when absent. Think of the pharmacy, the school, the local newspaper, the grocer, the tailor, and the traveling salesman. This is the energy of competence, cleverness, and expectation. It is energy too easily inhibited by stronger forces and trapped by its own standards.

Libra

Libra is the seventh sign. The mental energy that dominates Libra makes the environment in this part of the zodiac deceptively quiet. Physical and emotional activity are carefully weighed and measured. It is energy directed outward as well as inward in equal measure. Extremes are avoided. The middle course is always taken because when it is off-balance, this energy is paralyzed. The maturity gained in previous cycles is the energy in Libra focused on civility of behavior and attitude. As in Gemini, there is an emphasis on communication and ideas. In Libra, however, the energy is not as concerned with ideas and information as it is with the means by which they are shared—cooperation and interaction. Refinement and considered judgment hide the formidable strength of its strategy and manipulation. This is the environment of the general, not the foot soldier; the designer, not the builder; the judge, not the executioner. In the cycle of existence, Libra is energy that sustains the balance between the physical and mental, between spiritual and nonspiritual, and between the individual and society.

SCORPIO

From the mentally energized environment of Libra, we pass into the watery realm of Scorpio, the eighth zodiacal sign. Emotional energy is the ruling force here. It is not the obvious or wildly emotional environment of Cancer. Scorpio uses the balance acquired in Libra to exert control over the expression of its energy. It is more intense and more patient. It is the energy of observation, analysis, and penetration. It seeks to recognize its own motivation and behavior. It separates the relevant from the trivial, fathoms the depths, and unlocks the secrets. It is instincts and resourcefulness. As a stage in the cycle of existence, Scorpio is focused on emotional control as a means of becoming more powerful. The inclination to protect that prevails in Cancer is expanded in Scorpio's environment to the ultimate preservation, which is regeneration. It is the energy of transformation. It is development, conservation, and use of basic resources. Think of urban renewal, recycling, and waste management. Think of the cook, the butcher, the gardener, and the renovator.

SAGITTARIUS

Sagittarius is the ninth sign. The environment in this part of the zodiac is active, restless: an energy focused on the physical, intellectual, and emotional attainments acquired in previous stages. It seeks the total experience. Everything is the biggest and the boldest. It is adventure and passion, joy, and spiritual development. It turns information into knowledge and knowledge into truth. It is the creative force so dynamic and unique as to be almost a religious experience. It cannot or will not function when it is limited or confined. It is independent. The energy here is abundance, the grand gesture, exaggerated pageantry. Imagine a storm, thunder, and lightning. Think of universities and libraries, theaters, and museums. Think of publishers and art dealers. It is status-seeking, righteous, and fanatic. It is inspiring and prophetic. It is energy constantly reaching beyond its own environment. As part of the cycle of existence, Sagittarius is the spirit seeking its outer limits.

CAPRICORN

The energy of life has grown heavy by the time it reaches the tenth stage in the cycle of existence. Nothing is better suited to provide the proper focus at this stage than Capricorn, the zodiacal guardian of time and space. In this environment, the energy is focused on the big picture, the structure that contains the parts that make up the whole. It is the foundation. Imagine the bones that support the flesh and the walls that support the building. Think of the clock and the calendar, bound by the units of the time that they measure. The energy of Capricorn is the energy of limits, rules, and regulations that must be observed in order to be stable and to endure. It is the energy of authority and control. It is ambitious. Devious. Cunning. It is the end that justifies the means. It is longevity. The rewards of dedication and hard work. Its natural inclination is serious, formal, and never random. It is the energy of experience. It never assumes. It must merit what it attains, or suffer the consequences. It is patient. There is great and earthy passion, but never pleasure without responsibility. It is energy focused on the long term. Think of a virgin forest in awesome maturity, the pleasure of wine that has aged. Think of the richness of tradition and the legacy of remembrance.

AQUARIUS

From the mountains of Capricorn, the cycle of life passes into the ethereal environment of Aquarius, dominated by the energy of ideas and communication. The energy of the eleventh sign is focused on taking all that has been learned in previous cycles and making it function for all humankind. In this stage of existence, knowledge is transformed into principles and ideals. It is the energy of universal language and communication. This is a strange environment to the uninitiated because the principle force represents society but does not become society. Its task is to retain the many without sacrificing the one. If the uniqueness of one is lost, so is the uniqueness of all. It is energy unbiased, singular, and independent. It is communication that seeks the widest possible audience. Think of the radio, the telephone, the telegraph. Think of science, technology, and the computer. It is democratic and liberal, yet conservative and traditional. It is stability being upset by the unpredictable, and the unpredictable being made stable. It is the energy of groups and organizations who share the same interests and goals.

PISCES

The twelfth sign of the zodiac is Pisces. As the last stage in the cycle of existence, Pisces is the energy of the subconscious, and the power of spiritual and emotional ideals. It is an environment ruled by emotional energy—energy of a remarkable kind. Easily consumed by the action of fire, overwhelmed by the responsibility of earth, blown away by the air of confusion, and drowned in the water of need—it is able to survive them all. It is energy that must, however, devote itself to survival or risk its own destruction. Illusion is reality and reality is illusion in this environment. It is inner strength and unseen power. It is the energy of inner struggles and hidden dreams. Think of the fragile beauty and the incredible strength in a spider's web. Think of a flower growing out of a rock, and the world reflected in a rain drop.

THE PLANETS

Just as the energy of the signs represents the life cycle as well as the here and now, the planets also serve a dual role. They represent humanity in general as well as a single human being. In a natal chart, the planets embody the personality, temperament, and character traits of the individual. Outside the natal chart, the planets represent the behavior and experiences that all people share—physical pain and pleasure, emotional sorrow and joy, pride in human accomplishments and the shame of heinous acts, enjoyment of nature's bounty and the terror of earthquake, flood, famine, and fire. Early civilizations had only the power of their observation and imagination to cope with the awesome forces that surrounded them, so they created mythical gods and goddesses who controlled the universe and the lives of human beings. It was in these ancient days of thought and ideas that the planets were identified with gods and goddesses and the heavens became the theater in which they performed their roles. These mythical super beings also had human qualities, so, at least in part, they symbolized more powerful versions of men and women. Each planet was associated with a special nature that exemplified particular actions and circumstances and particular human traits and characteristics. The planets are no longer regarded as gods and goddesses, but this does not invalidate the drama that they once represented. Life still brings death, and all of our human needs and experiences are still the same. This is why we do not abandon what astrology has taught us.

SUN

The Sun is vitality and energy. The Sun is associated with pride—personal, public, and national pride. It describes leadership and acts of courage, loyalty, and integrity. It represents people with great influence or high position—supervisor, boss, president, king, as well as the government and similar agencies. The Sun signifies playfulness, leisure activities, and pleasurable pursuits. It also represents great ambitions and philanthropic enterprises. The sign Leo is ruled by the Sun.

MOON

The Moon represents emotional reactions and sensitivity. It describes fickleness and changeable moods, habits, needs, and desires. It is the public, public sentiment, public acceptance, and public rejection. The Moon is the collective subconscious, memory, intuition, and instincts. It is the rhythm and flow of daily life and its physical, emotional, and mental functions. The Moon represents food, diet, and acts of physical and emotional nurturing. It is infants and mothers. The Moon signifies homes, domestic environments, and domestic products. The sign Cancer is ruled by the Moon.

MERCURY

Mercury governs perceptions, mental outlook, and intellectual endeavors. It is information, facts, figures, and the spoken as well as the written word. It is the manner in which information is received and interpreted, as well as how and where learning and the exchange of information takes place. Mercury embodies ideas, opinions, and methods. It is perception and thought without judgment. Mercury describes the state and acts of youthfulness. It describes cleverness, imitation, physical dexterity, and mechanical skills. Mercury describes travel, transportation, and certain vehicles of transport: cars, trucks, bicycles, motorbikes, and roller skates. The signs Gemini and Virgo are ruled by Mercury.

VENUS

♀ Venus rules social attitudes, behavior, and interactions. It is physical beauty and gracefulness. It is aesthetic tastes and inclinations, artistic and musical talent, and related activities. Venus represents values, priorities, judgment, and moral sensitivities. It is the art of diplomacy and the spirit of cooperation. Venus is romantic adventure, love, companionship, marriage, partners, and allies. It describes merriment, luxuries, pursuit of physical ease, and sensual pleasure. Venus embodies females and female relationships. The signs Taurus and Libra are ruled by Venus.

MARS

♂ Mars is energy and efforts, physical force, power, and action. It describes strength and direction of physical force. Mars rules risky actions, competitiveness, and physical challenges. It is sexual drive and potency, aggressiveness, and the combative spirit. Mars signifies men, male relationships, and male associations. The sign Aries is ruled by Mars. Before Pluto was discovered, Mars also ruled Scorpio.

JUPITER

♃ Jupiter describes growth and expansion on many levels: physical, intellectual, spiritual, and cultural. It is the church, spiritual studies, and religious activities. It is the potential to reach beyond the ordinary, to exaggerate and enlarge. Jupiter is associated with good fortune, great wealth, material assets, professional and social status. It signifies enjoyment, optimism, and aspirations. It is sporting activities, horse racing, the theater, and art. It is related to clerics, fathers, actors, and politicians. The sign Sagittarius is ruled by Jupiter. Before the discovery of Neptune, Jupiter also ruled Pisces.

SATURN

Responsibilities, restrictions, obstacles, and limitations are the province of Saturn. It represents experience and maturity, hard work, and serious circumstances. It describes stability and longevity. Saturn is endurance, practicality, and conservative actions. Saturn governs elderly people, those who represent authority, and those who are strict, austere, and miserly. The sign Capricorn is ruled by Saturn. Before the discovery of Uranus, Saturn was also the ruler of Aquarius.

URANUS

Uranus rules freedom, independence, and originality of thought and expression. The status of situations in which Uranus is involved is subject to sudden changes and reversals. Uranus is associated with unpredictable and unexpected circumstances. It relates to the unusual or unique. It governs crowds, clubs, organizations and their activities, as well as the act of organizing. Uranus is science, technology, computers, and the media. The astrological sign Aquarius is ruled by Uranus.

NEPTUNE

Minority groups, criminals, the oppressed, and the misfits of society are connected with Neptune. It signifies despair, derangement, guilt, and persecution. Neptune is also charity and compassion as well as confinement, abandonment, and addiction. Neptune is sensitivity and psychic awareness. It rules visionaries and those who are glamorous and charismatic. Neptune represents heightened awareness, spirituality, abstract ideas, illusions, and disillusionment. It describes areas where things are not always what they seem. It represents spiritualism, mysticism, and certain ideals. The astrological sign Pisces is ruled by Neptune.

PLUTO

The power associated with Pluto is like atomic energy, it is never obvious until it is unleashed. Pluto represents intense energy. It describes physical, mental, and emotional power and control, the potency of sex, the violence and secrecy of rape or murder. It is hidden plots, espionage, coded messages, and spying. Assassins, kidnappers, and the underworld organizations are embodied by Pluto. It is total transformation, recuperation, rehabilitation, recycling, and renovation. Pluto is also linked to karma. The astrological sign Scorpio is ruled by Pluto.

ASTROLOGICAL SYMBOLS

It is easier to keep track of the planets and their various positions with shorthand symbols. Table 1 shows the symbols for each sign, and Table 2 depicts the symbols for the planets. Take time to familiarize yourself with the planets and signs and their symbols so that when you see such expressions as ☽♉ you know it means the Moon (☽) is in Taurus (♉), and a ☉♏ you know it means the Sun (☉) is in Scorpio (♏), and ☿♐ you know it means that Mercury (☿) is in Sagittarius (♐).

Aries	♈	Leo	♌	Sagittarius	♐
Taurus	♉	Virgo	♍	Capricorn	♑
Gemini	♊	Libra	♎	Aquarius	♒
Cancer	♋	Scorpio	♏	Pisces	♓

Table 1: Signs and their Symbols

Sun	☉	Moon	☽	Mercury	☿
Venus	♀	Mars	♂	Jupiter	♃
Saturn	♄	Uranus	♅	Neptune	♆
		Pluto	♇		

Table 2: Planets and their Symbols

PLANETARY RULERSHIP, ELEMENTS, AND QUALITIES

Planetary rulership of the astrological signs is worked out according to a system of compatible associations that are made between the planets and the signs. Table 3 lists the signs and their planetary rulers. Learning the nature and characteristics of each sign and each planet is the key to understanding how such a system was derived. A planet has a more powerful impact when it transits the sign (or signs) that it rules.

Sign	Ruler	Sign	Ruler
♈ is ruled by	♂	♎ is ruled by	♀
♉ is ruled by	♀	♏ is ruled by	♇
♊ is ruled by	☿	♐ is ruled by	♃
♋ is ruled by	☽	♑ is ruled by	♄
♌ is ruled by	☉	♒ is ruled by	♅
♍ is ruled by	☿	♓ is ruled by	♆

Table 3: Signs and their Planetary Rulers

In addition to the compatible associations they share with planets, the signs also share such associations with each other. To indicate the compatible nature that exists between certain signs, the signs are grouped into the *elements* and the *qualities*. If the majority of the transits are in fire signs, for example, it indicates a different energy in the general environment than would be described if the majority of transits happened to be in water signs. The same is true of the qualities. A *cardinal*-sign emphasis is different than when the majority of transits are found in *fixed* or *mutable* signs. Study these two groups and the categories within them to get a sense of the kind of energy that will be emphasized in the external environment.

The elements are fire, earth, air, and water (see Table 4). As a group, the energy of fire signs can be categorized as hasty, inspirational, initiatory, and active. The energy of earth signs as a group can be categorized as solid, tangible, materialistic, and purposeful. The energy of air signs as a group can be categorized as objective, analytical, and communicative. The energy of water signs as a group can be categorized as emotional, subjective, creative, and idealistic.

FIRE SIGNS	EARTH SIGNS	AIR SIGNS	WATER SIGNS
Aries ♈	Taurus ♉	Gemini ♊	Cancer ♋
Leo ♌	Virgo ♍	Libra ♎	Scorpio ♏
Sagittarius ♐	Capricorn ♑	Aquarius ♒	Pisces ♓

Table 4: The Elements

The qualities are cardinal, fixed, and mutable (see Table 5). When cardinal signs are emphasized, the energy is goal-oriented, self-directed, and authoritative. When fixed signs are emphasized, the energy is sustained, patient, and structured. When mutable signs are emphasized, the energy is adaptive, imitative, and changeable.

CARDINAL SIGNS	FIXED SIGNS	MUTABLE SIGNS
Aries ♈	Taurus ♉	Gemini ♊
Cancer ♋	Leo ♌	Virgo ♍
Libra ♎	Scorpio ♏	Sagittarius ♐
Capricorn ♑	Aquarius ♒	Pisces ♓

Table 5: The Qualities

Interpreting the planets in each sign means blending the characteristics of the planet with the special kind of energy associated with the sign. Learning to do this takes time, careful thought, and experience. As we move from interpreting an individual's natal chart to making predictions for that individual, we become more aware of how long the Sun, Moon, and planets appear in a sign and the time it takes them to complete their individual cycles through the zodiac. While the Sun's transit through the zodiac takes a year, the transit of the Moon is only about twenty-eight days. Table 6 lists the cycles or transits of the planets. The time that it takes each planet to complete one transit through the zodiac varies tremendously, from less than a month for the lunar cycle to 248 years for the cycle of slow-moving Pluto.

☽	transits the zodiac in approximately	28 days
☉	transits the zodiac in approximately	1 year
☿	transits the zodiac in approximately	1 year
♀	transits the zodiac in approximately	1 year
♂	transits the zodiac in approximately	22 months
♃	transits the zodiac in approximately	12 years
♄	transits the zodiac in approximately	29.5 years
♅	transits the zodiac in approximately	84 years
♆	transits the zodiac in approximately	165 years
♇	transits the zodiac in approximately	248 years

Table 6: Transit Cycles of the Planets

THE SOLAR MONTH VS. THE CALENDAR MONTH

The Sun appears in each sign for approximately one month, completing the zodiac in a year.(Of course, it is actually the earth that is moving around the Sun, but from the earth it appears as though it is the Sun that is moving. Astrology is based on celestial movements as they appear from the earth.) The Sun's journey through the zodiac begins each year when it appears at 0° Aries on or about March 20. Approximately one month later, the Sun has completed thirty degrees in Aries and begins its transit in Taurus. From Taurus, it continues through the rest of the signs until the following March when it completes the last degree of Pisces and is ready to begin its annual journey once again at 0° Aries. Each astrological sign represents a solar month, which begins not on the first day of the calendar month, but somewhere around the 20th when the Sun enters a sign. The zodiacal map in Figure 1.2 shows the date that the Sun enters each sign.

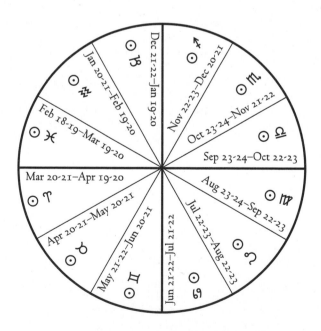

Figure 1.2: Sun's Entry into the Signs

THE DIFFERENCE BETWEEN TRANSITING PLANETS AND NATAL PLANETS

Most people know whether they are an Aries, Virgo, Capricorn, or whatever the astrological sign was when they were born. A person's astrological sign is also called their Sun sign because it indicates the Sun's location at birth. However, there are thirty degrees in each sign, so while most people know their Sun sign, they do not often know which degree of that sign the Sun occupied, or, for that matter, what sign and degree the Moon or any of the planets occupied when they were born. This is the information that comprises a person's horoscope or natal chart. Casting a chart requires the exact time, date, and location of birth. From this data, a natal chart is calculated showing the degree and sign of the Sun, Moon, Mercury, Venus, Mars, Jupiter, Saturn, Uranus, Neptune, and Pluto at the time of birth. The positions of planets, without reference to a particular chart, are referred to as transits. It is easy to find the location of transits by looking them up in an ephemeris, which is a daily or other periodic listing of the positions of the Sun, Moon, and planets. All ephemerides (plural for ephemeris) list planetary positions according to GMT (Greenwich Mean Time). The ephemeris in this book (see Appendix A) lists the date and time when planets enter the signs.

THE RELATIONSHIP BETWEEN TRANSITING PLANETS AND NATAL PLANETS

As the planets—each in their individual orbit and at their own speed—move through the zodiacal circle, they form geometric angles or *aspects* to one another. For example, when two planets are located in the same degree of the same sign, the aspect they form is a *conjunction*. In another instance, planets may be separated by as much as 180 degrees which puts them on opposite sides of the zodiacal circle. The aspect between them is an *opposition*. As transits move through the zodiac, they also form angles to the planets in a person's natal chart. This is a case of moving objects (transits) forming angles to stationary objects (natal planets). The movement of transits through the natal chart and the aspects they form to natal planets are significant factors in making predictions for an individual. Let us say, for example, that transit Jupiter is at 5° Libra and your natal Venus is at 5° Aquarius. The aspect that transit Jupiter makes to your natal Venus is a *trine*. Jupiter will keep moving through the rest of Libra while your natal Venus remains fixed at 5° Aquarius. However, at the time transit Jupiter trines your natal Venus, the potential is for favorable circumstances. What concepts are needed to explain this prediction and describe the kind of favorable circumstances it implies? There are four major considerations: the natal planet, the transiting planet, the aspect, and the house positions. The natal planet in this example is natal Venus. The meaning of natal Venus and other natal planets are mentioned briefly in context throughout this book, but understanding natal planets is part of learning how to interpret the horoscope which is covered in *The Instant Horoscope Reader*. The transit in this case is Jupiter, and the nature of Jupiter and the other transiting planets was described earlier. The aspect between transit Jupiter and natal Venus is a trine, which is explained along with the rest of the planetary aspects below. Even though (for the sake of brevity) I do not include them in this example, the house positions occupied by transit Jupiter and natal Venus are also important. Chapter Eleven discusses the transits in the natal houses.

Always remember that the planets do not cause things to happen. In the example, transit Jupiter trine your natal Venus only indicates the potential for certain situations: increased luck, growth, and optimism (transit Jupiter) may bring favorable circumstances (indicated by the trine) that favor you in matters of romance, marriage, partnership, and cooperative ventures (natal Venus). The biographical discussions of the four famous people in Chapter Twelve provide many detailed examples of how to assess all the potentials involved in making predictions.

HOW TO USE THIS BOOK

The material presented throughout this book will be more meaningful if you apply it to your natal chart and the charts of friends and family. Let us say you were born in 1960 with natal Sun in Taurus and you are going to read about transit Saturn conjunct natal Sun in Chapter Seven. Before you begin reading, refer to your natal chart or use the ephemeris in Appendix A to locate the position of Saturn when you were born. In 1960, Saturn was in Capricorn. Scan the following years as Saturn moved through Aquarius, Pisces, and Aries until 1969 when it entered Taurus on April 29. Table 7 represents the data from the ephemeris to help you follow Saturn as it made its way through Taurus.

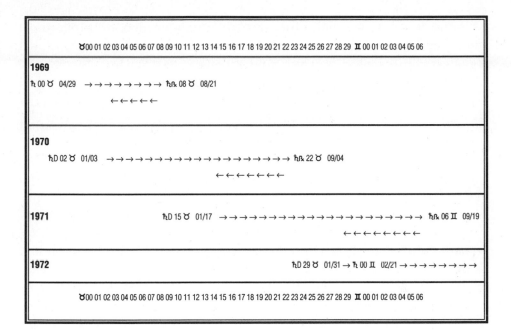

Table 7: Saturn's Transit through Taurus: 1969–1972

Saturn's transit in Taurus moved backward as well as forward due to a planetary phenomenon known as *retrograde motion*, which I will explain in a minute. (The planets do not really move backward, of course, they only appear to as we view them from the earth.) The point at which Saturn appeared to move backward is marked by ℞, and the point at which Saturn resumed forward motion is marked by D. The ephemeris for 1969 shows Saturn entered Taurus April 29, but only went as far as 8° Taurus before turning retrograde August 21. Transit Saturn went all the way back to 2° Taurus before it turned direct January 3, 1970. It reached 22° Taurus before turning retrograde again September 4. Resuming its forward motion at 15° Taurus on January 17, 1971, Saturn entered Gemini on June 18. On September 19, it turned retrograde at 6° Gemini, and reentered 29° Taurus January 10, 1972, where it turned direct again January 31 and left Taurus for good on February 21. If your natal Sun is in Taurus, this meant that at some point between April 29, 1969, and February 21, 1972, you experienced transit Saturn conjunct your natal Sun. Exactly when it occurred would depend on the degree of your Sun. Saturn takes 29.5 years to complete its cycle through the zodiac and will transit Taurus again between 1999 and 2001, at which time you will experience another transit Saturn-natal Sun conjunction. Recall the situations you experienced in 1969–1972 and compare them with the potential circumstances described for transit Saturn conjunct natal Sun in Chapter Seven. Do not be content merely to read the meaning of the transits and the aspects they make to natal planets. Use the ephemeris to determine when aspects from the transits occur in your natal chart, and record your own observations so that you can continually add to your understanding.

RETROGRADE PLANETS

Retrograde motion, which does not apply to the Sun and the Moon, occurs when a planet moving faster than the earth overtakes it or when a slower planet is overtaken by the faster movement of the earth. Since the planets do not actually move backward, retrograde is only an apparent motion, an illusion of planetary movement as we see it from the earth. Apparent retrograde periods occur at regular intervals and the frequency and duration of these periods is different for each planet. During its retrograde period, the energy and focus of a planet is said to be of a slower, more inward character, and the particular activities that are associated with the planet are repetitive and more reflective. Retrograde periods represent a time to retrace one's steps, discover errors, rethink, and review. Hasty or aggressive actions meet with delays and frustrations and their outcomes are likely to be unsatisfactory or unsuccessful. The retrograde periods of Mercury, Venus, and Mars offer the most evidence of certain patterns that are experienced on a personal level. Patterns associated with the retrograde periods of Jupiter and Saturn may be more evident in the affairs of business or activities of agencies and organizations and in weather and other natural phenomena. Retrograde periods of Uranus, Neptune, and Pluto may be linked perhaps to subtle shifts within large social, political, and economic movements. To understand the potentials of a retrograde planet, review your understanding of the planet itself. The transit of a retrograde planet in relation to a natal chart is also interpreted according to its house position and the aspects it makes to the natal planets. The following paragraphs contain short explanations of the potentials of retrograde planets and a table of their retrograde patterns through the end of the century. (The planetary positions are for midnight GMT.)

☿ ℞ MERCURY RETROGRADE

The retrograde periods of Mercury are the most readily observable and heavily documented. They provide examples of what happens when the dictates of a retrograde period, which are to move slower and with more deliberation, are ignored. When Mercury is retrograde, the potential increases for travel delays and other frustrations due to equipment failure, confusion, misdirection, and other errors. If you don't want to end up with a lemon, avoid buying new or used cars and other vehicles, appliances, computers, as well as electrical and

1989 12/30 ☿ ℞ 25 ♑	1993 02/27 ☿ ℞ 24 ♓	1996 01/09 ☿ ℞ 05 ♒	1999 03/10 ☿ ℞ 04 ♈
1990 01/20 ☿ D 09 ♑	1993 03/22 ☿ D 10 ♓	1996 01/30 ☿ D 19 ♑	1999 04/02 ☿ D 20 ♓
1990 04/23 ☿ ℞ 17 ♉	1993 07/01 ☿ ℞ 28 ♋	1996 05/03 ☿ ℞ 28 ♉	1999 07/12 ☿ ℞ 09 ♌
1990 05/17 ☿ D 07 ♉	1993 07/25 ☿ D 18 ♋	1996 05/27 ☿ D 19 ♉	1999 08/06 ☿ D 28 ♋
1990 08/25 ☿ ℞ 23 ♍	1993 10/25 ☿ ℞ 22 ♏	1996 09/04 ☿ ℞ 03 ♎	1999 11/05 ☿ ℞ 01 ♐
1990 09/17 ☿ D 09 ♍	1993 11/15 ☿ D 06 ♏	1996 09/26 ☿ D 19 ♍	1999 11/25 ☿ D 15 ♏
1990 12/14 ☿ ℞ 09 ♑	1994 02/11 ☿ ℞ 07 ♓	1996 12/23 ☿ ℞ 19 ♑	
1991 01/03 ☿ D 23 ♐	1994 03/05 ☿ D 22 ♒	1997 01/12 ☿ D 03 ♑	
1991 04/04 ☿ ℞ 28 ♈	1994 06/12 ☿ ℞ 08 ♋	1997 04/15 ☿ ℞ 09 ♉	
1991 04/28 ☿ D 17 ♈	1994 07/06 ☿ D 29 ♊	1997 05/08 ☿ D 29 ♈	
1991 08/07 ☿ ℞ 05 ♍	1994 10/09 ☿ ℞ 06 ♏	1997 08/17 ☿ ℞ 16 ♍	
1991 08/31 ☿ D 23 ♌	1994 10/30 ☿ D 20 ♎	1997 09/10 ☿ D 02 ♍	
1991 11/28 ☿ ℞ 24 ♐		1997 12/07 ☿ ℞ 03 ♑	
1991 12/18 ☿ D 07 ♐		1997 12/27 ☿ D 17 ♐	
1992 03/17 ☿ ℞ 11 ♈	1995 01/26 ☿ ℞ 21 ♒	1998 03/27 ☿ ℞ 21 ♈	
1992 04/09 ☿ D 28 ♓	1995 02/16 ☿ D 05 ♒	1998 04/20 ☿ D 09 ♈	
1992 07/20 ☿ ℞ 17 ♌	1995 05/24 ☿ ℞ 18 ♊	1998 07/31 ☿ ℞ 28 ♌	
1992 08/13 ☿ D 05 ♌	1995 06/17 ☿ D 09 ♊	1998 08/23 ☿ D 16 ♌	
1992 11/11 ☿ ℞ 08 ♐	1995 09/22 ☿ ℞ 20 ♎	1998 11/21 ☿ ℞ 17 ♐	
1992 12/01 ☿ D 22 ♏	1995 10/14 ☿ D 04 ♎	1998 12/11 ☿ D 01 ♐	

Table 8: Mercury Retrograde Periods: 1990 through 1999

mechanical devices for home and office. Events and meetings are delayed or canceled. The list of errors in communication is long. It is best to avoid finalizing contracts, placing mail or phone orders, responding to or placing advertisements, setting schedules, giving or receiving directions and instructions, and installing communication equipment such as telephones and fax machines. Books, keys, tickets, and documents are lost or misplaced, and people are more apt to change their minds. The potential is to make errors and lose things, but there is also increased potential to find errors and lost articles. It is a productive period to review material and clean out drawers and closets. It is a good time to gather information, become better organized, and do the background work for projects and activities.

Note in Table 8 that Mercury retrograde occurs three or four times a year. The interval between periods is about four months and the length of each period is twenty to twenty-four days.

♀ ℞ VENUS RETROGRADE

The periods of retrograde Venus are not as visibly troublesome as retrograde Mercury. Love and romance, social attitudes and behaviors, and affairs of business and politics may be less cooperative or even uncharacteristically rude and aggressive. Among the positive potentials is that some situations may require a

1980 05/24 ♀ ℞ 02 ♋	1985 03/13 ♀ ℞ 22 ♈	1989 12/29 ♀ ℞ 06 ♒	1994 10/13 ♀ ℞ 18 ♏
1980 07/06 ♀ D 16 ♊	1985 04/25 ♀ D 06 ♈	1990 02/08 ♀ D 20 ♑	1994 11/23 ♀ D 02 ♏
1981 12/31 ♀ ℞ 08 ♒	1986 10/15 ♀ ℞ 20 ♏	1991 08/01 ♀ ℞ 07 ♍	1996 05/20 ♀ ℞ 28 ♊
1982 02/10 ♀ D 23 ♑	1986 11/26 ♀ D 04 ♏	1991 09/13 ♀ D 21 ♌	1996 07/02 ♀ D 11 ♊
1983 08/03 ♀ ℞ 09 ♍	1988 05/22 ♀ ℞ 00 ♋	1993 03/11 ♀ ℞ 20 ♈	1997 12/26 ♀ ℞ 03 ♒
1983 09/15 ♀ D 23 ♌	1988 07/04 ♀ D 13 ♊	1993 04/22 ♀ D 03 ♈	1998 02/05 ♀ D 18 ♑
			1999 07/30 ♀ ℞ 05 ♍
			1999 09/11 ♀ D 18 ♌

Table 9: Venus Retrograde Periods: 1980 through 1999

more calculated or aggressive approach in order to restore or create a more equitable balance. Venus retrograde is not apt to favor cosmetic surgery or decorating projects, although this is a period in which such matters can be investigated, reviewed, and discussed.

The retrograde periods of Venus between 1980–1999 are shown in Table 9. Note that transit Venus is retrograde approximately every eighteen months for about forty days.

♂ ℞ Mars Retrograde

Transit Mars represents the animated energy of life, and when it is retrograde, the pace of everything seems slower. Whether it is a war between nations or the battle of the sexes, the aggressor can expect to lose if the hostilities were initiated during a retrograde period of Mars. Other concerns are the economic consequences of an industrial slowdown, rising unemployment, and the general lack of enthusiasm for accomplishing goals. Using the word energy in the widest sense, the positive potentials of slowing down include conserving energy, learning to apply it more productively, and improving methods.

Note in Table 10 that the period of retrograde Mars occurs every two years for a period of about ten weeks.

1969 04/27 ♂ ℞ 16 ♐	1977 12/12 ♂ ℞ 11 ♌	1986 06/08 ♂ ℞ 23 ♑	1995 01/02 ♂ ℞ 02 ♍
1969 07/08 ♂ D 01 ♐	1978 03/02 ♂ D 22 ♋	1986 08/12 ♂ D 11 ♑	1995 03/24 ♂ D 13 ♌
1971 07/11 ♂ ℞ 21 ♒	1980 01/16 ♂ ℞ 15 ♍	1988 08/26 ♂ ℞ 11 ♈	1997 02/06 ♂ ℞ 05 ♎
1971 09/09 ♂ D 11 ♒	1980 04/06 ♂ D 25 ♌	1988 10/28 ♂ D 29 ♓	1997 04/27 ♂ D 16 ♍
1973 09/19 ♂ ℞ 09 ♉	1982 02/20 ♂ ℞ 19 ♎	1990 10/20 ♂ ℞ 14 ♊	1999 03/18 ♂ ℞ 12 ♏
1973 11/26 ♂ D 25 ♈	1982 05/11 ♂ D 00 ♎	1991 01/01 ♂ D 27 ♉	1999 06/04 ♂ D 24 ♎
1975 11/06 ♂ ℞ 02 ♋	1984 04/05 ♂ ℞ 28 ♏	1992 11/28 ♂ ℞ 27 ♋	
1976 01/20 ♂ D 14 ♊	1984 06/19 ♂ D 11 ♏	1993 02/15 ♂ D 08 ♋	

Table 10: Mars Retrograde Periods: 1969 through 1999

♃ ℞ JUPITER RETROGRADE

Transit Jupiter represents optimism and generosity—two sentiments that are apt to be either missing or misapplied during the retrograde period of Jupiter. Failure to deliver what is promised is one of the best explanations of the potential of Jupiter retrograde. Freedom, material advantages, and status may not be lacking so much as the understanding of their purpose and value. Too much severity and unnecessary conservatism during this period becomes a deterrent that haunts future growth. The best use of Jupiter's retrograde period is achieving the proper perspective on growth and expansion.

Note in Table 11 that Jupiter retrograde occurs every year and lasts approximately 120 days.

1979 12/26 ♃ ℞ 10 ♍	1985 06/04 ♃ ℞ 16 ♒	1990 11/30 ♃ ℞ 13 ♌	1996 05/04 ♃ ℞ 17 ♑
1980 04/26 ♃ D 00 ♍	1985 10/03 ♃ D 07 ♒	1991 03/30 ♃ D 03 ♌	1996 09/03 ♃ D 07 ♑
1981 01/24 ♃ ℞ 10 ♎	1986 07/12 ♃ ℞ 22 ♓	1991 12/30 ♃ ℞ 14 ♍	1997 06/10 ♃ ℞ 21 ♒
1981 05/27 ♃ D 00 ♎	1986 11/08 ♃ D 12 ♓	1992 04/30 ♃ D 04 ♍	1997 10/08 ♃ D 12 ♒
1982 02/24 ♃ ℞ 10 ♏	1987 08/19 ♃ ℞ 29 ♈	1993 01/28 ♃ ℞ 14 ♎	1998 07/18 ♃ ℞ 28 ♓
1982 06/27 ♃ D 00 ♏	1987 12/15 ♃ D 19 ♈	1993 06/01 ♃ D 04 ♎	1998 11/13 ♃ D 18 ♓
1983 03/27 ♃ ℞ 10 ♐	1988 09/24 ♃ ℞ 06 ♊	1994 02/28 ♃ ℞ 14 ♏	1999 08/25 ♃ ℞ 04 ♉
1983 07/29 ♃ D 01 ♐	1989 01/20 ♃ D 26 ♉	1994 07/02 ♃ D 04 ♏	1999 12/20 ♃ D 25 ♈
1984 04/29 ♃ ℞ 12 ♑	1989 10/29 ♃ ℞ 10 ♋	1995 04/01 ♃ ℞ 15 ♐	
1984 08/29 ♃ D 03 ♑	1990 02/24 ♃ D 00 ♋	1995 08/02 ♃ D 05 ♐	

Table 11: Jupiter Retrograde Periods: 1980 through 1999

♄ ℞ SATURN RETROGRADE

Hard work, organization, experience and maturity, which are the usual associations of Saturn, may be lacking or the results that they are expected to achieve may not be forthcoming when Saturn is retrograde. Authority or authority figures may be gone or lost and the issue at hand becomes one of how best to compensate for it.

Table 12 lists the retrograde periods of Saturn between 1980 and 1999. Saturn is retrograde each year for approximately 140 days.

1980 01/06 ♄ ℞ 27 ♍	1985 03/07 ♄ ℞ 28 ♏	1990 05/04 ♄ ℞ 25 ♑	1995 07/06 ♄ ℞ 24 ♓
1980 05/22 ♄ D 20 ♍	1985 07/25 ♄ D 21 ♏	1990 09/23 ♄ D 18 ♑	1995 11/21 ♄ D 17 ♓
1981 01/18 ♄ ℞ 09 ♎	1986 03/19 ♄ ℞ 09 ♐	1991 05/17 ♄ ℞ 06 ♒	1996 07/18 ♄ ℞ 07 ♈
1981 06/05 ♄ D 02 ♎	1986 08/07 ♄ D 03 ♐	1991 10/05 ♄ D 00 ♒	1996 12/03 ♄ D 00 ♈
1982 01/31 ♄ ℞ 22 ♎	1987 03/31 ♄ ℞ 21 ♐	1992 05/28 ♄ ℞ 18 ♒	1997 08/01 ♄ ℞ 20 ♈
1982 06/18 ♄ D 15 ♎	1987 08/19 ♄ D 14 ♐	1992 10/16 ♄ D 11 ♒	1997 12/16 ♄ D 13 ♈
1983 02/12 ♄ ℞ 04 ♏	1988 04/11 ♄ ℞ 02 ♑	1993 06/10 ♄ ℞ 00 ♓	1998 08/15 ♄ ℞ 03 ♉
1983 07/01 ♄ D 27 ♎	1988 08/30 ♄ D 25 ♐	1993 10/28 ♄ D 23 ♒	1998 12/29 ♄ D 26 ♈
1984 02/24 ♄ ℞ 16 ♏	1989 04/22 ♄ ℞ 13 ♑	1994 06/23 ♄ ℞ 12 ♓	1999 08/30 ♄ ℞ 17 ♉
1984 07/13 ♄ D 09 ♏	1989 09/11 ♄ D 07 ♑	1994 11/09 ♄ D 05 ♓	2000 01/12 ♄ D 10 ♉

Table 12: Saturn Retrograde Periods: 1980 through 1999

♅ ℞ URANUS RETROGRADE

Freedom of expression, measures of reform, and technological advances that are currently abroad in society may be slowed down to accommodate unforeseen difficulties when Uranus is retrograde. Such backward or inwardly-directed energy can prove to be an inhibiting factor in the path of progress or represent time to gain a more enlightened approach.

Note in Table 13 that the retrograde periods of Uranus occur each year for approximately 148 days.

1980 02/29 ♅ ℞ 25 ♏	1985 03/22 ♅ ℞ 17 ♐	1990 04/13 ♅ ℞ 09 ♑	1995 05/05 ♅ ℞ 00 ♒
1980 07/30 ♅ D 21 ♏	1985 08/23 ♅ D 13 ♐	1990 09/14 ♅ D 05 ♑	1995 10/06 ♅ D 26 ♑
1981 03/05 ♅ ℞ 00 ♐	1986 03/27 ♅ ℞ 22 ♐	1991 04/18 ♅ ℞ 13 ♑	1996 05/08 ♅ ℞ 04 ♒
1981 08/04 ♅ D 26 ♏	1986 08/27 ♅ D 18 ♐	1991 09/19 ♅ D 09 ♑	1996 10/10 ♅ D 00 ♒
1982 03/09 ♅ ℞ 04 ♐	1987 04/01 ♅ ℞ 26 ♐	1992 04/21 ♅ ℞ 18 ♑	1997 05/13 ♅ ℞ 08 ♒
1982 08/09 ♅ D 00 ♐	1987 09/01 ♅ D 22 ♐	1992 09/22 ♅ D 14 ♑	1997 10/14 ♅ D 04 ♒
1983 03/14 ♅ ℞ 09 ♐	1988 04/04 ♅ ℞ 01 ♑	1993 04/26 ♅ ℞ 22 ♑	1998 05/17 ♅ ℞ 12 ♒
1983 08/14 ♅ D 05 ♐	1988 09/05 ♅ D 27 ♐	1993 09/27 ♅ D 18 ♑	1998 10/18 ♅ D 08 ♒
1984 03/18 ♅ ℞ 13 ♐	1989 04/09 ♅ ℞ 05 ♑	1994 04/30 ♅ ℞ 26 ♑	1999 05/21 ♅ ℞ 16 ♒
1984 08/18 ♅ D 09 ♐	1989 09/10 ♅ D 01 ♑	1994 10/02 ♅ D 22 ♑	1999 10/23 ♅ D 12 ♒

Table 13: Uranus Retrograde Periods: 1980 through 1999

♆ ℞ NEPTUNE RETROGRADE

The energy and activities associated with idealism, spirituality, and illusion may be forced by the reality of circumstances to find expression on a less obvious level. The elements of confusion and misplaced trust make it difficult to determine what can or is being accomplished when Neptune is retrograde. A period of inaction to allow time for deliberation and inspiration when Neptune is retrograde may be what is necessary to prevent catastrophe, and yet, it may also be a time when to do nothing can encourage more ill. Each period's circumstances must be assessed on their own merits.

Neptune is retrograde for about 150 days each year, as seen in Table 14.

1980 03/24 ♆ ℞ 22 ♐	1985 04/05 ♆ ℞ 03 ♑	1990 04/16 ♆ ℞ 14 ♑	1995 04/27 ♆ ℞ 25 ♑
1980 08/31 ♆ D 19 ♐	1985 09/12 ♆ D 00 ♑	1990 09/23 ♆ D 11 ♑	1995 10/05 ♆ D 22 ♑
1981 03/27 ♆ ℞ 24 ♐	1986 04/07 ♆ ℞ 05 ♑	1991 04/19 ♆ ℞ 16 ♑	1996 04/29 ♆ ℞ 27 ♑
1981 09/03 ♆ D 22 ♐	1986 09/14 ♆ D 03 ♑	1991 09/26 ♆ D 13 ♑	1996 10/06 ♆ D 24 ♑
1982 03/29 ♆ ℞ 27 ♐	1987 04/10 ♆ ℞ 08 ♑	1992 04/20 ♆ ℞ 18 ♑	1997 05/01 ♆ ℞ 29 ♑
1982 09/05 ♆ D 24 ♐	1987 09/17 ♆ D 05 ♑	1992 09/27 ♆ D 16 ♑	1997 10/09 ♆ D 27 ♑
1983 04/01 ♆ ℞ 29 ♐	1988 04/11 ♆ ℞ 10 ♑	1993 04/22 ♆ ℞ 21 ♑	1998 05/04 ♆ ℞ 02 ♒
1983 09/08 ♆ D 26 ♐	1988 09/18 ♆ D 07 ♑	1993 09/30 ♆ D 18 ♑	1998 10/11 ♆ D 29 ♑
1984 04/02 ♆ ℞ 01 ♑	1989 04/13 ♆ ℞ 12 ♑	1994 04/25 ♆ ℞ 23 ♑	1999 05/07 ♆ ℞ 04 ♒
1984 09/09 ♆ D 28 ♐	1989 09/21 ♆ D 09 ♑	1994 10/02 ♆ D 20 ♑	1999 10/14 ♆ D 01 ♒

Table 14: Neptune Retrograde Periods: 1980 through 1999

♇ ℞ PLUTO RETROGRADE

Available resources are used indirectly or their use is prevented by some shortfall or intervention. Resources are evaluated and there is a closer examination of their inventory, use, and abuse. All this may come by way of routine reports and investigations of course, and the only evidence of Pluto retrograde is that more of such tasks are scheduled. It has been suggested that this is a productive period to search for karmic links, a subtle message for those who are attuned to such things.

Table 15 lists the retrograde periods of Pluto between 1980 and 1999.

1980 01/24 ♇ ℞ 21 ♎	1985 02/05 ♇ ℞ 04 ♏	1990 02/19 ♇ ℞ 17 ♏	1995 03/04 ♇ ℞ 00 ♐
1980 06/28 ♇ D 18 ♎	1985 07/12 ♇ D 01 ♏	1990 07/26 ♇ D 14 ♏	1995 08/08 ♇ D 27 ♏
1981 01/26 ♇ ℞ 24 ♎	1986 02/08 ♇ ℞ 07 ♏	1991 02/22 ♇ ℞ 20 ♏	1996 03/05 ♇ ℞ 03 ♐
1981 07/01 ♇ D 21 ♎	1986 07/15 ♇ D 04 ♏	1991 07/28 ♇ D 17 ♏	1996 08/10 ♇ D 00 ♐
1982 01/29 ♇ ℞ 26 ♎	1987 02/11 ♇ ℞ 09 ♏	1992 02/24 ♇ ℞ 22 ♏	1997 03/08 ♇ ℞ 05 ♐
1982 07/04 ♇ D 24 ♎	1987 07/18 ♇ D 07 ♏	1992 07/30 ♇ D 20 ♏	1997 08/13 ♇ D 02 ♐
1983 02/01 ♇ ℞ 29 ♎	1988 02/14 ♇ ℞ 12 ♏	1993 02/26 ♇ ℞ 25 ♏	1998 03/11 ♇ ℞ 08 ♐
1983 07/07 ♇ D 26 ♎	1988 07/20 ♇ D 09 ♏	1993 08/02 ♇ D 22 ♏	1998 08/16 ♇ D 05 ♐
1984 02/04 ♇ ℞ 02 ♏	1989 02/16 ♇ ℞ 15 ♏	1994 03/01 ♇ ℞ 28 ♏	1999 03/13 ♇ ℞ 10 ♐
1984 07/09 ♇ D 29 ♎	1989 07/23 ♇ D 12 ♏	1994 08/05 ♇ D 25 ♏	1999 08/19 ♇ D 07 ♐

Table 15: Pluto Retrograde Periods: 1980 through 1999

The zodiac, the horoscope, and the planets are the structures that astrology uses to symbolize and explain the drama of life. The zodiac becomes the theater where the drama is performed, the horoscope is the stage where the action takes place, and the planets represent the actors and actresses. But what is a story without a plot? What is needed are the dynamics: patterns in which the energy can flow and create the circumstances that propel the actors forward to play the roles they were meant to perform. The plot thickens as you learn about the planetary aspects.

PLANETARY ASPECTS

As players in the human drama, we respond in some way to all the circumstances we experience in life. The dynamics that define and direct the energy of the circumstances we encounter are the planetary aspects; that is, the geometric angles formed by transiting planets to our natal planets.

In school we are introduced to basic geometric shapes such as the circle, triangle, and square, and we are taught how to measure them using degrees and angles. However, our elementary lessons in geometry do not prepare us to recognize the cosmic harmony that is inherent in it. Those with mathematical and philosophical skills may rush to unlock the mysteries of Phi and the Golden Section and achieve no more understanding of their cosmic significance than a first-year geometry student. The most complex ideas have humble origins and contain simple truths. The wisdom of Pythagoras and Plato (who regarded geometry as sacred) teaches us the harmony of numbers: the fundamental truths of a well ordered universe. In astrology, simple geometric angles are used to describe what in reality is an intricate pattern of circumstances that in turn, provokes an equally intricate pattern of human responses and interactions.

The meaning of the planetary aspects is the same whether we are talking about the planetary aspects between natal planets in someone's chart, the aspects between the transiting planets themselves, or aspects made from transiting planets to natal planets. In making predictions for an individual, which is the focus of this book, our concern is with the aspects from the transiting planets to the natal planets.

Understanding how the planetary aspects are derived is not difficult. The zodiac is a circle (360 degrees) divided into twelve sections of thirty degrees, each section represented by one of the astrological signs. Figure 1.3 shows the zodiacal

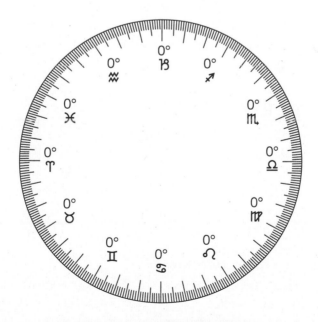

Figure 1.3: Zodiacal Circle

circle beginning with 0° Aries. Keep this figure in mind as a handy reference when you study the various aspects.

The opposition divides the circle by two, the trine divides the circle by three, the square divides the circle by four, the sextile divides the circle by six, and the conjunction occurs when planets are located in the same degree of the same sign. Study Table 16 to familiarize yourself with the planetary aspects and their short-hand symbols.

Opposition	☍	180°
Trine	△	120°
Square	□	90°
Sextile	✳	30°
Conjunction	☌	0°

Table 16: Planetary Aspects and their Symbols

The following paragraphs explain each of the five major planetary aspects plus some additional aspects that should be recognized and considered when interpreting the transits.

THE OPPOSITION

Looking at the zodiacal circle in Figure 1.4, you can see which signs are opposed. An opposition occurs when two planets are located 180 degrees apart. If, for example, you have natal Moon at 12° Aries, every time a transiting planet is at 12° Libra, it is exactly 180 degrees from your natal Moon. Transiting planets in Taurus will oppose natal planets in Scorpio, just as transiting planets in Scorpio will oppose natal planets in Taurus, and so on.

What Does the Opposition Mean?

The dynamics of an opposition presume difficult circumstances in which compromise is the only solution. Circumstances associated with an opposition cannot be changed or removed; they must be dealt with as they are. There is apt

Aries	☍	Libra
Taurus	☍	Scorpio
Gemini	☍	Sagittarius
Cancer	☍	Capricorn
Leo	☍	Aquarius
Virgo	☍	Pisces

Figure 1.4: Opposing Signs

to be separation or loss when this aspect occurs. In the case of transit Saturn opposed natal Mars, for example, Mars is associated with a person's energy and physical efforts, while transiting Saturn represents authority, responsibilities, and restrictions. One potential difficulty indicated for the individual experiencing transit Saturn opposed natal Mars is the loss of physical energy brought on by illness or overwork. Another possibility is rebellious acts against authority. Oppositions, no matter what planets are involved, present the greatest learning experiences because they present the greatest challenges.

THE TRINE

△ The zodiacal circles in Figure 1.5 show which signs are trine. A trine occurs when planets are 120 degrees apart. It is helpful here to recall that the twelve signs are divided into four elements. Aries, Leo, and Sagittarius are the fire signs, and, as a group, they indicate action, inspiration, and stimulation. Taurus, Virgo, and Capricorn are the earth signs and they represent structure, purpose, and the material or physical world. Ideas, information, and communication describe the air signs Gemini, Libra, and Aquarius. Cancer, Scorpio, and Pisces are water signs and they represent emotional acts and experiences. Notice in Figure 1.5 that trines occur naturally between signs of the same element. Let us use the same example of natal Moon at 12° Aries. Any transit in 12° Leo or 12° Sagittarius will trine your natal Moon in Aries. Transiting planets in Taurus trine natal planets in Virgo and Capricorn, and so on.

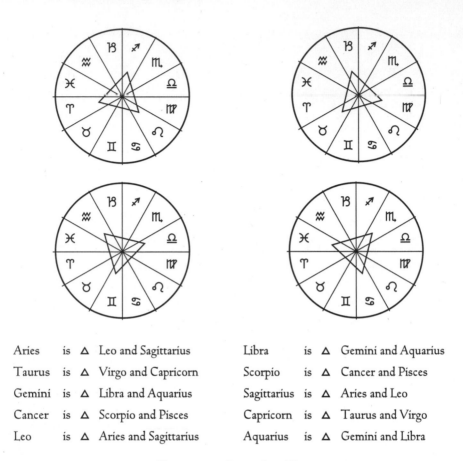

Aries	is	△	Leo and Sagittarius	Libra	is	△	Gemini and Aquarius
Taurus	is	△	Virgo and Capricorn	Scorpio	is	△	Cancer and Pisces
Gemini	is	△	Libra and Aquarius	Sagittarius	is	△	Aries and Leo
Cancer	is	△	Scorpio and Pisces	Capricorn	is	△	Taurus and Virgo
Leo	is	△	Aries and Sagittarius	Aquarius	is	△	Gemini and Libra

Figure 1.5: Signs that Trine

What Does the Trine Mean?

Dynamics of the trine, considered the most fortunate of aspects, allow energy to flow uninterrupted. This aspect is associated with harmonious circum-stances, cooperation, creativity, inspiration, and generosity. Human nature being what it is, however, there is an inherent disadvantage in the trine because it lacks challenge. Material wealth and easy success do not ordinarily induce need or desire for achievement. What is too easily gained is too easily lost.

THE SQUARE

A square occurs when two planets are located 90 degrees apart. The zodiacal circles in Figure 1.6 show which signs are square. Recall that the twelve signs are divided into three qualities. The cardinal signs—Aries, Cancer, Libra, and Capricorn—imply the push to get things done and no hesitation to change whatever stands in the way of attaining goals. Taurus, Leo, Scorpio, and Aquarius are the fixed signs, and they signify stability, patience, and reluctance to change. The mutable signs—Gemini, Virgo, Sagittarius, and Pisces—suggest compromise, adaptability, and flexibility. Notice in Figure 1.6 that squares occur naturally between signs of the same quality. Your natal Moon at 12° Aries will be squared by transits when they appear in 12° Cancer, 12° Libra, and 12° Capricorn. Transits in Taurus are square natal planets in Leo, Scorpio, and Aquarius, and so on.

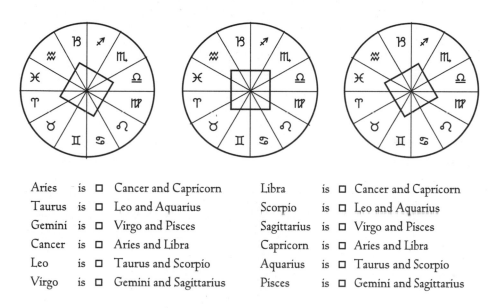

Aries	is □	Cancer and Capricorn	Libra	is □	Cancer and Capricorn
Taurus	is □	Leo and Aquarius	Scorpio	is □	Leo and Aquarius
Gemini	is □	Virgo and Pisces	Sagittarius	is □	Virgo and Pisces
Cancer	is □	Aries and Libra	Capricorn	is □	Aries and Libra
Leo	is □	Taurus and Scorpio	Aquarius	is □	Taurus and Scorpio
Virgo	is □	Gemini and Sagittarius	Pisces	is □	Gemini and Sagittarius

Figure 1.6: Signs that Square

What Does the Square Mean?

Unlike the circumstances associated with the trine which engender little need for achievement and action, the square describes frustrations and obstacles that demand immediate attention. Unlike the difficulties related to the opposition

33

which cannot be changed, the square is associated with problems that with effort and determination can be overcome and even turned into advantages.

THE SEXTILE

A sextile occurs when two planets are located 60 degrees apart. The zodiacal circles in Figure 1.7 show which signs are sextile. Figure 1.7 also illustrates that any transit at 12° Gemini or 12° Aquarius will sextile your natal Moon at 12° Aries. Planets in Taurus sextile natal planets in Cancer and Pisces, and so on.

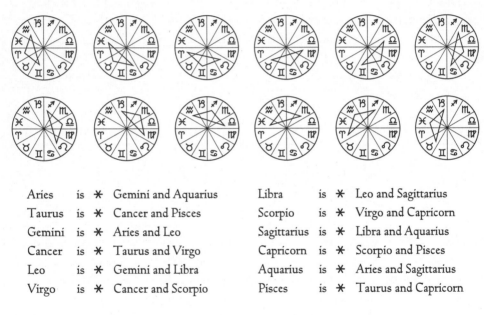

Aries	is	✳	Gemini and Aquarius	Libra	is	✳	Leo and Sagittarius
Taurus	is	✳	Cancer and Pisces	Scorpio	is	✳	Virgo and Capricorn
Gemini	is	✳	Aries and Leo	Sagittarius	is	✳	Libra and Aquarius
Cancer	is	✳	Taurus and Virgo	Capricorn	is	✳	Scorpio and Pisces
Leo	is	✳	Gemini and Libra	Aquarius	is	✳	Aries and Sagittarius
Virgo	is	✳	Cancer and Scorpio	Pisces	is	✳	Taurus and Capricorn

Figure 1.7: Signs that Sextile

What Does the Sextile Mean?

The sextile is similar to the trine in the sense that circumstances connected with it are generally of a positive nature. Prosperity and easy success are granted with little or no effort in the circumstances of a trine, while the sextile represents only an opportunity that can later become or lead to the success, not the success itself. Opportunity is the key word when it comes to the dynamics of a sextile.

THE CONJUNCTION

☌ The conjunction is easy to picture since the circle is not divided. Two planets in the same degree of the same sign are conjunct. The conjunction is powerful. The dynamics of this aspect combine and focus the energy of the planets involved, but the conjunction is susceptible in turn to other planets that may aspect it. For example, a conjunction between transit Jupiter and your natal Moon at 12° Aries is very fortunate. If, however, the conjunction is opposed by transit Saturn at 12° Libra, the conjunction's prospects for fortunate circumstances are reduced. On the other hand, if the transit Jupiter-natal Moon conjunction were trined by transit Saturn at 12° Leo, the potential for fortunate consequences increases.

OTHER ASPECTS

Although the opposition, trine, square, sextile, and conjunction are the five aspects primarily used in astrology, there are other aspects and patterns that deserve special attention. A few of these are discussed below.

QUINCUNX OR INCONJUNCT

⚻ This aspect occurs when two planets are 150 degrees apart. For instance, transits at 12° Virgo or 12° Scorpio would be quincunx your natal Moon at 12° Aries. The dynamics of this aspect present a situation of uneasiness or of an unexpected nature in which an adjustment must be made. It implies circumstances in which one thing must be given up in order to gain another. The solution to a quincunx is in the individual's willingness to pay a price for something that is gained. Even then, it is apt to mean having to settle for less than what may have been truly earned. Traditionally, the quincunx is not included with the five primary aspects, and it has not been included in this book. However, in recent years many astrologers have asserted that the quincunx should be given as much weight and attention as the other aspects, an assessment with which I am inclined to agree.

STELLIUM

When three or more transits are in the same sign, there is added emphasis and energy both in the natal house they occupy and the natal planets they aspect.

THE GRAND TRINE

When three or more planets trine each other from three signs, a Grand Trine is created. Transits at 12° Leo together with transits at 12° Sagittarius would form a Grand Trine with your natal Moon at 12° Aries. The trine is a fortunate aspect to begin with, and the Grand Trine enhances this prospect. However, as in the case of all trines, there may be wasted wealth and talent because the individual fails to preserve, develop, or use what has been so easily provided.

THE T-SQUARE

The T-Square is an aspect formed by an opposition and a square. Transits at 12° Capricorn and 12° Cancer oppose each other and would form a T-Square with your natal Moon at 12° Aries. The T-Square is a dynamic in which the stress of the opposition is afforded a release. The energy of the opposition flows out through the square. Note here, as in all aspects, the natal houses in which the aspects occur are an important part of how the pattern will be interpreted.

THE GRAND CROSS

The Grand Cross is a pattern that occurs when planets form two oppositions and four squares. Simultaneous transits at 12° Cancer, 12° Libra, and 12° Capricorn would form a Grand Cross with your natal Moon at 12° Aries. The Grand Cross involves the most stressful aspects—an indication of difficult circumstances in which one thing after another goes wrong, and it is only by seeing the big picture and concentrating on the ultimate goals that progress may be made.

PLANETARY ORBS AND APPLYING AND SEPARATING ASPECTS

Using the same example of the natal Moon at 12° Aries that we used in the previous paragraphs, let us say that the transit in Libra opposing the natal Moon was at 9° Libra or 13° Libra. Instead of being exactly 180 degrees apart, the transit at 9° Libra is only 177 degrees (three degrees away from making the aspect). At 13° Libra, the transit is now one degree past the aspect. Is the opposition still valid? Yes. However, the aspect is stronger when it is *applying* (about ready to make the exact aspect) than when it is *separating* (after the exact aspect has been made). How many degrees off (orbs) can the transit be and still make a valid aspect? Opinions differ about how many degrees to allow on either side of an aspect. Note that the orbs allowed with reference to aspects between natal planets are much wider, but when dealing with aspects from transiting planets to natal planets, the orbs should be no greater than three degrees when the aspect is applying and only one degree when it is separating as in our example.

Acquiring the necessary skills of prediction is a stimulating and challenging part of astrology. Now that you have been given the basic tools—the signs, the planets, and the planetary aspects—to work with, you are ready to begin. The extensive discussion of the transits in the natal charts of Ted Bundy, Grace Kelly, Mata Hari, and Theodore Roosevelt in Chapter Twelve includes many examples of how the information in this book can be applied.

Chapter Two

Transit Sun Aspects to the Natal Planets

The Sun moves approximately one degree per day, which means the impact of solar aspects to natal planets is going to be fleeting. The solar influence is stronger as an applying aspect than when it is separating. The solar aspect will gain strength if there are other transits around to support it.

SOLAR CONJUNCTIONS

TRANSIT SUN CONJOIN NATAL SUN

☉ ☌ ☉ Congratulations! It is the beginning of another personal year for you. The Sun is associated with vitality, ambition, and pride, and its transit touches off those areas as it conjoins your natal Sun on your birthday. Take advantage of its positive potential by renewing faith in yourself. Reflect on what the past has taught, look forward to where you want to be in the future. When you were born, others demanded nothing from you. Relive some of this freedom each year on your birthday. Forget what the world expects and concentrate on your own expectations. Are you the kind of person you want to be? Are you happy, successful, and productive, at least by your own standards? Are your standards too low? Too high? Too rigid? This is a day to start putting your life back on track if it has been derailed. This is also a day to enjoy a celebration of life, the affection of companions, the love of family and of those close to you.

TRANSIT SUN CONJOIN NATAL MOON

⊙ ♂ ☽ Whether or not circumstances give you a reason, the pride you have in your family, your residence, and your domestic skills becomes a focus when transit Sun conjoins your natal Moon. Determination and ego catch up with emotional desires and you are not to be denied. Success may seem like an incredible achievement and failure can cause bitter disappointment. More confident and certain of your goals, you can accomplish much today. You may, however, also tend to take everything too personally, which means you more easily attain success if you avoid self-centeredness, stubborn pride, and difficulties with supervisors or authority figures.

TRANSIT SUN CONJOIN NATAL MERCURY

⊙ ♂ ☿ This is a day to travel, to communicate, and to present ideas and opinions with confidence and enthusiasm. When transit Sun conjoins your natal Mercury, you may have reason to be proud of your intelligence, ideas, or skills. It is possible to benefit in some way from those in charge, so do not hesitate to consult them for advice, assistance, or other favors. Higher-ups may also ask you for information or assistance. Be prepared. Enhanced creative thinking encourages you to devise some very clever solutions or methods. Although there may be increased generosity in the sharing of knowledge and mechanical skills, do not get trapped in other situations that promote intellectual grandstanding and dishonesty.

TRANSIT SUN CONJOIN NATAL VENUS

⊙ ♂ ♀ During the period of transit Sun's conjunction with your natal Venus, you are, or should try to be, more outgoing, more attractive, and more appreciative of the beauty in all things. Relationships, especially romantic and marital relationships, are highlighted. An important alliance or partnership may be established, or, in the case of the negative potential, difficulties with a partner may arise due to stubborn pride, dominance, or selfish manipulation. Social activities, artistic endeavors, legal matters, negotiations, and diplomacy are likely to vie for time and attention. Self-indulgence is increased and you are more than a little tempted when it comes to the pursuit of pleasure, expensive clothes, luxury items, costly social activities, and entertainment.

TRANSIT SUN CONJOIN NATAL MARS

⊙ ☌ ♂ More animated and action-oriented as the transit Sun conjoins your natal Mars, you are likely to initiate new projects or act on the ideas or plans you have been talking or thinking about. This is a time to take pride in your work or other physical efforts. The negative side includes unpleasant consequences from being too hot-headed or impatient. Care must also be taken to avoid head injuries, cuts, stings, or contracting a fever. The physical vitality and enthusiasm you exhibit during this short period not only helps you to accomplish a lot, but also to attract and inspire others.

TRANSIT SUN CONJOIN NATAL JUPITER

⊙ ☌ ♃ Increased optimism and generosity are featured as transit Sun conjoins your natal Jupiter. Even if current circumstances turn out to be troublesome, something positive is apt to occur in spite of the difficulty. Spiritual awareness is enhanced and so is the potential for successful or enjoyable cultural events, artistic projects, long-distance travel, and activities that expand your intellectual horizons. You are more flamboyant and dramatic. Even though you may become too impressed with yourself, courage and confidence are also a part of your actions and attitudes at this time. Other potential situations may involve in-laws, your father, and the judicial system.

TRANSIT SUN CONJOIN NATAL SATURN

⊙ ☌ ♄ An urge to make daily tasks or responsibilities more interesting or meaningful is one of the likeliest motivations for your actions when transit Sun conjoins your natal Saturn. On the other hand, enjoyment may be stifled by serious situations that leave little time or inclination for fun. Circumstances call for reliability and trustworthiness. The hard work and loyalty you have demonstrated may earn you recognition or other rewards. The potential here suggests circumstances that involve the issue of your maturity, experience, and seniority, or a concern with the authority or senior position of others.

TRANSIT SUN CONJOIN NATAL URANUS

⊙ ☌ ♅ To be or not to be part of the group is the burning issue today. Negative potential includes difficulty organizing groups or participating in group activities, possibly caused by stubborn pride or lack of loyalty. Nevertheless, there are also potential benefits you may receive as a member of a group when transit Sun conjoins your natal Uranus. You may receive special attention from the group's leader or be invited to take a leadership role. You are more inclined to accept or seek that which is unusual or nontraditional. Others may show greater interest in you not because of how well you fit in, but because of qualities that make you unique or different. Other potential targets of your attention at this time involve social activities, technical subjects, the media, and computers.

TRANSIT SUN CONJOIN NATAL NEPTUNE

⊙ ☌ ♆ When there is a conjunction between transit Sun and your natal Neptune, spiritual matters, fantasies, and ideals become part of the environment. For example, you may feel more compassionate and visit those who are sick or confined, or you may volunteer your assistance to a charitable cause. You may decide to attend a religious service or spend the day on a sailboat to get some inner peace and tranquility. Be careful in whatever you do. You are inclined to conveniently lose sight of reality or others may hide the truth from you. Laziness, inattention, and flexible morals may creep into the picture and cause trouble. You may be able to avoid or minimize the harmful potential by going out of your way to be constructive and alert in all situations.

TRANSIT SUN CONJOIN NATAL PLUTO

⊙ ☌ ♇ As transit Sun conjoins your natal Pluto, you may be propelled by an urge to get to the bottom of motivations and to understand the reason for your ego drives. If you are strong-willed, you are even more formidable in getting things to go your way. If you are not so aggressive and tend to be easygoing and flexible, you become more aggressive and intense. Self-control, power, and the use of power are apt to be highlighted, either as concepts or because they have an important role to play in your present scenario. Circumstances may provoke you to resent others who are manipulative or who have more power or control.

SOLAR SEXTILES

TRANSIT SUN SEXTILE NATAL SUN

⊙ ✶ ⊙ Circumstances provide a measure of ego-gratification, a chance to feel good about yourself, to feel stronger and more vital. An attitude of helpfulness and generosity on your part will reflect well on you and inspire the same feelings in others, indirectly helping you progress toward your personal goals. When transit Sun sextiles your natal Sun, superiors or others with power or influence in your life are inclined to give you a boost, a chance to show what you can do. Unless negative situations suggest otherwise, it is a good time to ask for favors.

TRANSIT SUN SEXTILE NATAL MOON

⊙ ✶ ☽ Others show up to help you accomplish tasks, to keep you company, or to provide emotional support when transit Sun sextiles your natal Moon. Something or someone creates an emotional high for you, which in turn makes you feel physically more vital. Events in which you participate and information you receive enhance your creativity and imagination. Opportunities exist with regard to women, infants, home, and domestic projects. You may get the chance to express your feelings. In addition to smoother personal relationships, your interactions with most people are apt to be much easier. Take advantage of this atmosphere to establish better rapport. It is a good day to social-ize at home or to invite the boss or others with influence home for dinner.

TRANSIT SUN SEXTILE NATAL MERCURY

⊙ ✷ ☿ Participate in meetings, community activities, and any situation that gives you a chance to exchange ideas and information. Suc-cess is more likely to come along if you stay busy, mentally as well as physically. When transit Sun sextiles your natal Mercury, you may have the chance to con-tact or visit siblings or neighbors. If you need a car, this is a good time to look for one. Areas of opportunity are related to design and mechanical projects, writing, correspondence, business, and repair or maintenance of equipment and appli-ances. This is also the time that your schedule offers the best chance to get a haircut, have keys made, place or respond to advertisements, subscribe to peri-odicals, and reorganize.

TRANSIT SUN SEXTILE NATAL VENUS

⊙ ✷ ♀ If given a chance, superiors will be favorably disposed toward you when transit Sun sextiles your natal Venus. Socialize or at least initiate pleasant interactions with authority figures and those with influence. Opportunity today may also lead to partnership or alliance with an important individual. If you do not think such a situation is likely to come along, go out and create one. There is benefit in heeding those who advise on social matters or counsel you with regard to personal relationships. Luck is with you, but tak-ing advantage of it depends on being among people. Don't pass up any chance to exhibit personal charm and attractiveness. Watch for opportunities that may give you a chance to enjoy beautiful things, indulge in a little luxury, and pursue romance, pleasure, and entertainment.

TRANSIT SUN SEXTILE NATAL MARS

⊙ ✷ ♂ Circumstances provide opportunities to become more physi-cally active, more aggressive in pursuing goals, and better at accomplishing tasks. Masculine influences and those with energy and enthusi-asm in one form or another will provide encouragement as well as assistance in your physical accomplishments. When transit Sun sextiles your natal Mars, engaging in sports and other activities that contribute to physical fitness can ultimately lead to better health and more self-confidence. If you do not currently have a program of physical fitness or participate in sports or routine exercise, this is an opportune time to begin. The local health club or diet center may offer reduced rates or other incentives to get you started. No matter what opportunities you encounter, success is more likely to occur if you are physically assertive.

TRANSIT SUN SEXTILE NATAL JUPITER

⊙ ✶ ♃ When transit Sun sextiles your natal Jupiter, be ready to expand your intellectual horizons because success involves learning as well as demonstrating your knowledge or expertise. Children in your life are also favored with opportunities for higher education or advanced training. Advertising or direct-mail promotions are special avenues of opportunity. Spiritual guidance and participation in religious activities, cultural pursuits, and political activities are other possible sources of opportunity. Be alert to situations that enhance your influence or status. Superiors or authority figures are instrumental in helping you get something published or assisting you with long-distance travel plans. Opportunities today may also lead to success with regard to court decisions and to the job or health of a parent.

TRANSIT SUN SEXTILE NATAL SATURN

⊙ ✶ ♄ Pay attention. More creative ways to accomplish mundane responsibilities come along when transit Sun sextiles your natal Saturn. Hard work and planning result in a valuable opportunity. If you are in a business or profession, your maturity and expertise can mean new clients and invitations to consult or lecture. If you have not been a meticulous planner and organizer or have not worked hard in the past, this is the opportune time to begin. Circumstances may offer a chance to gain the wisdom, maturity, and experience that ultimately lead to greater productivity and success.

TRANSIT SUN SEXTILE NATAL URANUS

⊙ ✳ ♅ It is a good idea to get in touch with friends and to welcome the opportunity to make new ones when transit Sun sextiles your natal Uranus. Respond positively to the invitations or advice of friends. Favorable situations come through children and their activities, organizations to which you belong, or the network of acquaintances, family, and friends you have established. Joining an organization at this time may bring future opportunities. Attendance at meetings and social events is also advantageous. Other positive potentials in your present circumstances include superiors or other authority figures who suggest ways to gain more personal freedom, provide creative ideas and solutions, and offer a more visible format for your ideas.

TRANSIT SUN SEXTILE NATAL NEPTUNE

⊙ ✳ ♆ Opportunities you encounter when transit Sun sextiles your natal Neptune are very diverse. You may get a chance to swim, sail, and fish or to advantageously demonstrate your skills in such activities. You may be given a more effective prescription for an ailment or be directed to a physician or spiritual counselor who proves to be most helpful. Other possibilities include discovery of information that solves a problem or mystery. Favorable opportunity comes through helping someone less fortunate, working on artistic and photographic projects, or simply following your intuition and instincts.

TRANSIT SUN SEXTILE NATAL PLUTO

⊙ ✳ ♇ Transit Sun sextile your natal Pluto brings opportunity to use the past in some positive way. You may, for example, come across valuable information by reviewing old magazines or doing research. You may get a chance either to collect or repay an old debt or favor. Superiors or those with influence may provide an opportunity that results in better use of your special skills or increases monetary and other material resources. Present circumstances indicate there is benefit in getting rid of what you no longer need or want. If you are not certain of how to recycle or sell items, seek advice on how these tasks may be accomplished. It is also a good time to deal with self-control, engage in psychological analysis, make an effort to get to the bottom of things, and improve yourself and your personal environment.

SOLAR SQUARES

TRANSIT SUN SQUARE NATAL SUN

⊙ □ ⊙   Circumstances are likely to test your self-confidence and willpower. Success depends on your ability or willingness to withstand the demands of others, especially those in positions of authority. You may have to cope with situations that cause you to doubt that you are right or that you will succeed in what you are doing. Failure, however, is not necessarily destined to be the outcome of your endeavors when transit Sun squares your natal Sun. You can and will accomplish what you set out to do if you overcome frustration or discouragement. You may be particularly busy living up to promises or commitments you have made or that others have made for you.

TRANSIT SUN SQUARE NATAL MOON

⊙ □ ☽   Conflict arises between what you must do and what you would rather do when transit Sun squares your natal Moon. You encounter insensitive or arrogant people who make demands without realizing what the financial, emotional, or other cost may be to you. The key is not to let your feelings interfere with getting something accomplished. No matter what dislocation you are forced to cope with, you are likely to succeed because of it rather than in spite of it. You may be unusually sensitive to criticism, even very constructive criticism from those who have your best interests at heart.

TRANSIT SUN SQUARE NATAL MERCURY

⊙ □ ☿   You are busier than usual with writing or other communications. Others may seek your advice or opinion and you will have to scramble for the information they require. Pay closer attention to what you hear or read. It is likely to contain something worth knowing. When transit Sun squares your natal Mercury, those in charge may criticize your ideas and opinions, or perhaps their objection is the manner in which you express yourself. Take such discouragement in stride, it does not necessarily mean you are wrong. If your ideas are solid and well-organized, all you need is patience, determination, and the willingness to try various approaches until something works. Avoid engaging in false promises, boasting, or spreading misleading information, and do not get frustrated or distracted by others who do. If you find yourself in traffic, expect to encounter arrogant and careless drivers.

TRANSIT SUN SQUARE NATAL VENUS

⊙□♀ Enthusiasm does not quite gel, accompanied as it is by the lack of physical energy or strong emotional commitment. If this description does not altogether fit, it can easily apply to those you encounter. Refinement and beauty may be pushed aside by that which is coarse and gaudy. When transit Sun squares your natal Venus, it is a hectic and frustrating time for social activities. The proper pecking order may get screwed up in some way, and you get blamed or are the one elected to straighten things out. You might be stimulated by conflicts, chaos, or exciting events, but if nothing much seems to be going on, do not attempt to initiate more dynamic situations. Such attempts can put you in an unenviable position that might be compared to wanting to set the world on fire, attracting a crowd, and then finding you have misplaced the matches.

TRANSIT SUN SQUARE NATAL MARS

⊙□♂ Physical energy and stimulation arise either from within yourself or from the circumstances you encounter when transit Sun squares your natal Mars. The key to using this energy is not to push too hard. Avoid anger and frustration in carrying out the demands of superiors. If others challenge what you are doing or get in your way, do not stop to prove anything or engage in time- and energy-wasting maneuvers. Simply keep moving along. The spirit of competition is easily inspired, but nothing will be accomplished if aggressiveness gets out of control. Too much stress and strain could adversely affect your heart or your head.

TRANSIT SUN SQUARE NATAL JUPITER

⊙□♃ When transit Sun squares your natal Jupiter, you may be tempted to exaggerate your social status, professional position, intellectual accomplishments, or monetary assets. Restlessness or discontent may cause you to behave this way, or others whom you wish to impress may unwittingly serve as catalysts that inspire your overstatements. Whatever the reason or circumstance, if desire to identify yourself with some exalted position cannot be resisted, at least make an effort to minimize the damage. Use the energy of your desire to work harder in endeavors that may ultimately turn what was once a false boast into reality. Be prepared to demonstrate your knowledge or skills to those in charge. The chances of winning a contest or cashing in on speculative ventures at this time are slim. If you do emerge a winner, do not push your luck. Take the money or victory and quit while you are ahead.

TRANSIT SUN SQUARE NATAL SATURN

☉ □ ♄ This is a time when living by hard work, organization, and planning will stand you in good stead. If you have not previously conducted your affairs in this manner, you may now wish that you had. When there is a square between transit Sun and your natal Saturn, you may not initiate or be in control of circumstances, but you will nevertheless be called upon to measure up to them and to take a responsible position. Life may be, or seem to be, more somber than usual. Timing is off and you are more easily discouraged by problems that you usually regard as minor annoyances. The answer is to forge ahead. Forget instant gratification. Concentrate on the business at hand and let rewards or enjoyment come later.

TRANSIT SUN SQUARE NATAL URANUS

☉ □ ♅ You are unlikely to be able to control your life's circumstances when transit Sun squares your natal Uranus. Your normal schedule or plans you have made may be disrupted by the weather, war, or other forces in your outer environment. Although you may not be able to manipulate or control disruptions, they may stimulate you to adopt an unusual or different approach to things. You may be infused with a spirit of freedom or independence. Association with friends and organizations is apt to be part of the scenario.

TRANSIT SUN SQUARE NATAL NEPTUNE

☉ □ ♆ You are on your own when transit Sun squares your natal Neptune. Trusting those in charge right now can be a risky business

49

because they may be elusive and hard to find or they deliberately mislead you. There is also the potential that you are the one who appears to be elusive. Whatever the state of affairs, it is best to avoid all situations that require clear thinking, attention to detail, and confrontation with reality. Concentrate on artistic projects or spiritual studies. Be cautious with medicine and be more careful than usual if you are around water or if you find yourself in unfamiliar territory.

TRANSIT SUN SQUARE NATAL PLUTO

☉ □ ♇ Circumstances demand a show of willpower, stamina, and willingness on your part to investigate and get to the bottom of things. Thoroughness is a must if you want to succeed when transit Sun squares your natal Pluto. Direct confrontations, deliberate actions, and keen observations are the best strategies. Do not reveal plans or betray a confidence. Areas in which you have gained the most control may be challenged or invaded by others. A self-defeating attitude now can cause you to become your own worst enemy. A debt of honor may be due.

SOLAR TRINES

TRANSIT SUN TRINE NATAL SUN

☉ △ ☉ When transit Sun trines your natal Sun, you have a more positive sense of your uniqueness, an inner contentment. If current circumstances are troubling, you may escape at least some of the disappointment, anger, or dislocation. If, on the other hand, current circumstances are good, your increased self-confidence and vitality make them even better. It is a time to enjoy the world and your place in it.

TRANSIT SUN TRINE NATAL MOON

☉ △ ☽ Circumstances promote pride and emotional satisfaction in home, children and other family members. Female relationships are particularly meaningful, and a woman may provide valuable assistance.

When transit Sun trines your natal Moon, your emotional level is high and your intuition on target. Others will admire your home and family and your creativity. It is an excellent time to initiate artistic and other creative activities, start domestic projects, and take care of matters related to children, women, or a new venture. Should disappointments occur, they are apt to eventually work out to your advantage.

TRANSIT SUN TRINE NATAL MERCURY

⊙△☿ When transit Sun trines your natal Mercury, conditions favor travel, whether it involves running errands in your neighborhood or taking trips for business and pleasure. It is also a good time for the purchase, sale, or repair of equipment. Work that involves your mechanical or design skills is favored, as are business transactions, contracts, and negotiations. Writing, teaching, study, and communication are other areas of potential success. Relationships with co-workers, neighbors, and siblings are encouraged by the circumstances. Attendance at meetings and other group activities brings valuable contacts as well as an exchange of ideas and information.

TRANSIT SUN TRINE NATAL VENUS

⊙△♀ Others find you attractive and openly express their admiration or affection as transit Sun trines your natal Venus. Superiors are impressed and favorably disposed to recognize your talent, which makes this an appropriate day to ask them for favors or a promotion. Romantic relationships and female relationships are encouraged. You can move forward with social plans, artistic endeavors, and matters that pertain to luxury items and beautification projects. Luck is with you, especially when dealing with other people. Partnerships or other alliances, joint ventures, and public relations efforts that you initiate now are successful. You come out ahead in debates and judgments are in your favor. Do not let laziness, overindulgence, or taking too much for granted spoil what should be a fortunate and enjoyable period.

TRANSIT SUN TRINE NATAL MARS

☉ △ ♂ Positive energy and vitality accompany your physical efforts, the only drawback being a tendency for laziness which keeps you from initially making the efforts. Lacking sufficient aggressiveness or the competitive spirit, you may see no reason to take advantage of the favorable circumstances that are at hand. Avoiding indolence and a too passive attitude will net ample dividends. When transit Sun trines your natal Mars, superiors are impressed with your work. Male relationships and dealing with men or masculine products are favored. It is an excellent day to get a haircut, attend or participate in sporting events, and engage in open confrontation. If other factors do not negate the fortunate potential, this is a good time to undergo surgery or dental work.

TRANSIT SUN TRINE NATAL JUPITER

☉ △ ♃ Feel good about your own integrity, explore your spirituality, and broaden your intellectual horizons as transit Sun trines your natal Jupiter. These efforts are not only favored in and of themselves, but they are also likely to inspire the attention and admiration of those with influence. This is no time for false modesty and empty gestures on your part. Sincere generosity and devotion to the truth bring success. Enjoyment is enhanced and humor can be found in every situation. Cultural events, long-distance travel, religious activities, political interests, sports activities, banking and investment, speculative ventures, publishing, and advertising campaigns can be successfully launched. Judgments are in your favor.

TRANSIT SUN TRINE NATAL SATURN

☉ △ ♄ Hard work, planning, and organization pay off. Those in charge are suitably impressed by your past efforts, and that is only one of the potential rewards you reap when transit Sun trines your natal Saturn. If previous activities have not been carefully planned or organized, this can mark the successful beginning of such efforts. It will be worthwhile to accept whatever responsibilities come along and to initiate important projects that require long-term efforts, especially if they are related to real estate, business, building, or engineering. Seek favors from those in authority and those who are older, wiser, and have more experience. If you are the one with seniority and experience, you gain personal advantages from helping others.

TRANSIT SUN TRINE NATAL URANUS

⊙ △ ♅ A different or unique approach works to your advantage as transit Sun trines your natal Uranus, and, in fact, it might succeed better than you ever dreamed possible. However, being different just to be different is not likely to work at all. Your plan or idea must have a solid foundation. Participation in group efforts, organizational meetings, fund-raising, and political activities is favored.

TRANSIT SUN TRINE NATAL NEPTUNE

⊙ △ ♆ Others, especially superiors, are impressed with your imagination, spirituality, and sensitivity. They may also be impressed with your charitable acts or your skills in areas such as photography, swimming, sailing, water sports, therapy, and dancing. With or without the presence of superiors or other people around, all these activities may nevertheless work out well when transit Sun trines your natal Neptune. Also favored now are covert activities and highly confidential matters. Others may be attracted to you or you to them by something that seems unattainable or mysterious. Follow hunches, pay attention to dreams, and allow yourself to be inspired spiritually or artistically by whatever is offered by current circumstances.

TRANSIT SUN TRINE NATAL PLUTO

⊙ △ ♇ People or circumstances that you encounter when transit Sun trines your natal Pluto can be used to increase your self-control or gain additional power. Impressive determination, recuperative power, and concentration can be achieved. You will get to the bottom of things, perhaps with the fortunate assistance of those in charge. It is a time to develop and use your resourcefulness and to benefit from separating what is important from what is not.

SOLAR OPPOSITIONS

TRANSIT SUN OPPOSED NATAL SUN

☉ ☍ ☉ Although other circumstances may proceed smoothly today, you are not favored to emerge the winner in ego-related situations. This is not a fortuitous time to resist the authority of others and to exhibit arrogant or aggressive attitudes that at any other time would cause your opponents to back down. When transit Sun opposes your natal Sun, six months have passed since your birthday, which makes it a good time to measure your progress (or lack of it).

TRANSIT SUN OPPOSED NATAL MOON

☉ ☍ ☽ A tug-of-war exists between your desires or emotional needs and your ambitions when transit Sun opposes your natal Moon. Those in charge make impossible demands without knowing or caring what dislocation their demands cause, and trying to appeal to them on emotional terms will only result in a waste of time and energy. You are unlikely to succeed in direct confrontations with family or female associates. Appreciate whatever positive circumstances you encounter and do not believe you can easily overcome any negative ones.

TRANSIT SUN OPPOSED NATAL MERCURY

☉ ☍ ☿ Other people, especially supervisors or authority figures, are not likely to be on your wavelength right now. In fact, their ideas and opinions may directly conflict with your own. As transit Sun opposes your natal Mercury, efforts to debate issues, handle negotiations, or resolve contract disputes are thwarted. There is nothing constructive to be done about these situations except to leave them alone until an alternative or compromise becomes possible. It is not a favorable time for communications, writing, or travel.

TRANSIT SUN OPPOSED NATAL VENUS

☉ ☍ ♀ Friends, ex-partners, and former lovers are apt to be sharing their love and affections with other people today, and you may not be certain how you feel about the situation. A certain amount of loneliness creeps into your heart even if everything else in your life is fairly smooth when transit Sun opposes your natal Venus. Avoid letting ego reactions put you in conflict with a partner. Do not initiate legal matters, social events, romantic attachments, partnerships, or cooperative ventures. Do not accept gaudiness or ostentation as a substitute for true beauty.

TRANSIT SUN OPPOSED NATAL MARS

☉ ☍ ♂ As a result of laziness or careless behavior on your part or that of others, many of your physical efforts may be undone. The point is that you should not try too hard to accomplish something since it may be a lost cause. When transit Sun opposes your natal Mars, some vital force seems to be missing. Although you may or may not be able to point to exactly what it is, you will be frustrated if you try to stir things up to correct the situation. There is no pleasing anybody, including yourself. Open confrontations, especially with men, are likely to turn into disasters and solve nothing.

TRANSIT SUN OPPOSED NATAL JUPITER

☉ ☍ ♃ Others are not inclined to recognize your efforts or projects when transit Sun opposes your natal Jupiter. It may be the pride or jealousy of others that gets in the way of your progress, but whatever the reason, you are likely to waste your time if you try to arouse their interest or admiration. Situations and people you encounter may be all show and no substance. There is no productive way to expand your mental horizons or increase your personal status in this atmosphere. It is an unfavorable time for publishing, religious and political activities, advertising, long-distance travel, court decisions, and situations related to your father or his status. The most constructive thing is to stay put in your own sphere of influence and attend to routine business.

TRANSIT SUN OPPOSED NATAL SATURN

☉ ☍ ♄ The more work or responsibilities you take on, the more there will be as transit Sun opposes your natal Saturn. It may seem as though you are taking one step forward and eight steps back. Forget about receiving any show of thanks or gratitude. Nitpickers and those in charge seem to take it for granted that you have what they need and that you are fully prepared to execute their demands. Sloppy work or irresponsibility you exhibit is not only unacceptable now but will work against you in the future. It is not a good idea to seek favors or to count on luck to see you through. However, if your life is pretty smooth right now and you do not get unduly upset with anything that does turn up, circumstances are not apt to change for the worse.

TRANSIT SUN OPPOSED NATAL URANUS

☉ ☍ ♅ Superiors or those in charge will not be pleased if you attempt to change the schedule, suggest unorthodox or nontraditional ideas, or try to inspire them with new or unusual methods. This is not a favorable time to coordinate social events, conduct friendships, attend to children and their activities, or participate in organizational meetings and fund-raising activities. When transit Sun opposes your natal Uranus, things are not apt to come together the way they are supposed to or the way you thought they would. Concentrate on what is working instead of what is not.

TRANSIT SUN OPPOSED NATAL NEPTUNE

☉ ☍ ♆ When transit Sun opposes your natal Neptune, there is no telling what sort of impression you are making on others, especially superiors or authority figures. For no readily apparent reason, others find you vague or mysterious. This does not have to be a problem unless your present circumstances make it important that others do not form misconceptions about you. It is not a favorable time to seek spiritual counsel, take new medication, or be on, in, or around water.

TRANSIT SUN OPPOSED NATAL PLUTO

Others will stand firmly in your way if you try to get to the bottom of things when transit Sun opposes your natal Pluto. Save research, investigation, and power plays for another time. This is not a period to dig up the past, collect a debt, undergo psychological analysis, recycle materials, or start a renovation or restoration project. Others will be intimidated by or envious of your self-control or any power you have. It will not be to your advantage to inspire such feelings deliberately, but there is very little you will be able to do about it if others insist on feeling that way. Do not waste time trying to salvage anyone's ego, including your own.

Chapter Three

Transit Mercury Aspects to the Natal Planets

M ercury's aspects to natal planets usually last from the day before until the day after the exact aspect is made. An exception occurs when Mercury is retrograde and makes the same aspect to natal planets more than once. In this case, Mercury's influence will be stronger and of longer duration.

MERCURY CONJUNCTIONS

TRANSIT MERCURY CONJOIN NATAL SUN

☿ ☌ ☉ Self-esteem and willpower prompt you to express yourself in the most positive terms as transit Mercury conjoins your natal Sun. Communications and travel at this time are closely linked with the dictates of your ego and personal goals. You strongly identify with ideas that reflect your own thoughts or that provide a more aggressive or more dramatic forum in which you can express yourself. Increased self-focus in your intellectual endeavors and self-expression can inspire you to reach for higher levels of imagination and originality. You can take the ideas of others and add your input to create something entirely different and unique. However, the potential to avoid here is consciously or subconsciously appropriating the ideas of others and presenting them as your own. If situations that involve a car or travel happen to arise, you may be tempted to indulge in a more expensive automobile or first-class tickets.

TRANSIT MERCURY CONJOIN NATAL MOON

☿ ☌ ☽ There is likelihood of a spontaneous trip, a sudden decision to get in touch with people, or unexpected contact from others. Interactions with neighbors and siblings increase when transit Mercury conjoins your natal Moon. Neighbors or relatives offer transportation. You may take a trip with them or travel or run errands on their behalf. Information you give to others or seek to obtain for yourself at this time is apt to primarily concern home, family members, the education of children, and domestic items or activities. Business transactions involving the purchase or sale of a residence, domestic items, and family property may be on your agenda. Discussions or meetings involve dietary or health needs, childhood conditioning, and the past. This is also a time when you identify strongly with thoughts and ideas of others that reflect your own feelings.

TRANSIT MERCURY CONJOIN NATAL MERCURY

☿ ☌ ☿ While searching for ideas and methods that are similar or parallel to your own, you will find just the piece of information you are looking for. A constant stream of communication keeps coming at you from all directions. When transit Mercury conjoins your natal Mercury, you will not have to go very far to seek information because you are likely to find everything you need in your own neighborhood. Plans, designs, mechanical projects, and the purchase or repair of mechanical equipment (from cars to typewriters) are the most likely targets of your current plans and activities.

TRANSIT MERCURY CONJOIN NATAL VENUS

☿ ☌ ♀ You will either seek or be given ideas concerning your social life, proper etiquette, your appearance, and decorating or harmonizing your environment when transit Mercury conjoins your natal Venus. Discussing common goals with a partner or other allies is emphasized. If you are not very good at engaging in small talk, you may find it comes a little easier these days, especially since others may save you the trouble by doing most of the talking. Discussions and activities feature art or music instruction, romance, humor, and they tend to include more gossip than usual. Advice and information are at hand with regard to partnerships, joint ventures, contract negotiations, and legal matters. Other potential concerns you experience include wedding plans, divorce proceedings, social events, and eliciting the cooperation of others.

TRANSIT MERCURY CONJOIN NATAL MARS

☿ ☌ ♂ Things you hear or read motivate you to take physical action. By choice or circumstance, your plans and methods are put into action and your ideas become physical realities when transit Mercury conjoins your natal Mars. One of the most likely situations involves giving or receiving instructions on how to accomplish a physical task or goal, operate machinery, or go to a certain location. You may have some pressing need or urge to travel at this time. Business transactions are apt to include the sale or purchase of an automobile or other vehicle, communications equipment, sports equipment, or computers. Activities and discussions involve education, military service, a haircut, dental work, or a surgical procedure.

TRANSIT MERCURY CONJOIN NATAL JUPITER

☿ ☌ ♃ Information and ideas that come your way when transit Mercury conjoins your natal Jupiter are related to higher education, long-distance travel, religious and political activities, writing, publishing, or cultural pursuits. You seek to expand your monetary or business interests, language skills, or sports activities. One thing you can expect to come across is a lot of advertising, and you may place or respond to advertisements and direct-mail promotions. International communications may also play a role. Current news and concerns can involve a court decision, your father, and the health or employment of relatives.

TRANSIT MERCURY CONJOIN NATAL SATURN

☿ ☌ ♄ Ideas, information, and communications in general may be restricted because you either lack interest in learning or in making contacts with others. Your advice in certain matters may be sought by others. You may seek or use information and skills in order to become more experienced or to attain seniority status. Organization and preparation can become big issues as transit Mercury conjoins your natal Saturn. Contacts and travel these days relate to business or serious pursuits.

TRANSIT MERCURY CONJOIN NATAL URANUS

☿ ☌ ♅ Although the outcome of current circumstances may eventually filter down to you, most of the communications, ideas, and methods you handle are more relevant to societal issues and activities. When transit Mercury conjoins your natal Uranus, personal communications or travel may be unique, nontraditional, or out of synch with everything or everyone else. Technical information, computers, software, international finance, and the newsletters or business affairs of organizations to which you belong may be on the agenda.

TRANSIT MERCURY CONJOIN NATAL NEPTUNE

☿ ☌ ♆ It may be hard to grasp the true meaning or accuracy of information when transit Mercury conjoins your natal Neptune. Trying to get to the bottom of a situation ends in confusion and raises more questions than answers. Keys, reading material, papers, and correspondence can be misplaced. Ideas and information are taken or understood in a mystical or spiritual sense. Information you get or seek may involve spiritualism, mysticism, or the occult. Other potential targets of your current activities, communications, and contacts include charitable institutions, prisons, and hospitals. You may travel on or over water.

TRANSIT MERCURY CONJOIN NATAL PLUTO

☿ ☌ ♇ Information, ideas, and activities in which you are involved may relate directly to gaining personal power. You may, for example, be given instructions or develop strategies on diet and physical fitness that help you gain more control over your body. Information and activities also relate to finance and investment, organization and work methods, and development of self-discipline. When there is a conjunction between transit Mercury and your natal Pluto, you may gather valuable information or you may travel for purposes related to education, research, investigation, psychoanalysis, renovation, or property assessment.

Mercury Sextiles

Transit Mercury Sextile Natal Sun

☿ ✶ ☉ The flow of information and communications that come your way as transit Mercury sextiles your natal Sun contains helpful means by which you can better express your individuality and exert personal influence. Do not hesitate to take advantage of the ideas of others but be sure that you give them proper credit. The creative input, strength of character, or leadership you exhibit in meetings, group discussions, or with regard to community affairs and business transactions can make a big difference in how well situations turn out for you.

Transit Mercury Sextile Natal Moon

☿ ✶ ☽ You are emotionally influenced in some way by the information, opinions, and ideas that come to you during this period. As transit Mercury sextiles your natal Moon, the situations you experience represent a chance to express your feelings or fulfill some personal desire. Other possibilities include the opportunity to visit or communicate with out-of-town relatives and to interact more effectively with family members. Circumstances may present the chance to buy or sell a home and other real estate or domestic items. You may also get a chance to improve your diet, health, and physical fitness as a result of the people and situations you encounter.

Transit Mercury Sextile Natal Mercury

☿ ✶ ☿ These days, opportunity is apt to provide a way to improve basic skills, gather information, purchase or learn to operate computers, and engage in sales. Looking for a car? Need a job? Explore the possibilities. Situations that can lead to employment, travel, and education are at hand as transit Mercury sextiles your natal Mercury. They may not appear automatically. Do not wait for them to come to you. Go out and seek opportunity and the rest of the pieces will fall into place.

Transit Mercury Sextile Natal Venus

☿ ✶ ♀ This is a period of increased potential for an opportunity that leads to romance, making social contacts, establishing partnership and other alliances, and improving your physical appearance. You may also be given the chance to use your diplomatic skills or personal charm to great advantage. An opportunity now may involve luxury items, art, jewelry, and decorating or harmonizing your environment. When transit Mercury sextiles your natal Venus, someone may send you flowers or candy, or you can view this as an opportunity to send such gifts to someone special.

Transit Mercury Sextile Natal Mars

☿ ✶ ♂ Circumstances you encounter as transit Mercury sextiles your natal Mars represent a chance to take physical action of some kind. This opportunity covers a variety of possibilities. Your ideas become physical realities, theories are given physical application, or travel may be on your agenda in the future because of an advantage you gain now. Situations may also lead, for instance, to the purchase or sale of a car and other machinery and the chance to learn how to operate them. Circumstances may lead to the use or development of design, mechanical, or athletic skills. Ideas and methods that come your way enable you to accomplish work and other physical tasks more efficiently.

Transit Mercury Sextile Natal Jupiter

☿ ✶ ♃ When transit Mercury sextiles your natal Jupiter, letters, phone calls, and other communications are apt to contain an opportunity related to higher education, long-distance travel, people of another culture or race, religious or political activities, and cultural events. Circumstances may lead to news about relatives, in particular your father or your in-laws. Other opportunities can be found by placing or responding to advertisements and direct mail promotions.

Transit Mercury Sextile Natal Saturn

☿ ✶ ♄ You may learn how to become more organized and better pre-pared for the future when transit Mercury sextiles your natal Saturn. Information and activities that come along fit neatly into whatever organization or plans you have already laid out. Circumstances at this time may lead to easing current restrictions, provide some opportunity that will be useful to you later in life, or result in recognition of your authority and experience.

Transit Mercury Sextile Natal Uranus

☿ ✶ ♅ As transit Mercury sextiles your natal Uranus, you may get the chance either to demonstrate or to acquire some unique or special talent or knowledge. Other situations to watch for at this time include opportu-nities to gain or use technical expertise and sociological skills, to travel in some unusual capacity or to an unusual place, and to be involved in the finances or newsletters of an organization or club. Success that occurs now is apt to result from not being in synch with everyone else or having a nontraditional attitude or approach.

Transit Mercury Sextile Natal Neptune

☿ ✶ ♆ When a sextile occurs between transit Mercury and your natal Neptune, you can expand your spiritual awareness, improve artis-tic sensitivity, and develop intuitive skills. If you take advantage of the informa-tion and ideas that come your way during this period, you may profit from the sale or purchase of footwear, boats and marine equipment, swimming apparel, photographic equipment, or seafood. You may also have the opportunity to travel on or over water, get a chance to go dancing or skating, or receive instruc-tion in these activities.

TRANSIT MERCURY SEXTILE NATAL PLUTO

☿ ✶ ♇ Watch for information and ideas related to self-control and willpower as transit Mercury sextiles your natal Pluto. They represent opportunities that may lead to improvement in mental health and physical fitness, enhancement of organizational skills, effectiveness at work or at home, and the attainment of greater self-discipline. Such opportunities may not come automatically or appear in an obvious way, so you may have to go out and actively seek information or methods that will help you attain greater personal power. It may be in this very search that you find the opportunity you are looking for.

MERCURY SQUARES

TRANSIT MERCURY SQUARE NATAL SUN

☿ □ ☉ There is likely to be some problem or frustration in connection with information, ideas, or communications during this period. You will be offended if what you read or hear happens to be in the form of criticism. Even if it was not meant to be taken personally, you tend to react to it that way. When transit Mercury squares your natal Sun, those who give you instructions or directions must be careful not to impinge on your authority or damage your ego. On the other hand, if you refuse to let ego or stubbornness interfere with the ideas, methods, or information you are given, and you patiently overcome any other obstacles that turn up along the way, a great deal of progress is possible.

TRANSIT MERCURY SQUARE NATAL MOON

☿ □ ☽ You have to grapple with conflicting opinions, too much or too little information, and other annoying distractions when transit Mercury squares your natal Moon. If your stomach gets tied up in knots, simply take a deep breath, relax, patiently sort things out, and continue moving along. Before leaving home or office, prepare yourself mentally for the possibility of traffic jams and other delays in transportation, public as well as private. Projects may not get finished on time. If this is the case, notify those who need to know and keep working. Another strong potential is to lose or misplace keys, books, and important papers. Carefully retracing your steps is apt to result in successfully locating lost items. In spite of schedules that get turned upside down, plans that must be changed at the last minute, mechanical failures, or a hundred other things that go wrong, much can still be accomplished.

TRANSIT MERCURY SQUARE NATAL MERCURY

☿ □ ☿ Try to simplify things as much as possible during this period. Many ideas and much information may come your way but a lot of it is likely to be repetitious and will only waste your time. Lines of communication tend to get crossed or break down as transit Mercury squares your natal Mercury. Equipment fails just when you need it the most, and the purchase or delivery of machinery may be unavoidably delayed. Be sure to read the fine print in contracts and count your change in monetary transactions. Travel plans run into snags. Information, methods, or ideas you present may duplicate or parallel that of others. In spite of obstacles that must be overcome, success is not impossible. The idea is to keep moving forward.

TRANSIT MERCURY SQUARE NATAL VENUS

☿ □ ♀ It would be a mistake to discount the potential value of what others tell you or what you read or hear simply because it is distasteful or because you do not care for the manner in which it is presented. Contract negotiations and lines of communication between you and a partner or other allies tend to go awry when transit Mercury squares your natal Venus. Decorating projects can be plagued by misunderstanding or misinformation. Make sure you understand what is involved concerning proposed beauty treatments or methods to enhance your physical appearance. When it comes to romance, vacation plans, entertainment, and social events, you can expect frustration but not necessarily failure. The thing to keep in mind is that frustrations during this period are apt to disappear soon. Progress can be made in spite of them.

TRANSIT MERCURY SQUARE NATAL MARS

☿ □ ♂ Physically accomplishing something when transit Mercury squares your natal Mars is apt to be frustrating. Incorrect information or directions may cause you to be too early or too late to attain a certain goal. Your car breaks down or public transportation delays throw you off schedule. Purchase of a car or other equipment at this time can develop snags. You are apt to be more competitive or aggressive, which can help you accomplish more if you do not let it go too far. Others may say things or use methods that provoke your anger. It is to your ultimate advantage to avoid rash behavior and to make sure you understand the information you receive. No matter what headaches (literally and figuratively) turn up, you are still apt to make measurable progress. Protect yourself against colds and fever, and take extra precautions when handling electrical equipment and volatile materials.

TRANSIT MERCURY SQUARE NATAL JUPITER

☿ □ ♃ Information and ideas have to be gathered, methods discussed, and choices made. On top of that, you experience difficulty and frustration when you try to organize everything because of the volume of things that come your way. Details can easily slip away or be neglected when transit Mercury squares your natal Jupiter, so make sure you get all the information you need and that the information you get is accurate. Another possibility is that you become involved with so many details it becomes difficult to see the overall picture. Be aware of the tendency to exaggerate or expand a situation or the information at hand. All in all, measurable progress is likely to occur.

TRANSIT MERCURY SQUARE NATAL SATURN

☿ □ ♄ Information, ideas, or methods may seem very interesting and even valuable when transit Mercury squares your natal Saturn, but trying to use or apply them proves to be difficult or restricted in some way. Although you may not be able to put the idea or method to practical use for the time being, perhaps even for a long period of time, it will someday come in handy. Too much perfectionism or lack of time hampers organization and planning. Even if you are usually very efficient and organized, you cannot locate the very document, book, or other item you need. During this period you may be required to redo or complete a task you thought was finished. Eventually everything gets straightened out and you will have something to show for your efforts.

TRANSIT MERCURY SQUARE NATAL URANUS

☿ □ ♅ During this period you may find yourself a little out of synch with those who are trying to communicate with you, either because you are not in your usual location or following your normal schedule, or because they are not. Since your ideas about what is different or unique may be at odds with other people's notions when transit Mercury squares your natal Uranus, a certain amount of discussion and clarification becomes necessary. You understand or approach most things in a impersonal, societal way and thus misinterpret what others want you to understand on a personal level, or else others take what you say in a personal way when your only intention was to discuss the broader societal implications of some issue.

TRANSIT MERCURY SQUARE NATAL NEPTUNE

☿ □ ♆ Following instructions or directions is not easy to accomplish when transit Mercury squares your natal Neptune. Trying to assimilate information accurately is also apt to be difficult, though it does not necessarily lead to failure. You may arrive at the right conclusion for the wrong reasons, or come to the wrong conclusion but still have circumstances work out satisfactorily. This is not a favorable period to determine who is right and who is wrong since there is little likelihood it will make any difference in the long run. Although you may find it difficult, keep as much of a logical perspective as possible. Intuition or instincts may dictate one thing while the facts point to another. You may question whether the facts are real or an illusion. This is an unfavorable time for business transactions and travel on or over water.

TRANSIT MERCURY SQUARE NATAL PLUTO

☿ □ ♇ You take things too seriously. Do not try to read between the lines when there is really nothing to find, and do not waste time looking for hidden motives in others when their actions may be perfectly innocent. You may become too intense or place too much importance on what in reality is a relatively innocuous idea or piece of information when transit Mercury squares your natal Pluto. The reverse may also be true when others take your ideas or actions far more seriously than you had intended. Valuable time can be lost. You can jeopardize a position of personal power or control if you try to manipulate a situation or use the information and ideas you get from others for personal gain. This will also be true if you allow others to behave in such a manner. In spite of frustrating obstacles that turn up during this period, much progress can occur if you maintain a patient, reasonable attitude.

MERCURY TRINES

TRANSIT MERCURY TRINE NATAL SUN

☿ △ ☉   The news and information you receive or the way that you make use of them can greatly enhance your personal image and reputation during this period. Others look favorably on your accomplishments as well as your opinions when transit Mercury trines your natal Sun. Your approval will, no doubt, also be sought. There is a successful meshing of ideas and methods, the potential results of which include advancement in your social or professional position and an invitation to become the leading spokesperson of a group. This is an excellent time to launch a writing or communications project, engage in business transactions, or begin a journey.

TRANSIT MERCURY TRINE NATAL MOON

☿ △ ☾   Everything should flow smoothly and successfully as transit Mercury trines your natal Moon. Everyone in your world is where they are supposed to be and doing what they are supposed to be doing. Machinery hums along, your body functions well, and your mind is free from annoying distractions. Dissension is not likely to disrupt meetings and discussions. Business transactions that involve your home, real-estate property, and domestic items are favored. Your requests are granted and there is likely to be personal advantage when you grant others what they request. Teaching, as well as learning, is highly beneficial. This is an excellent period to contact or visit relatives. News or information you read or hear is emotionally satisfying.

TRANSIT MERCURY TRINE NATAL MERCURY

☿ △ ☿ Unbiased information and ideas lead the way. Devoid of emotional need or egotistical input, the ideas and information you apply and the activities in which you are involved make rapid progress when transit Mercury trines your natal Mercury. There is an easy exchange of talk and assistance at meetings and discussion groups. Mechanical projects proceed smoothly, and so does travel. It is a good time to take care of errands and correspondence, to gather information, and to launch neighborhood activities.

TRANSIT MERCURY TRINE NATAL VENUS

☿ △ ♀ Planning social events, discussing decorating projects, devising diplomatic maneuvers, negotiating contracts, and taking legal actions are favored during this period. It is a fortunate time for the sale or purchase of art, music, flowers, jewelry, clothes, and luxury items. Travel is pleasurable. You will benefit from instruction in art or music and succeed in exhibits of arts and crafts. When transit Mercury trines your natal Venus, you are more inspired than usual when it comes to saying the right things to the right people. Engendering cooperation among other people or between yourself and others should be an easy matter. Joint ventures and discussions with partners and allies are apt to be highly productive. Counseling, whether you are the giver or receiver of advice, produces excellent results.

TRANSIT MERCURY TRINE NATAL MARS

☿ △ ♂ When transit Mercury trines your natal Mars, ideas can successfully be turned into physical realities. Words cause actions to flow smoothly, and, in turn, actions give greater meaning to words. It is an excellent time to prepare, present, or receive travel plans, travel brochures, instructions related to physical tasks or goals, and written or verbal descriptions of physical events. Surgical procedures, especially those that involve the head, nerves, or sensory organs, are favored. Business transactions, manufacturing, sports events, military maneuvers, building, engineering, and mechanical projects are highly productive ventures. It is a favorable period for personal services such as a manicure or haircut. Too much talk and not enough action is the only real threat to success.

TRANSIT MERCURY TRINE NATAL JUPITER

☿ △ ♃ Information, ideas, and activities you encounter during this period have the potential to enhance your intellectual endeavors and boost your economic or social status. You may receive news from or about your father at this time. You may be in just the right place at the right time with the right information when transit Mercury trines your natal Jupiter. Ideas may tend toward the dramatic and grandiose, but they have their place in the scheme of things. What should be avoided, however, is overconfidence and being out of touch with reality and practicality. Favorable outcomes are predicted for religious or political activities, court decisions, publishing, advertising, long-distance travel, cultural pursuits, and dealing with those of other races or cultures.

TRANSIT MERCURY TRINE NATAL SATURN

☿ △ ♄ You begin to appreciate the organization you have worked to achieve and the knowledge you have managed to acquire. Others may reward you handsomely for your advice and consultation. Information and ideas you receive will be a valuable addition to what you have already learned, and you may acquire knowledge or develop basic skills you were unable or unwilling to learn when you were younger. When transit Mercury trines your natal Saturn, others support your promotion or increased authority. Attempts to find practical, long-lasting solutions are successful as are endeavors related to social security, insurance, taxes, and government officials or similar authority figures.

TRANSIT MERCURY TRINE NATAL URANUS

☿ △ ♅ Information, ideas, and activities you encounter when transit Mercury trines your natal Uranus deal with larger societal issues that are related to your personal affairs. It is an excellent time, for example, to attend meetings or organizational activities. Unexpected personal benefits may be gained through the information you pick up or as a result of the people you impress with your knowledge or ideas. Discuss your hopes and aspirations, join organizations, and expand your circle of friends. Success these days will favor work or other activities that involve scientific and technical projects, computers, travel by air, international finance, and sociological issues.

Transit Mercury Trine Natal Neptune

☿ △ ♆ This is a tricky time. Even though luck is on your side, there is no guarantee that you will make proper use of the information, ideas, or activities that come your way when transit Mercury trines your natal Neptune. Cold logic will not be allowed to intrude as inspiration and instincts are the primary elements in your current circumstances. Your imagination and intuition are enhanced and can prove highly useful by leading you to the right place at the right time. Certain activities are favored such as photography, endeavors that rely on the use of glamor or illusion, charitable causes, spiritual guidance, promotion, advertising, travel on or over water, and the sale or purchase of waterfront property, boats or marine equipment, swimwear or swim gear, footwear, seafood, oil, liquor, and drugs.

Transit Mercury Trine Natal Pluto

☿ △ ♇ Investigation and research yield satisfying results during this period. Digging for buried treasure is liable to bring rewards. Lost items are found and debts or favors repaid. Circumstances inspire shrewd business decisions, psychological analysis, and property assessment when transit Mercury trines your natal Pluto. You can learn self-discipline and how to successfully exert personal influence. If you keep in mind that "the pen is mightier than the sword," you will be able to use this period to great advantage.

Mercury Oppositions

Transit Mercury Opposed Natal Sun

☿ ☍ ☉ Your ego is apt to be bruised when transit Mercury opposes your natal Sun. Ideas and opinions that surround you are not likely to be compatible with your own. Neither are they apt to agree with the type of image you want to project or be affected by the personal influence you want to exert. You may ask, "Now what?" The answer is that you should not waste efforts trying to get others to change their minds and you should not dismiss their opinions as worthless; no one will listen to you. You might make productive use of this unfavorable period by learning what you can. If you are unable to find an agreeable or productive way of working within a situation or with certain people, be content to work quietly on your own.

TRANSIT MERCURY OPPOSED NATAL MOON

☿ ☍ ☽ Words are not destined to bring emotional satisfaction at this time. Be prepared to confront opinions and ideas that are in opposition to your feelings. Trying to get things to run smoothly will present a few problems. A change of heart can bring things to a halt. You have to cope with activities that conflict with those you have already scheduled. Even if you follow directions, you can end up in exactly the place you did not want to be. When transit Mercury opposes your natal Moon, you can expect to encounter people and situations that block the path of your progress at every turn, literally or figuratively. After leaving instructions with a tailor for a garment to be lengthened, you come back to find it has been shortened. This illustrates the kind of situation you may be up against during this period.

TRANSIT MERCURY OPPOSED NATAL MERCURY

☿ ☍ ☿ Attempts to mesh people and ideas in a meaningful way are useless for the time being. You become discouraged coping with diverse opinions and people running off in opposite directions. You hear or read about various ideas on a certain subject, but these ideas may not agree with each other or answer your questions. What is worse, they may be in total conflict with your own thinking. There is no mechanism for the easy flow or exchange of communication when transit Mercury opposes your natal Mercury. People keep changing their minds, or else you do. No one agrees on a price, a time to meet, or the best way to reach a destination. Trying to teach or trying to learn is difficult at best.

TRANSIT MERCURY OPPOSED NATAL VENUS

☿ ☍ ♀ When it comes to handling interpersonal relations, enhancing the beauty or harmony of an environment, or planning social events, this is an exceedingly difficult period. Things just do not come together.

Everyone has a different viewpoint. No one is in a mood to be tactful or of a mind to make an effort to please. Conflict and lack of cooperation can arise between you and a partner or other allies when transit Mercury opposes your natal Venus. Disagreement concerning common goals and other matters plagues the efforts of joint ventures, business transactions, counseling sessions, contractual negotiations, and legal matters.

Transit Mercury Opposed Natal Mars

☿ ☍ ♂ When an opposition occurs between transit Mercury and your natal Mars, information and ideas lead to incorrect actions, either because the information itself is erroneous or you misinterpret what it means. You are apt to do exactly the opposite of what you have been told, or, after correctly following instructions, it turns out you should have done exactly the opposite. Either way, the results are not likely to be happy or successful. You tend to act too rashly or fail to ascertain certain details, which leads to undesirable consequences. This is not a favorable time for the purchase or sale of a car and electrical or mechanical equipment, nor is it fortuitous to take a trip. Unfortunate potentials for travel include physical danger, equipment breakdown, and delays or cancellations.

Transit Mercury Opposed Natal Jupiter

☿ ☍ ♃ Resist signing up for continuing education, do not send away for books and other reading material, postpone long-distance travel, and avoid scheduling religious, political, and cultural activities during this period. Of course, any real choice of whether or not to engage in these things may be nonexistent since opposing forces may come along to effectively cancel such efforts or make it next to impossible to carry them out. When transit Mercury opposes your natal Jupiter, ideas and activities are not calculated to enhance your growth and expansion in any way—and that includes involvement in get-rich-quick schemes and so-called "promising" opportunities. Circumstances may include severe disagreement or conflicts with your father or a father figure.

TRANSIT MERCURY OPPOSED NATAL SATURN

☿ ☍ ♄ Information, ideas, and activities are apt to be diametrically opposed to the structures, tradition, and organization you have carefully built up. Others voice dissenting opinions concerning the status of your authority or experience. When transit Mercury opposes your natal Saturn, travel is curtailed and others are not apt to bring good news or say the things you want to hear. What you read or hear is not compatible with what you have learned from experience. The most productive action is to approach everything as philosophically as possible. Do not rush back to square one merely on the strength of opposing opinions or conflicting information. Unhappy or unpleasant situations may eventually right themselves again, and who is to say you will not be the wiser or better off for having experienced them?

TRANSIT MERCURY OPPOSED NATAL URANUS

☿ ☍ ♅ You are exposed to much disagreement, conflict, and turmoil. Presenting your thoughts to others may be made demonstrably more difficult by the fact that everyone is so distracted or at odds about other matters that they pay little heed or credence to what you are trying to get across. Serious conflicts arise with those of a different generation. When transit Mercury opposes your natal Uranus, it is not a good period to be involved with the newsletters or finances of an organization or the coordination of group activities. Avoid travel by air.

TRANSIT MERCURY OPPOSED NATAL NEPTUNE

☿ ☍ ♆ When transit Mercury opposes your natal Neptune, do not attempt to rely on logic and clear thinking. Information and ideas are elusive, intentionally deceptive, or even quite dangerous. Trying to make a wise decision or uncover the truth is impossible. You may not understand what others say or they may not understand what you mean. This is not a favorable period for travel on water, photography, business transactions (especially those that involve water-, drug-, or oil-related products or property), and spiritual studies or activities. There is an increased tendency for self-pity and despair or for suffering personal loss or disappointment. Avoid incurring debt or lending money to others. This is definitely a time for careful deliberation and cautious behavior.

Transit Mercury Opposed Natal Pluto

☿ ☍ ♇ There is intensity in the information or ideas you present as well as receive. It may be difficult to pinpoint the opposing forces that generate intensity, but they are there nonetheless when transit Mercury opposes your natal Pluto. You may be so intent on forcefully exerting your own thoughts that you refuse to listen, or others may attempt to manipulate your ideas to their advantage. It just is not the best time for easy exchanges or free thinking. Information may be withheld as a form of paranoia or protection and the wrong information may be deliberately given in an effort to mislead. This all seems a bit much for ordinary lives and pursuits, but you may experience the potential of this period in small ways. If, for instance, you are invited to dinner and enjoy a particular dish, do not be tempted to ask your hostess for the recipe. Nor, in the reverse situation, would you be willing to part with such information.

Chapter Four

Transit Venus Aspects to the Natal Planets

The aspects that transit Venus makes to natal planets usually last from the day before until the day after the actual aspect is made. Every eighteen months when transit Venus is retrograde, it can make the same aspect to a natal planet more than once which makes the influence of the aspect effective for a longer period of time.

VENUS CONJUNCTIONS

TRANSIT VENUS CONJOIN NATAL SUN

♀ ☌ ☉ Personal magnetism, physical attractiveness, or both are the focus of attention when transit Venus conjoins your natal Sun. Others find you more attractive and charming and you may be inclined to feel the same way about them. With no particular effort, you find yourself surrounded by beauty during this period. Perhaps it is beautiful people with whom you come in contact, but it could also be beautiful things, luxury items, music, or a well appointed environment. A concert and an art or fashion show may be on the agenda. A partner and other allies are apt to be very supportive, and, in turn, you may be willing to extend your cooperation in joint efforts. Romance can be part of your scenario at this time. The negative potentials include self-indulgence and too much emphasis on the pursuit of pleasure. Pride in your looks may well be in order in your present circumstances, but do not let it become selfish vanity or shallowness. This is a time to demonstrate integrity and principles since such characteristics will be noticed.

TRANSIT VENUS CONJOIN NATAL MOON

♀ ☌ ☽ Your popularity increases and you may get the urge to enhance your physical attractiveness or beautify your domestic environment when transit Venus conjoins your natal Moon. You may be fortunate enough to find just the right person to assist you in such projects. If negative circumstances do not occur at this time to spoil the otherwise positive potential, you should feel very sociable and amiably inclined when in the company of others. Romantic and sensual are other adjectives that can describe your mood. Harmony and peace within the family is enhanced. It is a period to entertain at home and initiate family activities. Dining in a beautiful setting with beautiful people lifts your spirits. You are lucky and may put yourself in a fortunate situation by following your instincts and intuition rather than relying totally on the cold, hard facts.

TRANSIT VENUS CONJOIN NATAL MERCURY

♀ ☌ ☿ When transit Venus conjoins your natal Mercury, you are encouraged to communicate with partners, allies, and those with whom you are involved in joint ventures. You experience a greater need to share your thoughts with others and there may be an increase in the number of people who want to share their ideas with you. Unless other factors ruin the fortunate potential of this period, public relations, debate, negotiations, counseling, and legal matters proceed well. You are apt to say or write the right thing to the right person at the right time. It should be an excellent time for correspondence, and messages you receive are likely to contain humor and good news. Cordial business relations, successful community activities, agreeable meetings and get-togethers, and art or music instruction are other possible highlights of your current agenda.

TRANSIT VENUS CONJOIN NATAL VENUS

♀ ☌ ♀ If you are alone, this is a period when you wish others were around. If you are in the company of others, you are more apt to appreciate their companionship, care, and affection. Everything operates on a mutual basis when transit Venus conjoins your natal Venus. No one wants to get too far off balance. You admire someone, they admire you; you like Chinese food, they like Chinese food. Whatever you give to others these days is what you would like to receive, and others will give you what they would like to get. It is an enjoyable period of polite manners and pleasant encounters.

TRANSIT VENUS CONJOIN NATAL MARS

♀ ☌ ♂ You are likely to be highly motivated to attain anything that catches your eye and pursue anyone to whom you are attracted when a conjunction occurs between transit Venus and your natal Mars. Desire for physical pleasures, as well as for music, literature, and beauty in all forms, is enhanced. Your physical activities may involve artistic projects. Joint efforts with a partner or allies make work more enjoyable these days, even if the tasks at hand are not all that pleasant. You are attracted to beautiful cars. If you travel during this period, a greater desire for luxurious transportation may prompt you to go first class. Aggressive tendencies, if they exist, may be muted by the elegance, charm, and amiability you encounter in others.

TRANSIT VENUS CONJOIN NATAL JUPITER

♀ ☌ ♃ This is an excellent, perhaps even fortuitous period to expand your appreciation and knowledge of art, music, religion, diplomacy, and law. It would be equally fortuitous to launch an important project in any of those areas. You may experience enhanced ability to inspire others. The good life is apt to be extremely appealing when transit Venus conjoins your natal Jupiter. There is, however, danger of overindulgence, overstatement, and exaggeration to the point where beauty and refinement are turned into gaudiness and ostentation—a tendency perhaps to "gild the lily." If you cannot trust your own sense of proportion, be willing to consider the opinions or judgment of those in a position to advise you. The potential here is a double-edged sword:

encountering good fortune in one form or another, you have also to contend with a temptation to waste it.

TRANSIT VENUS CONJOIN NATAL SATURN

♀ ☌ ♄ It can be difficult to admire beauty for its own sake when transit Venus conjoins your natal Saturn. It is not that you lack appreciation for the things or people that catch your eye. It is more likely to be a case of also realizing that responsibilities and commitments accompany these attractive visions. You are most appreciative of beauty that is traditional, structured, and orderly, or perhaps it is just your enhanced appreciation for the intrinsic harmony in tradition, structure, and order. If you are not usually inclined to lead a neat or organized existence, this may be one time when you appreciate the necessity of having some order in your life. Your participation in social events and fun activities is apt to be more enthusiastic if these activities also happen to serve some purpose in addition to enjoyment: a successful combination of business and pleasure. There is no one new you care to meet and nothing you care to do, and you may prefer to remain either alone or in the company of those who serve a purpose in your life.

TRANSIT VENUS CONJOIN NATAL URANUS

♀ ☌ ♅ An unorthodox or less-than-traditional partnership or alliance may be on the agenda, proposed either by you or to you. Romantic or social contacts may inspire you to adopt unique methods to achieve common goals. The social scene you encounter at this time can engender the spirit of egalitarianism in you, or you may be the one that prompts others to adopt such an attitude. Unless negative circumstances spoil its potential, this may be a fortuitous period for establishing friendships and coordinating group activities. Those viewed by most of society as different or eccentric may be the people that you find appealing when transit Venus conjoins your natal Uranus. In turn, others may be attracted to you for the characteristics that make you different or unique. Artistic or musical activities are not likely to follow along traditional lines.

TRANSIT VENUS CONJOIN NATAL NEPTUNE

♀☌♆ If you seek unearthly beauty or pleasures in present circumstances, you are apt to find them. If you desire inspirational beauty and pleasure, you are apt to find them as well. If you look for beauty and pleasure that is real and available, forget it. Elusive, mysterious, and spiritual describe the people and situations you are likely to encounter when transit Venus conjoins your natal Neptune. Photographs taken of you at this time are apt to be flattering as are pictures taken of you with your friends or at social events. This is an excellent time for freedom of imagination and disguise, but a difficult time to get one plus one to equal two. Your artistic temperament thrives and so does abstract thinking—both endeavors have the potential for profitable as well as satisfying results. Do others find you out of touch with reality, or do you find others hard to pin down? It may not matter since things are apt to work out well in either case.

TRANSIT VENUS CONJOIN NATAL PLUTO

♀☌♇ You may have an urge to gain control over social events or you may be forced by circumstances to take complete charge of them. Either way, it is an excellent time to plan every detail of a proposed event so that it proceeds as smoothly as possible. Charm has great power when transit Venus conjoins your natal Pluto. There is danger, however, that idle flattery can be interpreted as a serious overture. Since there is no telling whether you will be the one that engages in such flattery or the one that misinterprets its intent, you must remain aware of the possibility of being on either side. This is a period for the use of strategy in manipulating the control and outcome of situations, especially in situations where the demands of social groups or diplomatic purposes must be well served. Artistic endeavors can be as controlled as they are powerful in their impact.

VENUS SEXTILES

TRANSIT VENUS SEXTILE NATAL SUN

♀ ✶ ☉ When transit Venus sextiles your natal Sun, the social situations in which you find yourself can be ego-massaging experiences. Even better, they may be opportunities that lead to wider recognition of your personal integrity, special talent, and efforts. This potential is not a sure bet, mind you. It represents a chance you are either given outright or one that provides circumstances in which you can successfully create your own opportunity. You may get a chance to be in the driver's seat when it comes to gaining the cooperation and support of a partner or other allies. A chance encounter or situation may lead to a position of leadership, enhancement of your social status, or other personal success.

TRANSIT VENUS SEXTILE NATAL MOON

♀ ✶ ☽ Romance and the pleasant atmosphere of polite manners and agreeable dispositions that you encounter in current circumstances give you a chance to improve the quality and enjoyment of life. When transit Venus sextiles your natal Moon, it can mean an opportunity to express your feelings to a romantic partner, a spouse, family members, female friends, and children. A cooperative attitude and conciliatory gestures on your part may also result in better relationships with disgruntled relatives. Situations may ultimately lead to enhancing the attractiveness and harmony of your domestic environment, amiable dinner parties and other social activities in your home, or improvement in your diet, health, and physical attractiveness.

TRANSIT VENUS SEXTILE NATAL MERCURY

♀ ✶ ☿ If you have an urge to compose something romantic, the current circumstances may offer inspiration or opportunity. If you are not a writer of romantic prose or poetry, there is nevertheless likely to be opportunity at hand to speak, sing, or otherwise communicate your amorous thoughts and ideas. Circumstances may ultimately result in teaching or receiving instruction in art, music, interior design, or floral arrangement. Other potentials when transit Venus sextiles your natal Mercury are situations that lead to business opportunities, especially hairdressing and related services, fashion design, and the manufacture or sale of perfume and jewelry. You may further your interests or success in writing, illustrating, publishing, and the sale of books and magazines. Other areas include diplomacy, public relations, social planning, the law, partnership, and joint ventures.

TRANSIT VENUS SEXTILE NATAL VENUS

♀ ⚹ ♀ Taking advantage of situations when transit Venus sextiles your natal Venus, you may be able to persuade those around you to be more cooperative and agreeable. Or perhaps the people and situations you encounter will put you in this harmonious frame of mind. Whatever happens, everyone is likely to be on the same wavelength. Negotiations are smoother and joint ventures make progress. Opportunities that come along may lead to finding or attracting others of a similar mind concerning artistic or musical projects. Beauty attracts beauty, and you are not likely to be casting "pearls before swine" if you grab a chance to exhibit your looks, talent, and charm. Nor will such attempts on the part of others be lost on you.

TRANSIT VENUS SEXTILE NATAL MARS

♀ ⚹ ♂ Current circumstances offer a chance to turn romantic, artistic, or musical desires into physical realities—just an opportunity, mind you, not a sure thing. You must be willing to take advantage of situations and aggressively follow through. When transit Venus sextiles your natal Mars, others offer proposals for various types of affirmative action, any of which may turn out to be successful. No matter what happens, there may be a dynamic role for you to play somewhere along the line. If you grab or create the chance to play such a role and you play it well, the consequences are likely to be fortunate for everyone concerned. Watch for opportunities that could lead to success in joint ventures, diplomatic quests, and legal matters. This is a good period to take advantage of situations that involve sports, physical fitness, and work projects.

TRANSIT VENUS SEXTILE NATAL JUPITER

♀ ✶ ♃ Fortunate social opportunities are at hand. If they do not automatically come your way, go out and create opportunities. Participation in social events may turn out to be beneficial when transit Venus sextiles your natal Jupiter, especially if such activities are related to religious and political interests, cultural pursuits, higher education, long-distance travel, or involve your father or those of another race or culture. Opportunities may lead to success in publishing, advertising, or broadcasting. Joining a theater group, gourmet cooking class, or travel club may be on your agenda. Try your luck with the lottery, horse races, or other sporting events and you may emerge a winner.

TRANSIT VENUS SEXTILE NATAL SATURN

♀ ✶ ♄ When transit Venus sextiles your natal Saturn, it can mean an opportunity to successfully mix business with pleasure. Since people are likely to be more impressed by your maturity and experience, it is to your advantage to purposely emphasize these assets. Introducing some aspect of tradition, structure, and substance to your artistic endeavors and to the social situations or people you encounter leads to happy results. Interjecting the same elements into diplomatic gestures, counseling, public relations, partnerships, and joint ventures leads to future success in these areas.

TRANSIT VENUS SEXTILE NATAL URANUS

♀ ✶ ♅ Social situations emphasize the uniqueness of your generation when transit Venus sextiles your natal Uranus. You may experience unusual or nontraditional social contacts, romantic encounters, and proposals for partnerships or other alliances. Organizational activities may spontaneously turn into social events. The common factor in these situations is the opportunity they offer you to be a part of something outside of yourself while permitting you to retain your own individuality. You may be more egalitarian when it comes to accepting or judging others. Those you meet can engender this humanitarian attitude in you or you may inspire it in them.

TRANSIT VENUS SEXTILE NATAL NEPTUNE

♀ ⚹ ♆ Opportunity to acquire a glamorous image or to wrap yourself in an aura of mystery may come along. You may find yourself mystified by or strangely attracted to people or things of great beauty. Take advantage of opportunities that encourage your imagination. As transit Venus sextiles your natal Neptune, allow yourself to be inspired and take advantage of any chance to be inspiring to others. Let romantic encounters or social settings enhance your awareness and sensitivity to the subtleties of human relationships.

TRANSIT VENUS SEXTILE NATAL PLUTO

♀ ⚹ ♇ Interactions during this period, even on a casual basis, are apt to stimulate deeper responses than usual. They may lead to a closer examination of your reactions and motivations in dealing with other people, though you may or may not choose to share the results of this self-analysis with anyone. Current circumstances may engender the inclination and opportunity to measure how much personal influence and control you exert in partnerships and other alliances and with other people in general. When transit Venus sextiles your natal Pluto, it is a good time to test your ability to plan, control, and execute every detail of social events, negotiations, debates, diplomatic overtures, and legal matters.

VENUS SQUARES

TRANSIT VENUS SQUARE NATAL SUN

♀ □ ☉ You may find yourself in disagreement with others over principles or value judgments when a square occurs between transit Venus and your natal Sun. In the end, it may be a matter of having to explain your position artfully while letting others know they have a right to their own opinions. The potential for discord may cause strained relations, but it is not likely to inspire major upsets. A situation that initially seems to threaten your integrity or ego is apt to dissipate quickly in the atmosphere of highly stimulating interactions that occur. These interactions, for the most part, are likely to result in a tacit willingness to agree to disagree. Avoid exaggerating your own importance in social settings. Let others approach you. If they flatter and compliment you or offer a position of leadership, keep your responses modest. If, on the other hand, they offer insult or they object to your presence or status, the most effective strategy is not to respond in kind.

TRANSIT VENUS SQUARE NATAL MOON

♀ □ ☽ Do not expect instant gratification. Satisfaction or success may come, but not immediately or without some difficulty. There are apt to be problems or a lack of cooperation connected with household tasks, family-related activities, and social events, especially when such events involve entertaining at home. It is not that your endeavors cannot be accomplished; it is more a matter of having to work harder to achieve the desired result. You may have a tendency to be jealous of those who may be more attractive or possess more in the way of material wealth or status. You may also be the one to arouse such feelings in others. It is good to promote the idea that imitation is the sincerest form of flattery because you may be tempted to adopt the tastes or manners of others—though, once again, it is possible that it may be the other way around. Too much or too little emotional input, most likely on your part, can slow down many situations. When transit Venus squares your natal Moon, family responsibilities may interfere with socializing or other activities. You may not have as much confidence in yourself, your physical attractiveness, or your talents. Romance does not proceed smoothly, although trying to overcome the interfering obstacles may actually provide a stimulating challenge.

TRANSIT VENUS SQUARE NATAL MERCURY

♀ □ ☿ When transit Venus squares your natal Mercury, values become an issue. Circumstances can make it necessary to defend your values or demand that others explain theirs. Others may think your manner of expressing thoughts and ideas is too abrupt or even rude. There is potential that you may find the reverse, and it is others who lack adequate or polite forms of communication. If such interactions are allowed to proceed past any initially disagreeable impressions, the continuing contacts are apt to become intellectually stimulating and provocative. There are obstacles to overcome when traveling with others, working with a partner or other allies on intellectual or artistic endeavors, and planning meetings and social activities. However, keep in mind that not only is it possible for these endeavors to succeed, the challenges they present can turn out to be more fun than you anticipate. Compromise when negotiating contracts or establishing common goals in partnerships and other joint ventures is hard to achieve. Commercial activities related to the beauty business, art, music, jewelry, flowers, design, diplomacy, and the law may turn out successfully, but only after a certain amount of delay or resolution of discrepancies. Others seek your advice at inconvenient times.

TRANSIT VENUS SQUARE NATAL VENUS

♀□♀ Things come off pretty well during this period, though the timing may not be exquisite nor the setting one you prefer. For example, a woman who wishes her lover would give her a round diamond receives one that is square, or a man who dreams of falling in love with a tall brunette finds himself hopelessly attracted to a short, fair-haired woman. These are, after all, not losing situations. Do not apologize for or regret what is missing; enjoy what is there when transit Venus squares your natal Venus. If you turn up at the wrong party by mistake, it may be more fun than the one you were supposed to attend. This line of thinking should be applied to almost any situation you encounter at this time.

TRANSIT VENUS SQUARE NATAL MARS

♀□♂ Current circumstances arouse your competitive spirits. As long as you do not become overly aggressive or allow others to assume such a manner in dealing with you, the potential for excitement and stimulation of a physical nature can lead to adventure when transit Venus squares your natal Mars. You can use the added energy for many things, not the least of which are to burn off calories, accomplish the tasks at hand, and enjoy the stimulation of challenging interactions with the opposite sex. Do not overreact physically to insults or allow the pursuit of pleasure or revenge to rob you of what might have been just the right push you needed to get moving. Maturity is needed.

TRANSIT VENUS SQUARE NATAL JUPITER

♀□♃ Capacity for enjoyment increases, but keeping things manageable or in proper perspective can be difficult. You may be tempted to overstate your sentiments or overdo generosity when transit Venus squares your natal Jupiter. Shameless social climbing is a potential to avoid. Social gatherings can bring contact with those who admire your spirituality, knowledge, or sophistication. Do not ruin their image of you by immodestly agreeing with their flattering assessment. Pursuing the good life is an irresistible temptation and restraint is necessary. During this period, you may be of a mind to purchase shoes you do not need, lose money at the races, or settle for less than satisfactory theater tickets just so you can tell others that you saw the show. This is a good time to apply yourself seriously to the sometimes tricky issue of reconciling the law with actual justice. It would be bad timing to take relationships for granted or to dismiss the values of others as unimportant.

TRANSIT VENUS SQUARE NATAL SATURN

♀□♄ When transit Venus squares your natal Saturn, what seems like rejection may not be or what may actually be rejection can work to your advantage. Unhappiness at being unable to afford the cost of something may go much deeper than regretting the lack of money. Gaining love and affection or something that you want will not be easy, and once you achieve your wish, you may not want to accept the accompanying responsibilities. Socializing is difficult. You are not necessarily more antisocial, but since current circumstances prevent you from being able to enjoy yourself, you prefer to be alone. What seems most attractive may turn out to be the least desirable. In return for cooperation or favors you seek, you must be willing to give something of equal value in return—otherwise you may either get nothing at all or a poor imitation of what you wanted. Too much worry is possible, especially related to legal matters, romance, impending social engagements, or debates. The final result is apt to be success, but whether all goes smoothly, because or in spite of the fact that you worried so much, is debatable.

TRANSIT VENUS SQUARE NATAL URANUS

♀□♅ Interactions of all kinds—romantic, social, business, friendships, and even fleeting encounters with such people as salesclerks or bank tellers—can have a way of putting you in touch with the values and social mores of your own generation. It can work in many different ways and on many different levels. You may, for instance, be wearing a certain style of clothing and find yourself among those dressed in fashions that differ strikingly from your own. Your interactions with others may also differ enough to make social events awkward. When transit Venus squares your natal Uranus, these potential circumstances can end up being pleasant experiences, even if they are initially uncomfortable. Others are apt to eventually find you attractive and interesting, and you succeed because of your uniqueness not in spite of it. Coordinating group activities is apt to be frustrating, but if you rise to the challenge, your efforts may produce viable results.

TRANSIT VENUS SQUARE NATAL NEPTUNE

♀□♆ There is potential for mystical experiences at this time. However, it is apt to be a case of overlooking flaws or less than ideal circumstances in order to gain something pleasurable and achieve perfection. You are more vulnerable to false flattery and likely to suffer disillusionment when transit Venus squares your natal Neptune, so this is not the best time to make agreements or get involved socially, romantically, or legally. Although there may be rejection of social or romantic overtures, the rejection may be a lucky stroke for everyone concerned. The only real danger you may encounter at this time is an adverse reaction to drugs or alcohol.

TRANSIT VENUS SQUARE NATAL PLUTO

♀□♇ Interactions are apt to trigger more serious responses than circumstances indicate when transit Venus squares your natal Pluto. Something that is said or done in an innocent, social or light-hearted context, may stir up old memories, deep passions, anger, and resentment. Whether you are the one that is aroused or you inspire such reactions in others is not easy to predict. Being aware of the potential of such an occurrence and staying in control of your reactions will help you deal with whatever comes along. You should not, for instance, deliberately antagonize others or seek to arouse their jealousy, since such a plan would automatically backfire or result in something even worse. If your own internal conflicts are set off by innocent (and even not so innocent) gestures on the part of others, much will be gained if you can manage to rise to the challenge by turning such negative energy to some constructive purpose.

VENUS TRINES

TRANSIT VENUS TRINE NATAL SUN

♀ △ ☉ If others are ever to be impressed by your honesty, integrity, and worth as an individual, this is the time for you to demonstrate these qualities. If you ever wanted others to take note of your leadership ability, or even if all you want is to prove to yourself that you possess some measure of it, this is the time to go out of your way to seek situations that inspire you to exhibit this trait. Unless negative circumstances spoil the otherwise fortunate potential when transit Venus trines your natal Sun, this can be a very lucky time. Your inner vitality and self-image thrive. You are more generous to others, and others will tend to treat you in a similar fashion. The situations and interactions you experience are likely to give you reason to be proud of yourself. You are an enthusiastic entertainer and host. Social events, such as banquets and other formal affairs in which you participate, are apt to be joint ventures. There is also potential that such activities will be held in your honor, or in honor of your partner, allies, or superiors and other authority figures in your life. This is an excellent time to get married or establish other partnerships and cooperative ventures.

TRANSIT VENUS TRINE NATAL MOON

♀ △ ☽ This period is highly favorable for activities that enhance your physical appearance, beautify your home, or involve any aspect of art, music, or design. Your capacity for humor and enjoyment increases. Although you may have to fight a tendency for laziness or overindulgence, you have a positive outlook and feel more attractive and sociable when transit Venus trines your natal Moon. It is an excellent period to dine socially with others, especially if you entertain them in your home. If you ever wanted to take a chance on something, now is the time. Trust your instincts and intuition—they can lead to some fortunate as well as pleasurable situations. If your work involves sales, advertising, or public relations, this is a period of great success. You are highly favored in bonds of kinship, partnerships of an emotional nature, and your efforts to improve troubled relationships. This is one of those times when everything seems to fall effortlessly into place.

TRANSIT VENUS TRINE NATAL MERCURY

♀ △ ☿ When transit Venus trines your natal Mercury, you can expect to receive as well as to send good news and social invitations. Now is also the time to establish business partnerships and other joint ventures. You are apt to travel first class. Meetings and discussion groups can be particularly enjoyable. Communications flourish. You will know just what to say and when to say it. Letters you write are more creative and amusing. You may feel the urge to write a love letter, romance novel, song, poem, or biographical sketch, and you will enjoy reading such material. Success can be achieved in many endeavors, including public relations, community activities, counseling, legal matters, debates, and negotiations. There is potential for success should you be involved in commercial transactions related to beauty, jewelry, luxury items, books, flowers, fashions, interior design, architecture, the arts, and social planning.

TRANSIT VENUS TRINE NATAL VENUS

♀ △ ♀ It would be hard to find disagreeable circumstances at the present time. You are as attracted to others as they are to you. Situations you create are as pleasant as the situations you encounter when transit Venus trines your natal Venus. The only trouble, if you think there needs to be trouble, is that everything may be just a bit too nice. If you need a more competitive or aggressive atmosphere to stimulate you, this is not the time to expect it. Should you happen to find or stir up such agitated situations, they are not likely to result in anything productive or enjoyable. Activities related to fashion, design, and the arts are successful.

TRANSIT VENUS TRINE NATAL MARS

♀ △ ♂ Diplomacy and cooperative ventures are transformed into positive physical actions during this period. Enthusiasm is high for energetic interactions with others and for most physical activities. This is not the time to be alone. When transit Venus trines your natal Mars, work or play requires a partner, or, at the very least, being around others to get stimulation and feedback. You will be delighted to invest your efforts in a wedding, a party, or, for that matter, any social event. You experience enhanced appreciation for elegant cars, luxurious travel, or well-designed machinery. Compliments and appreciation for your talent, as well as the cooperation you may receive from others during this period, can make the difference between the success or failure of your efforts. Do not pass up the chance to pursue creative and artistic endeavors. Relations with the opposite sex are exceptionally smooth, and if they have not been, this is a time when you can successfully promote a more agreeable atmosphere. Life can be romantic, literally as well as in every other sense of the word. You are apt to emerge the winner in most risk-taking ventures.

TRANSIT VENUS TRINE NATAL JUPITER

♀ △ ♃ There is no telling what good thing can happen when transit Venus trines your natal Jupiter. Try your luck at the horse races and other sporting events or with lottery tickets. You could be the winner in a beauty or photography contest or emerge the favorite in a theater audition. Artistic and musical endeavors are successful. You are likely to receive the recognition or success you deserve for writing, publishing, advertising, higher education, politics, religion, direct-mail promotions, long-distance travel, dealing with those of another race or culture, and foreign languages. You are favored in court decisions and other judgments. Even though it is a favorable time, a certain amount of prudence is necessary. Potentially unhappy consequences can occur when there is too much of a good thing. Overindulgence, wastefulness, exaggeration, and physical laziness can prevent you from gaining the true benefits of this fortunate period.

TRANSIT VENUS TRINE NATAL SATURN

♀ △ ♄ You have a wonderful chance to succeed if you seek to establish solid, long-lasting relationships when a trine occurs between transit Venus and your natal Saturn. This is a period when romance as well as friendships are based on mutual commitment and responsibility along with love and affection. Others are attracted to your maturity and accomplishment. Endeavors that involve formal agreements, diplomacy, contracts, and other legal matters are likely to produce enduring, successful results. Efforts to bring organization and stability to social groups will not go unrewarded. Should you seek a position of greater authority at this time, others will favor your promotion.

TRANSIT VENUS TRINE NATAL URANUS

♀ △ ♅ Relationships with those of a different generation, particularly of a younger generation, are likely to be very pleasant, even stimulating. Other people may be attracted to you at this time because of something you reflect that is characteristic of your generation. You can be successful in activities that involve antiques, history, and technology. When transit Venus trines your natal Uranus, enthusiasm for equality and justice flourishes. Cooperation, diplomacy, and sociable dispositions are encouraged, making this a fortunate period for friendships, organizations, and group activities.

TRANSIT VENUS TRINE NATAL NEPTUNE

♀ △ ♆ You can be a master of disguise—become whatever others want you to be—and get away with it, at least when transit Venus trines your natal Neptune. There is no guarantee a charade of any kind will last beyond this period. However, for theatrical, artistic, and even spiritual purposes, you can be very inspired. The entire scenario may be just as true in reverse; the people and situations you encounter will take on certain characteristics you need them to have, whether or not they ordinarily possess these characteristics. In either case, you can take advantage of the positive possibilities while remaining aware of the illusionary effects. Romance, promotional activities, and joint ventures are intuitively in synch and can be highly successful. This is a good time to seek a more glamorous image, to photograph and be photographed, to dance or learn to dance, to participate in social events that benefit a charitable or religious organization, and to take a vacation by the sea.

Transit Venus Trine Natal Pluto

♀ △ ♇ Observing others, especially in social settings, will give you a clear idea of what is meant by body language. The subtleties of human interactions are readily apparent, and you can use them to your advantage. Others are attracted to you if you exhibit an attitude of self-containment—not aloofness or snobbishness—but an aura of self-possession and control. One of the potentials when transit Venus trines your natal Pluto is that you may be able to turn the tables on the past. Although there is no guarantee that you will regain control of something that was lost or turn a past failure into success, you may gain something equally valuable to make up for it.

Venus Oppositions

Transit Venus Opposed Natal Sun

♀ ☍ ☉ A need to establish your own identity may tempt you to show off. Social events can become nothing more than exercises in name-dropping, ostentatious displays of luxury, and similar ego-tripping behavior when transit Venus opposes your natal Sun. It is possible that other people will make determined efforts to impress you in the same manner. Beauty does not fare well these days. Refinement and elegance may be smothered by crudeness and gaudiness. Romantic encounters tend to be more a matter of ego satisfaction than emotional commitment. It is not a good time to put yourself in a situation that depends for its success on your popularity and acceptance by others. If you hold any position of leadership, you may expect that it will not be generally favored and may even be openly opposed. Circumstances can pose a threat to the sincerity of values, integrity, principles, relations and interactions with others. However, this potential does not have to leave a negative mark. You can, for instance, reduce the number of people you encounter by working alone or remaining quietly in the background.

TRANSIT VENUS OPPOSED NATAL MOON

♀ ☍ ☽ People drop in on you just when your house is a terrible mess. You are invited to a party or run into someone you want to impress just when you look the least attractive. This is one of the worst times to host a dinner party or attend one. Everyone has a different agenda. Promoting peace and harmony in your domestic environment is a fruitless gesture when transit Venus opposes your natal Moon. This is an unfavorable period for artistic activities and attempts to enhance your physical appearance or beautify your home. The pursuit of pleasure, romance, and amiable companions is likely to end in a no-win situation with little or nothing to show for your efforts. Self-discipline and maturity are not likely to be strong. Overindulgence, discouragement, self-pity, and too much sentimentality are the elements apt to dominate your current emotional environment. If you manage to achieve emotional satisfaction in some measure, you have beaten the odds.

TRANSIT VENUS OPPOSED NATAL MERCURY

♀ ☍ ☿ Rudeness or lack of communication is a viable potential when transit Venus opposes your natal Mercury. Presenting your thoughts and ideas to others is not a good idea. You are likely to encounter vigorous opposition, and, at the very least, you will waste your time. Conciliatory gestures are meaningless and perhaps even insulting. Do not expect to find others agreeable or willing to compromise. Commercial transactions are difficult. Failure to agree on a mutually satisfactory price or to resolve other conflicting opinions is apt to stymie progress. This is a time when the words do not go with the music. Concentration and learning are likely to suffer from too many distractions, mental laziness, or both. It is not an auspicious time for art and design projects or to purchase books, luxury items, and concert or theater tickets. Traveling is not apt to put you in the company of congenial companions. If it should happen that situations proceed more smoothly than the potential indicates, count yourself fortunate. The best advice is to realize what the negative potentials are and sidestep them whenever and wherever you can.

TRANSIT VENUS OPPOSED NATAL VENUS

♀ ☍ ♀ During this short period, do not expect to encounter people who agree or even sympathize with your proposals, opinions, or reactions, especially with regard to romantic, diplomatic, and artistic endeavors. On the other hand, the fact that others maintain an altogether different or even hostile position may have a stimulating effect in helping you more clearly define your own. This is a good time to see the other side of the coin when it comes to dealing with people, even if you cannot accept or agree with them. Partnerships and other alliances and joint ventures in which you are involved are plagued by opposing views and other conflicts. Determination to resolve differences may be greatly stymied but can eventually result in generating a better understanding of individual needs as well as establishing or re-establishing common goals.

TRANSIT VENUS OPPOSED NATAL MARS

♀ ☍ ♂ This period is best described as one that promotes the classic "battle of the sexes." Passions lie much closer to the surface when transit Venus opposes your natal Mars. The most innocent flirtation or gesture is apt to inspire a physically aggressive response. Jealous females are likely to intrude. The loser in competitive situations will not be gracious, and whether or not you are the winner, you may still lose. Social gatherings are not likely to be successful. The restless and aggressive energy that accompanies this period is an irresistible force in stirring things up. Spirited social interactions are certainly desirable, but, in this case, any party can turn into a brawl. Luxurious vehicles and travel accommodations are either unavailable or unaffordable. This is a most inauspicious time to undergo surgical procedures, especially cosmetic surgery. Overexertion when engaging in physical fitness and other strenuous activities may have serious consequences.

TRANSIT VENUS OPPOSED NATAL JUPITER

♀ ☍ ♃ When an opposition occurs between transit Venus and your natal Jupiter, you are almost certain to be sorely tempted to overindulge. There is always the chance that present circumstances will prevent you from personal disaster, but on one level or another, you have to cope with unnecessarily extravagant gestures and situations. Imagine the worst actor in the world—the phoniest, most pretentious, social-climbing person—and then, for good measure, throw in meaningless posturing, ostentatious displays, and pompous arrogance. After you have imagined such a person, do not allow yourself to become the one who fits the description. Even if you escape such a fate for yourself, be prepared to encounter those who have not. During this period, situations involving your father are adversely affected, justice is self-serving, diplomatic gestures fail, and what should be fine art is overdone and gaudy.

TRANSIT VENUS OPPOSED NATAL SATURN

♀ ☍ ♄ This period can be positive only if you have the maturity to understand that there is a certain kind of pleasure in self-discipline, performing thankless tasks, and staying home alone. Receiving little or no appreciation or affection and finding a total lack of humor in the people and situations you encounter can strengthen your character if you turn these situations into learning experiences. When transit Venus opposes your natal Saturn, forget about romance, fun and games, instant gratification, and the satisfaction that comes from dining sumptuously. There are few if any pleasures to be had right now without also incurring onerous responsibility—and, in the end, perhaps all you may get is the responsibility. Others may regard you as too serious, too old, too formal, or too inflexible. This is not a favorable time to ask others for their opinions, cooperation, or assistance. Go it alone. Do not take unnecessary risks of any kind because Lady Luck is not on your side. If something good does come your way, hold your breath and hope it will still be there in the morning.

TRANSIT VENUS OPPOSED NATAL URANUS

♀ ☍ ♅ When transit Venus opposes your natal Uranus, people are out of synch with each other and with you. You may feel the need for the company of others, and then, when other people are around, you want to be alone. Your values are apt to clash with those of a different generation or background. This is not an auspicious time for participating in organizational meetings, social events, or activities with friends. One of the worst mistakes is trying to be different just to be different. Even if you do not make this mistake, you may nevertheless find yourself unhappily dealing with those who do. Prejudice rears its ugly head, and it may belong to you. Temptation to judge the many by the sins of one can make interactions unfair and not worth trying to salvage, at least for the time being.

TRANSIT VENUS OPPOSED NATAL NEPTUNE

♀ ☌ ♆ Social diseases flourish when transit Venus opposes your natal Neptune—the physical ones that result from unhealthy sexual encounters as well as other kinds including vicious gossip, deliberate deception, and shameless exploitation. Illusion becomes disillusion. Diplomacy is an empty, self-serving gesture. Glamor is not based on real beauty. Religious fervor is not inspired by true spirituality. You can avoid the traps if you realize what they are, but the unfortunate potential is that you may not be aware of them. There is great danger involving water. Do not go sailing or swimming, especially if you have indulged in alcohol or drugs of any kind. It would also be in your best interests to avoid pool parties, cruises, or vacations by the ocean.

TRANSIT VENUS OPPOSED NATAL PLUTO

♀ ☌ ♇ Obsession, possessiveness, and jealousy find fertile ground in the situations you encounter during this period. Cut-throat competitiveness and underhanded manipulation lurk, ready to pounce. Things that may not normally have any deep significance can become passionate power struggles or worse when transit Venus opposes your natal Pluto. Partnerships and alliances, romantic or otherwise, as well as joint ventures suffer from lack of trust. It is a difficult period to describe since reactions can be subtle and impossible to detect. The most innocent gesture or scene can evoke destructive memories of past slights—slights that may have no connection with the present. Whether you are the perpetrator or the victim in any of the potential circumstances is not indicated. The idea is not to encourage such situations if they appear. Keep a low profile and sit this dance out.

Chapter Five

Transit Mars Aspects to the Natal Planets

Transit Mars is associated with action and, true to its nature, it is often a signal for circumstances to occur. Aspects made to natal planets from other transits may indicate the potential for circumstances that may have been building up in the background. Then, when transit Mars comes along, it is a signal for action. This is why the transit of Mars is important to watch as a timing mechanism. Mars takes about twenty-two months to complete the zodiac, and the aspects it makes to natal planets are slightly longer in duration than the Sun, Mercury, and Venus. Mars is retrograde every other year for a ten-week period, which will add emphasis to aspects it makes in the natal chart during that time.

MARS CONJUNCTIONS

TRANSIT MARS CONJOIN NATAL SUN

♂ ☌ ☉ A surge of vitality—a strong identification with so-called male energy—occurs when transit Mars conjoins your natal Sun.

Determination and ego gratification are the guiding forces behind many of your physical actions. Your actions may be the result of great courage, an aggressive push to get ahead, an enthusiastic endorsement, or a demonstration in one form or another of your integrity and principles. During this period, you may encounter physical challenges or purposely initiate direct confrontations and competitive or risky situations. You are well able and willing to physically handle whatever comes along (or at least believe that you can), but activities can strain your heart and spine or result in sunburn or injuries to your head or face.

TRANSIT MARS CONJOIN NATAL MOON

♂ ☌ ☽ Your pulse quickens and feelings lie much closer to the surface these days. Anger or frustration may incite you to throw temper tantrums, and the surge of emotional energy may inspire you to demonstrate your love and affection, depending on current circumstances. What can be expected, however, is that any exhibition of your feelings—positive or negative—is sure to be physically energetic. When transit Mars conjoins your natal Moon, the pace of life picks up, and family relationships and domestic activities are apt to be the main focus of physical efforts. You may decide to give a dinner party, clean the house, make home repairs, build an addition to your home or a barbecue pit in the back yard, or move to another residence altogether. If you are impulsive by nature, this trait is likely to be accentuated by increased tendencies to turn feelings into physical action. Inattention, restlessness, and a greater need for haste may have unpleasant consequences for you, your children, or other family members. During this period, avoid driving too fast and take precautions when using sharp instruments or handling flammable materials (especially household materials). When cooking and baking, monitor the time and temperature you use or your dish may be overdone or even burned. Check your home for possible fire hazards. The heating or cooling system of your home or car may require repairs or replacement. Make an effort to protect yourself from discomfort and danger—the greatest potentials being insect bites, excessive bleeding, colitis, ulcers, fever, digestive upsets, and insomnia.

TRANSIT MARS CONJOIN NATAL MERCURY

♂ ☌ ☿ Mental energies are high, urging you to turn thoughts into actions. An energetic stream of information and ideas flows through your immediate environment and there is strong potential that much of it is generated by you. As transit Mars conjoins your natal Mercury, the faster pace and increased volume of communications can become chaotic, and, at times, inspire an aggressive atmosphere—verbal combat being a likely prospect. You do not hesitate to speak your mind or demand that others do the same. It may be others who force you to defend your ideas or opinions. Meetings and discussion groups tend to be enthusiastic and energetic, or, if the conditions encourage such an atmosphere, they can become aggressive and combative. During this period, you put more physical effort into the use and development of your athletic, mechanical, computer, or artistic skills. Sales and other commercial transactions and business activities are more vigorous—though the competition encountered may also be more fierce. Your car or other motorized vehicles, office equipment, or computer may require repairs or replacement. A greater urge to travel is apt to be accompanied by increased tendency to speed. You are tempted to drive too fast or become unduly impatient when stuck in traffic jams or detained by delays in public transportation. There is potential for headaches and cuts or burns, especially to the head, face, hands, or fingers.

TRANSIT MARS CONJOIN NATAL VENUS

♂ ☌ ♀ New partnerships, alliances, and joint ventures may be established, or those in which you are currently involved are given renewed physical energy and enthusiasm when transit Mars conjoins your natal Venus. Unless negative situations are around to provoke unpleasant attitudes, your willingness to cooperate is enhanced, and, in return, you are just as likely to receive generous assistance from others. Interactions at all levels are more invigorating these days. Physical efforts are more enthusiastic with regard to art, music, design, or the beauty business. If you have been thinking of undergoing cosmetic surgery, enhancing your wardrobe, or decorating your home, you are apt to put such plans into action at this time. Romantic adventures, legal matters, and social events are prime targets of your energetic endeavors. There is nothing in any of these potential situations to suggest whether the efforts put forth are positive or negative, or whether they will have positive or negative consequences; other prevailing circumstances will have to determine the outcome.

TRANSIT MARS CONJOIN NATAL MARS

♂ ♂ ♂ The extremely active, potentially chaotic circumstances during this period can literally, as well as figuratively, give you a headache. Transit Mars conjoining your natal Mars promotes very energetic, sometimes overly-aggressive actions. The atmosphere you are apt to experience is one where everyone is likely to be busier than usual, and that includes you. It will be difficult to find passive participants in almost any situation. A new two-year cycle of energy begins and you will (or should) initiate new directions and new ventures.

TRANSIT MARS CONJOIN NATAL JUPITER

♂ ♂ ♃ You are likely to have an expansive or perhaps unnecessarily exaggerated part to play in some of the situations you encounter when transit Mars conjoins your natal Jupiter. You may be tempted to give people more credit than they deserve. The actions of others can inspire and expand the development of your own potential or that of your present circumstances. Unless negative factors interfere, you can improve your intellectual, monetary, and social status. You may have greater enthusiasm for expanding spiritual and cultural awareness and for engaging in sports or physical fitness. Some of your work or physical efforts may be for or concerned with your father. During this period, your appetite for obtaining the finer things in life is as enhanced as your capacity for enjoying them.

TRANSIT MARS CONJOIN NATAL SATURN

♂ ♂ ♄ This is a period in which you may be required to hurry, but obstacles in your path keep slowing you down. The most maddening prospect is that the obstacles you encounter are likely to be ones you bring on yourself. That is the negative potential. The positive side of the picture is that you will focus on becoming more structured and organized. You may be more willing to plan things carefully and to give greater credence to wisdom and experience before you act or allow others to act. When transit Mars conjoins your natal Saturn, it may be difficult to accept the authority or rules imposed on you—but then, you may not encounter such problems since your tendency for more careful actions these days may keep you from running afoul of others.

Dental work or minor surgery may be necessary. Wear clothing appropriate for the weather since there is increased potential for you to suffer from cold, flu, dermatitis, arthritis, and other chronic illness.

TRANSIT MARS CONJOIN NATAL URANUS

♂ ☌ ♅ When transit Mars conjoins your natal Uranus, the actions of others may inspire you positively or negatively (there is no telling which) to do something out of character. Energetic vibrations in the general atmosphere may urge you to emphasize your uniqueness or nontraditional approach to things. Of course, the reverse may also be true, and you will encounter some fairly unusual or nontraditional people and circumstances. Consider also that some actions that occur at this time may be quite dangerous, given the explosive potential for both Mars and Uranus. There may be more enthusiasm and energy in friendships and in your participation in groups and organizations. You may develop or be introduced by others to new techniques and methods. You may have more interest in (or perhaps more tolerance for) activities that involve astrology, the occult, or other unusual subjects, as well as more traditional topics such as history, sociology, finance, and antiques.

TRANSIT MARS CONJOIN NATAL NEPTUNE

♂ ☌ ♆ The best advice is to keep a low and cautious profile. Although it is possible for actions to be truly inspired, the potential is high for making unwise decisions and taking equally unwise actions. Others can become confused or misunderstand you, and you are not any more likely to understand the actions or motives of others. When transit Mars conjoins your natal Neptune, discovering who did what, where, when, or why is impossible. Physical efforts may be purposely secretive or may simply go undetected or unrecognized. Physical energy and efforts can become dissipated or undermined. The positive potential includes increased spiritual awareness and artistic sensitivity. Extreme caution is advised when around, on, or in the water and when dealing with drugs, chemicals, or gas.

TRANSIT MARS CONJOIN NATAL PLUTO

♂ ♂ ♇ The vitality of people and situations when transit Mars conjoins your natal Pluto is likely to be of an intense and purposeful nature. It is also true that they may inspire you to be more forceful than usual. This is a time, for example, when you can successfully tackle projects that require more patience and concentration. There is also karma here, of the sort that can bring something along that you were meant to do. Mars indicates a male figure may be the guiding force or the instigation behind your actions. From a negative point of view, interactions with others can be deeply jealous and vengeful, perhaps with truly perilous results. Thus, it would be unwise to confront or provoke a hostile situation. Several positive actions to take at this time include: rejuvenating certain aspects of your life, bringing out your hidden talents, finding new uses for old things, evaluating and investing assets, and conducting research and investigation—especially into the mysteries of science and nature.

MARS SEXTILES

TRANSIT MARS SEXTILE NATAL SUN

♂ ⚹ ☉ Use current opportunities to take physical action—advantageous action that can eventually lead to furthering your career or to gaining recognition for your individuality and talent. Do not pass up a chance to demonstrate courage, integrity, and loyalty or to defend your principles vigorously. The ultimate ego satisfaction you get or goals you attain when transit Mars sextiles your natal Sun may come through men and from being in situations that may be described as competitive or aggressive. Success is also likely to result from being a doer—which means you need to put yourself physically in different situations, participate in a variety of activities, and circulate among a wide variety of people in order to attract the kind of opportunity you seek.

TRANSIT MARS SEXTILE NATAL MOON

♂ ⚹ ☽ You may get the opportunity to turn feelings into physical actions when transit Mars sextiles your natal Moon. If you are involved in creative or artistic activities, your efforts may ultimately lead to exhibiting your work, developing your talent, or representing the talents of others. If your interest and instincts are aroused, follow them. Current circumstances may bring a chance to promote family relationships and activities and to accomplish domestic tasks. Your children or other family members may be given an opportunity to work or to participate in sports or other competitions. Do not miss an opportunity to invite male companions, male family members, and male business associates to dine. Avoid future problems with appliances and machinery by taking time now to repair them or provide the routine maintenance they require.

TRANSIT MARS SEXTILE NATAL MERCURY

♂ ✶ ☿ Current circumstances bring the opportunity to physically touch base with others—to exchange ideas and information. Contacts and activities with neighbors and siblings are apt to be especially stimulating, physically as well as mentally, when transit Mars sextiles your natal Mercury. Advantageous situations present a chance to initiate projects related to writing, direct-mail promotions, or publishing. You may run across a bargain that leads to the purchase or sale of a car or other vehicle. The opportunity to travel may come your way. Valuable information or ideas may be waiting if you catch up on correspondence and reading. Watch for any situation that allows you to use or develop mechanical, computer, or artistic skills. Meetings and discussion groups help you inspire others to take positive action, or your participation in such get-togethers can stimulate you to take such action.

TRANSIT MARS SEXTILE NATAL VENUS

♂ ✶ ♀ Opportunities that lead to romance, social activities, partnerships, and joint ventures are some of the potentials when transit Mars sextiles your natal Venus. There is no guarantee that such opportunities will automatically come. They are, in fact, more likely to result from deliberately putting yourself in situations that generate such opportunities. This favorable period encourages you to help others attain their goals, and, in return, you will be able to ask for their assistance in your own efforts. Present circumstances offer opportunity related to legal matters, contract negotiations, enhancement of your physical appearance, and artistic projects.

TRANSIT MARS SEXTILE NATAL MARS

♂ ✳ ♂ People and situations you encounter or that you attract at this time can help you accomplish physical tasks. When transit Mars sextiles your natal Mars, the attitude of "you scratch my back and I'll scratch yours" is the most successful approach to getting things done, and it keeps everyone busy. During this period, the more physical energy you use, the more you will generate. Accomplishing one task will lead to another.

TRANSIT MARS SEXTILE NATAL JUPITER

♂ ✳ ♃ Present circumstances bring an opportunity to demonstrate your knowledge or expertise. This period favors taking advantage of people and situations in ways that will lead to advancement in your professional status, the extension of your intellectual horizons, the attainment of cultural pursuits, greater spiritual awareness, success in sports, the realization of political ambitions, or international travel. Opportunity at this time may involve your father or his status. When transit Mars sextiles your natal Jupiter, physical efforts result in an opportunity to enjoy the good life, move up the social ladder, publish a book or other material, exhibit your sense of humor, or participate in theatrical productions.

TRANSIT MARS SEXTILE NATAL SATURN

♂ ✳ ♄ If you are a well-prepared, organized individual with definite goals, you are in the best position to take advantage of opportunities that come along when transit Mars sextiles your natal Saturn. Do not be reluctant to deliberately create opportunities that demonstrate your experience and maturity. If you are not such a highly structured, goal-oriented individual, the people and situations you encounter during this period can inspire you to become better organized and help you build a more solid foundation for the kind of success you wish to achieve. This period represents a chance to take advantage of any seniority or position of authority you have.

TRANSIT MARS SEXTILE NATAL URANUS

♂ ✶ ♅ Physical circumstances may give you a chance to introduce a change or new concept. This period implies opportunity to take advantage of new or nontraditional methods as well as a chance to demonstrate unique methods that you have devised. Other potentials when transit Mars sextiles your natal Uranus include circumstances that allow you to change current methods, machinery, or mechanical devices in such a way that more people will be able to take advantage of them. Either that, or you have a chance to benefit from such changes that are made by others. Taking advantage of this period, you can inspire and coordinate group efforts.

TRANSIT MARS SEXTILE NATAL NEPTUNE

♂ ✶ ♆ When transit Mars sextiles your natal Neptune, watch for opportunities that expand your spiritual and artistic awareness and allow you to develop and use your intuitive skills. The kind of people and situations you encounter during this period may also lead to more mundane opportunities, including a chance to go swimming, fishing, sailing, or dancing. Depending on your particular interests and the nature of the circumstances at this time, your efforts may mean eventual success in such areas as promotion, photography, magic, illusion, oil or gas industries, charitable institutions, bankruptcy proceedings, art, and entertainment. The only problem you encounter may be in distinguishing genuine opportunities from false or misleading promises, which means a certain amount of astuteness and caution must be applied.

TRANSIT MARS SEXTILE NATAL PLUTO

♂ ✶ ♇ Intense energy in the present circumstances represents a chance to gain a more powerful position. Your efforts may lead, for instance, to increased physical strength, more control over your actions, and greater resourcefulness. When transit Mars sextiles your natal Pluto, you may focus on physical efforts. Opportunities represent the potential for ultimate success in research and investigation, renovation, recycling, and the analysis and investment of financial assets.

MARS SQUARES

TRANSIT MARS SQUARE NATAL SUN

♂ □ ☉ Physical objects and physical actions frustrate your ego and challenge your willpower when transit Mars squares your natal Sun. You may be touchier than usual when others encroach on your territory, challenge your authority, or question your methods. Whether you stick to your way of doing things or decide to follow the suggestions of others, your desire for personal accomplishment is apt to be strong during this period. You seek ego-gratification from your efforts but not necessarily from the methods you use. Tension may occur when dealing with male companions or co-workers. The success of your efforts is likely to be delayed by unnecessarily aggressive or too hasty actions. Having found a way to restrain these tendencies and applying determination and patience, you will accomplish far more than you anticipated. Take precautions in all physical activities in order to avoid injury to your head or face and strain on your heart and spine.

TRANSIT MARS SQUARE NATAL MOON

♂ □ ☽ Things are not apt to run smoothly during this period. Equipment falters or breaks down, causing frustration and delay. Encountering traffic jams is a strong possibility, especially if you are homeward bound or if children or household errands are the reason for being out in the first place. Accidents or temper tantrums simply waste more time. When transit Mars squares your natal Moon, you may suffer from digestive complaints—the likely consequence of anger, frustration, or eating too fast. Take care not to arouse antagonism in male associates. Carelessness or neglect can cause fire and accidents at home. Caution is needed for the preparation of food since potentials here include the danger of cuts from knives or other sharp utensils, burns from a stove or oven, and ruined meals from cooking at too high a temperature. Disagreement between family members, whether or not the arguments involve you, can be enough to send you away until things quiet down. Even with this potential for trouble and frustration, it is possible to accomplish quite a bit. You may look back and realize that you probably got so much done because of the obstacles you had to overcome.

TRANSIT MARS SQUARE NATAL MERCURY

♂ □ ☿ Too much haste or aggressiveness causes tempers to flare when transit Mars squares your natal Mercury. Expect to encounter argumentative males, aggressive drivers, and frustration when trying to put ideas into action or implement new work methods. This is the time to check for faulty wiring and possible fire hazards in your workplace and in the equipment you use. Wrong directions, bad weather, and other physical obstacles can slow you down when traveling and interfere with the flow of information and other communications. Caution is advised to prevent burns or cuts, especially to your fingers and hands. Headaches and nervous tension are other potential complaints. In spite of potential problems, there is abundant and stimulating energy available during this period. Even if initially aroused by anger or frustration, this energy can, with determined efforts, be rechanneled into positive accomplishments.

TRANSIT MARS SQUARE NATAL VENUS

♂ □ ♀ There is much that is stimulating and exciting in the course of physical activities and interactions when transit Mars squares your natal Venus. Social activities, partnerships, cooperative efforts, romantic adventures, diplomatic maneuvers, and legal negotiations can be successful, but the potential is that these endeavors will not proceed altogether smoothly. Jealousy, envy, aggressiveness, and insensitivity are potential factors that must be avoided or eliminated before anything meaningful can be accomplished. Harmony and cooperation must be actively promoted to counterbalance negative forces. There is a potential for danger from or to a partner or other close ally, but there must be other factors in your present circumstances to strengthen this possibility.

TRANSIT MARS SQUARE NATAL MARS

♂ □ ♂ The raw energy in your present environment is stimulating, but the tension it implies can bring anger and frustration that slow efforts to get things done. Everyone may be too busy to pay enough attention to helping anyone else when transit Mars squares your natal Mars. It is not the time for indecisive actions or you run the risk that others will attain the success you had hoped to achieve. This period is one of a decidedly masculine influence. The methods required to accomplish a goal or task are apt to require physical strength, and the energy with which they are performed must be aggressive and, at times, inelegant—making up in forcefulness and determination for what may be lacking in caution or refinement.

TRANSIT MARS SQUARE NATAL JUPITER

♂ □ ♃ Restlessness and lack of attention to detail may best describe your actions—perhaps the consequence of responding too much to "the big picture." When a square occurs between transit Mars and your natal Jupiter, an increased tendency to overreach may result in your having to pay the consequences for exaggeration and extravagant gestures. Resist any temptation to accept more work than you are physically capable of handling and assignments for which you lack the proper skills or experience. Do not take risks if you cannot afford to suffer the potential loss. Avoid the tendency for overly-expansive gestures. If your gestures are prudent, you will overcome whatever physical obstacles block your path. Whether or not you succeed in the way you envisioned, at least you will not walk away empty-handed.

TRANSIT MARS SQUARE NATAL SATURN

♂ □ ♄ Difficulties and delays are likely to be caused by lack of preparation, planning, and organization—either on your part or that of others. The maddening thing is that even if you are the most careful individual, you are apt to be caught just when things are in disarray—or just when you need something, it cannot be located. Bad timing is, in fact, one of the biggest obstacles to progress when transit Mars squares your natal Saturn. Others may physically resist or even threaten your seniority or position of authority—and you are unlikely to take it graciously when they do. The best part of the present circumstances is the potential that you will eventually succeed, even if it is because maturity and experience dictate that you must keep going until everything proceeds as it should.

TRANSIT MARS SQUARE NATAL URANUS

♂ □ ♅ Circumstances may put you into such a tense or aggravated state as to make you do something you would not ordinarily do.

When Mars squares your natal Uranus, rash as well as unpredictable actions occur. Caution is advised. Keep in mind that not only are your actions unpredictable but so are their consequences—that is, whatever you hope to achieve is not likely to be what results. The performance of machinery and equipment, as well as that of the people who may work for or with you, is also unpredictable at this time. Changes in work schedules or new methods may result in more than a few frustrations. Another potential is that physical circumstances may challenge or alter the way you think or act.

TRANSIT MARS SQUARE NATAL NEPTUNE

♂ □ ♆ Your actions during this period may very well be inspired, but they are not apt to be organized, well-planned, or carefully executed. Under these conditions, the shortest distance between two points is not the expected straight line. The present atmosphere is not conducive to logical actions, although you may find plenty of rationalizations for the actions you do take when transit Mars squares your natal Neptune. You will have to make a determined effort if you wish to avoid wasting time and energy. Choosing methods must depend on intuition and instinct since there may be little else to go on. There is a certain amount of danger due to inattention or because you may simply be unaware of potentially perilous situations. Laziness is another obstacle you may have to overcome.

TRANSIT MARS SQUARE NATAL PLUTO

♂ □ ♇ When transit Mars squares your natal Pluto, power struggles, jealousy, and revenge may be the guiding forces behind some intense activities. During this period, past actions may cause obstacles that must be overcome before current actions can succeed. Anger, if it is aroused, can be formidably destructive. Transformed into positive energy, it can result in equally formidable accomplishments.

MARS TRINES

TRANSIT MARS TRINE NATAL SUN

♂ △ ☉ This can be an ego-boosting period in which you feel more confident that your efforts will succeed. In turn, this attitude attracts the kind of people and success you are looking for. Self-promotion works very well, as does using the efforts of others to your advantage. Other potentials imply that your physical efforts will bring recognition or a position of leadership and that you may be more generous in helping others. Although there is increased vitality when transit Mars trines your natal Sun, there is also a potential for laziness. If you are by nature a less-than-energetic individual, this period is not likely to galvanize you into action. It may be your good fortune, however, to get others to do the work for you. Some of the most highly favored activities involve men or products and services related to men, military maneuvers, sports, surgical procedures, manufacturing, and firearms. Just plain good luck can save you from accidents and other mishaps. The only word of warning is not to take things too much for granted or become too sure of yourself.

TRANSIT MARS TRINE NATAL MOON

♂ △ ☽ Your personal environment is likely to be untroubled when transit Mars trines your natal Moon. Schedules are not interrupted, machinery hums along as it should, everyone does what they are supposed to, and tasks are accomplished on time and with less effort. Creativity and imagination are enhanced. Your actions are more apt to be guided by instinct and intuition. Physical activities and efforts related to home, family, and nutrition are successful and emotionally satisfying. This is an excellent time for planting seeds—physically, emotionally, and mentally. Activities related to women and babies are highly favored. You do not feel the need to compete with anyone, not even yourself. If something comes along that you enjoy, you will have plenty of enthusiasm and energy to pursue it.

TRANSIT MARS TRINE NATAL MERCURY

♂ △ ☿ When a trine occurs between transit Mars and your natal Mercury, your mental faculties are energized. A surge of physical enthusiasm prompts you to turn thoughts and ideas into successful actions. During this period, the installation and repair of machinery or equipment are highly favored and sales of any kind are likely to be more energetic and successful. The same is true of travel, activities, meetings, and the physical dissemination of information. Your job or work, or a business that is owned or operated by you or your siblings is likely to flourish at this time, especially if it is located in your neighborhood. Good fortune or good news comes through the mail or by telephone. This is an auspicious period for writing, designing, buying a car or other motorized vehicle, and developing your mechanical or computer skills.

TRANSIT MARS TRINE NATAL VENUS

♂ △ ♀ This is an excellent time for a haircut, beauty treatment, dental work, or cosmetic surgery. Your physical actions and gestures are likely to be more graceful and elegant, literally as well as figuratively. The social scene is abuzz and everyone is animated and attractive. When transit Mars trines your natal Venus, romance, partnerships, and other alliances are more zestful and exciting. This is a time to do things with others because cooperative efforts may be able to accomplish what you have not been able to do by yourself. Activities that involve art, design, music, jewelry, flowers, the beauty business, debate, and legal matters are favored.

TRANSIT MARS TRINE NATAL MARS

♂ △ ♂ When transit Mars trines your natal Mars, you are surrounded by an abundance of free and easygoing energy. If you need help getting things done, it will appear. People you encounter are apt to be applying their physical efforts toward the same or very similar goals. Obstacles in your path are few or nonexistent. You can make one effort fit neatly into the next, resulting in a whole series of accomplishments. Your physical actions may have the fortunate consequence of putting you in the right place at the right time.

TRANSIT MARS TRINE NATAL JUPITER

♂ △ ♃ Your general status will greatly improve. Just about anything you attempt will succeed. Even a failed effort is likely to result in some better prospect. When transit Mars trines your natal Jupiter, it is definitely time to promote and demonstrate the status and knowledge you have achieved. You are highly favored in long-distance travel, writing, publishing, theater, dance, art, religion, politics, law, investment, finance, and sports. Gambling and other risk-taking ventures are likely to pay off. Men in your life, especially your father, are also favored, and your own good fortune may come through them. This is a period in which to grab and savor everything that brings enjoyment, humor, truth, and the good life. Do not, however, let overconfidence in your ability, the pursuit of pleasure, or laziness spoil the potential success of enterprises.

TRANSIT MARS TRINE NATAL SATURN

♂ △ ♄ You are apt to have more patience these days. If you require more time to accomplish a certain task, it will be granted. The maturity and experience you put into your efforts are what make them successful. If you have not achieved the maturity or experience needed in a given situation, someone who has achieved these qualities will help you. This is one of the most favorable periods. Your current efforts succeed and are likely to become solid, long-lasting accomplishments. When transit Mars trines your natal Saturn, it is an auspicious time to initiate long-term projects and those that are geared toward bringing security and other benefits in the future.

TRANSIT MARS TRINE NATAL URANUS

♂ △ ♅ Actions can have unusual or unexpected results when transit Mars trines your natal Uranus. It is difficult to predict what will happen, but the potential is for a beneficial outcome. Physical circumstances may be unusual or unexpected, but they create personal advantages. You may do something unique or unusual. Unless other circumstances discourage the fortunate potential, this is a good time to change your schedule, to try new methods and procedures, and to work with technical equipment, computers, and inventions. Travel by air, activities with friends, and organizing group efforts are also favored.

TRANSIT MARS TRINE NATAL NEPTUNE

♂ △ ♆ Use your intuitive abilities, increase your spiritual awareness, investigate dreams and the occult, and carry out as much of your work and other physical activities as possible behind the scenes. Exactly how or by what means some task or achievement is successfully accomplished may not be apparent, nor does it have to be when transit Mars trines your natal Neptune. The result of such actions will make everybody happy. Some of the most successful work and other physical activities in which you can engage include the arts and entertainment (especially dance), photography, charitable institutions, drugs, alcohol, oil, gas, marine life, water sports, and ocean cruises.

TRANSIT MARS TRINE NATAL PLUTO

♂ △ ♇ Research and investigation flourish when transit Mars trines your natal Pluto. You get the answers you seek with the help of the intense energy that surrounds you. You have all the control you need if you do not take it for granted and you recognize how to apply its subtle but deadly-accurate force. Recuperative powers, should you need them, are at a high level.

MARS OPPOSITIONS

TRANSIT MARS OPPOSED NATAL SUN

♂ ☍ ☉ There is a distinct possibility of ego-bruising opposition to your actions at this time. While failure does not have to be the final result, the present circumstances do not promise complete success. In the unlikely event that success occurs, it may be accompanied by a loss of integrity. When transit Mars opposes your natal Sun, the opinions and especially the actions of others are not likely to support your leadership, and, indeed, they may directly challenge it. Vitality and enthusiasm are either lacking or quickly burn out, leaving you with nothing to fuel further efforts. Male relationships may be strained—possibly as a result of anger or too much competitiveness. Even if you have no trouble rising to challenges, it is better if you keep a low profile and make plans for a more favorable time. Avoid being in the sun too long and engaging in activities that strain your heart or spine or that can result in injuries to your head or face.

TRANSIT MARS OPPOSED NATAL MOON

♂ ☍ ☽ Caution is advised. Avoid arousing antagonism in others or allowing others to excite such feelings in you. Emotions can get out of control. Anger becomes rage, desire turns into absolute need, infatuation masquerades as love, and love can be an excuse for venting violent passion. When transit Mars opposes your natal Moon, your domestic environment can become volatile and, at the very least, your life is not apt to be a calm or uninterrupted sequence of events. Trying to keep a schedule at work or at home is difficult at best. This can be a frustrating, even dangerous time to be running errands or chauffeuring children or other family members around. Household appliances and equipment break down and more than likely will have to be replaced instead of repaired. Too much haste and anger make household chores and participation in family activities difficult. Pay close attention or mishaps will occur, either in the kitchen or elsewhere in your home. When preparing meals, take care handling appliances and knives and setting temperatures for frying, cooking, or baking. Check your home for possible fire hazards and potentially dangerous chemicals. If you keep firearms in your home, make sure they are safely under lock and key to avoid the potential danger that some family member may accidentally discharge them. This is not a favorable time for surgery, open confrontations, and competitive situations. Physical complaints you may experience include digestive upsets, emotional fatigue, restlessness, insomnia, skin rash, and insect bites. Even if current circumstances do not seem to warrant it, you may feel tense and irritable. Should your efforts gain success or favor, you may be sure it will be accompanied by an enormous payback.

TRANSIT MARS OPPOSED NATAL MERCURY

♂ ☍ ☿ Your mental processes become paralyzed by tension in your physical environment when transit Mars opposes your natal Mercury. Intellectual efforts such as writing, teaching, and designing are not apt to succeed—that is, if they get anywhere at all. Your plans and ideas may be opposed or dismissed out of hand. It is not a favorable time to participate in meetings or discussions since they are apt to be disrupted by angry words, too-hasty exclamations, and an altogether unsatisfactory stream of communications. Neighbors and siblings may turn into temporary opponents. Bad weather is only one potential that makes this an inauspicious time to begin travel of any kind, even to run errands in your neighborhood. Machinery and equipment refuse to cooperate or they break down entirely. There is danger to your hands and fingers as well as the risk of respiratory infections. Move cautiously in all situations. Keep in mind this is a relatively short period and one that is best spent in concerted efforts to stay out of harm's way.

TRANSIT MARS OPPOSED NATAL VENUS

♂ ☍ ♀ Romance is not a likely or enjoyable prospect, nor for that matter are social activities or communications with co-workers, a partner, or other allies. This is not a favorable time for marriage and other alliances or joint ventures—and certainly not a period in which to initiate new ones. One potential suggests danger to or separation from a partner. When transit Mars opposes your natal Venus, everyone heads in opposite directions with no thought of cooperation or willingness to compromise. Elegance and refined actions are overwhelmed or replaced by bad taste and aggressiveness. You would be wise to avoid undergoing surgical procedures or beauty treatments to enhance your physical appearance at this time. Do not begin or expect to make progress in decorating projects or activities that involve diplomacy, art, or music. If you are traveling, do not expect to encounter amiable company along the way. Your work and other physical efforts are best accomplished alone, or current circumstances may force you to work alone. Energy is wasted on debate, negotiation, legal matters, and counseling. If the negative potential of this period fails to materialize or disrupt your routine, count yourself fortunate.

TRANSIT MARS OPPOSED NATAL MARS

♂ ☍ ♂ The biggest potential right now is that you constantly cope with people whose actions and purposes are diametrically opposed to your own. Your attempts to accomplish something physically may be appropriately compared to hitting your head against the proverbial stone wall. Making little or no headway, you end up wondering why you ever wasted your energy in the first place. Nor will you succeed any better with a show of strength or aggressiveness, since these efforts are met by the equally determined force of others. It is difficult to sustain controlled or stable physical efforts when transit Mars opposes your natal Mars, but things may be easier if you do not waste your energy with anything but the most routine, quietly carried out tasks.

TRANSIT MARS OPPOSED NATAL JUPITER

♂ ☍ ♃   It is easy to imagine the probable consequence of blowing up a balloon beyond its capacity. This image is also the easiest description of the circumstances when transit Mars opposes your natal Jupiter. There is a tendency to assume you are capable of greater abilities than a more honest estimation would suggest, or, knowing full well your real limitations, you may cave in to external pressure or temptation and let others make inflated assumptions of your capabilities. Either way, you are left trying to accomplish the impossible. Actions go too fast and too far. It is in your best interest to remember that there is more than a little potential here for unpleasant results if you experience too much of a good thing. This is not an auspicious time for court decisions, traveling abroad, higher education, writing, publishing, and participating in competitive sports. There is also the possibility of danger to or separation from your father. Physical efforts are either stymied by laziness and unwise actions, or they proceed with such extreme force as to invite dangerous consequences. Spirituality can turn into fanaticism, and intellectuality can become an arrogant display of superiority. Save grandstanding and bravado for another time.

TRANSIT MARS OPPOSED NATAL SATURN

♂ ☍ ♄   Any shortcut you attempt in order to make things easier is apt to have undesirable results. You waste more time and energy trying to get around the rules than if you comply with them in the first place. You resist and resent the authority of others and, what may be worse, you are just as likely to encounter the same attitude in others should you try to impose your authority. Attempts to organize or put structure and purpose into projects and other physical efforts will be difficult, and more than one task may be abandoned in discouragement. When transit Mars opposes your natal Saturn, delay turns into cancellation, and anger thwarts the prudent dictates of maturity and experience. Caution is necessary since there is increased potential for accidents to your teeth or bones and for flare-up of chronic illness.

Transit Mars Opposed Natal Uranus

♂ ☍ ♅ The physical energy surrounding you when transit Mars opposes your natal Uranus indicates it would be futile to try to coordinate group efforts. Although activities with friends and organizations are likely to be disrupted, other areas of your personal life may not be so disturbed. The instability of current circumstances makes it difficult to predict what actions you may unexpectedly take, or what actions may suddenly be taken against you. It is not a favorable period to act on the spur-of-the-moment or to participate in new or unusual experiences. The potential is high that such activities will be unsuccessful, perhaps even disastrous. Being in the middle of a crowd is unsettling and the same may be said for single encounters with strangers. Make no attempt to act out or impose egalitarian gestures to counteract prejudice. It is apt to inspire more than resentment in those with a deep bias who will not hesitate to attack you as well as your principles.

Transit Mars Opposed Natal Neptune

♂ ☍ ♆ Efforts are apt to come to nothing, or at least not accomplish the purpose for which they were intended. This unfortunate potential should not become an excuse for you to remain idle, since many daily or routine efforts are not necessarily threatened. However, the prospect of eroding physical energy and enthusiasm would suggest that it is not wise to invest your time and efforts in new activities or vague, disorganized projects. When transit Mars opposes your natal Neptune, charitable acts can be misguided. Work methods are inept, inefficient, or incorrect. Water sports pose the risk of danger, as do fishing trips, ocean cruises, and work that involves photography, gas, oil, and explosive or corrosive chemicals. It is not a favorable time to try new medication or use anesthetics, alcohol, and drugs. Illusion and deception are constant threats. There is a strong potential for unexpected attacks. Be alert but not paranoid.

TRANSIT MARS OPPOSED NATAL PLUTO

♂ ☍ ♇ Hostile forces you encounter when transit Mars opposes your natal Pluto can have an immobilizing effect. A contest of wills is to be avoided at all cost. Efforts to gain control of any kind are apt to have the opposite result. This is not a time to change or interfere with the status quo. Deliberately arousing the antagonism of another will create a formidable opponent that you might not otherwise have had to confront. Manipulation is a waste of time. Unfortunately, using the direct approach is not any more successful, though it may cast you in a more favorable light. If you realize that current circumstances do not present any means in which to gain the upper hand, you are correct. Act accordingly.

Chapter Six

Transit Jupiter Aspects to the Natal Planets

The transit of Jupiter takes twelve years to complete the zodiac. The twelve-year Jupiter cycle in your natal chart is (or can be) a period of intellectual, spiritual, and economic growth. Jupiter is retrograde each year for about 120 days and aspects it makes to natal planets can be effective for the better part of eight or nine months.

JUPITER CONJUNCTIONS

TRANSIT JUPITER CONJOIN NATAL SUN

♃ ☌ ☉ You have reached the culmination of something you began or gained approximately twelve years ago. Whatever it was—a marriage, a business venture, or some other endeavor—must either now move forward to a higher level of personal growth and happiness or it will begin to end at this point. What forces the issue is the conscious or subconscious expansion of your ego. When transit Jupiter conjoins your natal Sun, the pursuit of pleasure can become a much greater source of ego satisfaction, as can the attainment of knowledge and greater spiritual awareness. The tendency for self-indulgence as well as generosity to others is increased, which is not necessarily a bad thing unless you go too far. Avoid the temptation to get carried away with your own importance. Such self-inflating tactics are not likely to be necessary, since recognition and honor may come your way without having to demand them.

TRANSIT JUPITER CONJOIN NATAL MOON

♃ ☌ ☽ Emotional levels expand and your desires can become quite grand when transit Jupiter conjoins your natal Moon. You may effortlessly gain greater emotional commitment from those with whom you share close relationships and you will attract love and affection from many others as well. Emotional satisfaction can be achieved from practically everything these days. But everything is not necessarily desirable or practical. Too much physical pleasure in food, for example, can result in gaining weight. You may be tempted to indulge in lavish spending and other extravagant gestures in order to gain the admiration and approbation of others. This is an excellent period if your business or interests involve real estate, luxury items, domestic products, and goods and services related to women or children. You may attain higher social status and greater popularity. Your residence may be upgraded and your domestic environment improved by the introduction of educational materials, cultural pursuits, or spiritual activities. Your mother as well as your children prosper at this time.

TRANSIT JUPITER CONJOIN NATAL MERCURY

♃ ☌ ☿ Your range of interests and activities increases measurably when transit Jupiter conjoins your natal Mercury. Greater mental and physical restlessness can result in expanded communications, new methods, and new experiences, all of which contribute to broadening your intellectual horizons. Business ventures, travel, sales, advertising, higher education, religion, politics, law, languages, and drama represent at least some of the possible areas that grab your attention and inspire your participation. You travel more often and more luxuriously. This period represents an extremely wide variety of potential circumstances. Your neighborhood, for example, can become a place of expansion and development, contacts with siblings and neighbors are enhanced, and your interest and status in community affairs increase. You read, write, and communicate more. Some self-imposed restrictions may be necessary in order to avoid such negative potentials as mental laziness, intellectual arrogance, and taking on so many projects and activities that you achieve nothing of lasting value.

TRANSIT JUPITER CONJOIN NATAL VENUS

♃ ☌ ♀ Your capacity and desire for pleasure and luxury are enhanced, a situation that can lead to overindulgence and extravagance. It can also contribute to the expansion of your social life, establishment of fortunate partnerships and alliances, and success in writing, publishing, or the arts. Female relationships are favored. There is no doubt of the potential benefits that are possible as a result of your relationships and social interactions when transit Jupiter conjoins your natal Venus. However, the negative potential suggests physical laziness, taking too much for granted, and not being enterprising enough to take advantage of the contacts that are made. If this period finds you lacking the things you most desire, you may be all too willing to sacrifice long-term relationships or compromise your principles for what may be a short-lived reward. Another possibility is that you overestimate the true nature of relationships that come along, believing them to be more promising than they are. Wisdom, maturity, and prudence are needed to enjoy your added pleasures and good fortune without being trapped by them.

TRANSIT JUPITER CONJOIN NATAL MARS

♃ ☌ ♂ This period can be fortunate for your job or work and for most physical activities. In a sports competition, you will be on the winning team, a concept you can apply to any other area of your life these days. Wisdom and moderation must be imposed if you wish to avoid failing because you were too confident of your physical abilities or overestimated the potential success of an enterprise. When it comes to getting around, your enjoyment of speed as well as luxury increases, the result of which may be to indulge in a sports car or more luxurious means of travel. Male relationships are favored. Attraction to the dynamic force of physical energy and strength is greatly heightened, luring you to those who possess it and situations that inspire it in you.

TRANSIT JUPITER CONJOIN NATAL JUPITER

♃ ☌ ♃ Some type of personal growth and expansion is likely to occur, but there is no certain way to predict what form it will take. If your particular circumstances allow for such a likelihood, it may mean bearing children, an endeavor which can be seen as a form of personal expansion. It may also mean success in other areas such as higher education and advanced training or the growth of a commercial enterprise. Other potentials when transit Jupiter conjoins your natal Jupiter suggest that you may climb another rung of the social ladder or gain a position of higher professional status. Unless negative factors destroy the fortunate potential of this period, circumstances encourage you to pursue some form of personal advancement with the confidence that you will succeed.

TRANSIT JUPITER CONJOIN NATAL SATURN

♃ ☌ ♄ You may have the good fortune to rid yourself of restriction in one form or another when transit Jupiter conjoins your natal Saturn. The prevailing influence is an easing of the burden of responsibilities, though perhaps not removing them altogether. Whenever and wherever you have engaged in careful planning, hard work, organization, and patience, you will attain greater maturity and the wisdom of experience as well as the success and recognition you deserve. On the other hand, if you are possessed of a free-spirited nature that has found it difficult to acquire or apply the long-term efforts just described, circumstances may bring just the inspiration you need to develop a more practical, responsible attitude. If you have managed to acquire a position of authority or seniority, this is a period in which such a status may prove most advantageous.

TRANSIT JUPITER CONJOIN NATAL URANUS

♃ ☌ ♅ People and circumstances you encounter when transit Jupiter conjoins your natal Uranus make you more aware of freedom and independence. This can mean physical freedom as well as independence of thought. What inspires you cannot be predicted, but one potential suggests you may be encouraged to join or participate in groups or group causes. If negative factors do not interfere, the activities you undertake with groups will prove highly beneficial. Your attitudes and approach in dealing with people are more egalitarian and outgoing these days. The personal network of people who surround you expands. You seek to enlarge the role you play in the lives of others as friend, parent, lover, or associate. The potentials suggest success in finance, investment, fund-raising, computers, technology, astrology, travel (especially by air), and group activities.

Transit Jupiter Conjoin Natal Neptune

♃ ☌ ♆ Your psychic energy, instincts, spiritual awareness, and artistic sensitivity can reach unprecedented development if you choose to investigate and use them when transit Jupiter conjoins your natal Neptune. The facets of your nature that require illusion or pretense will be satisfied, but great caution is necessary if you are one that too easily loses touch with reality. Enhanced imagination can result in the most inspired ideas and actions, but unfortunately it can also be responsible for fanaticism and paranoia. People and situations that you encounter are likely to be associated with footwear, the feet, dancing, the ocean, drugs or alcohol, religion, promotion, bankruptcy, scandal, and mystery or illusion. Keep in mind that these associations may be of a positive as well as a negative nature. You must decide and act accordingly.

Transit Jupiter Conjoin Natal Pluto

♃ ☌ ♇ You can achieve a much greater knowledge of your potential when transit Jupiter conjoins your natal Pluto. Your personal resources as well as resourcefulness increase. You can develop more personal magnetism or achieve a position of greater power and control. Furthermore, you accomplish these things without working too hard to achieve them or else by receiving valuable assistance. Unless other factors destroy the positive potential, success will accompany your efforts, especially those that involve psychological analysis, research and investigation, and the evaluation or distribution of monetary assets and raw materials.

JUPITER SEXTILES

TRANSIT JUPITER SEXTILE NATAL SUN

♃ ✶ ☉ Circumstances that come along when transit Jupiter sextiles your natal Sun are likely to offer an opportunity to expand the range of your personal influence, to explore new ways or reasons to exert your will, and to give you a chance to be proud of yourself. The nature of this period is such that you do not or should not wait for such an opportunity to be handed to you, though that is also a potential. If the chance you need does not come along, find the best means and time available to create one. The implication is that your efforts will eventually lead to success. Do not hesitate to impose your own priorities and defend your integrity and principles.

TRANSIT JUPITER SEXTILE NATAL MOON

♃ ✶ ☽ Chance and circumstances these days afford the opportunity to express your emotions, to get what you want, and to follow your heart. Your emotional life is given a chance to grow and expand in one form or another when a sextile occurs between transit Jupiter and your natal Moon. This does not imply that you will actually succeed, only that you will find the opportunity that will lead to success. What are your desires, your fantasies, your requirements for emotional satisfaction? Money? Love? Power? Knowledge? The success of this period may come in the form of an opportunity to make your dreams come true, and perhaps to find out what you *do not want*, in itself a highly liberating situation.

TRANSIT JUPITER SEXTILE NATAL MERCURY

♃ ✶ ☿ Make an effort to increase your communications and contacts these days. If you are looking for a chance to be successful, you are most likely to find it in what you read and hear when transit Jupiter sextiles your natal Mercury. You will get valuable information and ideas at meetings, in your own neighborhood, as a result of travel, and in general by staying mentally alert and physically busy. It is an excellent time to look for opportunity to expand business enterprises, education, writing, publishing, mechanical and design projects, religious or spiritual studies, and political interests.

TRANSIT JUPITER SEXTILE NATAL VENUS

♃ ✶ ♀ When transit Jupiter sextiles your natal Venus, the people and situations you encounter offer the chance to expand your social activities, to establish partnerships or other alliances, to put some romance into your life, to obtain beautiful and luxurious possessions, and to enhance your own attractiveness. Finding such an opportunity (or creating one for yourself) depends, in this case, on your willingness to increase interactions with others. A current partner or ally may provide a chance to improve your social status or become more successful. This is also a period that can lead to negotiating better terms in legal affairs, diplomatic endeavors, contracts and other agreements.

TRANSIT JUPITER SEXTILE NATAL MARS

♃ ✶ ♂ Opportunity these days may be found in the form of employment, physical competition, or an increase of energy and physical strength. Circumstances may not automatically hand you these chances, but you can manipulate situations in order to create them for yourself. It is your physical efforts and actions that eventually lead to success when transit Jupiter sextiles your natal Mars. For this reason, it is worthwhile to be as physically enthusiastic and industrious as possible. Another situation you should not overlook is being given an opportunity through a male family member or acquaintance.

TRANSIT JUPITER SEXTILE NATAL JUPITER

♃ ✶ ♃ This period is usually not of particular strength or significance. Perhaps the most that might be said when transit Jupiter sextiles your natal Jupiter is that your success or prosperity will not be adversely affected by current circumstances. Considering the frustration and discouragement that can result from coping with opposing forces and other difficulties, perhaps the absence of such obstacles can in itself be all the benefit you need.

Transit Jupiter Sextile Natal Saturn

♃ ✶ ♄ People and situations you encounter when transit Jupiter sextiles your natal Saturn offer opportunities to use the experience you have acquired or to gain recognition or reward for your hard work, organization, and planning. If you lack maturity and the willingness to work hard, and have not gained much experience, it is wise to assume that what you are now being given is a chance to achieve these things.

Transit Jupiter Sextile Natal Uranus

♃ ✶ ♅ A chance to succeed may come as a result of demonstrating independence or a unique approach. It may be a person of a different generation who presents an opportunity you need now. When transit Jupiter sextiles your natal Uranus, you benefit by exhibiting an action or reaction appropriate to your generation but different from the ideas or methods of those with whom you are presently dealing. Do not pass up the opportunity to prove your loyalty and interest regarding friends or fellow club members. It may be through them that you are given a valuable opportunity for personal growth or success.

Transit Jupiter Sextile Natal Neptune

♃ ✶ ♆ The situations you can use to your advantage are no doubt going to be subtle when transit Jupiter sextiles your natal Neptune. The potential of a situation being able to lead to success may be missed merely because you were unaware of the facts or you were missing the needed perception. Pay attention to those who give you good advice. Opportunity is likely to be in the form of a chance to increase spiritual awareness, deepen artistic sensitivity, and enhance your imagination and intuition.

Transit Jupiter Sextile Natal Pluto

♃ ✶ ♇ When transit Jupiter sextiles your natal Pluto, it is a good time to analyze your talent and skills and find out how they may be developed and used more effectively. Current circumstances offer an opportunity to increase your personal power and control, or, at the very least, a chance to understand how to accomplish this goal.

JUPITER SQUARES

TRANSIT JUPITER SQUARE NATAL SUN

♃ □ ☉ You are confronted with obstacles that block your success when transit Jupiter squares your natal Sun. These obstacles could be caused by your own ego, stubborn pride, greed, self-indulgence, or overestimation. Avoiding such pitfalls in your attitude and behavior as well as avoiding those who indulge in them will help to minimize the negative potential. If your nature is not given to being paralyzed with anger or inaction when recognition or success is delayed or denied, you will pass the tests of this period with flying colors and no doubt obtain your goals in the process.

TRANSIT JUPITER SQUARE NATAL MOON

♃ □ ☽ The path to attaining the object of your heart's desires is littered with one obstacle or another during this period. You may have to deal with extravagance that has little redeeming value. Time is spent to no good purpose or useful result. Impatience at being denied instant gratification is out of proportion to the situation when transit Jupiter squares your natal Moon. If instant gratification is demanded and does occur, there may be a lack of appreciation or proper use of what was gained. No matter what the situation, the best advice is not to let your emotions go overboard. There are enough sentiments and emotional commitments to make everyone happy, but somehow nothing seems to fall into place. Avoid overcompensating when it is not necessary. Keep going and you will achieve whatever aims you have in mind.

TRANSIT JUPITER SQUARE NATAL MERCURY

♃ □ ☿ Progress is delayed by a variety of annoyances: too much of one thing and not enough of another, wrong information, paying too much or too little attention to details, having so much time that nothing gets finished or having too little time to accomplish something adequately. Tardiness or mechanical failure can cause frustration in travel. In spite of whatever snags develop, much can actually be accomplished when transit Jupiter squares your natal Mercury, especially if you avoid jumping to conclusions, acting with too much haste, or believing you already know the answers. Patience and a prudent manner in dealing with information and communications are rewarded with more progress than you thought could be accomplished when you started out.

TRANSIT JUPITER SQUARE NATAL VENUS

♃ □ ♀ When transit Jupiter squares your natal Venus, values and priorities get confused which results in your being either the perpetrator or the victim of shameless social climbing, ostentatiousness, laziness, wastefulness, and overindulgence. Success with regard to a partnership and other alliances, joint ventures, social events, and romance does not promise to be an easy matter, but there is the potential for progress if you persevere. Legal matters and negotiating contracts and other agreements during this period may turn to your advantage, but self-serving goals in the guise of concessions or other snags might have to be dealt with first.

TRANSIT JUPITER SQUARE NATAL MARS

♃ □ ♂ Moderation is needed to counteract the tendency to use too much force where none or very little is needed and to be too lazy to act when a demonstration of physical enthusiasm is required. Moderation will also prove useful in counteracting the tendency to overestimate physical strength and ability. If you have the control and common sense to avoid acting in haste and jumping to conclusions, your actions will succeed. When transit Jupiter squares your natal Mars, you can make progress if you do not not quit too early or work too long.

TRANSIT JUPITER SQUARE NATAL JUPITER

♃ □ ♃ When a square occurs between transit Jupiter and your natal Jupiter, you may think that certain unpleasant situations would not occur if only you were wealthier, more prominent, or more knowledgeable. If you allow such foolishness to discourage you from tackling obstacles and getting things accomplished, you have only yourself to blame. Skip the excuses and cynicism and you will get much further than you think.

Transit Jupiter Square Natal Saturn

♃ □ ♄ Circumstances can make it tempting to forego mature judgment and experience, to try shortcuts, and to avoid rules and regulations. Resist the temptation. In the end, the frustrations and delays that develop when transit Jupiter squares your natal Saturn make you realize it would have been simpler and more profitable to go by the book. In spite of this negative prospect, you can still make some progress, which is better than none at all.

Transit Jupiter Square Natal Uranus

♃ □ ♅ Meetings of any kind can be difficult to organize and coordinate. Although a spirit of generosity and togetherness may be encouraged by current circumstances, accomplishing group projects is difficult in spite of everyone's good intentions. When transit Jupiter squares your natal Uranus, progress can be made toward common goals or resolving disputes, but only by letting others act independently and then bringing all the separate efforts together.

Transit Jupiter Square Natal Neptune

♃ □ ♆ Details and reality get short shrift when transit Jupiter squares your natal Neptune. If you are a perfectionist, this can be an almost paralyzing period. If you are not a perfectionist, you are likely to be overwhelmed by admonitions from those who are. The potential for being victimized by illusions of one sort or another is increased. Avoid those who tell you to concentrate on the "big picture."

Transit Jupiter Square Natal Pluto

♃ □ ♇ The self-control you thought you had or the personal influence you wield may not seem to be working when transit Jupiter squares your natal Pluto. In reality, this may not be the case. It may only be a result of trying to cover too wide a base of desires and activities. Shorten your sights and you will be able to make progress.

JUPITER TRINES

TRANSIT JUPITER TRINE NATAL SUN

♃ △ ☉ The increased potential for fortunate circumstances when transit Jupiter trines your natal Sun brings you honor, recognition, and just plain good luck. Ego-gratifying experiences are what this period is all about. Your ambitions and goals expand and there is an excellent chance you will succeed in attaining them. The sphere of your personal influence grows with minimum effort on your part. If you want to attain a position of leadership, this is definitely a time to surge ahead with such a goal. Current circumstances not only enhance your generosity, integrity, and courage, but these traits will also be recognized and admired by others. As with all good fortune, however, there is danger of misusing it. You may feel too content with yourself or overconfident that things are going well. Taking things too much for granted, you may be not feel any necessity to change the status quo and thereby miss the advantages that come your way. Although most situations will no doubt be fortunate, some of the luck implied during this period may be a matter of keeping a bad situation from becoming worse. An example would be someone who is passed over for a promotion to supervisor—a seemingly unfortunate situation. However, two days later all the supervisors are fired.

TRANSIT JUPITER TRINE NATAL MOON

♃ △ ☽ Your instincts and intuition are enhanced these days and some of your fondest wishes may come true. Gaining emotional satisfaction on many different levels best describes the situation when transit Jupiter trines your natal Moon. Prosperity surrounds your home and family. Children and your mother or mother-figure may be especially favored, or they may contribute to your good luck. The sale or purchase of a home or domestic items is highly fortunate. If you have been looking for a residence and happen to find one at this time, the prospects favor acquiring it. Other fortunate circumstances involve the higher education of children, long-distance travel with family members, or traveling abroad to visit relatives or a childhood home. Your imagination and artistic or creative talents flourish. In spite of the promising circumstances, there are certain situations to avoid. The generosity and good feelings that prevail may prompt you to acquire more than you need, which, in turn, poses the danger of wastefulness. Food and nourishment are apt to be abundant and that may be a problem if your own consumption results in unwanted weight or other physical complaints that result from overeating.

TRANSIT JUPITER TRINE NATAL MERCURY

♃ △ ☿ The fortunate circumstances promised during this period involve broadening your intellectual horizons, developing new skills, and seeking new experiences. Communications increase and you are inundated with information and opinions. When transit Jupiter trines your natal Mercury, you are filled with new ideas and the enthusiasm to express them. New and better methods come along to make life easier and to increase your productivity. Although success may not be dropped in your lap, you are certain to run into it if you are involved in higher education, writing, publishing, computers, acting, political or religious activities, travel, broadcasting, direct mail, advertising, or the law. Business prospers, and if the enterprise happens to be in sales or located in your neighborhood, so much the better. This period can bring better forms of transportation and upgraded accommodations when you travel—which is a good thing since there is also the potential for doing a lot more traveling. There is more merriment and humor in your environment. Good fortune and increased contacts involve siblings and neighbors.

TRANSIT JUPITER TRINE NATAL VENUS

♃ △ ♀ If it is romance you seek, it is romance you will find when transit Jupiter trines your natal Venus. If it is more of a social life you want, a more active social life is what you will get. If you are looking for a suitable partner or ally, just the right person is apt to come along. And if the right person already has come along, this is an excellent time to marry, form a business partnership, and begin a joint venture. Other fortunate potentials of your current circumstances include success related to contracts and other legal matters, consultations, public relations, and diplomatic endeavors. Decisions are in your favor. Female friendships are more enthusiastic and enjoyable. The enhancement of your sense of humor, capacity for enjoyment, and cooperative spirit should be sufficient to bring you a measure of success in almost any situation. In spite of the fortunate prospects, the increased desire for wealth and luxury may tempt you to reach beyond your means or compromise yourself in some other way. Overindulgence in the pursuit of pleasure has pitfalls, not the least of which involves a wide range of minor physical complaints and illnesses. On the whole, however, you should prosper in many ways.

TRANSIT JUPITER TRINE NATAL MARS

♃ △ ♂ Difficult tasks are easier to accomplish when transit Jupiter trines your natal Mars. In other times and different societies, hunters and warriors who began their enterprises under this planetary aspect were expected to succeed. You may apply this to your current physical efforts and activities. In spite of the fortunate potential, there is a tendency for physical laziness and a state of contentment that discourages inclinations to compete. Knowing this, it would be in your best interest not to let inertia interfere with your physical industriousness. There is an element of luck to help your actions succeed. Even apparent failures have a way of being fortuitous. After all, it is better to miss the bus than to be hit by it. Good fortune may come to you through a man, and male relationships are favored at this time.

TRANSIT JUPITER TRINE NATAL JUPITER

♃ △ ♃ A trine between transit Jupiter and your natal Jupiter brings circumstances in which you enjoy a certain amount of ease or success. The people and situations you encounter are compatible, or at least they are not of such a negative nature as to interfere with your happiness or efforts to attain your goals.

TRANSIT JUPITER TRINE NATAL SATURN

♃ △ ♄ Although this can be a very fortunate period, its impact will be modified by your age, maturity, and past experiences. Current circumstances can bring the satisfaction as well as the rewards of hard work, sacrifice, and willingness to accept responsibility. If you have not been diligent in the past, you may find that present circumstances make it preferable to become that way now, which, in turn, ensures your success in the future. Restrictions and responsibilities can lessen, perhaps even disappear when transit Jupiter trines your natal Saturn. There are other possibilities. Benefits you get may be the result of your seniority or authority. Someone may come along and give you the kind of financial assistance or other lucky break that they themselves once received.

TRANSIT JUPITER TRINE NATAL URANUS

♃ △ ♅ It is easier to organize people and coordinate group activities when transit Jupiter trines your natal Uranus. Good fortune may come through friends and organizations. Success can be expected in financial dealings, but this success is likely to be associated with organizational efforts such as fund-raising rather than a private windfall that comes your way.

TRANSIT JUPITER TRINE NATAL NEPTUNE

♃ △ ♆ When transit Jupiter trines your natal Neptune, the circumstances are tricky and it becomes necessary to focus on reality. The magic of illusion and imagination, enhanced spirituality, or investigation of the paranormal can be enjoyable and even fortunate diversions if they pose no serious threat to life, limb, or your bank account. There is potential to experience the highest inspirations, as well as the kind of dumb luck that comes from unintentionally being in just the right place at the right time. You have the ability to be a master of disguise these days for whatever reasons you choose.

TRANSIT JUPITER TRINE NATAL PLUTO

♃ △ ♇ Knowledge you gain or the people and situations you encounter these days can be instrumental in helping you expand your personal influence and control, or, at the very least, they enable you to give the impression that you possess such power. When transit Jupiter trines your natal Pluto, an even likelier possibility is that you will gain a much better understanding of the value of power and control, how they can be attained, and how they can be used.

JUPITER OPPOSITIONS

TRANSIT JUPITER OPPOSED NATAL SUN

♃ ☍ ☉ Current circumstances are not likely to increase your prosperity. Situations that come along can deplete your material assets. When transit Jupiter opposes your natal Sun, your generosity benefits the wrong people or is wasted in worthless endeavors. Those who would like to help you may be rendered powerless or unwittingly steer you in the wrong direction. Those who come to you with grandiose ideas or the promise of some successful enterprise are not able to deliver, no matter how well-intentioned they are. Of course, this is not to say you have no choice in the matter. A conservative attitude may keep you from overreaching yourself in one way or another. Although unlikely, victories and other successes that are won during this period may compromise your principles or self-esteem. It is important to realize that you will probably not be able to remove the forces that oppose you, deflate your ego, and wound your pride, which only leaves you the option of finding a constructive way to work around them or with them. Your father or his status and influence are cast in a unfavorable light.

TRANSIT JUPITER OPPOSED NATAL MOON

♃ ☍ ☽ Emotional lows are a potential. If you are possessed of a fighting spirit, the loss of hope or promise when transit Jupiter opposes your natal Moon can inspire you to hang in there. It is unlikely that you will be able to overcome the people or situations that stymie your emotional satisfaction and block progress in emotional situations. Established relationships can be pulled apart by hysteria and vastly inflated emotional needs, but they may eventually emerge stronger for the experience. Weaker emotional commitments will, of course, be even more seriously threatened. If these commitments are dissolved, it will provide the freedom for you to seek new and stronger alliances. Freedom, at least on an emotional level, is an underlying factor in what occurs. It would be foolhardy to expect any tangible material gains. If your fondest desires are fulfilled, it will be at a very high price. Home and family are burdened by an overloaded or polarized emotional environment. Children are apt to be out of control. This is an unfavorable period for speculative ventures, especially those that deal with agricultural products, real estate, or domestic goods because there is liable to be a glut of these things in the market place. Perhaps the best thing to keep in mind is that more is not likely to mean better.

TRANSIT JUPITER OPPOSED NATAL MERCURY

♃ ☍ ☿ You may have a tendency to overrate or misjudge the value of your ideas or information. It may also be that you are perfectly reasonable and correct, but those to whom you present ideas or information misjudge its value or reject it out of hand. When transit Jupiter opposes your natal Mercury, you may be confronted with too much information and too many methods or none that are practical or efficient. Other potentials include grandiose plans and schemes, travel without purpose or pleasure, and lack of attention to detail. Be prepared for a lot of talk but no action and discussions or meetings that are all form and no substance. These are some of the threats that block your progress. Since there is little possibility of removing whatever stands in your path, try finding some constructive way to deal with it. Not apt to be favored by success are areas that include community activities, business dealings (especially sales, investment, and finance), writing, publishing, broadcasting, advertising, direct-mail promotions, travel, transportation, education, computers, and the use or development of your mechanical and design skills. Contacts or plans with siblings and neighbors are not apt to succeed at this time.

TRANSIT JUPITER OPPOSED NATAL VENUS

♃ ☍ ♀ The good life is apt to be disappointing. What should be pleasurable experiences fall flat. What should be stimulating social events turn into excesses that the participants would rather forget. When transit Jupiter opposes your natal Venus, it is probably one of the worst times to try to mix business with pleasure. Events that have been loudly and broadly promoted are not likely to live up to their promise. Partnerships, joint ventures, romance, and female friendships are not very successful or enjoyable. If you have been unhappy in a current partnership, you may become all the more discouraged with it during this period. Do not expect that others will want to cooperate with you, nor should you believe those who promise that they will. Trying to work in unison or in harmony with others is likely to be futile. Attempts to enhance your appearance or beautify some aspect of your environment end up as an extravagant waste of time and money. Your values, sincerity, proper perspective, and sense of proportion can all suffer during this period. Do what you can to minimize the damage.

TRANSIT JUPITER OPPOSED NATAL MARS

♃ ☍ ♂ Unless other powerful factors counteract the negative potential when transit Jupiter opposes your natal Mars, your physical actions and activities founder. Your efforts and activities may be conducted on too grand a scale and simply collapse under their own weight. Others may give you impossible tasks to perform. You may not possess the ability or expertise or you may lack the time or resources required to accomplish such tasks. This period does not favor competitive or risky sports, the physical aspects of long-distance travel, and male relationships. Legal actions or other maneuvers may prevent you from physically carrying out plans or goals. One way or another, you may be spinning your wheels these days. Be content with whatever does get done.

TRANSIT JUPITER OPPOSED NATAL JUPITER

♃ ☍ ♃ Discontent with wealth or personal achievement can creep into your environment when transit Jupiter opposes your natal Jupiter. It is difficult to find anyone who is the least bit impressed with you or your efforts. You may think you have achieved something worthwhile, only to find that someone else has already done the same thing, and, worse, they have done it better. In spite of the potential for overblown efforts or discouraging comparisons, if things do go along smoothly, you would be wise not to take anything for granted or push too hard.

TRANSIT JUPITER OPPOSED NATAL SATURN

♃ ☍ ♄ Responsibilities, restrictions, rules, and regulations are in direct conflict with freedom these days, and this situation is apt to be a key factor in blocking your progress, happiness, success, or whatever you seek. When transit Jupiter opposes your natal Saturn, you cannot count on maturity or experience to lead the way and, if you do, you are likely to be successfully challenged. A promising situation may tempt you to circumvent the rules or get around restrictions. It does not work. You refuse to bend the rules or relax your attentiveness to responsibilities and, as a result, you miss a valuable opportunity. Resist the promise of something new and hold on to what you have, at least for the time being.

TRANSIT JUPITER OPPOSED NATAL URANUS

♃ ☍ ♅   Business matters, especially with regard to organizational finances and fund-raising efforts, may come to a screeching halt due to lack of solidarity, common goals, or any number of other reasons that are impossible to reconcile for the time being. This is an unfavorable period for group activities. Everyone goes off in opposite directions in spite of the most rigorous efforts to coordinate everything. When transit Jupiter opposes your natal Uranus, circumstances make it difficult to be part of a group or function effectively in the role you play in the lives of others. There is too much conflict in the personal network of people who surround you. Greater need for freedom and independence may be the problem in these relationships and associations, or opposing views or goals may create the difficulties.

TRANSIT JUPITER OPPOSED NATAL NEPTUNE

♃ ☍ ♆   Be alert to the dangers of illusion and deception that make it difficult to keep track of reality when an opposition occurs between transit Jupiter and your natal Neptune. There is no predicting exactly what will happen, but it seems certain that those who propose fantastic schemes and, perhaps even more perilously, want to involve you in their fanatic ideas are to be avoided at all cost. Another discouraging potential is the tendency to use self-pity and guilt as an excuse for overindulgence and the use of drugs or alcohol. There will be serious consequences if you cannot manage to avoid this tendency. Confidential matters are either revealed or are completely distorted and misunderstood. This is a highly inauspicious time for long-distance travel on or over water.

TRANSIT JUPITER OPPOSED NATAL PLUTO

♃ ☍ ♇ Power and success are seductive traps when transit Jupiter opposes your natal Pluto. These things can be grossly mismanaged or overrated. People and situations that promise you greater personal influence or an opportunity to manipulate something to your advantage should be avoided. If such people or situations are still around once this period has ended, there will be time enough to consider or take advantage of what they offer. A contest of wills is the potential situation most likely to be encountered. You may either be the main participant in such a battle or the victim of being on the losing side. This is not a favorable time for matters that involve inheritance, taxes, insurance, and debt.

Chapter Seven

Transit Saturn Aspects to the Natal Planets

The transit of Saturn is a time of adjustment and willingness to accept responsibilities, but it is also a time when maturity and experience that come from hard work and coping with difficulties brings satisfaction and stability. Each year Saturn's retrograde cycle lasts for about 140 days, and its aspects to a natal planet can be effective from a few months to over a year.

SATURN CONJUNCTIONS

TRANSIT SATURN CONJOIN NATAL SUN

♄ ♂ ☉   This is a period that will test maturity and wisdom, as well as your willingness to correct mistakes and move forward. You develop an increasing need for recognition of your talents, abilities, and, most of all, for your efforts and achievements. You are apt to feel disappointment and discouragement, whether or not such feelings are justified. Worse than that, such negative feelings are apt to be directed toward yourself. Your achievements may be obvious to others, but even if they are praised and admired, this acknowledgement may not be enough to satisfy your pride and self-image. When transit Saturn conjoins your natal Sun, it can be especially difficult if you have devoted most of your efforts to a family or a marriage or business partner and given very little time to yourself as an individual. You become resentful and antagonistic toward those you believe are restricting your individuality and growth. The imposition of authority, rules, regulations, or other restrictions is not welcome just now. You may be given greater responsibilities—a situation that imposes further curtailment of freedom. However, in exchange for your acceptance of responsibilities at this time, you will gain higher status or a position of authority.

Transit Saturn Conjoin Natal Moon

ħ ☌ ☽ There is no doubt of the sobering effect this period can have on your emotions. You feel deprived—even if you cannot identify exactly what the deprivation is. When transit Saturn conjoins your natal Moon, emotional situations are apt to be more of a burden than a source of pleasure and satisfaction. You may feel old, tired, and undesirable no matter what is reflected in your mirror. Excessive worry and depression are likely, and current circumstances may or may not justify the sorrow and disappointment that you feel. The manner in which you cope with any of these potential situations will be a mark of your maturity and the nature of your character and personality. This is not a period in which to expect to gain money and material possessions. However, if wealth is already within your grasp, it is not apt to be a source of great satisfaction or pleasure because what you consciously or subconsciously suffer from right now is emotional deprivation. The attainment of desires is not totally out of the question, but only likely to occur if you truly deserve it. Even then, the cost of the prize you carry off is apt to be dear. Your mother or other female figures in your life, as well as children, may experience difficulty and your responsibilities regarding them may increase. Your domestic environment may be strained, restrictive, or devoid of emotional content. You may want to or be forced by circumstances to change your residence. Vulnerability to illness caused by emotional turmoil increases, and to some extent, such illness, if it occurs, may involve the breasts or digestive system.

Transit Saturn Conjoin Natal Mercury

ℏ☌☿ Your attitude toward such things as learning and the development and use of intellectual, communicative, or mechanical skills is apt to become more serious when transit Saturn conjoins your natal Mercury. If you are in the process of being educated or trained at this time, it may become necessary to switch instructors or schools. Current circumstances require the broadening of skills and knowledge. There may be increased responsibilities with regard to using your basic skills. This may be a good thing since the result may be to provide work or additional income, either now or in the future. This period also targets siblings, neighbors, and those you see on a daily basis. Relations with these people may become strained or restricted, and you may have to assume additional responsibilities for or because of them. Travel may be restricted or delayed by strikes and other problems, or lack of money may keep you at home. Daily transportation is threatened when your car or another vehicle requires repairs or must be replaced. You may be given less time to complete your tasks but also be expected to use greater care and organization in carrying them out.

Transit Saturn Conjoin Natal Venus

ℏ☌♀ Humor and lightheartedness are missing from many encounters and even the most casual interactions tend to become fraught with seriousness, intended or not. Female relationships, partnerships and other alliances, and joint ventures are especially vulnerable to this pattern. Diplomatic as well as social gestures are likely to be uninspiring and self-serving. Enjoyment, if it is found at all, is curtailed by attendant responsibilities. All this negativity paints a gloomy picture but much can also be said for the potentially positive circumstances. More structure and seriousness imposed on relationships can mean greater stability and commitment. While there may be little or no room for flirtation and whimsy in romantic or partnership proposals, there is also no doubt about their seriousness. A tendency to be more formal in your manner and perhaps even in your dress would not be unusual. When transit Saturn conjoins your natal Venus, socializing can become tedious, and if you are not one to take on a busy social life in the first place, circumstances during this period can turn you away from caring about it altogether. There is a greater attraction between you and those who are older or more mature. Artistic endeavors become more focused and organized, though originality and imagination can suffer from the tendency to stick to tradition or whatever methods or subjects you know best. This is an unfavorable time for beauty treatments, cosmetic surgery, or decorating projects.

TRANSIT SATURN CONJOIN NATAL MARS

♄ ☌ ♂ You experience a general lack of physical energy when transit Saturn conjoins your natal Mars. Although you are more vulnerable to physical complaints of one sort or another, there may be no real illness to account for your increased lassitude. Circumventing rules, regulations, or authority and attempting shortcuts at this time are ill-advised. Although you may think you are moving at a snail's pace, what you can actually accomplish may not justify discouragement over what you perceive as a lack of progress. All you need is firm determination to succeed no matter what the pace. Male relationships may be restricted or even broken off at this time. However, if a commitment is made to preserve these associations, then stronger and more lasting bonds can result. The seriousness and frustration that pervades your physical efforts—slowing them down or stopping them altogether—can just as well be turned to some constructive purpose. Direct your efforts toward improving physical strength and fitness. Difficulties may force you to realize that more organization and focus are needed to build a solid foundation for the success you wish to achieve. Physical ailments at this time are likely to involve bones, teeth, or chronic inflammations.

TRANSIT SATURN CONJOIN NATAL JUPITER

♄ ☌ ♃ Your usual sources of information may dry up, the path you were taking toward spiritual development may suddenly lose its appeal, or your economic growth and general prosperity may be restricted. However, there is also the implication that your ideas and attitudes concerning these things will be of a more serious nature, which in itself may be a positive change. When transit Saturn conjoins your natal Jupiter, you must give back some of what you have been given in life. If you have gained wealth, it is time to be philanthropic. If you have gained knowledge and experience, you must now share them with others. Tradition and authority rule against you if you previously indulged in too much individual freedom or divergence from the proper structure and form. Cultural pursuits are more serious, and you can become more realistically or solidly based in many areas. It will be to your ultimate benefit to accept a slower return on your efforts.

TRANSIT SATURN CONJOIN NATAL SATURN

♄ ☌ ♄ You are between twenty-five and thirty years of age when transit Saturn conjoins your natal Saturn and your life has come to a decisive point. You question your goals and the progress you have or have not made. It would not be unusual to start thinking in terms of a certain finality; a sense of lost youth, disappointment at the failure to accomplish or experience certain things, and a feeling that life has nothing exciting to offer. Confronting past failures and disappointments is necessary and equally important is learning what you can from these experiences. Barring any dalliance with depression or discouragement on your part—an unnecessary indulgence which should be avoided at any cost—you will begin to see a more structured and purposeful future. This is likely to lead to a serious attempt to change or terminate current relationships and situations that will not permit the future growth you envision. On the other hand, current circumstances being satisfactory, this is a period to reaffirm your commitment to your present course and long-range goals.

TRANSIT SATURN CONJOIN NATAL URANUS

♄ ☌ ♅ Circumstances conspire to restrict your personal freedom and independence when transit Saturn conjoins your natal Uranus. Attempts to take a new approach or introduce unorthodox methods do not meet with enthusiasm. In fact, they may be rejected altogether by those who insist on tradition or more structure. The key here is not to give up. This is also true if the reverse occurs and it is you who refuse to adopt a new approach. There is a positive potential in current circumstances suggesting that if your ideas or goals are carefully thought out and executed, you may eventually win over the reluctance of others. The initial reluctance or delays you experience may be the very frustration that inspires you to adopt more careful organization and to devise a plan that allows your unorthodox ideas and methods to work within an orthodox system. Efforts to organize groups or redistribute responsibility are slow going—hampered by delays and endless red tape. If you are a regular participant in group activities, you are apt to be given additional responsibilities at this time.

TRANSIT SATURN CONJOIN NATAL NEPTUNE

♄ ☌ ♆ Spiritual tendencies, artistic bents, and flights of imagination are overshadowed by the grim face of reality or disillusionment. When transit Saturn conjoins your natal Neptune, there is misinterpretation of what exactly you are supposed to be responsible for. You may fail to comprehend the reality of a situation and unnecessarily assume the burden of responsibilities that are not yours. This is a period in which to be especially wary of monetary matters. All is not negative, however. Artistic and creative projects can benefit from a strong dose of reality, structure, and organization. Spiritual growth is gained through more traditional understandings. Charitable efforts are put to practical and focused purposes.

TRANSIT SATURN CONJOIN NATAL PLUTO

♄ ☌ ♇ This period involves the use of power and control. When transit Saturn conjoins your natal Pluto, it can be a deeply psychological time. There may be a resurgence of disappointment over the past, or you may struggle to understand and control the current motivations and behavior that developed as a result of the past. You may experience the loss of control in a situation that is simply too large for you to handle readily or efficiently. Given more time and sufficient motivation, you will gain the control you desire. For the time being, however, do not be discouraged if you temporarily lack the resources to be the one in charge.

SATURN SEXTILES

TRANSIT SATURN SEXTILE NATAL SUN

♄ ✶ ☉ You are apt to be given the opportunity to demonstrate integrity, generosity, or your leadership ability when transit Saturn sextiles your natal Sun. In turn, this can lead to personal success and recognition. Whatever other factors attach themselves to the opportunities you are offered by current circumstances, they will also be a source of personal pride and ego fulfillment. Supervisors, authority figures, those who represent the government or similar institutions, and those who are older, more mature, and more experienced can give you advice or assistance that is instrumental in bringing about a chance for you to get ahead.

TRANSIT SATURN SEXTILE NATAL MOON

♄ ✶ ☽ When transit Saturn sextiles your natal Moon, watch for situations that give you a chance to improve your emotional life—opportunities that can lead to fulfilling a desire, becoming healthier or more physically fit, and establishing more stable relationships with family members, especially elderly family members. Benefits are ultimately gained from heeding the wisdom of those who are older and wiser. Patience is definitely a virtue that pays off. If patience is not normally a part of your personality, it would be in your best interest to adopt this approach. A potential opportunity may arise as a direct result of your careful work and patience in the past.

TRANSIT SATURN SEXTILE NATAL MERCURY

♄ ✶ ☿ Circumstances may give you the chance to make profitable use of your knowledge or training and to establish important business or personal contacts. However, such things will not happen by lightning strokes of good luck. This period is positive in that it implies a valuable opportunity, but such happenstance is connected with slow and methodical work, organization, and planning. Those you are more apt to impress and who will ultimately be of help to you are traditional thinkers with a formal, structured approach. When transit Saturn sextiles your natal Mercury, situations favor making business contacts, gathering and organizing information and statistics, and investigating commercial opportunities—all of which may provide the opportunity you need for success.

TRANSIT SATURN SEXTILE NATAL VENUS

♄ ✶ ♀ This is a good time to mix business with pleasure. When transit Saturn sextiles your natal Venus, social contacts can lead to business opportunities, and conversely, business contacts or activities may lead to opportunity for entertainment or socializing. Watch for other situations that lead to partnerships and joint ventures. If you are as attractive as possible and your behavior is polite and charming, you will make an impression on the people you encounter, especially on those with authority and positions of seniority. As a result of their being favorably impressed now, they may eventually provide valuable cooperation and assistance.

TRANSIT SATURN SEXTILE NATAL MARS

♄ ✶ ♂ Your physical efforts and enthusiasm must exhibit thoroughness, organization, strength, and determination during this period. In turn, this can create opportunity or allow you to take advantage of one that comes your way. When transit Saturn sextiles your natal Mars, you should base your actions on past experience and traditional methods. This is not the best time to try unproved theories or take shortcuts. Do not underestimate the value of advice you get from those who are older and wiser, especially men. One of the best things that could happen to you is getting or giving yourself the opportunity to engage in activities now that will have important implications later. A prime example of such an activity is engaging in exercise to improve physical fitness.

TRANSIT SATURN SEXTILE NATAL JUPITER

♄ ✶ ♃ This period offers opportunity that leads to some aspect of your personal growth. It may be a chance to increase your spirituality, expand your intellectual horizons, and gain new experiences through travel and dealing with those of another race or culture. When transit Saturn sextiles your natal Jupiter, the people and situations you encounter may ultimately improve your economic or professional status or lead to the expansion and success of cultural or political pursuits. Your father may also provide a valuable opportunity.

Transit Saturn Sextile Natal Saturn

♄ ✶ ♄   When a sextile occurs between transit Saturn and your natal Saturn, people and situations come along that can help you decide what is working and what is not as far as methods, activities, and attaining long-range goals are concerned. You come into contact with those who share similar goals, who are moving along similar paths, who use similar methods, and who will enlighten you as to what they have learned. The information and experiences they share allow you to move ahead with even more purpose and on more solid ground.

Transit Saturn Sextile Natal Uranus

♄ ✶ ♅   Potential opportunities that you encounter when transit Saturn sextiles your natal Uranus, may lead to friendships or business associations with older, more established people and authority figures. Other circumstances may lead to success in financial activities such as fund-raising or inspire you to establish or become a member of a group or organization. Watch for a situation that either gives you a chance to introduce new ideas or unorthodox methods into a traditional system or that allows you to apply traditional methods to a new or nontraditional system.

Transit Saturn Sextile Natal Neptune

♄ ✶ ♆   Current circumstances present the opportunity to turn fantasy into reality, a chance to use imagination and inspiration in some structured, meaningful way. It is only the opportunity that eventually leads to accomplishment—not the accomplishment itself. When transit Saturn sextiles your natal Neptune, you may either give or receive help regarding spirituality, addictions, and charitable activities.

TRANSIT SATURN SEXTILE NATAL PLUTO

♄ ⚹ ♇ The potential circumstances when transit Saturn sextiles your natal Pluto are likely to pass unnoticed unless you are engaged at this time in some intense mental, emotional, or physical activity. If you are involved in such a struggle, this is a period when you can encounter an opportunity to resolve the situation. You may learn the value of patience and determination. Ultimately it can mean you will gain even greater control, quite possibly through the help and advice of those older and wiser.

SATURN SQUARES

TRANSIT SATURN SQUARE NATAL SUN

♄ □ ☉ This is not a period that is apt to bolster your self-confidence, and you encounter more than a few obstacles in your path if you expect to easily gain anything in the nature of ego-satisfying success. Red tape, rules and regulations, delays, and authority figures who insist on being given their due are some of the likely frustrations that test your determination and distract you from the business at hand. When transit Saturn squares your natal Sun, an annoying situation becomes worse if you give in to time-wasting impatience or discouragement when something or someone challenges you or threatens the success of your goals. Avoid letting arrogance or anger keep you from listening to what may be good advice from those who are older and wiser. If you hold a position of leadership, it would not be prudent to use it to defy tradition and authority. The key to handling current circumstances is to pay attention to what is necessary and proper and continue on a steady course.

TRANSIT SATURN SQUARE NATAL MOON

♄ □ ☽ The things you choose to do or the times you choose to do them are almost sure to present endless difficulties when transit Saturn squares your natal Moon. Systems and schedules do not function as well as they should or as you had planned. You may not feel well. Household tasks are endless and boring. Family and other close relationships become strained by unnecessary nagging and nitpicking. Older machinery and appliances break down, possibly because you failed to give them routine maintenance or should have replaced them long ago. There is a certain vitality missing in your environment, at least on an emotional level. One day you are up, the next day you are down. One day others are enthusiastic and interested and the next day they are nowhere to be found. People seem to lack a sense of humor these days—including you. Fear can become the shaper of your opinions. Unless strong positive factors override the potential frustrations, it is not the best time to buy or sell a home, to plant a garden or undertake big domestic tasks, and to deal with women or children. If you have children, they are more vulnerable to illness and may become more fearful or frustrated than usual. Creative projects are endlessly delayed. There is a positive side to current circumstances. Most of what goes wrong, or at least does not go well, is likely to be only a temporary malfunctioning of one sort or another. Refuse to admit defeat. Resist depression and discouragement. Your efforts will be rewarded.

TRANSIT SATURN SQUARE NATAL MERCURY

♄ □ ☿ Getting from one place to another is not going to be very easy. Lack of a car or other transportation limits your mobility when transit Saturn squares your natal Mercury. If you are currently involved with computers, communications, writing assignments, mechanical and design projects, education, and training, these activities are likely to be plagued by delays or frustrations of one sort or another. Correspondence does not arrive on time or seems to contain only bad news or a negative slant. The material or assignments you are given may be more difficult than usual or other circumstances make it hard for you to give sufficient time and attention to the tasks at hand. Similar frustrations may accompany business or commercial enterprises, community activities, meetings or seminars, and projects or contacts with siblings and neighbors. Your normal pace may be slowed by respiratory ailments, hearing or speech difficulties, arthritis, and other complaints that you may experience yourself or have to cope with in others. The positive potential is that you can actually accomplish what you set out to do. If travel is delayed and other obstacles interfere with your plans, work your schedule around the changes or inconveniences. All you need are patience and the determination to overcome whatever challenges turn up.

TRANSIT SATURN SQUARE NATAL VENUS

♄ □ ♀ Your mood or current circumstances are not conducive to relaxation and being entertained or entertaining. Romance is difficult and social activities are likely to be viewed as obligatory rather than enjoyable experiences. You may be tempted to throw aside morality and polite behavior as a result of frustrating situations in which you are denied or rejected. When transit Saturn squares your natal Venus, the pursuit of pleasure is stymied by lack of motivation, experience, and opportunity. But then, this is precisely what may lead you to try harder to provide a little excitement for yourself. Such efforts may not go unrewarded since the more determination you have, the more likely you are to succeed. What may be meant as harmless flirtations may be interpreted as serious intentions. Since you have as much potential to be the initiator of flattery as you have for being its victim, it is well to keep from becoming either one. Marriage, a business partnership, joint ventures, and female relationships can become strained. However, if you approach others with a cooperative attitude and conciliatory gestures, much can be accomplished—mutual commitments are strengthened, common goals are clarified, dissatisfaction (real or imagined) is put to rest, and relationships are put on a more solid footing.

TRANSIT SATURN SQUARE NATAL MARS

♄ □ ♂ Physical actions are apt to be thwarted by a maddening series of delays and other frustrations. Impatience may tempt you to circumvent authority, rules and regulations. When transit Saturn squares your natal Mars, you may experience a lack of energy and time, which, in turn, can make shortcuts very appealing—shortcuts that are not likely to work. The methods you use or the goals you try to accomplish conflict with the established system and traditional ideas, and valuable time and energy are lost in arguments about who is right and who is wrong. Older people may require your physical assistance. Anger and resentment can make things very unpleasant unless you make an effort to rechannel the negative energy. Authority figures will not appreciate aggressiveness on your part and you become very resentful of them. Avoid overwork, stress, and strain, especially since you are more vulnerable these days to flu, fever, and accidental injury, especially to the head, bones, or teeth. This period is not, however, one that should be viewed as totally defeating. The obstacles it implies also represent the seeds of possible success if you are determined to rise to the challenge. Giving in to anger or discouragement is your worst enemy. Dogged patience and a serious, careful approach will help you eventually accomplish your goals.

TRANSIT SATURN SQUARE NATAL JUPITER

♄ □ ♃ The path to personal and economic growth, intellectual accomplishment or recognition, political success, and spiritual fulfillment is likely to be hampered by one frustration or another during this period. Endless rules and regulations, imposing authority figures, or just plain hard work that seems endless as well as useless may be the inhibitory factors that block your progress. When transit Saturn squares your natal Jupiter, some of the potential frustration may be connected to your father or his influence. You may be required to give back some of the success and prosperity you have been given, and even if you are more than willing to do this, you do not have the means to do it just now. In spite of the negative potentials, there is also an implication that frustrating circumstances may be only a temporary test of your strength and determination—a test you have the ability to pass.

TRANSIT SATURN SQUARE NATAL SATURN

♄ □ ♄ There is little flexibility in current circumstances. The key is to find the little that is there. When transit Saturn squares your natal Saturn, the people and situations you encounter are too much alike, imposing too many of the same restrictions, fears, and formalities to allow for new growth or overwhelming success. The positive side is that these situations are only temporary and should not be allowed to interfere drastically with your plans and goals.

TRANSIT SATURN SQUARE NATAL URANUS

♄ □ ♅ Dealing with older people can become frustrating during this period. You will be in trouble if you are too liberal, and yet stymied by taking a too conservative approach. When transit Saturn squares your natal Uranus, authority, experience, and tradition clash with the present and the plans that are being proposed for the future. Whether it is you who is stuck in the past or the one who seeks a new order and new ideas is hard to tell. Perhaps you are the luckless individual who must cope with others who fit these descriptions. The inability to organize a coalition in favor of settling differences or working for solutions can be overcome if a serious effort is made. There is a generational battle going on: stand back and let situations reach a level that seems comfortable for everyone.

TRANSIT SATURN SQUARE NATAL NEPTUNE

♄ □ ♆ Be wary of false hopes or false promises when transit Saturn squares your natal Neptune. If you are not one to be easily taken in, you may not be particularly affected, but it is wise to be mindful that some deception or disillusionment in your general circumstances is possible during this period. Imposing reality and structure on ideas and situations that are incompatible or severely discouraged by such limitations will not work out to anyone's advantage or satisfaction. Take heart that obstacles you encounter are likely to be temporary.

TRANSIT SATURN SQUARE NATAL PLUTO

♄ □ ♇ Too much intensity or contrivance to manipulate can hamper situations these days. When transit Saturn squares your natal Pluto, the potential is subtle and may pass unnoticed unless power or control is a primary factor in whatever you happen to be doing. Psychological factors may block attempts to clearly analyze matters at hand. Getting around the frustrations is possible by immediately slowing down and allowing yourself more time to gain through shrewd observation which cannot be accomplished by open confrontation.

SATURN TRINES

TRANSIT SATURN TRINE NATAL SUN

♄ △ ☉ This is a period of positive energy. Anything of a favorable nature that occurs now is likely to be solid and long-lasting. The fortunate potentials must be viewed from two vantage points: the past and the present. When transit Saturn trines your natal Sun, the hard work, planning, and organization that have marked your efforts in the past may now bring the rewards you deserve. Others bestow praise and admiration for the loyalty, honesty, generosity, and integrity you have demonstrated. You can correct mistakes that led to past failures and use what you learned from these experiences to begin another enterprise. This period has to do with the success of your ego drive and the satisfaction of indelibly stamping your individuality on situations as well as relationships. While emotional demands may have a part to play, it is more a case of pride in yourself and gaining recognition for your accomplishments. If you have long sought a position of leadership, this is a time when you are apt to attain it.

TRANSIT SATURN TRINE NATAL MOON

♄ △ ☽ The potential circumstances are fortunate when transit Saturn trines your natal Moon. Although it does not rule out the possibility of an astounding piece of good luck, the odds favor a quieter, but extremely beneficial time. Emotional levels can be high and stimulating, but they are more likely to be unusually content and reflective. This is a period to use the maturity and experience you have developed to decide present actions and plan for the future. Decisions made and actions taken these days will no doubt be successful, but it is also a good time to develop patience and understanding in emotional commitments. Fortunate consequences are likely to accompany activities related to nutrition, home, domestic items, real estate, women, babies and young children, creative projects, and historical preservation. To take maximum advantage of this positive period, fulfill your long-term needs and forego instant gratification. For the most part, the functioning of everyday affairs is smooth and efficient. Supervisors, authority figures, and those more mature and experienced may be the means of your good fortune through their assistance or advice.

TRANSIT SATURN TRINE NATAL MERCURY

♄ △ ☿ Activities concerned with communication, education, writing, mechanical skills, design, commerce, computers, and travel are favored when transit Saturn trines your natal Mercury. It can mean success in some new venture in these areas and that you can put past efforts and experience to some profitable use. Networks you have established may turn out to be highly valuable in providing information or assistance. Most contacts at this time tend to be favorable with a minimum of false promise in what is said, and honest efforts in what is done. Your ideas and thinking are more organized and practical. Plans and methods tend to be well thought out, which in itself is the reason for their success. Applying traditional ideas and methods is your most successful approach. If you champion something more nontraditional that you feel has real merit, it may be successfully integrated into the scheme of things.

TRANSIT SATURN TRINE NATAL VENUS

♄ △ ♀ Those who are older find you appealing and attractive these days. Entertain them. Socialize with them. Everyone will benefit in the nicest possible way. Romance, partnerships, female relationships, and joint ventures are highly favored. Long-established alliances will benefit. If marriage, romance, a business partnership, social contact, or friendship is initiated when transit Saturn trines your natal Venus, it has an excellent chance for longevity and fruitful consequences. Beauty treatments, decorating, design, and art projects are likely to have long-lasting and successful results. Social and diplomatic gestures are sincere as well as substantial. This is an excellent period to mix business and pleasure.

TRANSIT SATURN TRINE NATAL MARS

♄ △ ♂ Physical actions are favored with success. Efforts most likely to succeed are of two kinds: those that represent the culmination of hard work and experience and those that occur now and are undertaken in a careful, methodical way with an eye toward eventual success. When transit Saturn trines your natal Mars, male relationships are stable and well favored. Dental work (including oral surgery) or removal of cataracts is successful if undertaken at this time. This is a period of smooth functioning for mechanical and physical systems. A car and any other mechanical equipment you buy at this time will give you many years of solid service. Tradition and authority are given proper attention and respect and, as a result, substantial benefits are gained.

TRANSIT SATURN TRINE NATAL JUPITER

♄ △ ♃ There is a fortunate application of tradition, maturity, and past experience in your current circumstances that contributes to your personal growth and prosperity. If you lack the necessary tradition, experience, or maturity to contribute to your own progress when a trine occurs between transit Saturn and your natal Jupiter, it is possible to be helped by those who do possess such traits. This is not an automatic kind of luck. Lest such a beneficial atmosphere slip away unnoticed, you have to consciously attempt to take advantage of it.

TRANSIT SATURN TRINE NATAL SATURN

♄ △ ♄ Although this is a generally fortunate period, you are not certain to benefit from favorable circumstances or lucky breaks. However, when transit Saturn trines your natal Saturn, you can expect to gain some satisfaction from finding that your past reliance on work, tradition, and organization now puts you in touch with like-minded people and situations. Thus a certain stability is formed and your life-style is more comfortable.

TRANSIT SATURN TRINE NATAL URANUS

♄ △ ♅ Business and finance benefit from current circumstances. Although the fortunate potential may or may not extend to your personal finances, it may favor the financial fortunes of groups and organizations to which you belong when transit Saturn trines your natal Uranus. As an individual, you may be the beneficiary of lower interest rates or some other monetary break caused by thriving economic conditions that exist at this time.

TRANSIT SATURN TRINE NATAL NEPTUNE

♄ △ ♆ Aesthetic sensitivities that have been developed in the past may be put to some profitable use in current circumstances. Other situations you encounter when transit Saturn trines your natal Neptune may contribute to your spiritual development, especially if these situations represent traditional ideas and institutions. Although you may only indirectly benefit on a personal level, other fortunate potentials for this period suggest that success will favor organized charities; repayment, collection, or settlement of financial debts; maritime science or industry; photography; and cinematography.

TRANSIT SATURN TRINE NATAL PLUTO

♄ △ ♇ When transit Saturn trines your natal Pluto, it may mean the satisfaction of overcoming fear and settling old scores. Although you may not be aware of it, your endeavors at this time may eventually put you in a more powerful position. The influences you encounter are subtle and related to the gaining of personal power and deliberately manipulated control. If you are engaged in high-level politics, research and technology, conservation, mining, psychological analysis, or motivational research, this period is highly beneficial.

SATURN OPPOSITIONS

TRANSIT SATURN OPPOSED NATAL SUN

♄ ☍ ☉ If you are willing to put aside your own goals, individuality, and perhaps even your pride, you may not fare too badly when an opposition occurs between transit Saturn and your natal Sun. Failure to live up to your promises or accept responsibilities in the past may come back to haunt you. Expect to encounter discouragement from authority, rules and regulations, endless delays, and other frustrations. Your leadership, integrity, honesty, or generosity are challenged by those who are older or in positions of seniority. Vitality and willpower are either lacking or too ineffective to deal with current circumstances. Success or other rewards that do happen to come along will not be enough to satisfy you. If you break the rules or do whatever it takes to gain something at any cost, it can mean the loss of something more valuable. Over-work and stress may pose a serious health problem.

TRANSIT SATURN OPPOSED NATAL MOON

♄ ☍ ☽ There is an unfortunate negativity in the circumstances during this period. Perhaps the best way to describe it is an atmosphere devoid of nurture—lack of physical nourishment, lack of sentiments, and lack of optimism. Emotional deprivation and loss that occur may be linked to the past. As a result of abandonment, neglect, or abuse, close relationships are seriously threatened or even severed. The most likely targets of the ill-disposed atmo-sphere surrounding you are family relationships, your domestic environment, and creative projects. There may, for example, be separation or estrangement from your mother or a mother figure as well as illness or difficulties regarding children. Home is not the happiest place to be when transit Saturn opposes your natal Moon. Family responsibilities and burdens may be overwhelming. It is use-less to expect appreciation for your past or present efforts. Your general health may also suffer, especially if you have been heedless of physical fitness. Physical complaints include digestive ailments and chronic conditions that flare up or new ones that appear. Desires are thwarted. Whatever is gained will only come at an extremely high price, a price you may come to regret paying. Even if this period finds you in the best of circumstances on other levels, you are still going to be vulnerable to feelings of loneliness or depression. Is there a positive side to this? Your attitude and maturity will determine how well you handle your cir-cumstances at this time.

TRANSIT SATURN OPPOSED NATAL MERCURY

♄ ☍ ☿ Current circumstances suggest serious frustrations involved with education, communication, and travel or transportation. Your cir-culation—that is, your ability to move freely within your immediate environ-ment—is likely to be hampered when transit Saturn opposes your natal Mercury. Contacts and activities with siblings and neighbors are restricted or troublesome. Mechanical, design, and computer projects or the development of your skills in these areas may falter. Any type of mechanical or other equipment that you use on a daily basis is apt to need repair or replacement at this time, especially if it is old or has not been properly maintained. The pace of business transactions, especially sales, is slow. Your ideas, thoughts, and manner of self-expression will tend to be on the sober side. Even if you do manage to inject humor or lightheartedness into the proceedings, it will be difficult to sustain. If you lacked organization, careful planning, and attention to details in the past, it is likely to catch up with you now. Bad timing, especially tardiness, can become a problem. What to do about this negative potential? Avoid anger and resentment since they are useless and will only make things worse. Approach everything with patience, and do not force issues or openly confront difficult situations that may be more easily resolved at another time.

Transit Saturn Opposed Natal Venus

♄ ☍ ♀ This can be an extremely difficult period for marriage, partnerships, female relationships, and joint ventures—and perhaps the very worst period in which to establish new associations of this type. You or those you must deal with when transit Saturn opposes your natal Venus are not likely to be in the mood for compromise since the chance of that has, in all likelihood, long since passed. For one reason or another, you are not likely to look your most attractive or be on your best behavior. Everyone seems to have lost their sense of humor. What should be enjoyable experiences fail to measure up to expectations. The pursuit of beauty, luxury, cooperation, and harmony is likely to either fail outright or be gained at such a cost as not to be worth your efforts. Romance is burdened by anger, resentment, lack of enthusiasm and opportunity, or a combination of these things. Social activities lose their appeal or may be lacking altogether. By choice or circumstances, you may work or spend time alone: a not altogether unpleasant prospect since you may get more accomplished. The most positive way to approach potentially negative situations is to turn your attention as much as possible to other things.

Transit Saturn Opposed Natal Mars

♄ ☍ ♂ A serious lack of energy slows you down. Circumstances may be such that they promote lack of motivation to accomplish anything, or physical illness may be responsible for keeping you out of action. It may not even be you but those you rely upon who lack enthusiasm or become ill. This is a likely time for cars and other vehicles as well as other machinery to require repair or replacement. Whatever the case may be, work and other physical efforts are hampered at every turn when transit Saturn opposes your natal Mars. Life these days may be described as one enormous gridlock. Resentment, anger, resistance to authority, circumvention of rules and regulations, or attempts to avoid red tape are all a waste of time and whatever energy is available. If you become upset, it is important to find a healthy way to release your feelings through physical exercise because there is potential for anger to build to a point that it erupts in a violent way. It can be a difficult time for male relationships and dealing with men in general. The pace of business is apt to be slower. Irresponsibility now or in the past is apt to make matters worse. Avoid competitive sports and any risk-taking physical activity—you are not favored to win, and, what is worse, you may be injured in the process. Overwork and stress may result in headaches, heart problems, inflammations, and injuries to bones or teeth. Take an extra measure of precaution around fire or when handling volatile materials. Should you happen to be in favorable circumstances when this period comes along, you may fare better than the negative potential would suggest. It would be foolish however, to go out of your way to take on additional responsibilities and burdens at this time.

TRANSIT SATURN OPPOSED NATAL JUPITER

♄ ☍ ♃ Bad timing, past failures, authority figures, or a lack of generosity somewhere along the line frustrate your personal growth, economic prosperity, spiritual fulfillment, and intellectual endeavors when transit Saturn opposes your natal Jupiter. You may be expected to give back some of the prosperity or success you have attained to help others get ahead, but you do not have the means to do it. Your father or an authority figure is not favored, and some of the problems that turn up may be due to an inability to resolve conflicts you have with or because of him. You may be separated from or have to take responsibility for your father. If most situations seem to flow smoothly in spite of this potentially negative period, it is not a good idea to take your favorable status quo for granted or further defy the odds by going out of your way to invite situations that could threaten you in the areas described above.

TRANSIT SATURN OPPOSED NATAL SATURN

♄ ☍ ♄ If there are things to regret about the past, this is a period when you are most likely to regret them. The potentially negative circumstances you may encounter when transit Saturn opposes your natal Saturn can and should be viewed as lessons to be learned in life: lessons related to what failed in the past and what is obviously not working in the present. There is little or no room for real freedom or actual progress except by analyzing your lessons and planning what positive and constructive actions may be profitably accomplished once this period is over.

TRANSIT SATURN OPPOSED NATAL URANUS

♄ ☍ ♅ Current circumstances suggest an unfavorable atmosphere. The target of its negative potential is your generation rather than you as an individual. It may, for instance, mean the passage of legislation that imposes restrictions or additional responsibilities on those of your generation. It may mean the collapse of institutional structures that might otherwise have benefited your age group. Other potentials when transit Saturn opposes your natal Uranus include restrictions related to the groups and organizations to which you belong.

TRANSIT SATURN OPPOSED NATAL NEPTUNE

♄ ☍ ♆ This is not a period designed to facilitate or tolerate secret activities of any kind. It is highly unfavorable for spiritual activities, financial speculation, and learning the truth. Unnecessary fears or hidden agendas can confuse and even paralyze the circumstances when transit Saturn opposes your natal Neptune. Disappointment or loss leads to a morass of guilt and desperation.

TRANSIT SATURN OPPOSED NATAL PLUTO

♄ ☍ ♇ When transit Saturn opposes your natal Pluto, you may witness struggles in which neither side emerges victorious. Authority challenges power, the past opposes the present and future. Somewhere along the line you may find yourself embattled. The probability is that, although you are not directly involved, your control in some smaller sphere of influence is threatened as a result of the struggle between larger forces. The potential of this period may not occur or may pass relatively unnoticed, but it is not to be discounted altogether. Despite whatever else may be humming smoothly along, remember that this is an unfavorable time to attempt to manipulate circumstances to your personal advantage, collect debts, exact satisfaction or revenge, and directly challenge the position of tradition or authority.

Chapter Eight

Transit Uranus Aspects to the Natal Planets

Before you read the transits of the outer planets, please note that the currently available ephemeris for the 21st century does not go past the year 2050. This fact is reflected in the tables for Uranus, Neptune, and Pluto. The cycle of Uranus is eighty-four years, so you will be that old when it returns to its natal position in your chart. As transit Uranus moves through the natal houses and makes aspects to your natal planets, it signals unexpected changes and issues of personal independence. Because of its long cycle, the aspects that transit Uranus makes are part of the long-term circumstances for over a year.

URANUS CONJUNCTIONS

TRANSIT URANUS CONJOIN NATAL SUN

⛢ ☌ ☉ Whoever or whatever has been a source of ego fulfillment and encouragement no longer plays this role. The separation may be unexpected and leave you to fend for yourself, or you may rebel and go off in a completely different direction to find a new identity. You are restless and will not tolerate rejection or restriction. Since it is not a search for emotional satisfaction, it may not have a devastating effect on personal relationships—but this is not a certainty. You find it hard to be with those who offer no stimulation. When transit Uranus conjoins your natal Sun, nothing is a certainty. That which is unusual or different from what you have known becomes increasingly appealing. This is an ego awakening period to develop your skills and talents and find new ways to express them.

TRANSIT URANUS CONJOIN NATAL MOON

♅ ☌ ☽ You may be heading for a very different life-style these days as home and family situations and relationships with females and children change. New emotional commitments are established or current ones suddenly terminated. You may suddenly acquire a home or abruptly decide to get rid of one. This can be a chaotic period, especially if you suffer from nervousness, insomnia, and rash behavior. When transit Uranus conjoins your natal Moon, knowing what or who will make you happy is difficult and unpredictable, but independence on an emotional level plays a significant role. Possessiveness in relationships, no matter on whose part, will not be tolerated. Although the kind of emotional environment you inhabit during this period is impossible to predict, you can become more original and unique in creative and artistic efforts.

TRANSIT URANUS CONJOIN NATAL MERCURY

♅ ☌ ☿ Current ideas, methods, and travel are disrupted, causing you to venture into new and unusual places. You seek freedom to develop and express your thoughts and opinions. Since your mind is more open to nontraditional views, you may come up with original ideas. It is hard to say exactly what direction your mind or your activities will take or what subject may interest you, but learning new technology, developing mechanical or design skills, and studying astrology or psychology are some of the potentials. When transit Uranus conjoins your natal Mercury, your senses are keener but your nerves are more easily frazzled. The character of your neighborhood may change during this period, as might your contacts with neighbors and siblings. Restlessness may cause you to keep on the move from one project or activity to another. When traveling, expect the unexpected.

Transit Uranus Conjoin Natal Venus

♅ ☌ ♀ This period can signal the end of a romance, partnership, female relationship, or joint venture, but it can also mark the establishment of a new one. The significance is on the unpredictable change in the status of these matters, not on the particular direction they take. Freedom in partnership is needed, but there is no indication of whether it will be you, your partner, or both of you who require more independence. When transit Uranus conjoins your natal Venus, unusual or unexpected alliances may be established, and your interactions with people in general are more unpredictable or unusual. The style of your clothes and other aspects of your physical appearance during this period may reflect to a greater degree your individuality and independence. Your social activities and attitudes can also take new directions, some of them becoming rather unorthodox. Your activities and preferences in art and music may also take new directions.

Transit Uranus Conjoin Natal Mars

♅ ☌ ♂ New directions you take these days inspire your physical efforts and activities, perhaps even an entirely different line of work. Current activities can come to a halt and new endeavors can unexpectedly begin when transit Uranus conjoins your natal Mars. You seek greater autonomy on the job or in carrying out responsibilities, and you are apt to become restless with routine and repetitive procedures. Your present circumstances imply a potential separation from males or a change in the status of male relationships. Physical actions are highly charged and unpredictable, and the result of such actions may be totally different than what was intended or anticipated. For this reason, there is a potential for accidents, missteps, or finding yourself in other regrettable situations. This is a period when more than the usual caution must be taken while operating machinery and handling sharp instruments or explosive materials and when confronting adversaries.

TRANSIT URANUS CONJOIN NATAL JUPITER

♅ ☌ ♃ Your intellectual horizons and the situations you experience are considerably broadened, if not altered completely, as circumstances cause you to head down entirely new and unexpected paths. When transit Uranus conjoins your natal Jupiter, there is increased emphasis on independent education, which can occur by studying on your own, traveling to new places, seeking new experiences, or taking up some unusual type of training. This is an unstable period for your father and matters related to him. Freedom and independence, especially in the choice of a life-style and religious and political affiliations, can become strong issues. You are not likely to be able to control or manipulate the situations you encounter or the people you meet. You can, however, control your reactions to their influence, and, in the process, achieve a significant measure of personal, economic, and intellectual growth.

TRANSIT URANUS CONJOIN NATAL SATURN

♅ ☌ ♄ This period is liable to bring circumstances that challenge or change areas of your life that are governed by tradition, rules, regulations, and restrictions. However necessary such structures might otherwise be in your scheme of things, when transit Uranus conjoins your natal Saturn, you may be required to reevaluate and perhaps alter them considerably. The area of your present responsibilities may undergo a significant change. For example, you may seek or be introduced to new and unorthodox ideas and methods for handling responsibilities—methods that can successfully work within a system without destroying its basic structure.

TRANSIT URANUS CONJOIN NATAL URANUS

♅ ☌ ♅ Since you will be more than eighty years old when transit Uranus conjoins your natal Uranus, you can and should have the freedom to pursue anything you wish. By this time you have learned much about life's traditional patterns and coped with its many responsibilities. Now you can leave these things to others to carry on and free yourself to take the road less traveled, explore the unorthodox, and enjoy higher planes of thought and existence.

TRANSIT URANUS CONJOIN NATAL NEPTUNE

♅ ☌ ♆ There is an increased need to fulfill ideals and spiritual inspirations when transit Uranus conjoins your natal Neptune—though exactly how this will be accomplished or exactly what you are after is likely to be unclear. Uranus upsets the status quo and you are a creature of circumstances over which you have no control. The freedom to express religious, political, or other ideals disappears. In the long run, it is others who make decisions or take actions and you who will react. For example, those born with natal Neptune in Taurus and Gemini experienced transit Uranus conjunct natal Neptune between 1934 and 1949, when they were in their late forties and early sixties. The demented ideals espoused in Germany that resulted in World War II made a tragic mockery of personal freedom and equality. People born from 1928 to 1943 were between twenty-six and thirty-three years of age when transit Uranus conjoined their natal Neptune in Virgo from 1961 to 1969. The image of hard-working, patriotic citizens was challenged in the '60's by the pacifist "flower children," the emerging drug culture, and civil rights activists. Study this table in light of this aspect's interpretation for insights into societal conditions that your generation experienced

Transit ♅	conjoins in years	Natal ♆	of those born in:	at age:
♅ ♏	1890–1897	♆ ♏	1792–1807	90–98
♅ ♐	1897–1904	♆ ♐	1806–1820	84–91
♅ ♑	1904–1912	♆ ♑	1820–1834	78–84
♅ ♒	1912–1920	♆ ♒	1834–1848	72–78
♅ ♓	1919–1928	♆ ♓	1848–1862	66–71
♅ ♈	1927–1935	♆ ♈	1861–1875	60–66
♅ ♉	1934–1942	♆ ♉	1874–1889	53–60
♅ ♊	1941–1949	♆ ♊	1887–1902	47–54
♅ ♋	1948–1956	♆ ♋	1901–1915	41–47
♅ ♌	1955–1962	♆ ♌	1914–1928	34–41
♅ ♍	1961–1969	♆ ♍	1928–1943	26–33
♅ ♎	1968–1975	♆ ♎	1942–1957	18–26
♅ ♏	1974–1981	♆ ♏	1955–1970	11–19

Table 17: Transit Uranus Conjunctions to Natal Neptune

when transit Uranus conjoined natal Neptune. Table 17 covers the transits of Uranus conjoined the natal Neptune of those born with Neptune in Scorpio (1792–1807) to when it conjoined the next generation born with Neptune in Scorpio (1955–1970).

TRANSIT URANUS CONJOIN NATAL PLUTO

♅ ☌ ♇ The actions or sentiments you encounter when transit Uranus conjoins your natal Pluto are best understood as part of general social conditions. They can, however, affect you on a personal level, bringing an abrupt change in a familiar way of life. Situations that are forced upon you can make it necessary for serious psychological adjustments to new people and patterns, and, as a consequence, these situations disturb or create hidden fears that you may not be prepared to confront. The areas you could control or manipulate in the past are lost in the transitions that take place. An excellent example of this aspect is the birth of the atomic age. Nothing in the history of the world has put ultimate physical power on such a different footing than gaining access to atomic energy. The generations born with Pluto in Taurus (1851–1884), Gemini (1882–1914), and Cancer (1912–1939) experienced Uranus conjunct natal Pluto between 1934 and 1956 (see Table 18). From these generations came the chemists and physicists responsible for the horror of the atomic bomb as well as the peaceful use of atomic energy.

Transit ♅	conjoins in years	Natal ♇	of those born in	at age
♅ ♈	1927–1935	♇ ♈	1822–1853	82–105
♅ ♉	1934–1942	♇ ♉	1851–1884	58–83
♅ ♊	1941–1949	♇ ♊	1882–1914	35–59
♅ ♋	1948–1956	♇ ♋	1912–1939	17–36
♅ ♌	1955–1962	♇ ♌	1937–1958	04–18
♅ ♌	2039–2046	♇ ♌	1937–1958	88–102
♅ ♍	1961–1969	♇ ♍	1956–1972	00–05
♅ ♍	2045–	♇ ♍	1956–1972	–89

Table 18: Transit Uranus Conjunctions to Natal Pluto

URANUS SEXTILES

TRANSIT URANUS SEXTILE NATAL SUN

⛢ ⚹ ☉   When a sextile occurs between transit Uranus and your natal Sun, the potential will not necessarily be obvious, but it can bring an opportunity that leads to gaining recognition or a position of leadership. When this period comes along, you encounter situations in which you find out how dynamic and vital you can be or that give you a chance to change the way your life is headed. Other possibilities include a chance to gain friends and join groups or to attain a more advantageous or prestigious position either through them or in association with them.

TRANSIT URANUS SEXTILE NATAL MOON

⛢ ⚹ ☽   When transit Uranus sextiles your natal Moon, circumstances can lead to achieving emotional satisfaction or fulfilling a desire. Remember, these circumstances bring opportunity that can lead to achievement. You may, for instance, run into an advantageous situation that leads to exciting new relationships, perhaps unusual or nontraditional relationships. Current relationships can attain a unique level you might not have thought possible. Females or children may play a role in opportunities that come along. Situations can lead to your use or understanding of new technology, computer systems, or unorthodox methods that help you accomplish daily tasks. You may get a chance to adopt more freedom and originality in your domestic environment or a whole new and different living arrangement or life-style. Circumstances may offer the chance to try a new diet or nontraditional approach to nutrition.

TRANSIT URANUS SEXTILE NATAL MERCURY

⛢ ⚹ ☿   The current situation is not likely to change measurably by the way things are going, unless other influences at this time contribute to such a change. There is positive energy in the form of opportunities to travel and to develop new methods when transit Uranus sextiles your natal Mercury. Because of the particular nature of this aspect, the chance to travel includes unusual places and nontraditional or unorthodox methods. You may gain unusual or unorthodox knowledge and information or acquire it in some unique or different way. Other opportunities to look for during this period include the use or development of new technology and activities related to computers and trade or commerce.

TRANSIT URANUS SEXTILE NATAL VENUS

The potential when transit Uranus sextiles your natal Venus is of a positive nature. It can mean an opportunity to socialize or interact with unusual or unique people. It is a period that may ultimately result in a joint venture, marriage, business partnership or other kind of alliance—but it is apt to be a unique partnership or one with a different or unorthodox partner. The unique or different quality associated with this period can extend to your friends and the groups to which you belong, or it can indicate the activities in which you participate with friends or associations.

TRANSIT URANUS SEXTILE NATAL MARS

When transit Uranus sextiles your natal Mars, you might find an opportunity to make your physical efforts succeed. Given the offbeat nature of the potential circumstances, you may run across a chance to engage in unusual or nontraditional work or activities, or the methods used to accomplish a physical goal may be unusual or nontraditional. This period may bring opportunities that include involvement with technical machinery or equipment, computers, sports, risk-taking ventures, military maneuvers, and commercial enterprises.

TRANSIT URANUS SEXTILE NATAL JUPITER

This period can bring an opportunity that leads to economic expansion, success in sports and cultural or political pursuits, and increased intellectual, spiritual, and other types of personal growth. A chance encounter may result, for example, in successful publishing, sales, advertising, and higher education or advanced training. You may be offered knowledge or training in unusual subjects or there may be something unique or different about where or how you obtain such experience. It will be up to you to recognize and take advantage of situations and people who offer opportunity when transit Uranus sextiles your natal Jupiter.

Transit Uranus Sextile Natal Saturn

⛢ ✶ ♄ A sextile between transit Uranus and your natal Saturn adds positive energy to circumstances that lead to successfully attaining or exercising a position of seniority. This may also be your chance to make use of previous hard work and long-term planning or to develop such habits that will lead to greater success in the future. Other opportunities to look for relate to business or the chance to make nontraditional or unorthodox methods or ideas work within traditional systems.

Transit Uranus Sextile Natal Uranus

⛢ ✶ ⛢ There are three periods in your life when transit Uranus sextiles natal Uranus. The first period occurs at approximately fifteen years of age, the second around age seventy, and the third around age ninety-eight (see Table 19 on page 176). Since the focus of circumstances when transit Uranus sextiles your natal Uranus is so broad, its impact on you as an individual may be minimal. However, the aspect implies an opportunity for beneficial change, a change that is apt to be particularly relevant to the people in your generation.

Transit ♅	sextiles in years	Natal ♅	of those born in:
♅♒ ♅♎ ♅♒	1912–1920 1968–1975 1995–2003	♅♐	1897–1904
♅♓ ♅♏ ♅♓	1919–1928 1974–1981 2003–2011	♅♑	1904–1912
♅♈ ♅♐ ♅♈	1927–1935 1981–1988 2010–2019	♅♒	1912–1920
♅♉ ♅♑ ♅♉	1934–1942 1988–1996 2018–2026	♅♓	1919–1928
♅♊ ♅♒ ♅♊	1941–1949 1995–2003 2025–2033	♅♈	1927–1935
♅♋ ♅♓ ♅♋	1948–1956 2003–2011 2032–2040	♅♉	1934–1942
♅♌ ♅♈ ♅♌	1955–1962 2010–2019 2039–2046	♅♊	1941–1949
♅♍ ♅♉ ♅♍	1961–1969 2018–2026 2045–	♅♋	1948–1956
♅♎ ♅♊	1968–1975 2025–2033	♅♌	1955–1962
♅♏ ♅♋	1974–1981 2032–2040	♅♍	1961–1969
♅♐ ♅♌	1981–1988 2039–2046	♅♎	1968–1975
♅♑ ♅♍	1988–1996 2045–	♅♏	1974–1981
♅♒	1995–2003	♅♐	1981–1988
♅♓	2003–2011	♅♑	1988–1996

Table 19: Transit Uranus Sextiles to Natal Uranus

TRANSIT URANUS SEXTILE NATAL NEPTUNE

⛢ ✶ ♆ When transit Uranus sextiles your natal Neptune, the prevalent ideals, spiritual directions, ideas, and illusions in society are its primary focus. Circumstances are usually of a positive nature, but sometimes fear and paranoia can emerge. You may have little occasion to observe its impact on your personal life, but there is potential for an opportunity that may allow you to play a more active role in civil rights, care for those who are hungry and homeless, or contribute to other charitable goals. Table 20 lists eight generations born between 1887 with natal Neptune in Gemini and 1984 with natal Neptune in Capricorn. Most generations will experience this aspect twice. But generations born close to the period when the sextile occurs between transit Uranus and transit Neptune will experience it three times. The age when this

Transit ⛢	sextiles in years	Natal ♆	of those born in:	at age:
⛢ ♈	1927–1935	♆ ♊	1887–1902	33–40
⛢ ♌	1955–1962			60–68
⛢ ♉	1934–1942	♆ ♋	1901–1915	27–33
⛢ ♍	1961–1969			54–60
⛢ ♊	1941–1949	♆ ♌	1914–1928	21–27
⛢ ♎	1968–1975			47–54
⛢ ♋	1948–1956	♆ ♍	1928–1943	13–20
⛢ ♏	1974–1981			38–46
⛢ ♋	2032–2040			97–104
⛢ ♌	1955–1962	♆ ♎	1942–1957	05–13
⛢ ♐	1981–1988			31–39
⛢ ♌	2039–2046			89–97
⛢ ♍	1961–1969	♆ ♏	1955–1970	00–06
⛢ ♑	1988–1996			26–33
⛢ ♍	2045–			–90
⛢ ♒	1995–2003	♆ ♐	1970–1984	19–25
⛢ ♓	2003–2011	♆ ♑	1984–1998	13–19

Table 20: Transit Uranus Sextiles to Natal Neptune

aspect occurs is different for different generations. Examine the interpretation of this aspect to shed light on some of the circumstances your generation and other generations experienced when transit Uranus sextiled natal Neptune.

TRANSIT URANUS SEXTILE NATAL PLUTO

♅ ✶ ♇ This is a period that signals the potential of circumstances that will change the status of power and control. Although its focus is society as a whole, this time frame may nevertheless bring opportunity for you to participate in or benefit from changes concerning natural resources, environmental issues, political issues, crime, and corruption. Locate Pluto's sign position for your birth in Table 21. Most generations will experience this transit twice. Compare the circumstances you encountered when natal Pluto was sextiled by transit Uranus with the kind of environment with which this aspect is associated

Transit ♅	sextiles in years	Natal ♇	of those born in:	at age:
♅ ♈	1927–1935	♇ ♊	1882–1914	21–45
♅ ♌	1955–1962			48–73
♅ ♉	1934–1942	♇ ♋	1912–1939	03–22
♅ ♍	1961–1969			30–49
♅ ♊	1941–1949	♇ ♌	1937–1958	00–04
♅ ♎	1968–1975			17–31
♅ ♊	2025–2033			75–88
♅ ♏	1974–1981	♇ ♍	1956–1972	09–18
♅ ♋	2032–2040			68–76
♅ ♐	1981–1988	♇ ♎	1971–1984	04–10
♅ ♌	2039–2046			62–68
♅ ♑	1988–1996	♇ ♏	1983–1995	01–05
♅ ♍	2045–			–62
♅ ♒	1995–2003	♇ ♐	1995–2008	00–05

Table 21: Transit Uranus Sextiles to Natal Pluto

Uranus Squares

Transit Uranus Square Natal Sun

⛢ □ ☉ Circumstances may severely test your willpower and determination to succeed. One of your biggest frustrations is not being able to control or manipulate situations. It is the actions and decisions of others that initiate a situation; the only control you have is over your own reactions. To describe the potential when a square occurs between transit Uranus and your natal Sun as a test is appropriate since that is all it may be. Havoc and challenges occur but do not necessarily signal an end to your present course or the futility of further attempts to attain your goals. Since the potential is for situations to be unpredictable and unexpected, it is hard to be prepared. It may be difficult to assert or maintain your leadership or status. You can and should, however, be prepared to stand up for your integrity, principles, and decisions.

Transit Uranus Square Natal Moon

⛢ □ ☽ Regard the status of relationships, emotional commitments, domestic arrangements, and the place where you reside as vulnerable to sudden or unexpected changes during the unstable period when transit Uranus squares your natal Moon. One of the most troublesome problems may be keeping your feelings, urges, and emotional reactions under control. Circumstances are unpredictable and what may be worse, you cannot manipulate them. The actions and decisions of others can intrude on your current emotional commitment to relationships and other endeavors. Relationships are not necessarily terminated and the chance to fulfill your desires is not denied, but there are sure to be disruptions that involve these matters. In the face of changing circumstances, stay flexible in your attitudes and feelings and hold on to what has always been a source of emotional satisfaction. Your health may be adversely affected by increased restlessness, nervousness, irritability, and digestive disorders. During this period, women and children in your life are apt to be unpredictable, you may experience separation from them, or they may be difficult to control.

Transit Uranus Square Natal Mercury

⛢ □ ☿ Circumstances challenge your current methods and ideas and dis-rupt the status or character and activities of your education, writing, sales, communications, and the mode or frequency of travel. Relationships and activities with siblings or contacts with neighbors are disrupted or changed in some way. You may encounter situations that require computer or other mechanical or design skills that you do not possess. Meetings and discussion groups can be frustrating and chaotic because everyone is intent on introducing a different course of action and independent ideas. Unexpected developments frequently plague scheduled events when transit Uranus squares your natal Mercury. Although this period does not bring an end to your present involvement in any of these areas, outside forces over which you have no control are likely to require you to make some adjustment or change. Keeping activities organized and information available and at hand when it is needed is difficult. Malfunctions in computers, electrical systems, and technical equipment are apt to occur. Your work may be slowed by physical fatigue and soreness of your hands or fingers as a result of using them to operate a computer or other technical equipment.

Transit Uranus Square Natal Venus

⛢ □ ♀ Friendships (especially with females), romantic attachments, social contacts, or marriage and other partnerships are subjected to unstable circumstances. Relationships may not necessarily come to an end when transit Uranus squares your natal Venus, but the mutual goals and other conditions that determine these associations are likely to take new directions. Joint ventures and cooperative efforts develop unanticipated problems. Social events, diplomatic maneuvers, or artistic pursuits that you undertake are plagued by obstacles that are caused by the actions or decisions of others. This is not a favorable time for beauty treatments or cosmetic surgery, since the results of such endeavors may not be what you anticipated. Unusual social circumstances may occur, an unorthodox alliance may be offered, and you may be taken by surprise at the unpleasant or unhappy reactions of others to what you say or do.

TRANSIT URANUS SQUARE NATAL MARS

♅□♂ Rash actions can lead to accidents and injury, especially to the head or face, and caution must be taken while operating machinery and when handling explosive materials (as well as people) during the unpredictable period when transit Uranus squares your natal Mars. Associations with men, even on a casual or fleeting basis, may become difficult or troublesome. Close male relationships may be disrupted, though not severed completely. If there is a reason for such relationships to continue, they will, but perhaps under completely different conditions and terms. Your physical progress may be impeded by a crowd, as when you get caught in a traffic jam or need to rush through a busy place. At times, your efforts succeed while at other times they miss the mark. Work habits may be erratic due to circumstances beyond your control. Make your actions slower and more deliberate, not only to prevent accidents but also to make sure you actually accomplish something. Efforts that fail in one way may have unexpected results that succeed in a way you had not planned. Group activities are more stimulating, more unusual, or unanticipated.

TRANSIT URANUS SQUARE NATAL JUPITER

♅□♃ There is an element of rebelliousness in your circumstances. At the center is the issue of your independence. The more obstacles prevent you from exercising your right to think or behave in the manner you choose, the more you seek to assert your freedom when transit Uranus squares your natal Jupiter. The seriousness of the situation depends on many other factors. It may be a case of wanting to leave home and be on your own, or it may involve your refusal to perform an obligatory function such as serving in the military, or it may be dissatisfaction with traditional religious or political views. Your relationship with your father and matters related to him may change. Other status-altering potentials may occur that involve higher education, long-distance travel, professional ambitions, and writing or publishing. Your generosity and optimism may be erratic or misplaced. You may be given increased status or recognition even though you may not deserve it, or, if recognition is deserved, you fail to receive it. The interruptions or changes that occur may turn out to be positive and so this period should not be viewed as preventing success.

TRANSIT URANUS SQUARE NATAL SATURN

♅□♄ When transit Uranus squares your natal Saturn, an event or situation creates a generation gap. There is a threat to the status of seniority or authority. These potentials are not likely to be caused by you so much as they are by the actions or decisions made by other people. There may be conflict between new ideas or methods and the traditions which you as well as others near your age embrace. The thing to understand, however, is that one system does not have to destroy the other. There are workable alternatives if you choose to find them.

TRANSIT URANUS SQUARE NATAL URANUS

♅□♅ A square between transit Uranus and your natal Uranus implies circumstances that are disruptive. The outlook, methods, and lifestyle that are unique to you and your generation clash with the thinking and lifestyle currently in vogue. Obstacles to personal independence seem to get in everyone's way—each generation blaming another one for the problems. The circumstances that occur are not, however, likely to be catastrophic or without solution. The extent to which such disturbances matter to you will depend on other factors. Table 22 lists all the squares that have been and will be made from transit Uranus to the natal Uranus of those born between 1897 and 1981. The two periods in life when transit Uranus squares natal Uranus occur between nineteen and twenty-four years of age and between sixty and sixty-five years of age. Locate your birth year and compare the interpretation for this aspect with the circumstances you experienced when transit Uranus squared your natal Uranus.

Transit ♅	squares in years	Natal ♅	of those born in:
♅ ♓ ♅ ♍	1919–1928 1961–1969	♅ ♐	1897–1904
♅ ♈ ♅ ♎	1927–1935 1968–1975	♅ ♑	1904–1912
♅ ♉ ♅ ♏	1934–1942 1974–1981	♅ ♒	1912–1920
♅ ♊ ♅ ♐	1941–1949 1981–1988	♅ ♓	1919–1928
♅ ♋ ♅ ♑	1948–1956 1988–1996	♅ ♈	1927–1935
♅ ♌ ♅ ♒	1955–1962 1995–2003	♅ ♉	1934–1942
♅ ♍ ♅ ♓	1961–1969 2003–2011	♅ ♊	1941–1949
♅ ♎ ♅ ♈	1968–1975 2010–2019	♅ ♋	1948–1956
♅ ♏ ♅ ♉	1974–1981 2018–2026	♅ ♌	1955–1962
♅ ♐ ♅ ♊	1981–1988 2025–2033	♅ ♍	1961–1969
♅ ♑ ♅ ♋	1988–1996 2032–2040	♅ ♎	1968–1975
♅ ♒ ♅ ♌	1995–2003 2039–2046	♅ ♏	1974–1981

Table 22: Transit Uranus Squares to Natal Uranus

TRANSIT URANUS SQUARE NATAL NEPTUNE

♅ □ ♆ One might say that a rebellion is going on, but drawing clear lines of battle is hampered. Who is the real enemy? What are the terms or conditions sought? In spite of the elusive nature of the situation, some determinations can be made. Ideas and methods regarding religion or spiritual growth, and attitudes and institutions that are concerned with minority groups and civil rights are the main targets of unrest in the societal conditions you experience when transit Uranus squares your natal Neptune (see Table 23). On an intellectual and artistic level, the prevailing circumstances disrupt ideas and representations of reality, romanticism, and idealism. The end result is not apt to be the elimination of one system replaced by another, but a combination that allows both systems to exist, at least for a time. How much

Transit ♅	squares in years	Natal ♆	of those born in:	at age:
♅ ♓	1919–1928	♆ ♊	1887–1902	26–32
♅ ♍	1961–1969			67–74
♅ ♈	1927–1935	♆ ♋	1901–1915	20–26
♅ ♎	1968–1975			60–67
♅ ♉	1934–1942	♆ ♌	1914–1928	14–20
♅ ♏	1974–1981			53–60
♅ ♊	1941–1949	♆ ♍	1928–1943	06–13
♅ ♐	1981–1988			45–53
♅ ♊	2025–2033			90–97
♅ ♋	1948–1956	♆ ♎	1942–1957	00–06
♅ ♑	1988–1996			39–46
♅ ♋	2032–2040			83–90
♅ ♒	1995–2003	♆ ♏	1955–1970	33–40
♅ ♌	2039–2046			76–84
♅ ♓	2003–2011	♆ ♐	1970–1984	27–33
♅ ♍	2045–			–75

Table 23: Transit Uranus Squares to Natal Neptune

impact such situations can be expected to have on your personal life will depend on the degree to which you are involved with the areas that are affected.

TRANSIT URANUS SQUARE NATAL PLUTO

♅ □ ♇ There are two periods when transit Uranus squares your natal Pluto (see Table 24), bringing circumstances that are likely to be more generational than personal—circumstances that represent movements in the outer environment disrupting the status and sources of political, economic, or physical power. How much a shift in political power, control of resources, or military activity will affect your personal life is determined by your life-style and circumstances at the time the aspect occurs. If you were born between 1912 and 1939, transit Uranus in Libra squared your natal Pluto in Cancer between 1968 and 1975. During this period, antiwar protests and civil rights struggles in the United States, Africa, and elsewhere were some of the social problems that may have impacted you. The generation born between 1937 and 1958 experienced transit Uranus in Scorpio square natal Pluto in Leo between 1974 and 1981, a period that witnessed great shifts in political control with the deaths of China's Mao Zedong and Premier Zhou en Lai, the downfall and subsequent death of the Shah of Iran, and the disgrace and resignation of U.S. President Nixon. Both generations were affected during the overlapping years between 1973 and 1975,

Transit ♅	squares in years	Natal ♇	of those born in:	at age:
♅ ♓	1919–1928	♇ ♊	1882–1914	14–37
♅ ♍	1961–1969			55–79
♅ ♎	1968–1975	♇ ♋	1912–1939	36–56
♅ ♈	2010–2019			80–98
♅ ♏	1974–1981	♇ ♌	1937–1958	23–37
♅ ♉	2018–2026			68–81
♅ ♐	1981–1988	♇ ♍	1956–1972	16–25
♅ ♊	2025–2033			61–69

Table 24: Transit Uranus Squares to Natal Pluto

when transit Uranus was retrograde in late degrees of Libra and early degrees of Scorpio. At this juncture, the first generation with Pluto in Cancer was between the ages of thirty-six and fifty-six and the second generation was between the ages of twenty-three and thirty-seven. The age spread of both generations, covering twenty-three to fifty-six years of age, constitutes almost the entire adult working population, a population of people who may recall the manner in which they personally were affected by a worldwide recession brought on by rising food prices and a global energy crisis precipitated when Arab nations imposed an oil embargo. If you are a member of the generation born between 1956 and 1972, recall the circumstances that you experienced between 1981 and 1988 when transit Uranus in Sagittarius squared your natal Pluto in Virgo.

URANUS TRINES

TRANSIT URANUS TRINE NATAL SUN

♅ △ ☉ When transit Uranus trines your natal Sun, good fortune may come by default or through your meritorious efforts or a combination of both these things, but the tricky part is that you are not likely to be the one who controls or manipulates the overall circumstances by which you benefit. The target of this period has little to do with enhancing your emotional life or fulfilling desires, at least not directly. More in focus these days are the promotion of your individuality, the favorable application of your will, and the enjoyment of ego-satisfying success. If you seek leadership, advanced position, or the attainment of career goals, this is the period to move forward in appropriate directions. Expect the unexpected since it is likely to be a good thing.

TRANSIT URANUS TRINE NATAL MOON

♅ △ ☽ Your emotional life may be greatly improved in unexpected and unpredictable ways during this period. When transit Uranus trines your natal Moon, you are more attracted to what is new or unique, and thus there may be something of the unorthodox or unusual in your emotional attachments and commitments. Your domestic environment is apt to change or become more emotionally stimulating, and should this occasion introduce children into your life, they will be welcome. No matter how strange or unexpected the circumstances are that provide emotional satisfaction, the outlook is favorable.

TRANSIT URANUS TRINE NATAL MERCURY

♅ △ ☿ If you are looking for a more exciting sales approach, more stimulating avenues in which to express your ideas and opinions, the latest methods to handle your tasks, or better transportation, you will find just what you need. New, perhaps radically different ideas, methods, machinery, technology, and information come your way when transit Uranus trines your natal Mercury. Other areas of favorable focus include computers, information and communication systems, travel, and electronics. Contacts and relationships with siblings, neighbors, and those you deal with routinely may suddenly prove highly stimulating or take on some other unexpected but favorable changes. This is an excellent period for group activities and involvement with a newsletter or information issued by a group or association.

TRANSIT URANUS TRINE NATAL VENUS

♅ △ ♀ Interactions include exciting and unusual people, any one of whom may turn out to be a new business or marriage partner or ally in joint ventures and other cooperative efforts. Finding a romantic partner and forming congenial female relationships are also strong possibilities. Relationships may be with those of a different culture or generation, or the relationships themselves may be unorthodox or nontraditional. During the stimulating and favorable, if somewhat unpredictable, period when transit Uranus trines your natal Venus, your social life and activities include an element of the unexpected or unusual. Artistic and creative projects and commercial or diplomatic endeavors are apt to be successful, but they too may involve a different or unexpected approach. Staying home alone or in isolated spots reduces the favorable odds. You cannot control or bring about the circumstances of your good fortune since they are apt to hinge on the actions or decisions made by others, but you can attract good fortune by putting yourself in social or public situations among many different people. Be willing to try new experiences and to travel to new and exotic places.

TRANSIT URANUS TRINE NATAL MARS

♅ △ ♂ Physical efforts and activities can take some unexpected, unusual, or unorthodox turns these days, but for the better. Do not be surprised if you become more physically stimulated by unusual or unfamiliar situations. When transit Uranus trines your natal Mars, it is important to remain busy and active. Your actions have an unpredictable nature and their conclusions may not bring the results you anticipate, but they will benefit you nonetheless. Be prepared for anything to happen, and when it does, act on it. Male relationships are favored, although, as in most things these days, men or your associations with them may be unorthodox. The character of your physical endeavors that involve men is subject to unstable or unpredictable conditions, but with fortunate results. This is an excellent period for work in general and, in particular, work that involves electronics, computers, television or radio, and the latest technology.

TRANSIT URANUS TRINE NATAL JUPITER

♅ △ ♃ Your generosity pays off handsomely but in a way you might not have imagined. This is a generally favorable time in which your social or professional status may increase, success may attend your travel and educational endeavors, important recognition is given to your writing or publishing efforts, and there is the potential for economic prosperity as well as cultural and spiritual growth. You are favorably involved with your father or situations related to him when transit Uranus trines your natal Jupiter. As a result of other people, fortunate circumstances occur, and they may develop unexpectedly or arise in an unusual or unorthodox manner. Whether you are the initiator or simply react to favorable situations caused by others, you can gain a new independence, philosophy, and optimistic outlook.

TRANSIT URANUS TRINE NATAL SATURN

♅ △ ♄ Accumulated experience, organization, past efforts, and hard work are emphasized and may be expected to count in your favor when transit Uranus trines your natal Saturn. People (often older people) and circumstances come along to provide you with recognition and rewards. It is possible that present circumstances may upset your traditional structures or ideas, but the key is to incorporate the old with the new—getting rid of what is no longer viable or useful and adding the benefits of new people, new ideas, and new technology. You cannot manipulate people or events to bring about your own good fortune. They will come on their own and then it is up to you to react expediently.

TRANSIT URANUS TRINE NATAL URANUS

⛢ △ ⛢ This is a favorable period for those in your generation. A trine occurs between your natal Uranus and transit Uranus twice, the first time between twenty-seven and thirty-one years of age and the second time between fifty-three and fifty-nine years of age (see Table 25). Your generation will get the most benefit from new methods, new technology, and political and social changes that occur at this time. What impact such beneficial circumstances have on your private life is determined by other factors.

Transit ⛢	trines in years	Natal ⛢	of those born in:
⛢ ♊	1941–1949	⛢ ♒	1912–1920
⛢ ♎	1968–1975		
⛢ ♋	1948–1956	⛢ ♓	1919–1928
⛢ ♏	1974–1981		
⛢ ♌	1955–1962	⛢ ♈	1927–1935
⛢ ♐	1981–1988		
⛢ ♍	1961–1969	⛢ ♉	1934–1942
⛢ ♑	1988–1996		
⛢ ♎	1968–1975	⛢ ♊	1941–1949
⛢ ♒	1995–2003		
⛢ ♏	1974–1981	⛢ ♋	1948–1956
⛢ ♓	2003f–2011		
⛢ ♐	1981–1988	⛢ ♌	1955–1962
⛢ ♈	2010–2019		
⛢ ♑	1988–1996	⛢ ♍	1961–1969
⛢ ♉	2018–2026		
⛢ ♒	1995–2003	⛢ ♎	1968–1975
⛢ ♊	2025–2033		

Table 25: Transit Uranus Trines to Natal Uranus

TRANSIT URANUS TRINE NATAL NEPTUNE

♅ △ ♆ This period must be thought of as a broad-based time that benefits your generation rather than you as an individual. Potential circumstances encourage favorable trends in charitable institutions and their activities, in civil rights and other minority issues, and in literature and art. There is a reaching out for greater spiritual awareness. If these particular areas are of unusual importance in your life's work or in the lives of those close to you, then you may reap benefits from the new trends in society in a more personal way. So that you may study the circumstances from an historical point of view, Table 26 lists the transit of Uranus for the generations born between 1887 with natal Neptune in Gemini and 1984 with natal Neptune in Sagittarius.

Transit ♅	trines in years	Natal ♆	of those born in:	at age:
♅ ♒	1912–1920	♆ ♊	1887–1902	18–25
♅ ♎	1968–1975			73–81
♅ ♓	1919–1928	♆ ♋	1901–1915	13–18
♅ ♏	1974–1981			66–73
♅ ♈	1927–1935	♆ ♌	1914–1928	07–13
♅ ♐	1981–1988			60–67
♅ ♈	2010–2019			91–96
♅ ♑	1988–1996	♆ ♍	1928–1943	53–60
♅ ♉	2018–2026			83–90
♅ ♒	1995–2003	♆ ♎	1942–1957	46–53
♅ ♊	2025–2033			76–83
♅ ♓	2003–2011	♆ ♏	1955–1970	41–48
♅ ♋	2032–2040			70–77
♅ ♈	2010–2019	♆ ♐	1970–1984	35–40
♅ ♌	2039–2046			62–69

Table 26: Transit Uranus Trines to Natal Neptune

TRANSIT URANUS TRINE NATAL PLUTO

♅ △ ♇ This period specifically targets power and control. However, unless you occupy a high-level position in government or industry, you are apt to benefit from favorable power shifts only indirectly when transit Uranus trines your natal Pluto (see Table 27). Since this period also involves regeneration and conservation, the trend in society is one that favors successful control and distribution of the earth's natural resources.

Transit ♅	trines in years	Natal ♇	of those born in:	at age:
♅ ♒	1912–1920	♇ ♊	1882–1914	06–30
♅ ♎	1968–1975			61–86
♅ ♒	1995–2003			89–113
♅ ♏	1974–1981	♇ ♋	1912–1939	42–62
♅ ♓	2003–2011			72–91
♅ ♐	1981–1988	♇ ♌	1937–1958	30–44
♅ ♈	2010–2019			61–73
♅ ♑	1988–1996	♇ ♍	1956–1972	24–32
♅ ♉	2018–2026			54–62

Table 27: Transit Uranus Trines to Natal Pluto

URANUS OPPOSITIONS

TRANSIT URANUS OPPOSED NATAL SUN

♅ ☍ ☉ There is no telling in which direction your ego will lead you when an opposition occurs between transit Uranus and your natal Sun. Circumstances provoke you to act in ways that do not necessarily reflect attempts to satisfy deep emotional desires but are reflective of a bruised or errant ego. Separation from someone or something important to you is a more than a likely prospect. The potential separation may be an action you unexpectedly decide to take or a separation occurs which you are forced to accept, and, as a result, you react by going off in a totally new or surprising direction. Expect your leadership or your will to be challenged. You may not be able to control or manipulate the people or circumstances that come along, you can only try to control your reactions. Supposedly permanent changes and situations that occur during this period are not apt to survive for long. In fairly short order, they may either be completely reversed or else the results will turn out to be different than you had anticipated.

Transit Uranus Opposed Natal Moon

⛢ ☍ ☽ Home and family status are almost certain to be disrupted by the circumstances of this period. Although not an absolute certainty, you may change your residence or become separated from home, children and other family members, and even family pets—actions which would have been highly unlikely just a short time ago. When transit Uranus opposes your natal Moon, your normal routine and the functioning of many things become erratic, forcing you to find new methods and a new approach. Your emotional life is highly unstable and unpredictable, making your commitment to anyone or anything difficult if not impossible to establish or maintain. Your general health may suffer as a result of emotional turmoil, and, if you are female and of the appropriate age and circumstances to be pregnant, it will be difficult to carry the baby to full term. Your diet and digestion are apt to be less efficient, which in turn may cause you to lose weight or suffer from other digestive and stress-related difficulties. It is wise to avoid making permanent decisions or important changes until this period has passed.

Transit Uranus Opposed Natal Mercury

⛢ ☍ ☿ Be prepared for radical changes in thinking, methods, and communication. Although something of value may ultimately come from the chaotic circumstances you experience, there is also the danger that what is useful or good will be discarded in favor of something new or different. This is unlikely to be an easy time. When transit Uranus opposes your natal Mercury, it is hard to express or organize thoughts and ideas, your mind races so far ahead of what you say or write that others find it difficult to fill in the missing gaps. You may be plagued by nerves, restlessness, accidents, and turbulent confrontations. Electrical equipment is potentially dangerous, your neighborhood is disturbed, and contacts with siblings may be broken off. Travel and even running errands can unexpectedly result in accidents or chaos. What can be done? You cannot control the disruptions, but you can take precautions to counterbalance their influence by tempering your own reactions with as much calmness and good sense as you can muster.

TRANSIT URANUS OPPOSED NATAL VENUS

♅ ☍ ♀ The prospect of interactions when transit Uranus opposes your natal Venus is not to be taken lightly since unstable or unpredictable reactions, attitudes, and actions either on your part or on the part of others occur frequently. Female relationships, marital or business partnership, cooperative efforts or joint ventures are subject to changes that might include a separation. A current romantic attachment may be severely strained by outside forces, and romance that begins now may not withstand unstable circumstances—ending as abruptly as it started. Social contacts are unstable, and social events may not come off as planned. This is not a favorable time to launch artistic or design projects. Legal suits and contracts or other agreements are not likely to be of a permanent nature and may even be reversed.

TRANSIT URANUS OPPOSED NATAL MARS

♅ ☍ ♂ The physical urge to act is compelling. You may be a rebel without a cause, or else everything becomes a cause when transit Uranus opposes your natal Mars. Physical efforts and activities are erratic and unpredictable, as are the results of these actions. Actions taken against you may be unexpected. The danger they can pose, if not certain, is a strong possibility. The prospect of separation from male relatives or companions increases. Your job or other physical work in which you engage brings increased stress and chaos, which, in turn, negatively impact your health. Headaches, fevers, and injury to the face or eyes are possible. This is not a favorable period to undergo surgery since its results are unpredictable. The outcome of a hostile physical confrontation will not favor you. Aggressive tendencies and rash behavior with respect to sexual encounters, sports activities, and any highly competitive situations should without exception be strictly avoided.

TRANSIT URANUS OPPOSED NATAL JUPITER

♅ ☍ ♃ Caution is advised. Your generosity or optimism may be disastrously misplaced. Sources of information, intellectual progress in general, economic expansion, and even spiritual growth are vulnerable to sudden change and other elements of instability. It would be unwise to vigorously pursue advancement in your personal or professional status since the outcome is not only unpredictable but also likely to be unfavorable. There is a potential of separation from or unexpected changes involving your father. The people and circumstances responsible for introducing alterations and inconveniences that you experience when transit Uranus opposes your natal Jupiter cannot be controlled or manipulated by you to any better advantage. It is wiser to react in as low-key a manner and as judiciously as possible whenever and wherever you encounter difficulty.

TRANSIT URANUS OPPOSED NATAL SATURN

♅ ☍ ♄ Whatever you have managed to gain thus far in matters of seniority, experience, and authority (especially if these achievements have been won by some manner of default rather than through hard work and attention to business) is liable to be unexpectedly threatened, perhaps completely disrupted, by people and circumstances over which you have no control. There is little likelihood of improving a situation if you attempt to impose your seniority or authority. When transit Uranus opposes your natal Saturn, your traditions and methods are under fire and the opposing forces press for change and a new order. Although you may not totally escape some measure of the potential that has been described, your flexibility, careful observance, and cautious response to threats can minimize the unpleasant impact of this unstable and unfavorable period.

TRANSIT URANUS OPPOSED NATAL URANUS

♅ ☍ ♅ The potential of your current circumstances can best be described as a midlife crisis. This is primarily because transit Uranus opposes your natal Uranus at about forty years of age, an age when most people experience some trepidation regarding the future as well as the past. It is a time when generations clash. Although you may feel somewhat outdated by the so-called new wave, this is not a period calculated to make you feel old, only different. You may be as unwilling to give up the unique qualities that belong to your age group as another generation is to give up their special character. There is little meeting of the minds (or tastes).

TRANSIT URANUS OPPOSED NATAL NEPTUNE

♅ ☍ ♆ Circumstances and movements in society these days will reverse ideas and methods with regard to religion and spiritual growth, attitudes and institutions concerned with minority groups, and the arts. The end result is that one ideology is eliminated and replaced by another. The generation born in 1887–1902 no doubt regretted the loss of their ideals when they experienced transit Uranus in Sagittarius opposed their natal Neptune in Gemini in 1981–1988. However, for generations that experience this aspect at younger ages (see Table 28), the loss of ideals may have more serious implications.

Transit ♅	opposes in years	Natal ♆	of those born in:	at age:
♅ ♐	1981–1988	♆ ♊	1887–1902	86–94
♅ ♑	1988–1996	♆ ♋	1901–1915	81–87
♅ ♒	1995–2003	♆ ♌	1914–1928	75–81
♅ ♓	2003–2011	♆ ♍	1928–1943	68–75
♅ ♈	2010–2019	♆ ♎	1942–1957	62–68
♅ ♉	2018–2026	♆ ♏	1955–1970	56–63
♅ ♊	2025–2033	♆ ♐	1970–1984	49–55

Table 28: Transit Uranus Oppositions to Natal Neptune

TRANSIT URANUS OPPOSED NATAL PLUTO

♅ ☍ ♇ By the time an opposition between transit Uranus and your natal Pluto occurs, you have acquired resources in some form (see Table 29 on page 196). The problem now may be a clash between you and members of younger generations who have different ideas about how resources should be handled. Movements in society that disrupt and even eliminate established sources of power are apt to occur. Hopefully you have gained enough experience to be able to cope successfully with shifts in the power of political and social institutions that may impact you.

Transit ♅	opposes in years	Natal ♇	of those born in:	at age:
♅ ♐	1981–1988	♇ ♊	1882–1914	74–99
♅ ♑	1988–1996	♇ ♋	1912–1939	57–76
♅ ♒	1995–2003	♇ ♌	1937–1958	45–58
♅ ♓	2003–2011	♇ ♍	1956–1972	39–47
♅ ♈	2010–2019	♇ ♎	1971–1984	35–39

Table 29: Transit Uranus Oppositions to Natal Pluto

Chapter Nine

Transit Neptune Aspects to the Natal Planets

The transit of Neptune through the zodiac takes one hundred sixty-four years, too long for it to complete a cycle through your natal chart. Neptune's slow-moving journey makes it an important factor in the background of circumstances you experience. Its aspects to natal planets can be in effect for several years.

NEPTUNE CONJUNCTIONS

TRANSIT NEPTUNE CONJOIN NATAL SUN

♆ ☌ ☉ The period in which transit Neptune conjoins your natal Sun can be confusing, especially with regard to its primary focus, which is your ego. Goals that prompt your ego drive during this period fail to crystallize for lack of any solid purpose or because they are inspired by misguided or unrealistic notions. The problems that confront or confound you are maintaining a clear self-image and understanding the nature and reasonableness of your ambitions. Your leadership, ideals, and personal integrity may become eroded or brought into question at this time. Illusions encourage fanciful ideas and expectations and there is a danger of fanaticism—either on your part or the part of others. Avoid using drugs, alcohol, or other addictive substances to bolster your ego. Not every instance of this aspect's occurrence is negative. There is the potential for greater sensitivity, increased spiritual awareness, imagination, and inspiration of the highest order.

TRANSIT NEPTUNE CONJOIN NATAL MOON

♆ ☌ ☽ You experience a sense of rootlessness, of being unable to make strong emotional commitments to anything or anyone, and of being unable to get others to make such commitments to you when transit Neptune conjoins your natal Moon. Depending on your particular situation, family relationships and other close ties, especially with maternal or strong female figures, can either become eroded or become much closer, more spiritual, and even clairvoyant. Some mystery or confusion regarding your family or background may emerge. It is hard to pinpoint exactly what you want or what will make you happy which, in turn, may prompt you to indulge in daydreaming—even if fantasizing has never been your habit. Creative and promotional talents can flourish. Spirituality increases and your instincts and intuition are developed to a remarkable degree. However, trying to stick to the routine business of life is a struggle even in the most positive circumstances. Physical complaints that occur at this time are difficult to diagnose or they may be psychosomatic. Your home may be damaged by flood or gas leaks or you may take up residence near a penal institution or hospital, in an isolated spot, or near the ocean. Keep a close eye on your possessions since there is increased potential to lose them through carelessness or theft. Dwell on the negative possibilities only long enough to protect yourself from falling victim to them, but concentrate your efforts on promoting the positive potentials.

TRANSIT NEPTUNE CONJOIN NATAL MERCURY

♆ ☌ ☿ Clear and rational thinking is hard to achieve when transit Neptune conjoins your natal Mercury. The positive and negative potentials of this period affect your mental outlook, the way you express yourself, ideas you originate as well as receive, information you disseminate as well as information you are given, and methods you use as well as methods you devise. The positive potential suggests that you can develop mechanical, design, and communicative skills; more imagination; greater spirituality; higher mental planes; and keener intuition—any or all of which can successfully be applied to education, computers, languages, information systems, publishing or distribution of magazines and other reading material, travel, transportation, advertising, direct-mail promotions, broadcasting, communication systems and equipment, and sales and other commercial transactions. The negative potentials imply confusion, disorganization, lack of attention to detail, mental laziness, inability to grasp reality, and outright deception. Keeping schedules efficient, sticking to the agenda, and being on time are challenges you face on a constant basis during this period. Circumstances related to neighbors, siblings, co-workers, and fellow travelers can be confusing, strange, or mysterious, but they may also become inspirational or highly spiritual.

TRANSIT NEPTUNE CONJOIN NATAL VENUS

♆☌♀ When a conjunction occurs between transit Neptune and your natal Venus, the focus of its circumstances includes your social behavior and attitudes, your partner (business as well as marriage) and other allies, romantic attachments, and female friends. The greater imagination, sensitivity, and instinctual responses that you develop during this period can create close and successful relationships, but there is also the potential that misunderstanding, confusion, obsessiveness, or paranoia can undermine your success with others. You may lack the ability to recognize your own worth or the worth of other people, and your ideals or expectations may be unrealistic. The possibility of disillusionment and deception at this time puts you at a disadvantage in joint ventures, artistic projects, legal negotiations, and romantic adventures. Your talent and appreciation for art and beauty may be greatly enhanced. The pursuit of physical pleasures, luxury, and wealth can be ruinous these days unless you apply prudence and moderation. Negative circumstances may cause your entire value system to disintegrate, while positive circumstances can help you establish more insightful values.

TRANSIT NEPTUNE CONJOIN NATAL MARS

♆☌♂ Physical accomplishments are difficult when transit Neptune conjoins your natal Mars. Your maturity can contribute in a positive way to your behavior and to the final outcome of your actions, especially if you become frustrated when you don't make headway and keep running up against others who misunderstand your methods or goals. Your physical energy, physical endeavors, and male relationships can be negatively or positively affected during this period depending on what other factors are at work in your current circumstances. Deception or confusion can undermine your efforts, you may fail to receive recognition, or the things you do don't seem (at least to you) to make any difference or have a long-lasting effect. In turn, this can make you reluctant to make any effort at all. You may engage in impractical or unrealistic enterprises. The bright side offers the potential that your actions and activities succeed as a result of the inspiration, intuition, sensitivity, or spirituality that you invest in them. Even when your actions miss the intended target, they may hit one that is just as successful or meaningful. Your work or the men in your life may be involved during this period with the ocean, fishing industry, footwear, photography, dance, drugs, alcohol, fraud, bankruptcy, charitable institutions, or the penal system.

Transit Neptune Conjoin Natal Jupiter

Ψ ☌ ♃ Your spiritual, intellectual, and economic growth are the focus when transit Neptune conjoins your natal Jupiter. Combining illusion with exaggeration and extravagance (which is what can happen during this time) can be disastrous unless held at bay by more prudent facets of your character and personality. Idealism is enhanced but can too easily be encouraged to the point of fanaticism. A search for knowledge and truth can be truly inspired but also the basis for intellectual snobbery. Avoid get-rich-quick schemes since there is no sure method for separating the facts from the fiction of overestimation and outright deception. If you mount a determined effort to keep yourself and your circumstances within the limits of proper proportion and perspective, this can be a phenomenal period for personal growth and success. Some areas that offer you increased benefits include writing, publishing, advertising, sales, long-distance travel, drama, dance, religion, the stock market, the ocean or maritime industries, your father, the justice system, footwear, drugs, or alcohol.

Transit Neptune Conjoin Natal Saturn

Ψ ☌ ♄ If you are very young when transit Neptune conjoins your natal Saturn, the authority figures in your life and the structures and traditions with which you are being raised may be of two kinds. They may either be highly idealistic or strange and misguided. If you have gained maturity and a position of authority by the time this aspect occurs, you may be inspired by circumstances that add a new dimension to your maturity and a new approach to how you handle your authority. Another potential is that the tradition and structures you have adopted to this point in life begin to disintegrate in the atmosphere of what you are currently experiencing. There is always the potential, even if you are an adult, that those who represent authority will be affected positively or negatively by their ideals and, in turn, this has an impact on your life or activities.

TRANSIT NEPTUNE CONJOIN NATAL URANUS

♆ ☌ ♅   When transit Neptune conjoins your natal Uranus, confusion, disorientation, or unrealistic expectations arise to cause certain changes in society. Ideals and spiritual goals conflict with technical and economic considerations and almost anything can happen. Eventually, of course, this conflict can mean significant changes in how things get done—and how society gets things done may have some impact on you. As Table 30 indicates, this aspect occurs at different ages for different generations. The generation born between

Transit ♆	conjuncts in years	Natal ♅	of those born in:	at age:
♆ ♈	1861–1875	♅ ♈	1844–1851	17–24
♆ ♉	1874–1889	♅ ♉	1851–1859	23–30
♆ ♊	1887–1902	♅ ♊	1858–1865	29–37
♆ ♋	1901–1915	♅ ♋	1865–1872	36–43
♆ ♌	1914–1928	♅ ♌	1872–1878	42–50
♆ ♍	1928–1943	♅ ♍	1878–1884	50–59
♆ ♎	1942–1957	♅ ♎	1884–1890	58–67
♆ ♏	1955–1970	♅ ♏	1890–1897	65–73
♆ ♐	1970–1984	♅ ♐	1897–1904	73–80
♆ ♑	1984–1998	♅ ♑	1904–1912	80–86
♆ ♒	1998–2012	♅ ♒	1912–1920	86–92
♆ ♓	2011–2026	♅ ♓	1919–1928	92–98
♆ ♈	2025–2039	♅ ♈	1927–1935	98–104
♆ ♉	2038–	♅ ♉	1934–1942	–104

Table 30: Transit Neptune Conjunctions to Natal Uranus

1844 and 1851 was between the ages of seventeen and twenty-four when transit Neptune conjoined their natal Uranus in Aries. Each subsequent 19th-century generation experienced this aspect at increasingly advanced ages. By the time the first generation in the 20th century was born, this aspect did not occur until they were between seventy-three and eighty years of age. For us, this aspect is of interest when its implied circumstances can be related historically to past generations and to the projected potential for future generations.

Transit Neptune Conjoin Natal Neptune

♆ ☌ ♆ This planetary aspect is not applicable for the simple reason that it takes Neptune approximately 165 years to transit the entire zodiac. You would have to live at least that long to experience transit Neptune's conjunction with your natal Neptune.

Transit Neptune Conjoin Natal Pluto

♆ ☌ ♇ The dissolving of power, but not necessarily by means of anarchy, is the potential of circumstances when transit Neptune conjoins natal Pluto. Treachery, poison, or plague could remove the current ruler or system of power and control. Circumstances associated with this aspect may also encourage the rise of those who bring a religious message or favor reincarnation, spiritualism, and psychic power. The effect on your personal environment will be dictated by your behavior and attitude toward these trends in society. Not all of these potentials are necessarily negative in their prospects. Interpreting the conjunction between transit Neptune and natal Pluto has value in analyzing history but, as shown in Table 31, it will not be experienced by any generation in this century.

Transit ♆	conjuncts in years	Natal ♇	of those born in:	at age:
♆ ♊	1724–1738	♇ ♊	1640–1669	69–84
♆ ♋	1737–1752	♇ ♋	1669–1693	59–68
♆ ♌	1751–1765	♇ ♌	1692–1711	54–59
♆ ♍	1764–1779	♇ ♍	1710–1725	54
♆ ♎	1778–1793	♇ ♎	1724–1737	54–56
♆ ♏	1792–1807	♇ ♏	1736–1749	56–58
♆ ♐	1806–1820	♇ ♐	1748–1762	58
♆ ♑	1820–1834	♇ ♑	1762–1778	56–58
♆ ♒	1834–1848	♇ ♒	1777–1798	50–57
♆ ♓	1848–1862	♇ ♓	1797–1823	39–51
♆ ♈	1861–1875	♇ ♈	1822–1853	22–39
♆ ♉	1874–1889	♇ ♉	1851–1884	05–23
♆ ♊	1887–1902	♇ ♊	1882–1914	00–05

Table 31: Transit Neptune Conjunctions to Natal Pluto

NEPTUNE SEXTILES

TRANSIT NEPTUNE SEXTILE NATAL SUN

♆ ✶ ☉   When transit Neptune sextiles your natal Sun, an element of mystery, glamor, illusion, or spirituality turns up in what otherwise may be fairly routine circumstances, and when it does, you have an opportunity to demonstrate leadership, integrity, individuality, and generosity. Recognition and success do not automatically occur. But this is a positive dynamic, so it improves the odds that the opportunity you take advantage of now will ultimately lead to personal recognition and increased status.

TRANSIT NEPTUNE SEXTILE NATAL MOON

♆ ✶ ☽   Creativity develops in strange ways and a watery environment may lead to inspiration when transit Neptune sextiles your natal

Moon. The potential of this period is for opportune circumstances that enhance your emotional life, help you obtain your desires, and promote greater awareness and sensitivity. An important female figure may give you a boost. A chance meeting or occurrence may lead to beginning a family, obtaining a residence or improving your current home, and establishing more meaningful emotional ties and commitments.

TRANSIT NEPTUNE SEXTILE NATAL MERCURY

♆ ✶ ☿ Watch for situations that stir your imagination and lead you to higher planes of thought and self-expression. When transit Neptune sextiles your natal Mercury, the opportunity is one in which you may be able to inspire others with your thoughts and ideas, or it may lead you to those who will inspire you. Either way, the situation is advantageous because of the potential benefit you derive. Possibilities include a chance to travel, especially on or over water. Opportunity may lead to improving your prospects in business or writing, ocean or marine industries, dance, religion, drugs, alcohol, charitable institutions, dream studies, photography, or footwear.

TRANSIT NEPTUNE SEXTILE NATAL VENUS

♆ ✶ ♀ The potential areas of opportunity when transit Neptune sextiles your natal Venus are related to marriage, joint ventures, relationships with women, social contacts, and romantic encounters—either new or current ones. Although weak, this aspect is nevertheless of a positive nature. It suggests that if you make use of the elements of imagination, mystery, glamor, illusion, or spirituality in your current circumstances, it can lead to success in legal matters, contract negotiations, social activities, and getting others to cooperate.

TRANSIT NEPTUNE SEXTILE NATAL MARS

♆ ✶ ♂ When a sextile occurs between transit Neptune and your natal Mars, it signals a time for you to take advantage of any opportunity related to physical activities, male relationships, and men in general. Greater imagination, mystery, glamor, illusion, or spirituality in your work, physical efforts, and associations with males offer a chance to attain health- or work-related benefits.

TRANSIT NEPTUNE SEXTILE NATAL JUPITER

Ψ ✶ ♃ Take advantage of any opportunity to gain new experiences. Although the prospects are not strong when transit Neptune sextiles your natal Jupiter, their energy is positive. If you are shrewd enough to recognize the favorable atmosphere in your present circumstances, they may lead to personal growth, economic expansion, the broadening of your intellectual horizons, and increased professional status. There are prospects that favor long-distance travel, politics, writing, publishing, cultural pursuits, and a situation related to your father.

TRANSIT NEPTUNE SEXTILE NATAL SATURN

Ψ ✶ ♄ There may be only the subtlest of clues to the opportunities that exist when transit Neptune sextiles your natal Saturn, and only your realization of what is possible that keeps them from slipping away unnoticed. It will be up to you to find some element of imagination, mystery, glamor, illusion, or spirituality in the current circumstances and use it to your advantage in gaining greater authority, seniority, maturity, and in promoting the traditions and structures on which your life-style is based.

TRANSIT NEPTUNE SEXTILE NATAL URANUS

Ψ ✶ ♅ Strange and whimsical fads in fashion, behavior, and attitudes may indirectly represent a personal advantage when transit Neptune sextiles your natal Uranus. The freedom associated with Uranus combined with the illusion and imagination of Neptune can, for example, inspire a trend in the design of clothing that is flattering while it also gives your body more freedom of movement. But there are more important possibilities to contemplate than clothes. The idealism of Neptune and the freedom of Uranus can have a positive impact on your life in matters that involve civil rights, welfare, religious tolerance, and better opportunities for employment. The age when individuals experience this aspect varies for each generation as they are born either during, close to, or further from the period when a sextile is formed between the two transiting planets. For purposes of study and comparison, the transits of Neptune are listed in Table 32 on the next page.

Transit ♆	sextiles in years	Natal ♅	of those born in:	at age:
♆ ♎	1942–1957	♅ ♌	1872–1878	70–79
		♅ ♐	1897–1904	15–53
♆ ♏	1955–1970	♅ ♍	1878–1884	77–86
		♅ ♑	1904–1912	58–64
♆ ♐	1970–1984	♅ ♎	1884–1890	86–94
		♅ ♒	1912–1920	58–64
♆ ♑	1984–1998	♅ ♏	1890–1897	94–101
		♅ ♓	1919–1928	65–70
♆ ♒	1998–2012	♅ ♐	1897–1904	101–108
		♅ ♈	1927–1935	71–77
♆ ♓	2011–2026	♅ ♉	1934–1942	77–84
		♅ ♑	1988–1996	23–30
♆ ♈	2025–2039	♅ ♊	1941–1949	84–90
		♅ ♒	1995–2003	30–36
♆ ♉	2038–	♅ ♋	1948–1956	90–
		♅ ♓	2003–2011	35–

Table 32: Transit Neptune Sextiles to Natal Uranus

TRANSIT NEPTUNE SEXTILE NATAL NEPTUNE

♆ ✳ ♆ Transit Neptune forms a sextile to your natal Neptune when you are between twenty-eight and thirty years old. The ideals and spiritual values you have maintained in life will be favored at this time by the concepts that are being promoted in society.

TRANSIT NEPTUNE SEXTILE NATAL PLUTO

♆ ✳ ♇ The combining of mystery, glamor, or illusion with the structures of power and control describes the potential of circumstances when transit Neptune sextiles your natal Pluto. With the exception of people born between 1884 and 1914 who experienced this aspect between 1914 and 1929, the subsequent generations of this century were born while the sextile was being created between the two transiting planets. Since most of the 20th century consisted of the long period in which the Neptune-Pluto sextile was formed, perhaps the century itself will historically represent an opportunity for generations of the 21st century to change the world.

NEPTUNE SQUARES

TRANSIT NEPTUNE SQUARE NATAL SUN

♆ □ ☉ When transit Neptune squares your natal Sun, there is confusion, disorientation, or a sense of unreality connected with your self-image. You may be unsure of how to satisfy your ego demands or where to direct your willpower during this period. Positions of leadership or situations that recommend you as an individual—your integrity, honesty, and principles—are difficult to attain or sustain. The sources that usually provide the necessities of life, whatever they may be for you (food, money, courage, ambition) become elusive and difficult to define or rely on. There is a positive side which will become apparent if you are by nature a determined and capable individual, one who is able to realize that what seems like reality may not always actually be reality. The illusive obstacles in your path eventually disappear and the fact that you tried your best to overcome them is enough to assure your eventual success.

TRANSIT NEPTUNE SQUARE NATAL MOON

♆ □ ☽ Undermining obstacles keep tripping you up when you try to obtain your heart's desire. When you get what you want, you may not want it, or it may not be what you thought it was. Your emotional life, your domestic environment, and your family ties are at the mercy of what can only be described as confusing situations. When transit Neptune squares your natal Moon, it is difficult to establish solid commitment, steadfast loyalty, and unwavering priorities and principles. However, having to cope with constantly shifting alliances and a lack of confidence can eventually lead to the recognition of what is truly important to you, to the need for stronger emotional bonds, and to more sensitivity and deeper understanding. By the time your struggles have ended, you may not have any clearer notion of what you want, but you will have gained a much better understanding of what you do not want.

TRANSIT NEPTUNE SQUARE NATAL MERCURY

♆ □ ☿ Clear and rational thinking is increasingly difficult to achieve. Your age and maturity will no doubt contribute to the overall outcome, but, in the end, disorganization, disorientation, unreality, and other undermining influences can creep into ideas, communications, and methods. The increased potential for misunderstanding others as well as for being misunderstood yourself, causes frustration and, at times, needless hurt. Inefficiency or ineffectiveness attends the employment of your mechanical, design, computer, or other manual skills. The best-laid plans go awry, especially in such areas as transportation, travel, writing, education, and trade. Who should be blamed when things go wrong? Is it your fault? The fault of others? It is best not to waste time looking for culprits, since none may be found. To get from point A to point B may not be a simple process these days. In fact, when transit Neptune squares your natal Mercury, getting anywhere, mentally as well as physically, may turn out to be pretty much of a maze in which you wind your way past one obstacle after another. The positive potential of this influence suggests that through diligent attention and devotion to detail you can proceed cautiously and eventually achieve success.

TRANSIT NEPTUNE SQUARE NATAL VENUS

♆ □ ♀ Dealing with others on a clear and rational basis is not easy when transit Neptune squares your natal Venus. Hopefully, your maturity and past experiences will help as you cope with confusion, deception, or other undermining influences in legal matters, counseling you give or receive, social contacts, romantic attachments, partnerships (business or marriage), joint ventures, and female friendships. Others may misunderstand your values, or circumstances may undermine them. Your ideals or expectations concerning others (or theirs concerning you) may be unrealistic. It is difficult to get or depend on the cooperation of others, or even be sure that, if asked, you will be in a position to offer such assistance. The pursuit of pleasure and the finer things in life may be misguided or marred by one thing or another. This period presents obstacles, but they are only challenges to stimulate your determination to succeed.

TRANSIT NEPTUNE SQUARE NATAL MARS

Ψ □ ♂ Your physical energy and enthusiasm may be slowly drained as disorientation, laziness, and other undermining influences impact your physical efforts. The frustration of seeing endeavors come to nothing or fail to make much of a difference is something you should expect these days. The point is to keep moving along with cautious, steady efforts toward definite and realistic goals. In the long run, you may be making more progress than you think. Overcoming obstacles and the frustration of not attaining immediate success is the key to progress when transit Neptune squares your natal Mars. Associations with men may be confused, or circumstances surrounding your activities with men may be undermined. Keep as clear a perspective as possible on your work and physical activities. Be careful when traveling in or over water and when participating in water sports. There is potential for pneumonia, fever, and injury to your head

TRANSIT NEPTUNE SQUARE NATAL JUPITER

Ψ □ ♃ Disorganization, unwarranted optimism, or unrealistic expectations can undermine your spiritual, intellectual, and economic growth when transit Neptune squares your natal Jupiter. The potential of current circumstances may be described as combining inspiration and illusion with exaggeration and extravagance. Such a situation can become a disaster unless more prudent facets of your character and personality are able to prevent it. Fanaticism can masquerade as idealism. The search for knowledge and truth can be stymied by false prophets and blind devotion. Some scandal or other confusing circumstance may involve your father and his status or achievements. Wild and unrealistic get-rich-quick schemes must be avoided. Obstacles that turn up can be hard to recognize and thus impossible to overcome.

TRANSIT NEPTUNE SQUARE NATAL SATURN

Ψ □ ♄ Hidden fears and worries increase, and to make matters worse, confronting them openly and honestly is not easily accomplished. Traditions, structures, and the usual restrictions and limitations become vague or misguided when transit Neptune squares your natal Saturn. Deception, disorientation, and unrealistic expectations can impact your life-style, authority, experience, hard work, and organization. How well you are able or willing to cope with disappointment, loss, and failure is tested. This is a highly unfavorable period for risky business ventures or acquiring any kind of debt. Yet all is not totally negative. With patience and determination you can hold on to what is real and what is truly worthwhile. If your actions fail, let them fail on the side of conservatism and morally correct behavior.

TRANSIT NEPTUNE SQUARE NATAL URANUS

Ψ□♅ When a square occurs between transit Neptune and your natal Uranus (see Table 33), it represents a period when idealism and spirituality clash with technical and economic considerations, permitting almost anything to happen. Eventually, the results may be looked back upon and referred to as an "inspired revolution" but while the revolution occurs, the battles may be confusing as well as chaotic.

Transit Ψ	squares in years	Natal ♅	of those born in:	at age:
Ψ ♍	1928–1943	♅ ♐	1897–1904	31–39
Ψ ♎	1942–1957	♅ ♑	1904–1912	38–45
Ψ ♏	1955–1970	♅ ♒	1912–1920	43–50
Ψ ♐	1970–1984	♅ ♓	1919–1928	51–56
Ψ ♑	1984–1998	♅ ♈	1927–1935	57–63
Ψ ♒	1998–2012	♅ ♉	1934–1942	64–70
Ψ ♓	2011–2026	♅ ♊	1941–1949	70–77
Ψ ♈	2025–2039	♅ ♋	1948–1956	77–83
Ψ ♉	2038–	♅ ♌	1955–1962	83–
Ψ ♐	1970–1984	♅ ♍	1961–1969	09–15
Ψ ♑	1984–1998	♅ ♎	1968–1975	16–23
Ψ ♒	1998–2012	♅ ♏	1974–1981	24–31
Ψ ♓	2011–2026	♅ ♐	1981–1988	30–38
Ψ ♈	2025–2039	♅ ♑	1988–1996	37–43

Table 33: Transit Neptune Squares to Natal Uranus

TRANSIT NEPTUNE SQUARE NATAL NEPTUNE

♆ □ ♆ Some confusion or disappointment is likely to result from the obstacles that society throws in the path of your spiritual and aesthetic goals during this period. Other factors must decide how much you as an individual will become involved with or influenced by such broad implications. This aspect occurs when you are in your early forties. By this time, you have established certain goals and ideals and if societal conditions prevent you from expressing and pursuing them, there is potential for dissatisfaction.

TRANSIT NEPTUNE SQUARE NATAL PLUTO

♆ □ ♇ Undermining influences infiltrate control and power structures in society during the period when transit Neptune squares your natal Pluto. Only secondarily is it likely to disrupt your personal environment. There are some possibilities to consider, however. Just when you think, for instance, that you have gained mastery over something, it may suddenly fall apart or elude you. Should this occur, the key is to realize that loss of control or the resources that gave you control may be only an illusion. If, in fact, there is loss, it may only be temporary, perhaps to remind you of the importance of staying in control, of not abusing power, and of preserving your resources. In Table 34, locate the period in which transit Neptune squared your natal Pluto and compare your circumstances at that time to the interpretation described for this aspect. Note that as the 20th century progressed, generations have experienced this aspect at increasingly younger ages.

Transit ♆	squares in years	Natal ♇	of those born in:	at age:
♆ ♍	1928–1943	♇ ♊	1882–1914	29–46
♆ ♎	1942–1957	♇ ♋	1912–1939	18–30
♆ ♏	1955–1970	♇ ♌	1937–1958	12–18
♆ ♐	1970–1984	♇ ♍	1956–1972	12–14
♆ ♑	1984–1998	♇ ♎	1971–1984	13–14

Table 34: Transit Neptune Squares to Natal Pluto

NEPTUNE TRINES

TRANSIT NEPTUNE TRINE NATAL SUN

♆ △ ☉ The positive potential of this period is for circumstances to boost your ego. You may be surrounded with an aura of glamor, mystery, or spirituality that attracts others and opens doors that might otherwise have been closed to you. Your aesthetic tastes are greatly enhanced as well as recognized by others. If these qualities are used in your work or profession, this is a favorable period to promote them. Wine, perfume, drugs, art, photography, religion, promotion, dance, footwear, charitable foundations, penal institutions, hospitals, the navy, marine equipment, and any activities or items related to the ocean are some of the specific areas where you will have an excellent chance to succeed. Trying to pinpoint the source of your good fortune when it occurs, or explain exactly how you happen to be at the right place at the right time is when transit Neptune trines your natal Sun. You can achieve your ambitions with no effort just as easily as you can by working hard.

TRANSIT NEPTUNE TRINE NATAL MOON

♆ △ ☽ Intuition and instincts are greatly heightened, and depending on your inclination to develop and pay heed to such inner talents, they may even reach a state of clairvoyance when transit Neptune trines your natal Moon. Some inner voice or whim that you do not quite understand can lead you to fortunate circumstances. Aesthetic and spiritual sensibilities are aroused, but the potential of this period does not indicate whether you will seek religion, art, or some other path to accommodate your increasing sensitivity and awareness. If you possess artistic and creative talents, however, they will flourish. Deception and disguise become an art. Desires may be fulfilled and emotional satisfaction achieved. Your fantasies and ideals regarding family and home life take wing. The inspiration you get from your mother or a strong female figure can play a significant role in your success.

TRANSIT NEPTUNE TRINE NATAL MERCURY

♆ △ ☿ Your thoughts and ideas, methods, and communications are more imaginative and inspired during this period. The favorable circumstances that occur when transit Neptune trines your natal Mercury encourage you to put effort into writing, publishing, sales, computers, education, and any activity that involves communication and associated areas. Commerce, travel, and trade are highly favored, as are the development and use of mechanical and design skills. Your methods, ideas, and expressions are likely to be based more on intuition, instincts, and imagination than on structured, fact-based analysis. You will succeed with neighbors and community activities or operating a neighborhood business—but, given the nature of Neptune, it may be difficult to say why. You can be a master of disguise and illusion and almost clairvoyant in knowing what others want to know and what they want to hear.

TRANSIT NEPTUNE TRINE NATAL VENUS

♆ △ ♀ There is no doubt that an application of charm, tact, and personal attractiveness will take you far these days. Oddly, even if you choose not to exhibit any of these qualities, others may perceive them in you. An aura of great spirituality, mystery, or glamor surrounds you and, though you may not be aware of it, others can be inspired and enraptured by you when transit Neptune trines your natal Venus. It may be difficult to discern exactly why or how your interactions and relationships work as well as they do. Good fortune is apt to smile upon your marriage, joint ventures, legal pursuits, contract negotiations, artistic and creative projects, and social events (especially if they are undertaken to benefit charitable foundations). At the highest level, your spiritual values and ideals are enhanced—and you may even prosper in some tangible way because of them.

TRANSIT NEPTUNE TRINE NATAL MARS

♆ △ ♂ When transit Neptune trines your natal Mars, you are encouraged to use spiritual and other inspirations as motivation for your physical efforts. Some of the most likely targets for success are your job or profession and activities that involve the ocean, marine equipment, sports and other competitive contests, dance, photography, footwear, charitable causes, the penal system, hospitals, magic and illusion, armed services, explosives, drugs, alcohol, and the design or manufacture of machinery, cars, and other motorized vehicles. Travel by water is stimulating, and physical therapy in water is especially effective. In spite of the luck that can accompany you, there are warnings that must be heeded. Avoid the tendency for physical laziness, lack of attention to details, the assumption that others will take care of things, and underestimation of danger in risk-taking activities.

TRANSIT NEPTUNE TRINE NATAL JUPITER

Ψ △ ♃ Your economic prospects, intellectual horizons, political ambitions, spiritual awareness, and cultural pursuits are likely to increase when transit Neptune trines your natal Jupiter. If you have any sort of personal flair for the dramatic, it will no doubt be accentuated. Extravagant gestures may be successful from one point of view, but, in some situations, they may later be the source of embarrassment or ultimately turn away those you have initially impressed. During this period, your father may prosper or he may be the source of increased inspiration in your life.

TRANSIT NEPTUNE TRINE NATAL SATURN

Ψ △ ♄ Your good fortune these days is likely to involve gaining recognition as well as material rewards for hard work and experience, past efforts, organization and planning. You may attain a position of seniority and authority. When transit Neptune trines your natal Saturn, you may not be aware of how you managed to succeed when others who worked as hard and deserve to do just as well do not achieve success. Some of the benefits that come along will be provided by those who are older. Others will be favorably impressed if you exhibit a strong preference for traditional thinking and ideals. Whether or not you actually believe in these ideals does not matter since transit Neptune requires only the illusion, not the reality.

TRANSIT NEPTUNE TRINE NATAL URANUS

Ψ △ ♅ A trine that occurs between transit Neptune and your natal Uranus is a fortunate dynamic and, as you can see in Table 35, you may experience it more than once in your lifetime. It is a harmonious com-bination of idealism and inspiration with such practical considerations as finances and technology. These elements create fortunate situations such as employment opportunities for minorities and the disadvantaged, increased schol-arships and endowments for the arts and sciences, or medical and technological breakthroughs. How much of this you actually experience on a personal level depends on the extent to which you are directly involved in these areas. Check Table 35 for the period when transit Neptune trined your natal Uranus and compare your experiences at that time with the circumstances that are described in the interpretation for this aspect.

Transit ♆	trines in years	Natal ♅	of those born in:	at age:
♆ ♌	1914–1928	♅ ♐	1897–1904	17–24
♆ ♍	1928–1943	♅ ♑	1904–1912	24–31
♆ ♎	1942–1957	♅ ♒	1912–1920	30–37
♆ ♏	1955–1970	♅ ♓	1919–1928	36–42
♆ ♐	1970–1984	♅ ♈	1927–1935	43–49
♆ ♑	1984–1998	♅ ♉	1934–1942	50–56
♆ ♒	1998–2012	♅ ♊	1941–1949	57–63
♆ ♏	1955–1970	♅ ♋	1948–1956	07–14
♆ ♓	2011–2026			63–70
♆ ♐	1970–1984	♅ ♌	1955–1962	15–22
♆ ♈	2025–2039			70–77
♆ ♑	1984–1998	♅ ♍	1961–1969	23–29
♆ ♉	2038–			77–
♆ ♒	1998–2012	♅ ♎	1968–1975	30–37
♆ ♓	2011–2026	♅ ♏	1974–1981	37–45
♆ ♈	2025–2039	♅ ♐	1981–1988	44–51

Table 35: Transit Neptune Trines to Natal Uranus

TRANSIT NEPTUNE TRINE NATAL NEPTUNE

♆ △ ♆ When transit Neptune forms a trine to your natal Neptune, you are in your mid-fifties. This is likely to be a generalized experience that either targets or is initiated for the most part by your generation. However, it is a positive energy and has the potential to allow your ideals to become a major force of inspiration in current circumstances.

TRANSIT NEPTUNE TRINE NATAL PLUTO

♆ △ ♇ If you have managed to gain a position of substantial power or control, you may experience some inspired understanding of how to use it to an even greater advantage when transit Neptune trines your natal Pluto. Societal conditions are conveniently suited to offer the means as well as reward the efforts to increase inner power and control. Apply this to circumstances experienced by you and those of other generations during the periods when transit Neptune trined natal Pluto. These periods are listed in Table 36.

Transit ♆	trines in years	Natal ♇	of those born in:	at age:
♆ ♌	1942–1957	♇ ♊	1882–1914	43–60
♆ ♒	1998–2012			116–98
♆ ♏	1995–1970	♇ ♋	1912–1939	31–43
♆ ♓	2011–2026			87–99
♆ ♐	1970–1984	♇ ♌	1937–1958	26–33
♆ ♈	2025–2039			81–88
♆ ♑	1984–1998	♇ ♍	1956–1972	26–28
♆ ♉	2038––			–82

Table 36: Transit Neptune Trines to Natal Pluto

NEPTUNE OPPOSITIONS

TRANSIT NEPTUNE OPPOSED NATAL SUN

♆ ☌ ☉ You may be unsure of how to satisfy your ego demands or where to direct your willpower. It is a period when your ambitions are not realized. You may succeed in other areas, but when transit Neptune opposes your natal Sun, your main goal or purposes are not attained, and they may be undermined or even disappear. It is possible that your goals were unrealistic or unattainable in the first place, but, even if this is true, you may not see it that way right now. There is a tendency for unrealistic expectations as to what you can accomplish, and you are vulnerable to false flattery or those who promise more than they can deliver. The best advice is to be as patient and philosophical as possible. You may, for instance, not be given the job or recognition you seek, but you may get another type of job or recognition that is acceptable for the time being. If you hold an administrative or other position of leadership, you must try to prevent or forestall situations that could undermine or erode your effectiveness as a leader. Avoid any potentially scandalous or dishonest people or situations that could damage your reputation.

TRANSIT NEPTUNE OPPOSED NATAL MOON

♆ ☌ ☽ Self-pity, guilt, and deception can become pervasive. Desires and needs may be undermined by physical indulgence and addictions. It is to be hoped that your maturity and common sense are sufficiently developed to have a positive influence on your behavior and attitudes during the confusing period when transit Neptune opposes your natal Moon. Your emotional life, domestic environment, family ties, and the children and women in your life are not favored. You may become inexplicably or unreasonably sensitive and moody. Emotional commitments are drained of enthusiasm and depth. You may become involved in secret emotional attachments. Your desires are not apt to be fulfilled these days, and if they are, they will not bring you the satisfaction and happiness you anticipated. After this influence has passed, you may emerge the stronger for experiencing the loss (or the threat of loss) of your emotional security and other desires. One potential of this period is the danger of water or gas leaks in your home. This is definitely an unfavorable time to purchase real estate, especially if it happens to be waterfront property. Your health is more vulnerable and you may experience food poisoning, food allergies, and either retention of water or dehydration. You are more susceptible to adverse reactions from anesthetics, drugs, and alcohol, and you may develop a variety of physical complaints that are difficult or impossible to diagnose.

TRANSIT NEPTUNE OPPOSED NATAL MERCURY

♆ ☍ ☿ The potential for misunderstanding and being misunderstood increases during this period, and the inability to organize your thoughts and ideas is endlessly frustrating as is trying to make sense of facts and figures. Accurate records of sales and other business transactions, or, for that matter, any type of records are vulnerable to error, deception, and loss. Ideas may be strange or fanatic when transit Neptune opposes your natal Mercury. Travel is often apt to be pointless, even when you begin a trip with definite goals or purposes in mind. This is not a favorable period in which to travel on or over water. Any type of network you have developed—friends, business associates, social contacts—may become increasingly elusive or even disappear. Education, specialized training, and the development and use of your basic skills may be a waste of time or unable to serve the purpose you had intended. Disintegration of your neighborhood or its goals may also occur. Determination, diligence, and keeping close to others who can be trusted to point out inaccuracies, mistakes, or delusions is necessary. Take precautions against pneumonia, pleurisy, edema, and possible injury to your hearing or other senses.

TRANSIT NEPTUNE OPPOSED NATAL VENUS

♆ ☍ ♀ You are going to have to cope with some very unclear and downright confusing situations in your relationship with a marriage partner or with any kind of partner or close ally. Interactions with other people in general are not likely to be any better. Deception, mistrust, and other undermining influences infiltrate attempts to resolve difficulties. Cooperation you promise to give as well as cooperation you seek is definitely on shaky ground since it may never materialize. Not everyone will fail to come through for you, but the potential is high for mix-ups, misconceptions, and deception when it comes to others. Care must be taken in all monetary matters since bankruptcy is a possibility. Common goals and values must be clearly defined. The pursuit of romance and other pleasures as well as the finer things in life may be marred by deception or false promises. Diplomatic and social gestures are empty or self-serving, and your social reputation and status are not likely to be advanced in any sort of healthy or meaningful way. Artistic skills as well as projects and activities in which you are involved are subject to strange circumstances, misunderstandings, confusion, and loss.

TRANSIT NEPTUNE OPPOSED NATAL MARS

♆ ☍ ♂ Physical efforts and activities have a disturbing way of being absolutely futile when transit Neptune opposes your natal Mars. Physical energy and strength are undermined by illness, laziness, or other debilitating factors. There is also potential for loss of your job for reasons you do not fully understand. Physical actions may be seriously flawed by unreasonable urges, so you must avoid becoming either the victim or the perpetrator of misguided ideals that inspire acts of aggression or revenge. Cars and other means of transportation, including boats, may give you trouble and develop mechanical problems no one seems able to identify or fix. This is a highly unfavorable time to be involved with risk-taking activities or to initiate hostile confrontations since you may not understand exactly what you are up against. Men with whom you have contact may be confused, and the circumstances surrounding your relationships and activities with men are vulnerable to scandal, mistrust, or deception. There is danger when traveling in or over water, when participating in water sports, and when handling poisonous materials. Headaches or fever that occur may be difficult to diagnose.

TRANSIT NEPTUNE OPPOSED NATAL JUPITER

♆ ☍ ♃ Your spiritual growth, intellectual endeavors, and economic prosperity are opposed by the undermining influences of deception, disorganization, and unrealistic expectations when transit Neptune opposes your natal Jupiter. How these potentially ruinous dynamics will emerge from your current circumstances will vary according to your age, maturity, and your personality and character. The point here is that you need courage, logic, and prudent wisdom to avoid the more serious consequences of overblown thinking and actions. This is a vulnerable time when you can become involved in or the victim of substance abuse, false promises, fanatical ideals, and deceptive advertising.

TRANSIT NEPTUNE OPPOSED NATAL SATURN

♆ ☍ ♄ The record of your hard work, the stability of your experience and mature judgment, and the strength of your authority are threatened by illegal actions, deception, bankruptcy, and unknown or disillusioned people when transit Neptune opposes your natal Saturn. It is possible that this same description can involve those who represent authority figures in your life. Circumstances during this period present severe challenges that test your ability or willingness to overcome inner fear and worry. Traditions and structures that have developed and guided you in the past can become ambiguous or misguided. Restrictions and limitations that were important threads in the fabric of your character and life-style may disappear. Be suspicious if your responsibilities are removed or appear to dissolve since nothing good is apt to take their place.

TRANSIT NEPTUNE OPPOSED NATAL URANUS

♆ ☍ ♅ Spirituality and idealism conflict with the freedom of thought, life-style, and societal institutions. The problem with this conflict is that there is not likely to be any motivation (or at least the right kind of motivation) to find a compromise, which makes the outcome impossible to predict. If you were born after 1920, check Table 37 for the period when transit Neptune opposed your natal Uranus and interpret this aspect as it was reflected in the circumstances you experienced at that time.

Transit ♆	opposes in years	Natal ♅	of those born in:	at age:
♆ ♋	1901–1915	♅ ♑	1904–1912	00–03
♆ ♌	1914–1928	♅ ♒	1912–1920	02–08
♆ ♍	1928–1943	♅ ♓	1919–1928	09–15
♆ ♎	1942–1957	♅ ♈	1927–1935	15–22
♆ ♏	1955–1970	♅ ♉	1934–1942	21–28
♆ ♐	1970–1984	♅ ♊	1941–1949	29–35
♆ ♑	1984–1998	♅ ♋	1948–1956	36–42
♆ ♒	1998–2012	♅ ♌	1955–1962	43–50
♆ ♓	2011–2026	♅ ♍	1961–1969	50–57
♆ ♈	2025–2039	♅ ♎	1968–1975	57–64
♆ ♉	2038–	♅ ♏	1974–1981	64–

Table 37: Transit Neptune Oppositions to Natal Uranus

TRANSIT NEPTUNE OPPOSED NATAL NEPTUNE

♆ ☌ ♆ An opposition between transit Neptune and your natal Neptune does not occur until you are past the age of eighty and it is apt to have little effect on you as an individual. Circumstances during this period pit the current ideals against the ideals of your generation. Only to the extent that you wish to get involved in this conflict-at-large are you likely to become upset by it, unless time and misfortune have placed you in a position where you become a victim of religious or racial persecution.

TRANSIT NEPTUNE OPPOSED NATAL PLUTO

♆ ☌ ♇ Power which includes natural resources as well as political and economic power is eroded by current trends in the thinking and ideals of current society when transit Neptune opposes your natal Pluto. How much effect this condition has on your personal life will depend on how closely you are associated with the power structures being threatened. Table 38 lists the periods when each generation born between 1882 and 1984 will or has experienced this aspect.

Transit ♆	opposes in years	Natal ♇	of those born in:	at age:
♆ ♐	1970–1984	♇ ♊	1882–1914	70–88
♆ ♑	1984–1998	♇ ♋	1912–1939	59–72
♆ ♒	1998–2012	♇ ♌	1937–1958	54–61
♆ ♓	2011–2026	♇ ♍	1956–1972	54–55
♆ ♈	2025–2039	♇ ♎	1971–1984	54–55

Table 38: Transit Neptune Oppositions to Natal Pluto

Chapter Ten

Transit Pluto Aspects to the Natal Planets

The transit of Pluto through the zodiac is 248 years. Its influence is strong and intense. Pluto has such an erratic orbit that it spends from over thirty years in some signs to about a dozen years in others.

PLUTO CONJUNCTIONS

TRANSIT PLUTO CONJOIN NATAL SUN

♇ ☌ ☉ When a conjunction occurs between transit Pluto and your natal Sun, you experience intense self-awareness and the urge to attain recognition as an individual with influence and power. Much, of course, depends on the strength and power you develop and exert before this period comes along. If you are already a determined, dominating, and independent person, your actions may become only a little more aggressive than usual. However, if you have not been able or willing to exert yourself, to take chances with your destiny, and to control the people and situations in your life, the independent actions you take now may be quite courageous. One potential of your present circumstances is that they will force or motivate you to make a new start or transform your life-style. There is no guarantee that you will succeed when you strike out on your own, but it may not matter because you cannot escape the need to do whatever it takes to gain more control over yourself and what happens to you. The past will have much influence on the present, especially if you have allowed others to take control of your life to escape the responsibility of doing so yourself. Although your emotional life provides some motivation for what you do, your ego is the real focus and driving force. If, for example, a relationship comes apart at this time, it may not be due to the lack of love or affection, but because your ego was not allowed to grow or exert itself within the relationship. You believe that you and you alone must solve your own problems. In turn, this makes it difficult or impossible for you to accept help or even consolation from others. You retreat inwardly, becoming more and more isolated. You cannot hide from your inner self—who you are, what you have become, and, most of all, what you want to become. Your pride can take a severe beating and you become intimately acquainted with fear and self-recrimination. Whatever happens, you will emerge a changed person—stronger, more determined and independent.

TRANSIT PLUTO CONJOIN NATAL MOON

♇ ☌ ☽ Emotional transition is the primary focus when transit Pluto conjoins your natal Moon. The reflections of and reactions to family relationships, childhood conditioning, and upbringing in which you engage are on deeper levels than you have wanted or been able to reach in the past. If there has been emotional trauma or abuse, it must now be confronted, understood, and put to rest. Your mother (or other strong female figure) has profound influence, though it cannot be said whether her influence will be positive, negative, or perhaps both. All emotional attachments intensify. Physical aspects of your home and domestic environment may be transformed, possibly as a result of emotional changes that take place. Although you may undergo intense turmoil, the potential rewards include emotional strength and fulfillment. There can be devastating consequences during this period if you attempt to emotionally manipulate others or allow others (especially females) to manipulate or control you. This is such an overpowering emotional time that pursuing your desires may outweigh everything else. Being so powerfully motivated can lead to impressive achievements, but if you become too recklessly determined to fulfill a desire, you may lose everything else. The urge to develop your psychic powers may occur, but even if you are not inclined toward the occult, your basic instincts and intuition will no doubt become exceptionally keen.

TRANSIT PLUTO CONJOIN NATAL MERCURY

♇ ☌ ☿ Greater personal power and control are achieved through knowledge, and especially the understanding you gain about yourself as well as others during this period. Thoughts, ideas, and self-expression become more intense and focused as your intellectual awareness deepens. When transit Pluto conjoins your natal Mercury, you gain increased ability to recognize the hidden meanings and motivations behind your own words and the words of others and to separate what is important from what is not. Previous concepts and methods are altered as you become more concerned with what is efficient and relevant. Your interest and activities may involve investigation, research, development of ideas, psychological analysis, or occult studies. Circumstances may increase your influence within the community, and there may be more intense or karmic links with neighbors and siblings.

TRANSIT PLUTO CONJOIN NATAL VENUS

♇ ☌ ♀ Romantic attachments tend to be consuming, and even if you are happily married or already involved with a romantic partner, it would not be unusual to become attracted to someone else. When transit Pluto conjoins your natal Venus, you may find your true soul mate. It is a time when you may establish extremely powerful, karmic partnerships (business or marriage) and other close relationships. Circumstances and experiences cause you to seek greater personal influence and power in and through your interactions with others. You may come to view partnerships, romantic attachments, female relationships, and social contacts as means to enhance your personal status. If a self-serving approach is your only motivation for seeking a relationship during this period, it can have ruinous consequences. You cannot hope to get away with idle flattery and should be aware of the possibility that the reverse may occur and you become too aroused by the words and gestures of those whose only intention is to flatter you. Pleasure and the good life can become desires to be indulged at any cost. The nature of circumstances may be such that you are starkly confronted by your values, principles, and priorities. Joint ventures, negotiations, and attempts to gain the cooperation of others can become intense and involve a power struggle.

TRANSIT PLUTO CONJOIN NATAL MARS

♇ ☌ ♂ You consciously or subconsciously seek greater control over your physical energy and efforts, and, as a result, you become more focused when transit Pluto conjoins your natal Mars. There is no guarantee that a particular direction or channel for your efforts will automatically come along; there is only a heightened potential that the interests you already have or develop will be pursued with greater physical stamina and determination. It is difficult to turn away from what you are intent on doing, which may not be harmful if you have a constructive purpose in mind, but such a single-minded approach can be dangerous if revenge or anger is the driving force. Successful or not, more intense, competitive, and aggressive physical actions and activities characterize this period. Physical passions are potent and some discretion may be necessary to avoid misguided or unhealthy sexual involvements. Physical tasks and other activities these days may involve secrecy, renovation, conservation, physical analysis, research and development. Associations with men are more intense and competitive and, in some cases, of a karmic nature.

TRANSIT PLUTO CONJOIN NATAL JUPITER

♇ ☌ ♃ Intellectual endeavors, spiritual growth, political ambitions, and economic expansion may or may not succeed, but they are the likely areas through which you seek to attain greater power and influence. If you or your family has suffered loss of status and been forced to begin again, circumstances offer the possibility of regaining what was lost. Your father or his influence may have a subtle and significant karmic role in what happens at this time. Although you may extend your sphere of influence, taking yourself too seriously or exaggerating your own importance will backfire since this period demands total honesty. If you become involved with ideas and activities concerning social or religious reform, you must remain alert to the danger of intolerance and fanaticism.

TRANSIT PLUTO CONJOIN NATAL SATURN

♇ ☌ ♄ The past becomes significantly important to the present when transit Pluto conjoins your natal Saturn. The structures and traditions upon which your work and life-style are based may be significantly altered or even completely transformed by current circumstances. If you have been unable or unwilling to accept responsibilities or to work hard for what you wanted, you will learn the importance of such efforts. If you have refused to accept the necessary restrictions and limitations that were necessary for progress to be made, this is a time when you regret your resistance and you must correct your attitude. Self-discipline plays a major role. Abuse of authority is confronted and corrected. Ambitions must be tempered with patience and control.

TRANSIT PLUTO CONJOIN NATAL URANUS

♇ ☌ ♅ When transit Pluto conjoins your natal Uranus, your life is affected by technological advances and issues related to individual freedom. The power of government is made to yield to the people for whom it was created. Much depends on the age at which you experience this aspect, but your life will in some way be affected by changes that occur in the status of federal jobs or federal programs. Table 39 shows transit Pluto beginning in Virgo in 1956–1972 and ending in Pisces in 2043. No one born in this century before 1961 experienced this aspect. The 1961–1969 generation was born when the conjunction was made in Virgo between transiting Pluto and transiting Uranus. Note that after 1969, subsequent generations experience the aspect at increasingly advanced ages.

Transit ♇	conjuncts in years	Natal ♅	of those born in:	at age:
♇ ♍	1956–1972	♅ ♍	1961-1969	00–03
♇ ♎	1971–1984	♅ ♎	1968–1975	03–09
♇ ♏	1983–1995	♅ ♏	1974–1981	09–14
♇ ♐	1995–2008	♅ ♐	1981–1988	14–20
♇ ♑	2008–2024	♅ ♑	1988–1996	20–28
♇ ♒	2023–2044	♅ ♒	1995–2003	28–41
♇ ♓	2043–	♅ ♓	2003–2011	40–

Table 39: Transit Pluto Conjunctions to Natal Uranus

TRANSIT PLUTO CONJOIN NATAL NEPTUNE

♇ ☌ ♆ Circumstances bring political, economic, and even physical power struggles, but essentially they are struggles for spiritual control and ideals. For example, abortion, mercy killing, genetic engineering, and civil rights become religious and moral issues rather than economic or technical considerations. When transit Pluto conjoins your natal Neptune, power can become an illusion or it can slowly become eroded by undermining forces that go undetected. Table 40 lists the transits of Pluto between its period in Gemini from 1882–1914 until it enters Pisces in 2043. The first generation in this century (1887–1902) was born when the actual conjunction was made between transit Pluto and transit Neptune in Gemini so those people had this aspect in their natal charts. Study the conditions in society when your generation experienced this aspect.

Transit ♇	conjuncts in years	Natal ♆	of those born in:	at age:
♇ ♊	1882–1914	♆ ♊	1887–1902	00–12
♇ ♋	1912–1939	♆ ♋	1901–1915	11–24
♇ ♌	1937–1958	♆ ♌	1914–1928	23–30
♇ ♍	1956–1972	♆ ♍	1928–1943	28–29
♇ ♎	1971–1984	♆ ♎	1942–1957	27–29
♇ ♏	1983–1995	♆ ♏	1955–1970	25–28
♇ ♐	1995–2008	♆ ♐	1970–1984	24–25
♇ ♑	2008–2024	♆ ♑	1984–1998	24–26
♇ ♒	2023–2044	♆ ♒	1988–2012	25–32
♇ ♓	2043–	♆ ♓	2011–2026	32–

Table 40: Transit Pluto Conjunctions to Natal Neptune

TRANSIT PLUTO CONJOIN NATAL PLUTO

♇ ☌ ♇ Transit Pluto will not conjoin your natal Pluto in your lifetime since Pluto takes 248 years to complete its journey through the twelve signs of the zodiac.

PLUTO SEXTILES

TRANSIT PLUTO SEXTILE NATAL SUN

♇ ⚹ ☉ The planetary dynamics during this period are not strong enough to cause much change unless they are supplemented by other factors that encourage their energy and particular focus. When transit Pluto sextiles your natal Sun, the potential circumstances are associated with an opportunity to gain power or control, to revitalize something that has been lost, or to make a new start. The particular focus is your ego and situations that lead to attaining a more powerful status, a position of leadership, enhanced professional reputation, and recognition for your generosity, integrity, and individuality. Opportunities may also lead to resolving (or getting out of) relationships and situations where your ego cannot grow or is being stifled, and they may bring a chance to strike out on your own. It is up to you to be on the lookout for such possibilities and to take advantage of them.

TRANSIT PLUTO SEXTILE NATAL MOON

♇ ⚹ ☽ A sextile that occurs between transit Pluto and your natal Moon represents opportunity related to your emotional life and to situations that may eventually lead to the attainment of desires or a higher level of emotional satisfaction. Opportunities can bring about more satisfactory family relationships, a change for the better in your domestic environment, improvement in a family business, and a chance to sell or restore homes and domestic items. You may find a better diet or other ways to improve your health. Circumstances may lead to a better understanding of your childhood conditioning and to better relationships with your mother, other important female figures, and children.

TRANSIT PLUTO SEXTILE NATAL MERCURY

♇ ⚹ ☿ Current conditions bring opportunities that involve education, psychology, research, communications, writing, computers, travel, transportation, sales and other business transactions, community affairs, and contacts with siblings. When transit Pluto sextiles your natal Mercury, you may also encounter situations that bring a chance to develop and make advantageous use of ideas, methods, and basic mechanical or design skills.

TRANSIT PLUTO SEXTILE NATAL VENUS

During the period that transit Pluto sextiles your natal Venus, the potential of your circumstances includes opportunities related to partnership (business or marriage) and other alliances, romantic attachments, female relationships, your ability to cooperate and interact with others, legal matters, and joint ventures. There is no guarantee that luck will come from out of the blue and dramatically change your life, but if you are willing to press forward when something does come along, you will ultimately reap some benefit.

TRANSIT PLUTO SEXTILE NATAL MARS

The energy of circumstances when a sextile occurs between transit Pluto and your natal Mars is favorable. As with its sextile to natal Sun, Pluto's sextile to natal Mars represents an opportunity to gain power or control, to revitalize something that has been lost, or to make a new start, but, in this case, its focus is related to your job or work, to physical activities, and to male relationships. Circumstances require physical action and they may bring the chance you have been waiting for to take such action.

TRANSIT PLUTO SEXTILE NATAL JUPITER

The favorable circumstances at this time may bring increased optimism and inspiration. Since great luck is not apt to jump into your lap without some help, you have to put yourself in situations that could engender a more optimistic outlook or provide new sources of inspiration. When transit Pluto sextiles your natal Jupiter, you may find the opportunity to increase your stature through participation in sports and religious, political, or cultural activities. The opportunity you need may also involve higher education or be related to your father.

TRANSIT PLUTO SEXTILE NATAL SATURN

Opportunity is made possible during this period as a result of your maturity and experience, recognition of your authority, hard work, sacrifice, and the traditions and structures that support your life-style. If you have not managed to become industrious and hardworking by the time tran-sit Pluto sextiles your natal Saturn, circumstances may provide the chance for you to change your habits.

TRANSIT PLUTO SEXTILE NATAL URANUS

♇ ⚹ ♅ Changes that occur in society when transit Pluto sextiles your natal Uranus involve political, social, and economic structures and institutions that may present you with a beneficial opportunity you might not otherwise have had. Note in Table 41 that the age at which this aspect occurs is different for the various generations. Many members of the generation born between 1934–1942 with natal Uranus in Taurus, for example, are not likely to experience this aspect at all. The 1941–1949 generation with natal Uranus in Gemini was born as the sextile was made between transit Uranus and transit Pluto, which means they have this aspect in their natal chart. Subsequent generations experience this aspect at increasingly advanced ages. The circum-stances associated with this aspect are of historic interest and it is worthwhile reviewing what political or financial conditions in society occurred.

Transit ♇	sextiles in years	Natal ♅	of those born in:	at age:
♇ ♎	1971–1984	♅ ♐	1897–1904	74–80
♇ ♏	1983–1995	♅ ♑	1904–1912	79–83
♇ ♐	1995–2008	♅ ♒	1912–1920	83–88
♇ ♑	2008–2024	♅ ♓	1919–1928	89–96
♇ ♒	2023–2044	♅ ♈	1927–1935	96–109
♇ ♓	2043–	♅ ♉	1934–1942	109–
♇ ♌	1937–1958	♅ ♊	1941–1949	00–09
♇ ♍	1956–1972	♅ ♋	1948–1956	08–16
♇ ♎	1971–1984	♅ ♌	1955–1962	16–22
♇ ♏	1983–1995	♅ ♍	1961–1969	22–26
♇ ♐	1995–2008	♅ ♎	1968–1975	27–33
♇ ♑	2008–2024	♅ ♏	1974–1981	34–43
♇ ♒	2023–2044	♅ ♐	1981–1988	42–56
♇ ♓	2043–	♅ ♑	1988–1996	55–

Table 41: Transit Pluto Sextiles to Natal Uranus

TRANSIT PLUTO SEXTILE NATAL NEPTUNE

♇ ⚹ ♆   When transit Pluto sextiles your natal Neptune (see Table 42), the energy is favorable and is associated with engendering circumstances that lead to the expression and development of positive ideals and spiritual aspirations in society. These sentiments are likely to benefit your generation as a whole rather than have a dramatic impact on you as an individual. However, being aware of the positive nature of this period may inspire you to find a way to use it on a personal level.

Transit ♇	sextiles in years	Natal ♆	of those born in:	at age:
♇ ♌	1937–1958	♆ ♊	1887–1902	50–56
♇ ♍	1956–1972	♆ ♋	1901–1915	55–57
♇ ♎	1971–1984	♆ ♌	1914–1928	56–57
♇ ♏	1983–1995	♆ ♍	1928–1943	52–55
♇ ♐	1995–2008	♆ ♎	1942–1957	51–53
♇ ♑	2008–2024	♆ ♏	1955–1970	53–54
♇ ♒	2023–2044	♆ ♐	1970–1984	53–60
♇ ♓	2043–	♆ ♑	1984–1998	59–

Table 42: Transit Pluto Sextiles to Natal Neptune

TRANSIT PLUTO SEXTILE NATAL PLUTO

♇ ⚹ ♇   Your generation is apt to be the beneficiary of a change in the power structure in society. When transit Pluto sextiles your natal Pluto, advances enable you to make better use of available resources or gain control of resources. Although it is instructive to make historical comparisons between different generations as they experience this aspect, it cannot be said with any certainty that when it occurs, you will be influenced on a personal level by the opportunistic circumstances associated with it. Table 43 shows the transits of Pluto between 1937 and 2024.

Transit ♇	sextiles in years	Natal ♇	of those born in:	at age:
♇ ♌	1937–1958	♇ ♊	1882–1914	44–55
♇ ♍	1956–1972	♇ ♋	1912–1939	33–44
♇ ♎	1971–1984	♇ ♌	1937–1958	26–34
♇ ♏	1983–1995	♇ ♍	1956–1972	23–27
♇ ♐	1995–2008	♇ ♎	1971–1984	24–24
♇ ♑	2008–2024	♇ ♏	1983–1995	25–29

Table 43: Transit Pluto Sextiles to Natal Pluto

PLUTO SQUARES

TRANSIT PLUTO SQUARE NATAL SUN

♇ □ ☉ Circumstances bring difficult but not insurmountable situations, the nature of which involves overcoming those with more power and influence or having to deal with the threatened loss of your own influence or power. Those who once provided the power structure and resources you need may no longer be available. As transit Pluto squares your natal Sun, much strength and other benefits are gained, but not without frustrations or setbacks that test your determination and inner drive, humble your egotistical attitudes and ambitions, and challenge your integrity and generosity.

TRANSIT PLUTO SQUARE NATAL MOON

♇ □ ☽ Obstacles you encounter when transit Pluto squares your natal Moon are likely to involve compulsions and obsessions, the negative influence of a strong female figure, or negative attitudes and behavior caused by childhood conditioning. This is a period when your ability to overcome depression or disappointment will be tested, as well as your determination to fulfill your desires and make your dreams come true. Emotional commitments, family relationships, and your home or domestic environment are surrounded by intense energy that requires deeper understanding and greater attention on your part. The general state of your health and physical fitness can be greatly affected by your emotional outlook at this time.

TRANSIT PLUTO SQUARE NATAL MERCURY

♇ □ ☿ You must be willing to change previous concepts, adopt better ways to express yourself, find more efficient methods of getting things done, and increase your ability to separate what is important from what is not when transit Pluto squares your natal Mercury. As always when Pluto is involved, there is an element of control in circumstances you encounter. Overcoming obstacles or obtaining your goals is a matter of learning to be more observant, control your responses, express yourself in precise terms, and perfect your mechanical skills. This is not an altogether harmful period and it may provide circumstances that prompt you to increase your ability and determination to succeed, especially in such areas as education, writing, communications, travel, transportation, computers, sales and other business transactions, community affairs, and contacts with siblings.

TRANSIT PLUTO SQUARE NATAL VENUS

♇ □ ♀ Your principles, priorities, or values are important issues as well as potential obstacles when transit Pluto squares your natal Venus. You may be confronted with past actions and attitudes that result from embracing the wrong values, especially in areas that relate to partnerships (business or marriage) and other alliances, romantic attachments, female relationships, legal matters, and your ability to interact effectively with others. What is the nature of the positive potential? It is taking advantage of situations that enable you to distinguish between gaining control through destructive manipulation and achieving it through true cooperation and commitment to common goals.

TRANSIT PLUTO SQUARE NATAL MARS

♇ □ ♂ Obstacles that stand in your way at this time may be the result of wrongful physical actions. If you physically abuse others or yourself, this must be corrected. If you engage in dishonest actions, they, too, must be corrected. The waste of time or energy is going to cause some problems when transit Pluto squares your natal Mars. Circumstances require that methods you use must be more efficient. Your competitive spirit and aggressiveness increase, which can mean physical struggles of one sort or another and the possibility of unpleasant confrontations in male relationships or in your contacts and activities that involve men. Increased competitiveness can be a good thing if it helps you to accomplish some worthwhile goal you might not otherwise have tackled.

TRANSIT PLUTO SQUARE NATAL JUPITER

♇ □ ♃ Taking yourself too seriously or exaggerating your own importance will be squelched by those with more power and influence. When transit Pluto squares your natal Jupiter, your father or his influence and status can represent obstacles that must be overcome. The biggest frustrations you encounter are apt to be in areas such as higher education, politics, advertising, publishing, drama, diplomacy, religion, cultural pursuits and projects, or philanthropy and endowment.

TRANSIT PLUTO SQUARE NATAL SATURN

♇ □ ♄ The abuse of your authority or position of control will be troublesome and prevent you from obtaining your present goals. If restrictions or heavy burdens are placed upon you when transit Pluto squares your natal Saturn, you may have only yourself to blame. If you have done nothing to deserve these burdens, you will still have to accept the responsibility. You cannot hide your long-range ambitions because they will emerge from the circumstances surrounding you, and, unless your goals are almost saintly in nature, you can expect to be severely criticized. Obstacles challenge your right to the rewards of age and experience, hard work, and sacrifice.

TRANSIT PLUTO SQUARE NATAL URANUS

♇ □ ♅ When transit Pluto squares your natal Uranus (see Table 44 on the next page), political and economic structures and institutions are under fire from those with power who threaten to restrict or withhold resources that are needed for those institutions to function. These threats exist, but they will not necessarily be carried out. The fact that Pluto squares two different generations as it transits a sign is worthy of study. For example, did circumstances associated with transit Pluto in Virgo (1956–1972) cause the

1897–1904 generation to initiate changes felt by the 1941–1949 generation? Do the changes initiated by the older generation cause problems that compel the younger generation to find solutions? Or, are these two generations linked in some other way? Students of history as well as astrology find this an intriguing possibility, although by no means the only one.

Transit ♇	squares in years	Natal ♅	of those born in:	at age:
♇ ♍	1956–1972	♅ ♐	1897–1904	59–68
		♅ ♊	1941–1949	15–23
♇ ♎	1971–1984	♅ ♑	1904–1912	67–72
		♅ ♋	1948–1956	23–28
♇ ♏	1983–1995	♅ ♒	1912–1920	71–75
		♅ ♌	1955–1962	28–33
♇ ♐	1995–2008	♅ ♓	1919–1928	76–80
		♅ ♍	1961–1969	34–39
♇ ♑	2008–2024	♅ ♈	1927–1935	81–89
		♅ ♎	1968–1975	40–49
♇ ♒	2023–2044	♅ ♉	1934–1942	89–102
		♅ ♏	1974–1981	49–63
♇ ♓	2043–	♅ ♊	1941–1949	102–
		♅ ♐	1981–1988	62–

Table 44: Transit Pluto Squares to Natal Uranus

TRANSIT PLUTO SQUARE NATAL NEPTUNE

♇ □ ♆ When transit Pluto squares your natal Neptune, a dynamic is set up that is similar to the one that occurs when transit Pluto squares your natal Uranus. Changes or restrictions that involve economic and political power and the conservation and distribution of resources are at odds with ideals and spiritual goals. Table 45 lists the transits of Pluto beginning with Virgo in 1956 through Pisces in 2043. The generations born since the turn of the century have all been or will be in their mid- to late '60's when this aspect occurs. The first generation with natal Neptune in Gemini (1887–1902) was the first to experience the square from Pluto as it transited Virgo (1956–1972).

The first worldwide awareness of resources and the fragile ecosystem began in the early '70's and has grown in strength and scope since that time. Subsequent Neptune generations will continue to feel the pressure to do something about the world's environment when transit Pluto squares their natal Neptune.

Transit ♇	squares in years	Natal ♆	of those born in:	at age:
♇ ♍	1956–1972	♆ ♊	1887–1902	69–70
♇ ♎	1971–1984	♆ ♋	1901–1915	69–70
♇ ♏	1983–1995	♆ ♌	1914–1928	67–69
♇ ♐	1995–2008	♆ ♍	1928–1943	65–67
♇ ♑	2008–2024	♆ ♎	1942–1957	66–67
♇ ♒	2023–2044	♆ ♏	1955–1970	68–74
♇ ♓	2043–	♆ ♐	1970–1984	73–

Table 45: Transit Pluto Squares to Natal Neptune

TRANSIT PLUTO SQUARE NATAL PLUTO

♇ □ ♇ When transit Pluto squares your natal Pluto, circumstances present problems that involve the nature or source of power. Some generations may be forced to deal with political power and its abuse. Others may deal with issues involving physical power (atomic energy) and natural resources. Note the

Transit ♇	squares in years	Natal ♇	of those born in:	at age:
♇ ♍	1956–1972	♇ ♊	1882–1914	58–74
♇ ♎	1971–1984	♇ ♋	1912–1939	45–59
♇ ♏	1983–1995	♇ ♌	1937–1958	37–46
♇ ♐	1995–2008	♇ ♍	1956–1972	36–39
♇ ♑	2008–2024	♇ ♎	1971–1984	37–40
♇ ♒	2023–2044	♇ ♏	1983–1995	40–49
♇ ♓	2043–	♇ ♐	1995–2008	48–

Table 46: Transit Pluto Squares to Natal Pluto

generations in Table 46 and study the power struggles or struggles over power that occurred when the various generations experienced Pluto square their natal Pluto.

PLUTO TRINES

TRANSIT PLUTO TRINE NATAL SUN

♇ △ ☉ This is an excellent period for advancement and a time for you to seek a more powerful, dynamic image. At hand are the means to accomplish these goals. Those who can provide for you or help you advance are also favored, and their increased prospects may generate the means to improve your own. A trine between transit Pluto and your natal Sun indicates you should not have to work hard to acquire success and the favor of others; but beyond having the means and opportunity, you must be motivated to take advantage of your resources. The trine can make current circumstances so comfortable that you may not feel any pressure or need to exploit your easy options. You may, of course, be at an age when such advantageous circumstances have little meaning. Just as important as immediate victories or good fortune, current circumstances can play a significant role in giving you the power or influence to maintain or regain success in the future.

TRANSIT PLUTO TRINE NATAL MOON

♇ △ ☽ If you want to attract the affections of others, you are favored to succeed when transit Pluto trines your natal Moon. Your emotional life can definitely improve, but how much or by what means depends on your particular circumstances. If you are married, for example, you may be tempted to get involved with someone other than your spouse. If you are not married, this is a time when you should make an effort to find your true soul mate since Pluto's involvement implies a karmic connection in your emotional commitments. While you have advantageous circumstances in your favor, focus your efforts on home and family, relationships that provide emotional security and support, beginning a family business, developing creative talents, or providing yourself with better nutrition and health practices. During this period, your mother or a strong female figure as well as children in your life are favored, and they may be the means of your good fortune.

TRANSIT PLUTO TRINE NATAL MERCURY

♇ △ ☿ Current circumstances are favorable, especially those related to the development or use of your ideas, methods, and basic mechanical skills. It is a positive period for education, writing, computers, communications, travel, transportation, sales and other business transactions, and community affairs. Available advantages may come from almost anywhere. Achieving the maximum benefits when transit Pluto trines your natal Mercury depends largely on your willingness to understand and participate in what is happening around you and on your motivation to succeed. Significant progress will occur if you make good choices in the appropriate areas and set about achieving your goals with a definite plan and purpose. Your siblings, your neighbors, and those with whom you work or deal on a daily basis are favored, and their fortunate prospects may prove to be the means by which you can improve your own. Do not overlook the benefits of the more subtle karmic influence that the people and circumstances that come along during this period can have on your perceptions and understanding.

TRANSIT PLUTO TRINE NATAL VENUS

♇ △ ♀ Commitment to solid values and high principles works to your great benefit in the current circumstances. There are other positive potentials depending on you and what you want to achieve. Would you like more cooperation from others? You can get it. Do you want more equality in your partnerships? You can have it. Do you want to achieve a more powerful social status? You can. The depth of friendships, partnerships, and interactions with others becomes much deeper. When transit Pluto trines your natal Venus, your romantic partner, spouse, and female friends are favored—and it may be through them or because of them that you benefit. There is much you can achieve through personal magnetism. Even if you never thought of yourself as possessing such appeal, you may nevertheless exhibit it now. The situations you encounter or the interests you pursue may be responsible for making you more interesting and attractive as an individual. The potential is high for success in joint ventures, legal matters, public relations, and counseling.

TRANSIT PLUTO TRINE NATAL MARS

♇ △ ♂ This is an excellent period to increase physical strength and stamina. The trine implies fortunate circumstances, but ease and comfort do not present a challenge, and, without a challenge, there is no need or motivation to act. The focus is on physical actions and activities, which means that work, physical fitness, and athletic endeavors are likely to succeed when transit Pluto trines your natal Mars. It is a favorable time for work that involves recycling or renovation. Methods you use become more efficient as well as effective. This is the time to turn ideas into physical realities and develop or use your mechanical skills. Your actions can have favorable implications for the future as well as the present. Male relationships and contacts with men take on new meaning and depth, and it is likely to be a male that is responsible for benefits that come your way. Should there be physical confrontations, the result of the battles will be in your favor.

TRANSIT PLUTO TRINE NATAL JUPITER

♇ △ ♃ What you should concentrate on right now is broadening your intellectual horizons, gaining new experiences, increasing your spirituality, and enhancing your cultural appreciation. This is a period to enlarge your outlook, to reach beyond your immediate environment in order to gain greater understanding of the world at large. When a trine is formed between transit Pluto and your natal Jupiter, circumstances favor advancement in your profession, political goals, advertising, writing, publishing, drama, diplomacy, philanthropy and endowment. Your father and his status is favored or he may be the contributing factor in whatever benefits come to you.

TRANSIT PLUTO TRINE NATAL SATURN

♇ △ ♄ Seniority, the rewards of hard work and sacrifice, and established traditions are the focus of as well as the favored areas when transit Pluto trines your natal Saturn. If ever there was a period in which benefit is gained by heeding the lessons you have learned from the past, this is it. The long-term positive effects of your willingness to accept responsibilities and overcome restrictions will be evident in the situations you encounter, and engaging in these activities now has positive implications for the future.

TRANSIT PLUTO TRINE NATAL URANUS

♇ △ ♅ The energy when transit Pluto trines your natal Uranus is positive. Changes that occur are related to political, intellectual, and physical power, and these changes are highly beneficial to your generation. As with other aspects between transit Pluto and natal Uranus, it is worth noting that the natal Uranus of individuals born in two different generations are trined by Pluto as it transits a sign (see Table 47). This brings up the intriguing possibility that the older generation's reaction to the circumstances associated with transit Pluto's aspect may benefit the younger generation. Is there some beneficial continuity between generations that experience Pluto's trine at the same time? Asking questions that involve such historical implications is the appropriate way to study Pluto and the other outer planets.

Transit ♇	trines in years	Natal ♅	of those born in:	at age:
♇ ♍	1956–1972	♅ ♑	1904–1912	52–60
		♅ ♉	1934–1942	22–30
♇ ♎	1971–1984	♅ ♒	1912–1920	59–64
		♅ ♊	1941–1949	30–35
♇ ♏	1983–1995	♅ ♓	1919–1928	64–67
		♅ ♋	1948–1956	35–39
♇ ♐	1995–2008	♅ ♈	1927–1935	68–73
		♅ ♌	1955–1962	40–46
♇ ♑	2008–2024	♅ ♉	1934–1942	74–82
		♅ ♍	1961–1969	47–55
♇ ♒	2023–2044	♅ ♊	1941–1949	82–95
		♅ ♎	1968–1975	55–69
♇ ♓	2043–	♅ ♋	1948–1956	95–
		♅ ♏	1974–1981	69–

Table 47: Transit Pluto Trines to Natal Uranus

TRANSIT PLUTO TRINE NATAL NEPTUNE

♇ △ ♆ As you can see in Table 48, most people experience this aspect when they are quite elderly, but there are benefits to be gained when transit Pluto trines your natal Neptune. The positive nature of the circumstances should, most likely, be attributed to societal institutions that provide a measure of happiness and comfort that conforms to the ideals and spiritual aspirations of your generation.

Transit ♇	trines in years	Natal ♆	of those born in:	at age:
♇ ♊	1882–1914	♆ ♒	1834–1848	48–66
♇ ♋	1912–1939	♆ ♓	1848–1862	64–77
♇ ♌	1937–1958	♆ ♈	1861–1875	76–83
♇ ♍	1956–1972	♆ ♉	1874–1889	82–83
♇ ♎	1971–1984	♆ ♊	1887–1902	82–84
♇ ♏	1983–1995	♆ ♋	1901–1915	80–82
♇ ♐	1995–2008	♆ ♌	1914–1928	80–81
♇ ♑	2008–2024	♆ ♍	1928–1943	80–81
♇ ♒	2023–2044	♆ ♎	1942–1957	81–87
♇ ♓	2043–	♆ ♏	1955–1970	88–

Table 48: Transit Pluto Trines to Natal Neptune

TRANSIT PLUTO TRINE NATAL PLUTO

♇ △ ♇ The fortunate circumstances that come along when transit Pluto trines your natal Pluto grant more power and resources to that which has already been established or is being maintained by members of your generation. Table 49 shows that the generations born during the last of the 19th century and all of this century have or will experience this aspect past the age of fifty. Check this table to see when your generation was affected and compare your circumstances to what has been described for this aspect.

Transit ♇	trines in years	Natal ♇	of those born in:	at age:
♇ ♍	1956–1972	♇ ♉	1851–1884	85–105
♇ ♎	1971–1984	♇ ♊	1882–1914	70–89
♇ ♏	1983–1995	♇ ♋	1912–1939	56–71
♇ ♐	1995–2008	♇ ♌	1937–1958	50–58
♇ ♑	2008–2024	♇ ♍	1956–1972	52–52
♇ ♒	2023–2044	♇ ♎	1971–1984	52–60
♇ ♓	2043–	♇ ♏	1983–1995	60–

Table 49: Transit Pluto Trines to Natal Pluto

PLUTO OPPOSITIONS

TRANSIT PLUTO OPPOSED NATAL SUN

♇ ☍ ☉ This is an unfavorable period in which the circumstances may be described as a struggle between opposing forces, a contest of wills, and no-compromise situations. Manipulation of an unhealthy nature plays a prominent role when transit Pluto opposes your natal Sun, and anything gained by such tactics is likely to be at the expense of losing something far more valuable. Intense self-awareness develops and relentlessly pressures you to seek recognition of your individuality and worth; when such recognition does not occur, your self-image can degenerate into one of impotency and self-denigration. A bruised and defeated ego may cause you to retreat inwardly, becoming more and more isolated. The worst part is that you will not succeed in removing the negative situations, so save your struggle and strategies for the time being. Even if your determination is compulsive and your actions are ruthless, in the end you may not have the power or resources necessary to succeed. The most positive approach is to find a constructive way to work around situations that threaten your ego. If you are normally of a mild and easygoing disposition, this is a time to simply refuse to be a victim of those who would manipulate or oppose you. If, on the other hand, you possess a strong and manipulative nature, do not be tempted to abuse your power or influence.

TRANSIT PLUTO OPPOSED NATAL MOON

♇ ☍ ☽ Vigorously pursuing unreasonable desires is foolhardy since this is a period when you are likely to intimately and regrettably come to understand exactly what is meant by the phrase, "be careful what you wish for." When transit Pluto opposes your natal Moon, it will serve you well to remember that nothing stays the same forever. Emotional manipulation, trauma, or abuse are potentials with which you may be confronted. The struggles or strife you experience relates to family relationships, your childhood and upbringing, and control of your feelings. Retribution occurs if your attempts to achieve emotional satisfaction or control were unsavory. Your children and your mother or another strong female in your life are not favored at this time and their difficulties may either cause or be part of your own discomforts. It is possible that your domestic environment will be significantly affected. Because of constant struggles, there is not much emotional satisfaction in the development or use of your creative talents, establishing a home or family, starting a family enterprise, or engaging in anything but the simplest, common sense nutritional and health practices. In spite of the implied severity of your circumstances, believing or behaving as though your very life is in jeopardy does nothing to improve your prospects. Take a positive attitude and any actions necessary to hold on to whatever and whomever is important. Act with wisdom and caution in all situations, even if it means taking no action.

TRANSIT PLUTO OPPOSED NATAL MERCURY

♇ ☍ ☿ Mental manipulation is a strong potential when transit Pluto opposes your natal Mercury. Another strong possibility is that self-expression, thoughts, and ideas are more intense and serious and they may become obsessed and troubled. A significant transition in the way you think or express yourself and in your methods will occur; the implications must be interpreted according to your particular circumstances and background. However, since this is a negative period, it is hard to believe that any transitions will be for the better. Consciously or subconsciously, you seek greater personal power and control through the use of knowledge and information. Investigation, research and development, and secret or confidential information is misused. There will be struggles to control your education, writing, computers, communications, travel, transportation, sales and other business transactions, community affairs, contacts with siblings or neighbors, or the development or use of your mechanical or design skills.

TRANSIT PLUTO OPPOSED NATAL VENUS

♇ ☍ ♀ Marriage, romance, social intercourse, legal matters, and joint ventures are not lighthearted or pleasurable when transit Pluto opposes your natal Venus. Even if you are happily married or already involved with a romantic partner, you may become involved with someone else and, if this occurs, the outcome is not promising. The unpleasant prospect of jealousy and manipulation during this period targets your lovers, friends, and social acquaintances. Motivations behind your interest in people as well as those who show an interest in you are questionable at best. Your values, principles, priorities, material possessions, and relationships are in conflict with current circumstances. The unbridled pursuit of pleasure, luxuries, and the good life has disastrous consequences. If you find yourself pressured or plagued by any of the negative situations associated with this period, do not waste your time in useless attempts to gain an advantage or change the way things are going. Retreat to a safe distance and be content to stay there.

TRANSIT PLUTO OPPOSED NATAL MARS

♇ ☍ ♂ Powerful forces can paralyze your actions and prevent your efforts from reaching completion or achieving success. Whatever or whoever these opposing forces might be depends upon your particular circumstances, but potentials include aggressive competitors, manipulators, and those with potent physical passions. If the intense energy of this period is channeled constructively, you can be more successful than the potential suggests. When transit Pluto opposes your natal Mars, your efforts become so focused on getting back at someone, or achieving other misguided goals, that you end up with nothing. Male relationships and associations with men involve power struggles, a physical struggle being the most likely (but not the only) type of confrontation. There is potential for physical manipulation or physical abuse, and, in either situation, you may play the role of culprit or victim. Do not initiate or provoke such situations. Keep a firm control over your actions and be ever mindful of those who may rise against you.

Transit Pluto Opposed Natal Jupiter

♇ ☍ ♃ Current circumstances do not favor your professional or economic status. You may not know what or who is standing in the way of your success during this period, but be content in the knowledge that nothing you have already achieved may be destroyed. However, the measures you take to increase your prospects at this time will be soundly defeated. Optimism is discouraged by situations that halt your progress. This is not a favorable time for sales, advertising, and long-distance travel. Keep your aspirations subdued or on hold for the time being if they relate to politics, higher education, writing, religion, or the theater. Your father is not favored when transit Pluto opposes your natal Jupiter, and you may be locked in a power struggle with him or adversely affected by him.

Transit Pluto Opposed Natal Saturn

♇ ☍ ♄ Other factors notwithstanding, the structures and traditions upon which your work and life-style are based may be significantly altered or completely transformed by the character of current circumstances. There are no obvious comforts or rewards to be gained for having sacrificed, worked hard, or attained seniority, nor is this a time to demand such things. Attempts to impose your authority will be met with unwavering resistance. When transit Pluto opposes your natal Saturn, the time to stand up and be counted has passed. It you have been unwilling or unable to accept past failure, loss, and disappointment, it will work against you. There are always positive options, even in the most negative situations.

Transit Pluto Opposed Natal Uranus

♇ ☍ ♅ When transit Pluto opposes your natal Uranus, you may not experience any personal dislocation or frustration, but the outer environmental circumstances involve great conflicts in which those with power and resources are pitted against established financial and political institutions. Table 50 lists the transit of Pluto from Gemini (1882–1914) through Pisces (2043). As successive Uranus generations have come along, they experienced this aspect at increasingly older ages. Study the various generations and the conflicts in society that occurred when transit Pluto opposed their natal Uranus.

Transit ♇	opposes in years	Natal ⛢	of those born in:	at age:
♇ ♊	1882–1914	⛢ ♐	1897–1904	00–10
♇ ♋	1912–1939	⛢ ♑	1904–1912	08–27
♇ ♌	1937–1958	⛢ ♒	1912–1920	25–38
♇ ♍	1956–1972	⛢ ♓	1919–1928	37–44
♇ ♎	1971–1984	⛢ ♈	1927–1935	44–49
♇ ♏	1983–1995	⛢ ♉	1934–1942	49–53
♇ ♐	1995–2008	⛢ ♊	1941–1949	54–59
♇ ♑	2008–2024	⛢ ♋	1948–1956	60–68
♇ ♒	2023–2044	⛢ ♌	1955–1962	68–82
♇ ♓	2043–	⛢ ♍	1961–1969	82–

Table 50: Transit Pluto Oppositions to Natal Uranus

TRANSIT PLUTO OPPOSED NATAL NEPTUNE

♇ ☍ ♆ No Neptune generation since 1820 has experienced transit Pluto opposite their natal Neptune. The generations between 1778 and 1820 might be studied, however, with a view to understanding what circumstances arose when the ruling powers were challenged by those who held conflicting ideals and spiritual aspirations (see Table 51).

Transit ♇	opposes in years	Natal ♆	of those born in:	at age:
♇ ♈	1822–1853	♆ ♎	1778–1793	44–60
♇ ♉	1851–1884	♆ ♏	1792–1807	59–77
♇ ♊	1882–1914	♆ ♐	1806–1820	76–94

Table 51: Transit Pluto Oppositions to Natal Neptune

TRANSIT PLUTO OPPOSED NATAL PLUTO

♇ ☍ ♇ There is every likelihood that one great power will be locked in a no-compromise struggle with another power when transit Pluto opposes your natal Pluto (see Table 52). You will be of such an advanced age when this aspect occurs that circumstances will make little difference in your personal life.

Transit ♇	opposes in years	Natal ♇	of those born in:	at age:
♇ ♐	1995–2008	♇ ♊	1882–1914	94–113
♇ ♑	2008–2024	♇ ♋	1912–1939	85–96
♇ ♒	2023–2044	♇ ♌	1937–1958	86–86
♇ ♓	2043–	♇ ♍	1956–1972	–87

Table 52: Transit Pluto Oppositions to Natal Pluto

Chapter Eleven

Transit Planets Through the Natal Houses

Circumstances that we associate with transiting planets in the natal houses and with the aspects the transits make to natal planets do not exist on a plane separate from reality. The astrologer interprets the transit within the context of an individual's circumstances at the time.

As the Sun transits the natal houses, its focus emphasizes the vitality of the people and circumstances that you encounter. The delineation of transit Mercury outlines movement from one place to another and the expression of ideas and thinking. Social interactions as well as whatever and whoever is valued, desired, and enjoyed are included in the transits of Venus. Mars is associated with the direction of physical energy and in the behavior and activities that occur. Transit Jupiter implies the potential growth and optimism in current circumstances. Restrictions and obstacles that must be overcome or worked around and the attainment of maturity and experience are defined by Saturn. Transit Uranus suggests the possibility of unexpected or unique developments that disrupt the status quo. Transit Neptune involves the spiritual nature, ideals, and mystery to be found in present circumstances. The transit of Pluto adds the karmic potential as well as the development, use, or abuse of power and control.

TRANSIT SUN THROUGH NATAL HOUSES

SUN TRANSIT HOUSE ONE

It is time for an unemotional assessment of your personal attributes, time to take greater pride in yourself and, if necessary, time to develop or improve your self-image. The solar emphasis is on you and the personal goals you want to achieve.

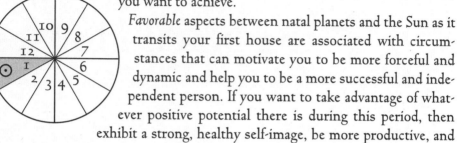

Favorable aspects between natal planets and the Sun as it transits your first house are associated with circumstances that can motivate you to be more forceful and dynamic and help you to be a more successful and independent person. If you want to take advantage of whatever positive potential there is during this period, then exhibit a strong, healthy self-image, be more productive, and treat others with generosity. Doing these things now will help you achieve personal goals and attract those you want to impress.

Unfavorable aspects between your natal planets and the Sun as it transits your first house are associated with circumstances in which your self-centered behavior, competitiveness, or arrogance prevents others from seeing your positive traits.

SUN TRANSIT HOUSE TWO

Are you making progress toward your monetary goals? Do you have other important priorities besides money? Your principles and the value system you have established are as important as income and other financial matters that may be emphasized by the solar focus during this period.

Favorable aspects between natal planets and the Sun as it transits your second house are associated with circumstances that improve your financial status, either through your own efforts or through the assistance of a parent, boss, or other authority figure. Others are more apt to recognize your personal integrity and generosity, which, in turn, will add to your stature.

Unfavorable aspects between natal planets and the Sun as it transits your second house are associated with circumstances that can engender a tendency to overspend in an effort to impress others. You may be tempted to use money or status as a wedge to gain the cooperation or affection of others. Money may be lost as a result of false pride which prevents you from backing away from unwise expenditures.

SUN TRANSIT HOUSE THREE

The flow of information and ideas is energized. A car or other means of transportation, travel, computers, communications equipment, appliances for home and office, contacts, and correspondence are the most likely areas of your interest and activities these days.

Favorable aspects between natal planets and the Sun as it transits your third house are associated with circumstances that can prompt you to develop or improve basic skills, to read more, and to gather information. Interactions and social activities with siblings as well as neighbors may increase, and you may be asked to assume a position of leadership in community affairs. A greater urge to express your ideas and opinions enhances your effectiveness in doing so.

Unfavorable aspects between natal planets and the Sun as it transits your third house are associated with circumstances that can require assertiveness in expressing yourself which, if you are mild of disposition and disinclined to force yourself or your opinions on others, is going to be difficult. If, on the other hand, you are more aggressive to begin with, there is the danger that you will behave as though your ideas and opinions are the only ones worth listening to.

SUN TRANSIT HOUSE FOUR

The focus of solar energy in this period targets your family, domestic chores, and matters related to home or property. Interest and participation in family relationships and activities increase. You are more aware of your role and influence in the family and the need to assert yourself within this group. If you do not have strong family ties or your life-style places little importance on your domestic environment, the solar focus is directed to whatever real or psychological elements you have substituted for these things.

Favorable aspects between natal planets and the Sun as it transits your fourth house are associated with circumstances that can promote family pride and strengthen family goals. Family support and the advantage of family connections can contribute to your success as an individual. It is a good period for real estate and activities that involve the purchase or sale of domestic items.

Unfavorable aspects between natal planets and the Sun as it transits your fourth house are associated with circumstances that engender arrogance or stubborn pride. In turn, this kind of attitude and behavior can either cause or add to problems with parents or other family members.

SUN TRANSIT HOUSE FIVE

Even if you are not usually self-indulgent, your capacity for enjoyment and the pursuit of pleasure increases. The emphasis during this period is on romance, humor, and imagination. Children may play a more dramatic role. Taking monetary as well as other kinds of risks is also part of the scenario.

Favorable aspects between natal planets and the Sun as it transits your fifth house are associated with circumstances that can cause you to become more creative and flamboyant. Creative or artistic projects are successful as are social events, entertainment, or leisure-time activities. Your luck in general improves.

Unfavorable aspects between natal planets and the Sun as it transits your fifth house are associated with circumstances that can make mundane responsibilities seem too tedious and uninspiring, and you are more interested in fun and games than in taking care of business or other serious matters. Increased self-indulgence makes it hard to stay on a diet or be moderate in your pursuit of pleasure. If you have children, you regard them as extensions of yourself instead of individuals in their own right, and you view their actions as being a direct reflection on you. Romantic encounters are apt to be ego involvements rather than emotional commitments. If your creative projects are criticized or romance becomes difficult, your suffering is more likely to be a bruised ego than a broken heart.

Sun Transit House Six

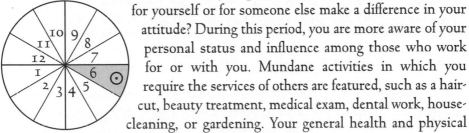

Increased concern with employment makes this a good time to examine what does or does not motivate you to work. Do you take pride in efficiently carrying out tasks and daily responsibilities? Does whether you work for yourself or for someone else make a difference in your attitude? During this period, you are more aware of your personal status and influence among those who work for or with you. Mundane activities in which you require the services of others are featured, such as a haircut, beauty treatment, medical exam, dental work, housecleaning, or gardening. Your general health and physical fitness are also emphasized.

Favorable aspects between natal planets and the Sun as it transits your sixth house are associated with circumstances in which you take pride in tasks and enjoy work and those with whom you work. Greater awareness of your vitality may lead to a healthier diet and exercise.

Unfavorable aspects between natal planets and the Sun as it transits your sixth house are associated with circumstances that can engender stubborn pride and the need to assert yourself when it comes to how and when you perform your tasks. Ego can disrupt relations with employees and co-workers.

Sun Transit House Seven

The influence you exercise over other people and your ability to elicit their cooperation are highlighted. Do others regard you as strong, forceful, and independent? If you are married or living with someone, you are likely to assess the union from a purely egotistical point of view. Do you dominate your partner or is it the other way around? Does the partnership help or impede your growth as an individual? Has your monetary potential or social status been improved as a result of the relationship? These issues also apply to business alliances. Your ego causes you to be more assertive in legal matters, contracts, negotiations, and interactions with people in general.

Favorable aspects between natal planets and the Sun as it transits your seventh house are associated with circumstances that can encourage others to cooperate with you, that promote the willingness to compromise, and that facilitate agreement about common goals.

Unfavorable aspects between natal planets and the Sun as it transits your seventh house are associated with circumstances in which you are likely to engage in open conflict and opposition. Stubborn or antagonistic behavior makes trying to resolve conflicts or reach compromises an unpleasant prospect.

SUN TRANSIT HOUSE EIGHT

Money and status gained through family connections, inheritance, business partnerships, or marriage are prominently featured these days. The payment or collection of debts, borrowing money, and the use or development of skills that make you more independent financially or otherwise are other possibilities. There may be issues concerned with surgery, psychological analysis, or sexual situations. *Favorable* aspects between natal planets and the Sun as it transits your eighth house are associated with circumstances that enhance focus and concentration, contribute to the progress of research and investigation, and increase your understanding of psychological motives and behavior.

Unfavorable aspects between natal planets and the Sun as it transits your eighth house are associated with increased determination and willpower that make you too demanding and critical. A medical emergency may arise.

SUN TRANSIT HOUSE NINE

Intellectual or professional status becomes a bigger priority and, as a result, you focus on communicating information and opinions to others either directly or through writing and publishing. Religious or philosophical beliefs, cultural pursuits, long-distance travel, the job or health of a parent, in-laws, and matters related to a second marriage are areas demanding time and attention during this period.

Favorable aspects between natal planets and the Sun as it transits your ninth house are associated with circumstances that cause you to be more generous in contributing your time and talents to religious, educational, or political institutions. You may have a greater desire to pursue higher education or advanced training, and you are more willing to indulge in speculation or other risk-taking ventures. You are more outgoing and assertive when traveling abroad or dealing with those of a different race or culture.

Unfavorable aspects between natal planets and the Sun as it transits your ninth house are associated with increased competitiveness that can make you a formidable opponent but a less able team player. Judgments are not apt to be in your favor.

SUN TRANSIT HOUSE TEN

Is your life going in the direction you want it to take? Your reputation may be of greater concern to you these days. You assess your major ambitions and how your ability to achieve them is being enhanced or restricted by current circumstances.

Favorable aspects between natal planets and the Sun as it transits your tenth house are associated with circumstances that bring public recognition and honor for your achievements. Relations with supervisors, authority figures, and those with influence are favored.

Unfavorable aspects between natal planets and the Sun as it transits your tenth house are associated with difficult circumstances related to parents, supervisors, and other authority figures. Problems can arise from your behavior and attitude toward responsibilities imposed by state and government agencies. Promoting your own goals and reputation is not favored, and you are apt to be disappointed at not attaining the level of achievement or status you want.

SUN TRANSIT HOUSE ELEVEN

The material rewards or other tangible recognition you receive for your efforts are highlighted, and you may become more aggressive in seeking greater financial compensation from your career or work in other areas. This is a period of understanding whatever and whoever you need in order to be a happy, productive individual. Part of the answer is found in the roles you play in the lives of others as friend, lover, parent, child, fellow club member, social contact, or business associate. The quality of these relationships and the importance you attach to them are more vital these days. If you tend to be a loner, you may have a desire for companionship. If you have many friends and contacts, you tend to identify your personal influence and status with them, and you may become more assertive in these relationships.

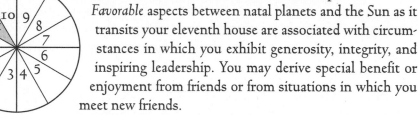

Favorable aspects between natal planets and the Sun as it transits your eleventh house are associated with circumstances in which you exhibit generosity, integrity, and inspiring leadership. You may derive special benefit or enjoyment from friends or from situations in which you meet new friends.

Unfavorable aspects between natal planets and the Sun as it transits your eleventh house are associated with circumstances that promote stubborn pride and arrogance—a potential you may wish to avoid or risk severely straining your relationships and organizational affiliations.

SUN TRANSIT HOUSE TWELVE

This is a period that targets unconscious motivations and the influence these hidden factors have on your conscious ego drive. If your outward behavior, for instance, suggests the possibility of an unconscious resentment of authority, then analyze why you may have developed such hidden resentment. This is a time for the private side of your life, for the struggles and successes you experience that are hidden from the outside world. *Favorable* aspects between natal planets and the Sun as it transits your twelfth house are associated with gaining more understanding of your subconscious, courageously dealing with failure or shame, and accepting necessary limitations or restrictions. You may gain remarkable inner strength and determination.

Unfavorable aspects between natal planets and the Sun as it transits your twelfth house are associated with circumstances that promote secrecy of an unhealthy nature, self-pity, inner fears and worry, and finding ways to hide from problems rather than solve them. You may experience confinement or be isolated due to illness or as a result of obligations that must be fulfilled. A family member may experience job- or health-related difficulties.

TRANSIT MERCURY THROUGH NATAL HOUSES

MERCURY TRANSIT HOUSE ONE

Circumstances during this period involve information that is primarily either for or about you. Consciously or subconsciously, your thoughts and discussions will be self-centered. You may not be the initiator of this personal focus; others may present a written review of your appearance, personality, or performance or speak to you about these matters.

Others are impressed with the information they receive about you, with your conduct during interviews, or with the intellectual or verbal ability you exhibit when Mercury makes *favorable* aspects to natal planets as it transits your first house.

There is the potential danger of injury to your hands and fingers or to your eyes, you may experience nervousness and irritability, unpleasant discussions that include being asked questions you would rather not answer, and negative reports concerning you when Mercury makes *unfavorable* aspects to natal planets as it transits your first house.

MERCURY TRANSIT HOUSE TWO

The majority of paperwork, writing, meetings, and discussions during this period is likely to involve finances and issues of high priority, and others may require information regarding your financial status. Transacting business, going to pick up a paycheck, monitoring expenditures, paying of bills, and comparison shopping are potential activities on your current agenda.

There are benefits to be gained by talking about your values and priorities when Mercury makes *favorable* aspects to natal planets as it transits your second house. A monetary error may be found and it will be in your favor. Money for travel or traveling for money is another possibility.

Circumstances may require you to define and defend your values when Mercury makes *unfavorable* aspects to natal planets as it transits your second house. Difficulties are caused by errors in billing, banking, or business deals.

MERCURY TRANSIT HOUSE THREE

Physically this is a "hands on" period. Your hands are not apt to be idle and your attention is pulled in a variety of directions. Some of the likely targets of your efforts include business projects (especially sales), contacts with siblings, correspondence, educational meetings, neighborhood activities, errands, or short trips. Talk increases and information and ideas flow. Your time and attention may be taken up with cars and other vehicles, computers, or mechanical and electrical equipment for home and office.

Meetings and short trips are successful and you find greater ease in writing and speaking when Mercury makes *favorable* aspects to natal planets as it transits your third house. You will learn better methods and receive enthusiastic reactions to your ideas and opinions. News or information you receive either from or about your neighbors and siblings is positive.

Angry words and gestures, accidents, car trouble, and the loss of documents, books, and keys are some of the potential difficulties that can occur when Mercury makes *unfavorable* aspects to natal planets as it transits your third house. Others may bring or send bad news or you may be the one who has to convey unpleasant information.

MERCURY TRANSIT HOUSE FOUR

Talking about your family, family discussions and travel or matters of family transportation are highlighted in current circumstances. Other activities include real-estate transactions, logistics of changing your residence, household repairs, purchase or sale of household goods, or a family business. You may be occupied with family heirlooms, your family's history, or a visit to your childhood home.

Real-estate dealings, contacting relatives, family travel, and planning family projects are successful endeavors when Mercury makes *favorable* aspects to natal planets as it transits your fourth house. This is a good time to install phones and other communications equipment in your home or to purchase computers and printers for home use.

Errors are likely to delay real-estate transactions, family trips may be canceled or postponed, and letters, house keys, and deeds or other household documents may be misplaced when Mercury makes *unfavorable* aspects to natal planets as it transits your fourth house. Conflicting opinions or lack of communication can be the cause of angry family discussions. Disgruntled relatives are difficult, if not impossible, to please.

MERCURY TRANSIT HOUSE FIVE

Creative writing or speaking projects may be part of your scenario. This may also be a time of communication or travel with a romantic partner, children, or social groups. A vacation taken during this period is apt to include a guided tour or some other type of educational experience. Plans, discussions, and even business transactions may be related to entertainment projects, social events, children's education and activities, or speculative ventures. Stimulating conversations of a social or romantic nature occur when Mercury makes *favorable* aspects to natal planets as it transits your fifth house. Information or news you receive concerning your lover or child, a speculative venture, or creative endeavor will be positive.

Important facts and other information related to speculative ventures may be lacking or incorrect causing such activities to fail when Mercury makes *unfavorable* aspects to natal planets as it transits your fifth house. Difficulties related to vacation travel or leisure activities can arise. Tickets for shows and other entertainment may be misplaced, and scheduling or travel problems may occur with regard to a child's education.

MERCURY TRANSIT HOUSE SIX

This period is likely to focus on schedules and the assignment of tasks and responsibilities related to your own work as well as to those who may work for or with you. Your daily routine is filled with an increasing number of details, messages, and information. Whether or not your focus is on a job, you will or should be more concerned with organization, methods, and planning in general. Other potential activities may involve discussions concerning the state of your health, gathering information about health and physical fitness, or consultations with professionals in these areas.

You may receive some good news related to a job assignment when Mercury makes *favorable* aspects to natal planets as it transits your sixth house. This is a good time to inquire about the services of a health care professional, barber, beautician, or domestic helper. Gather information on animals (to be kept as pets or for breeding purposes), advertise for employees, and seek employment yourself or advertise your services.

Difficulties may arise with office equipment and the completion of reports or work assignments when Mercury makes *unfavorable* aspects to natal planets as it transits your sixth house. Information or news regarding your health is not apt to be good. Lack of attention to detail or failure to communicate properly can cause problems in matters of health, physical fitness, and your job.

MERCURY TRANSIT HOUSE SEVEN

Lawyers and legal matters, debates, contract negotiations, partnerships, alliances, and joint ventures are the focus of your current circumstances. Your activities at this time may be initiated by or made possible through a partner. There is a potential for meeting with consultants and for sharing spontaneous conversations with retail clerks, bank tellers, those waiting in line with you at the supermarket, and other people you happen to meet.

A partnership or joint venture is harmonious and mutually beneficial when Mercury makes *favorable* aspects to natal planets as it transits your seventh house. You can negotiate favorable terms in contracts, succeed in formal debate, and establish better communication with partners or allies during this period.

Requests for cooperation may be rejected and there is a disregard of mutually agreed upon goals when Mercury makes *unfavorable* aspects to natal planets as it transits your seventh house.

MERCURY TRANSIT HOUSE EIGHT

Assessment and the development of your talent and skills may claim your time and attention. Joint income may be the subject of your plans or discussions. Activities may include psychological analysis; handling matters of inheritance, taxes, or insurance; analyzing investments; and collection or repayment of debts. You may seek information and ideas with regard to research and investigation projects or surgical procedures you are contemplating. Investigations produce positive results, loan applications are approved, and you may collect a debt when Mercury makes *favorable* aspects to natal planets as it transits your eighth house. If there is a test of your resourcefulness during this period, you will not be found wanting.

You may receive news of a death or negative reports regarding the status of joint income and tax or insurance benefits when Mercury makes *unfavorable* aspects to natal planets as it transits your eighth house.

MERCURY TRANSIT HOUSE NINE

Circumstances require you to reach beyond your immediate environment for a broader understanding and perspective. You are apt to have contact with others who live far away or are of a different culture or race. Subjects that occupy your time and attention may include travel, advanced training, the study or use of foreign languages, religious or political interests, publishing, direct-mail promotions, or advertising. There is increased correspondence or discussions regarding a second marriage, in-laws, or the health or job of a parent.

Your long-distance travel plans work out well, international trade or correspondence is successful, political speeches are well received, and publishing and advertising projects are a hit when Mercury makes *favorable* aspects to natal planets as it transits your ninth house.

When Mercury makes *unfavorable* aspects to natal planets as it transits your ninth house, the news or information you receive is not apt to be of a positive nature, especially if it relates to a court decision, in-laws, a second marriage, the job or health of a parent, and religious or political interests.

MERCURY TRANSIT HOUSE TEN

Your mental outlook or intellectual abilities may be the main topic of public recognition or discussion at this time. You may seek, or be given, a public forum

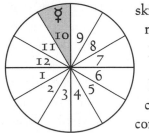

in which to express your ideas or share your knowledge and skills. This can involve writing a letter to the editor of a newspaper, making a speech, or expanding the use of your skills and knowledge beyond your family or those with whom you have daily contact. Circumstances are likely to increase your communications with superiors, clients, and a parent. There is potential for having to comply with government regulations or those imposed by some similar authoritative agency.

The news or information you receive regarding a career or other important ambition is likely to be good when Mercury makes *favorable* aspects to natal planets as it transits your tenth house. This is an excellent time to handle the paperwork or reports related to your request for promotion or other favors from a supervisor or public agency.

Forget about keeping information secret when Mercury makes *unfavorable* aspects to natal planets as it transits your tenth house. Your ideas and methods are open to public scrutiny, and this scrutiny does not serve your purposes. You are required to explain your actions and the timing is very inconvenient, or you take an unpopular point of view for which you are criticized.

MERCURY TRANSIT HOUSE ELEVEN

Your communications are focused on the personal network of people who surround you: family, friends, business associates, fellow club members, and those

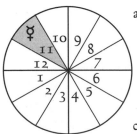

with whom you have daily contact. They have information for and about you and you may be required to provide information to or about them. Other potential activities include increased interactions or travel with children, especially children that are not biologically yours but for whom you have responsibility. Your interest and participation may also increase with regard to clubs and associations. Activities such as fund-raising, membership drives, and newsletters may be on your agenda.

It is an excellent time for association meetings and other group discussions when Mercury makes *favorable* aspects to natal planets as it transits your eleventh house. You are inspired to outline and articulate clearly what will make you happy and productive.

Disorganization and lack of information makes getting down to business difficult when Mercury makes *unfavorable* aspects to natal planets as it transits your eleventh house. Social events or meetings may have to be canceled or postponed. Others are very selective in what they choose to say to or about you and this behavior will not be in your best interest.

Mercury Transit House Twelve

Your information or activities must be kept confidential or you may not be inclined to share your thoughts or ideas with others during this period. Gathering information about the past or contact with people from your past is also a possibility. Messages you receive may be subtle or contain hidden meanings meant only for you. Your intuition, subconscious, and dreams are highlighted. There may be secret travel and contacts with strangers.

You can learn from the past and discover higher levels of consciousness when Mercury makes *favorable* aspects to natal planets as it transits your twelfth house. At this time, you may also discover information that would normally be hidden from you.

Your thoughts and ideas are restricted or censored or they focus heavily on loss and disappointment when Mercury makes *unfavorable* aspects to natal planets as it transits your twelfth house.

Transit Venus Through Natal Houses

Venus Transit House One

There is no question that you can attract the attention of others during this period. How interested do you want them to be? It pays to make an effort to exert your personal influence. The charm of your personality, willingness to cooperate with others, and sense of humor can make a big difference in the way things turn out. It is important to look as neat and attractive as possible since your physical appearance will have as big an impact as your personality.

Your luck in general gets a boost when Venus makes *favorable* aspects to natal planets as it transits your first house. You exhibit an easy charm and grace that appeals to others. It does not guarantee others will fall at your feet, but you can at least get their attention. Take advantage of this favorable time to enhance your appearance and make the most of your personality and people skills.

When Venus makes *unfavorable* aspects to natal planets as it transits your first house, you may attract the attention of others, but their interest in you may be unwelcome or their association with you not of a viable or positive nature.

VENUS TRANSIT HOUSE TWO

Personal finances, friendships, and values are going to be emphasized. You may have a greater tendency to purchase luxury items. Expenditures are also apt to include social or cultural events as well as products and services for the enhancement of your appearance or to improve the attractiveness of your environment. The issue of wealth connected with social status may arise in some form. Should financial matters be disrupted by disagreement, you will have to play the role of peacemaker. Your income may increase when Venus makes *favorable* aspects to natal planets as it transits your second house.

Other potentials are benefits attained through joint ventures and the purchase or sale of art or luxury items. Money may come to you through a female.

Circumstances do not favor monetary matters, nor will they be likely to honor your priorities or values when Venus makes *unfavorable* aspects to natal planets as it transits your second house.

VENUS TRANSIT HOUSE THREE

The use of flattery, charm, and a sense of humor can be persuasive during this period. There is a social emphasis on relations with neighbors and people with whom you have daily contact. You may also have a greater urge or perhaps opportunity to increase contacts or improve relationships with brothers, sisters, cousins, and in-laws. You may visit or contact nieces or nephews away at college. Some of the best opportunities for socializing these days are in your immediate environment.

Participate in community activities and neighborhood beautification when Venus makes *favorable* aspects to natal planets as it transits your third house. Take music or art lessons at a local school, visit an art museum, or attend a music festival. If contacts with neighbors or siblings have been troubled in the past, this is a good time to improve them.

If your immediate environment changes when Venus makes *unfavorable* aspects to natal planets as it transits your third house, it is not apt to be a change that you will find pleasing. Siblings, neighbors, or those with whom you must associate on a daily basis do not offer humor, companionship, or pleasant manners.

VENUS TRANSIT HOUSE FOUR

Pleasure and enjoyment centers around entertaining at home or participating in social gatherings with family members. Other potential situations at this time include decorating your home and the addition of books, music, or art to improve the quality as well as the look of your domestic environment. Legal matters connected with a family business or the artistic endeavors of a parent may be on the agenda.

Circumstances encourage harmonious family relationships when Venus makes *favorable* aspects to natal planets as it transits your fourth house. Successful real- estate transactions are possible as is the sale or purchase of luxury items for the home.

Home is not apt to be where your heart is, or, you would like to be home but you have to be somewhere else when Venus makes *unfavorable* aspects to natal planets as it transits your fourth house. Lack of cooperation and enthusiasm discourages social activities at home. This is not the best time to launch a new enterprise.

VENUS TRANSIT HOUSE FIVE

Current circumstances emphasize the pursuit of pleasure: a vacation, social event, hobby, or risk-taking adventure. Other potential situations that engage your time and attention may be triggered by a friend, a child, or a romantic partner.

If you want to put a little romance in your life, do not pass up social invitations when Venus makes *favorable* aspects to natal planets as it transits your fifth house. It is a period that encourages relationships with children, rapport with a romantic partner, and expansion of social contacts. Enhanced imagination and artistic urges can make it a period of successful creative endeavors, carried out on your own or with a partner. Your luck in general improves.

You may have to face the consequences of too much self-indulgence or extravagance when Venus makes *unfavorable* aspects to natal planets as it transits your fifth house. Avoid speculations and idle flattery; they are losing propositions.

VENUS TRANSIT HOUSE SIX

Harmony in your working environment is highlighted this period. Even if current circumstances do not demand such harmony, it is nevertheless a good idea to promote cordial relationships with those who work for or with you. Your job may involve legal matters. An office romance or social events connected with co-workers may be on the agenda. Beautifying your workplace is another potential activity that may include anything from major renovation and decorating projects to putting a fresh coat of paint on the walls, adding background music, and installing plants or artwork to brighten the surroundings.

This is also a period when you are likely to be more concerned with your health and physical fitness.

Physical enhancements such as beauty treatments, a new hairstyle, dental work, and cosmetic surgery are successful when Venus makes *favorable* aspects to natal planets as it transits your sixth house. Your work is more enjoyable, and the atmosphere there is more sociable. If the circumstances fit, this is a good time to seek employment, begin a new job, or hire others.

Work may take you into unfriendly territory, and relations with those who work for or with you can deteriorate when Venus makes *unfavorable* aspects to natal planets as it transits your sixth house. Cooperation and compromise may be hard to come by on the job, so do not waste time arguing or forcing issues.

VENUS TRANSIT HOUSE SEVEN

This is a period when the focus of circumstances shifts away from you as an individual and emphasizes other people, especially those with whom you are allied in marriage or business. Other potential concerns include legal matters, contracts, public relations, the income of a relative, and situations in which you must seek as well as offer cooperation.

Promote harmony and cooperation in achieving common goals when Venus makes *favorable* aspects to natal planets as it transits your seventh house. This is a good time to form a partnership or initiate legal matters.

Do not expect advantageous terms in agreements you sign when Venus makes *unfavorable* aspects to natal planets as it transits your seventh house. Others may fail to keep their word or they may disappoint you. Although there is pressure to resolve disagreements, there is no room for compromise. This is not a good time to retain an attorney.

VENUS TRANSIT HOUSE EIGHT

Joint income and social status, acquired either through marriage or a business partnership, are two issues likely to surface. Common goals and values are also apt to play a part in the circumstances that occur. There is more intensity with regard to social contacts as well as romance or sexual encounters at this time.

Your loan application is likely to be approved or you may receive tax or insurance benefits when Venus makes *favorable* aspects to natal planets as it transits your eighth house. If marriage takes place at this time, there is an indication that the alliance will increase your income or social status. This can be a productive period to participate in group therapy.

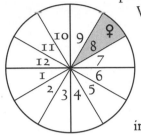

When Venus makes *unfavorable* aspects to natal planets as it transits your eighth house, you may be required to handle matters of inheritance or make financial arrangements for a funeral. This is not a fortunate time for joint income or the collection of debts you are owed. This is a period when the values of others will be imposed on you.

VENUS TRANSIT HOUSE NINE

Higher education, religious activities, political interests, and cultural pursuits are not only highlighted these days, they are apt to take on a more social atmosphere. Other potential circumstances include romance, marriage, or a joint venture in a foreign country or with an individual who is of a different race or culture. Issues or activities connected with a second marriage or a court decision may arise. You may write, publish, or purchase books—especially books on art, music, or biography. You may seek cooperation in joint efforts related to the health or employment of a parent. Socializing and establishing cordial relationships with in-laws are other potential activities on your agenda.

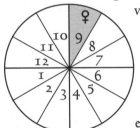

When Venus makes *favorable* aspects to natal planets as it transits your ninth house, it can mean success with advertising or mail campaigns that are aimed at romantic or other relationships. Present circumstances are most encouraging for an art or music recital and for other cultural pursuits.

Issues or activities connected with a second marriage or a court decision will not be to your advantage if Venus makes *unfavorable* aspects to natal planets as it transits your ninth house. Do not expect to encounter amiable companions on a long-distance journey.

VENUS TRANSIT HOUSE TEN

Public social events may put you in the spotlight these days, which means others will notice your physical beauty, artistic talent, and charming personality. Indicate to others that you are a cooperative and interested as well as an interesting individual. Do not wait for others to notice you, take every opportunity you can to be in their direct line of vision. "If you have it, flaunt it," accurately describes what your attitude should be. This is also a period that emphasizes relationships and social activities with older family members, superiors, and authority figures. The status of female relationships at this time can deeply affect your future. There is also the potential that your allies, a spouse, or other partners may receive recognition or a special promotion.

Ask for a promotion or other favors from those with influence when Venus makes *favorable* aspects to natal planets as it transits your tenth house.

You may find yourself in the public eye, but the reason you attract such attention may not be very pleasant when Venus makes *unfavorable* aspects to natal planets as it transits your tenth house.

VENUS TRANSIT HOUSE ELEVEN

You are likely to be more concerned with personal aspirations and happiness, especially the satisfaction you derive (or do not derive, as the case may be) from the role you play in the lives of others—as spouse, child, parent, friend, lover, or associate. The people who count on you in these roles are the targets of your efforts to coordinate activities, promote harmony, and encourage cooperation. The social aspects of romance may be on your agenda. Some of your fondest aspirations may be realized when Venus makes *favorable* aspects to natal planets as it transits your eleventh house. Joining organizations and participating in group activities can be socially rewarding.

When Venus makes *unfavorable* aspects to natal planets as it transits your eleventh house, friendships can develop problems, and lack of cooperation can make organizing meetings and events difficult.

VENUS TRANSIT HOUSE TWELVE

You may withdraw from society using all kinds of excuses, legitimate or otherwise, to pass up invitations to go out: you are too ill, you are too overweight to fit into the clothes you wanted to wear, you have too much work to do. Romance may be secret or relegated to the world of fantasy and dreams. Love relationships from the past, especially those in which you suffered a loss, can intrude on the present.

Charitable work and fund-raisers for charitable causes are successful when Venus makes *favorable* aspects to natal planets as it transits your twelfth house.

You are more susceptible to false flattery or unworthy attentions when Venus makes *unfavorable* aspects to natal planets as it transits your twelfth house.

TRANSIT MARS THROUGH NATAL HOUSES

MARS TRANSIT HOUSE ONE

This is a physically active period. Energizing circumstances arouse your competitive spirit and inspire you to be more aggressive, perhaps even physically combative. Should contrary influences in the current circumstances prevent you from actually being more energetic, you are still likely to want to give others the impression of being very busy. You are impatient and restless. Physical activities these days are involved with satisfying your personal needs and goals.

Demonstrations of physical skill are successful when *favorable* aspects occur between natal planets and Mars as it transits your first house.

When *unfavorable* aspects occur between natal planets and Mars as it transits your first house, be careful handling sharp objects and hot or explosive materials.

Your head or face may be injured. You may suffer stings, bites, burns, and cuts. Fevers, headaches, or toothaches may occur.

MARS TRANSIT HOUSE TWO

Time and energy is devoted to financial and business concerns these days. You may be inspired to organize your bank and financial papers, sort through bills and accounts, make payments, or initiate actions regarding debts, assets, and income. Another focus may be to increase income by working overtime, seeking an additional job, or doing whatever is necessary to earn more money. Other potentials include actions to either attain or hold on to something or someone you deem highly worthwhile. Other activities are geared toward meeting priorities or establishing new ones. You seek ways to stimulate or increase your physical energy, since you have more of a tendency these days to view energy itself as a valuable commodity.

Shop for a car or other equipment when *favorable* aspects occur between natal planets and Mars as it transits your second house. Money may come to you through a male.

Unwise actions and rash behavior can result in monetary loss if *unfavorable* aspects occur between natal planets and Mars as it transits your second house.

MARS TRANSIT HOUSE THREE

The physically energized atmosphere surrounding you during this period engenders more than the usual volume of communications and activities, especially with siblings and neighbors. You are apt to be swamped with information and ideas, not to mention the number of ideas you develop on your own. Travel and public as well as private transportation are highlighted. You may develop skills with machinery or computers. Other projects that inspire your physical actions include writing, design, arts and crafts, and business enterprises. You are more of a doer than a thinker—eager to turn ideas into physical reality and more than ready to speak your mind. If words will not suffice, you will not hesitate to use physical means to express yourself.

You will accomplish a multitude of errands and other business when *favorable* aspects occur between natal planets and Mars as it transits your third house. This is a good time to begin a short trip.

Should *unfavorable* factors enter the picture when Mars transits your third house, you may either be tempted to physically demonstrate your anger and frustration or you may become the victim of those who resort to physical retaliation. Rash actions can cause accidents, particularly burns, cuts, or driving mishaps.

MARS TRANSIT HOUSE FOUR

Physical endeavors involve your home, personal possessions, domestic arrangements, family relationships, family-owned property or business, and real-estate transactions in general. Enthusiasm for doing things as a group may encourage more family activities. You may be inspired to collect or restore family heirlooms. The potential of this period may also be described as the start of another energy cycle—a time you can direct your endeavors into new areas. If you have been thinking about a new business venture or achieving some personal physical goal, this is a time when you are likely to put such plans in motion.

When *favorable* aspects occur between natal planets and Mars as it transits your fourth house, take care of household repairs or other chores. If you are planning to move, this is a good time to do so.

There are negative circumstances at work when *unfavorable* aspects occur between natal planets and Mars as it transits your fourth house. It would be wise to make sure your household insurance is in effect and check your home for possible fire hazards. Watch your step to prevent falls, cuts, and other mishaps around the house, and go out of your way to avoid angry domestic scenes.

MARS TRANSIT HOUSE FIVE

Circumstances during this period encourage your pursuit of pleasure. You will need little urging to put physical enthusiasm into speculative ventures, social events, and activities related to entertainment or a vacation. Creative juices flow, but there is no telling exactly how or where you will direct them. Romantic notions are apt to be physically carried out. Inspiration and imagination spark artistic endeavors and activities related to children.

Romance is given vitality and enthusiasm, your enjoyment of good food and merry companions does not go unsatisfied, and risky adventures leave you in the winner's circle when *favorable* aspects occur between natal planets and Mars as it transits your fifth house.

There are apt to be unpleasant, perhaps dangerous, consequences of overindulgence and taking risks when *unfavorable* aspects occur between natal planets and Mars as it transits your fifth house.

MARS TRANSIT HOUSE SIX

You may feel more energetic and enthusiastic about your work these days, which is good since there are plenty of things for you to do—on the job as well as around the house. Circumstances may put you in a position to hire others. The flow of physical energy can make you more aggressive or competitive concerning work, co-workers, or employees. If there are problems, you confront them directly and seek an immediate solution, or if such attempts are thwarted, you may be tempted to give in to angry outbursts or rash actions. Other potentials at this time include a haircut, a medical or dental check-up, and any procedure that entails cutting or burning.

Physical tasks are easier to accomplish and work proceeds well when *favorable* aspects occur between natal planets and Mars as it transits your sixth house. This is a period of success for a sports team sponsored by the company you work for. It is a good time to get involved in an exercise program to improve physical fitness. Be sure to consult a physician or other health expert before you start. Enthusiasm can easily get out of hand. If your body is not used to regular or vigorous exercise, be careful not to overexert yourself.

There is the potential for headache, fever, or inflammation when *unfavorable* aspects occur between natal planets and Mars as it transits your sixth house.

Accidents on the job are another potential, so caution is necessary if your work requires you to handle sharp objects, volatile materials, or dangerous machinery.

MARS TRANSIT HOUSE SEVEN

Energy and enthusiasm center around partnerships and other alliances, cooperative efforts, and interactions with others. The inspiration you gain from others stimulates you to physical action. You can ignore this type of energy focus of course, or other factors may prevent you from taking advantage of it. However, there is every likelihood that getting things done will be more difficult to accomplish by yourself than it might be with a partner or partners. Even if you want to be left alone, other people will find a way to intrude. In most situations other people make the first move, leaving you to react. More than one open confrontation is apt to occur, but this potential does not necessarily indicate that such encounters will be hostile.

Vigorously pursue the physical aspects of setting up a partnership or joint venture and negotiate contracts with energy and enthusiasm when *favorable* aspects occur between natal planets and Mars as it transits your seventh house.

Legal proceedings and direct physical confrontations are not apt to be pleasant or advantageous when *unfavorable* aspects occur between natal planets and Mars as it transits your seventh house.

MARS TRANSIT HOUSE EIGHT

Energy can be intense during this period. Closer attention to details and enhanced awareness of subtleties mark your physical efforts. The most likely areas of these efforts include sex, money, and financial as well as psychological analysis. A partner's income or jointly-held property may require more attention than usual. By choice or circumstance, you may be forced to collect debts and favors owed to you or make arrangements for repayment of your own debts. Issues concerning insurance, taxes, inheritance, or money that you manage for others may also demand more of your time and attention these days. Situations you may encounter with regard to sex include several possibilities—the physical act itself, counseling, or surgical procedures.

Activities related to research and investigation are successful and your physical resourcefulness is enhanced when *favorable* aspects occur between natal planets and Mars as it transits your eighth house.

When *unfavorable* aspects occur between natal planets and Mars as it transits your eighth house, you may be denied the resources you need or you may be confronted with the physical aspects of death.

MARS TRANSIT HOUSE NINE

The energy-filled atmosphere can inspire your enthusiasm in so many potential directions that it is impossible to predict which path or paths you will choose. Physical efforts may focus on higher education, religion, politics, long-distance travel, cultural pursuits, foreign languages, writing, and publishing. However, there are numerous other categories that can just as easily arouse your interest and physical participation—speculative ventures, sports contests, court decisions, a second marriage, and activities or relations with in-laws. The most positive way to approach this period is to use whatever circumstances and activities you encounter as a way to broaden your spiritual and intellectual horizons.

Begin a journey, publish your writings, and advertise your goods or services when *favorable* aspects occur between natal planets and Mars as it transits your ninth house.

The outcome will not be fortunate if you go to court or marry for the second time when *unfavorable* aspects occur between natal planets and Mars as it transits your ninth house.

MARS TRANSIT HOUSE TEN

The energy and enthusiasm of current circumstances are directed primarily toward self-promotion. Career or other long-range ambitions are emphasized and your actions can have an important impact on your future. You work hard to get attention from the public and those with power and influence. You may not necessarily desire to call attention to yourself, but public attention is well within the realm of possibility during this period. Even if you have no access to a public forum, you may experience an increased urge to have others notice what you are doing. Activities that involve superiors or authority figures increase. This can means you may do a lot of extra work with your boss or for the government or similar authority. Largely because of your efforts, a male relative or superior may receive recognition or enhanced status at this time.

Promote yourself or launch a campaign on behalf of another person or a cause in which you believe, when *favorable* aspects occur between natal planets and Mars as it transits your tenth house.

Do not engage in activities you do not wish others to know about when *unfavorable* aspects occur between natal planets and Mars as it transits your tenth house. There may be physical confrontations with male authority figures.

Mars Transit House Eleven

The most likely targets of your energetic efforts during this period include friends, organizations, and children, especially those who are not your biological offspring but for whom you may have responsibility. Activities are apt to involve the role you play in the lives of others. Your schedule may become overloaded and nothing gets accomplished, making it necessary for you to place some restraints on the number of activities and people you decide to accommodate. You may be concerned with what is or is not making you happy, and such concern is apt to go beyond the stage of just thinking about it. You may actually go after what you want or get rid of what you do not want.

You will have more success if you work outward through others—as part of a group rather than as an individual—when *favorable* aspects occur between natal planets and Mars as it transits your eleventh house.

When *unfavorable* aspects occur between natal planets and Mars as it transits your eleventh house, you can become too aggressive toward others and lose patience when things become too hectic or do not proceed as planned. There may be difficult physical confrontations, especially with male friends or associates.

MARS TRANSIT HOUSE TWELVE

Past actions, good or bad, catch up to you during this period. You may prefer that others do not observe some of your activities, either because these efforts actually concern secret matters or merely because you may accomplish more by working alone. Even if you do not experience the need to take covert actions, adopting this approach is the most positive way to make use of the available energy. You can explore and develop inner strengths and gain a deeper understanding of your childhood conditioning, subconscious mind, hidden fears, and dreams. Yet another potential during this period is for increased involvement with the activities of charitable organizations, hospitals, prisons, and institutions that are concerned with minorities and the underprivileged.

When *favorable* aspects occur between natal planets and Mars as it transits your twelfth house, much can be accomplished from behind the scenes or by giving others physical power to act on your behalf from such a hidden position.

You may suffer from insomnia and your physical activities may become restricted through illness or other confinement when *unfavorable* aspects occur between natal planets and Mars as it transits your twelfth house.

TRANSIT JUPITER THROUGH NATAL HOUSES

JUPITER TRANSIT HOUSE ONE

This is a period to appreciate your uniqueness as an individual, your physical appearance, and the various facets of your personality. You may have more of a tendency to make overly grand gestures while trying to impress others—perhaps what you are really trying to do is impress yourself. Even if you do not engage in grandiose actions, people may get the idea that you have a higher status or importance than may really be the case. This can and should be a period to gain a much better understanding of yourself and to explore other avenues of self-improvement. One potential is a tendency for overindulgence and to put on weight. If you can resist the temptation to go overboard, your efforts will result in a much healthier self-image. Your father or his status may have a more prominent role to play in helping you accomplish your personal goals.

Favorable aspects made to natal planets from Jupiter as it transits your first house can mean a release from personally restricting influences and the achievement of personal goals.

Unfavorable aspects made to natal planets from Jupiter as it transits your first house can mean difficult situations in which you can no longer grow or expand your personal influence and unpleasant consequences occur because of your greed or self-indulgence.

JUPITER TRANSIT HOUSE TWO

This can be a tricky, even ruinous, period. Money is or becomes the source of pleasure, which is fine if you can afford to spend it. If you cannot, restrictions must be rigorously applied to all purchases. Potential budgetary disasters may be avoided if you can make an enjoyable experience out of learning how to conserve and invest current assets and find ways to increase your income. You may exaggerate your wealth or status to impress others—a tendency that may tempt you to indulge in unnecessary purchases of luxury items and other status symbols. Other expenditures at this time are likely to involve higher education, political interests, religious or spiritual activities, travel, publishing, and cultural pursuits.

Favorable aspects made to natal planets from Jupiter as it transits your second house can mean circumstances that encourage an expansion of your value system and priorities. Money may come to you through your father or his side of the family.

Unfavorable aspects made to natal planets from Jupiter as it transits your second house can mean bankruptcy, the loss of perspective as far as values are concerned, and the loss of social status, an important relationship, or precious possessions.

JUPITER TRANSIT HOUSE THREE

This is an excellent period to develop your knowledge and skills with computers or any type of machinery and mechanical equipment. Communications as well as travel prospects increase—widening your circle of contacts and encouraging the exchange of ideas and information. You may expand your artistic and design talents or writing ability, or you may decide to continue your education or broaden the scope of your present course of study. Other potentials include greater interest in neighbors or community activities as well as increased contacts with siblings. Your status among neighbors may increase in some way, and there is the possibility that you may seek to relocate to a more influential neighborhood. As a secondary potential, your neighbors and siblings may become more prosperous. Participation in meetings and discussion groups may demand more of your time and attention. Reading increases and a growing pile of magazines, newspapers, and mail begins to clutter your environment. If such equipment happens to fit your needs and interests, there is a possibility that you will acquire telephones, computers, answering machines, and other communication devices.

Begin a short trip, launch community activities or a learning program, and exhibit the ability to interpret information and ideas when there are *favorable* aspects made to natal planets from Jupiter as it transits your third house.

Unfavorable aspects made to natal planets from Jupiter as it transits your third house can mean loss of status in your immediate environment and negative prospects for a neighborhood business, advertising, or a newsletter.

JUPITER TRANSIT HOUSE FOUR

This period marks the beginning of a twelve-year cycle of learning and gaining new experiences The people and circumstances that you encounter during this initial period are likely to be catalysts that inspire you to start new projects, a business venture, a new career, higher education or the study of a particular subject, advanced training, writing, publishing, or promotion. Whatever you begin now can eventually expand your personal, professional, and intellectual horizons. The introduction of greater spirituality and cultural appreciation into your domestic environment is an expected result of the twelve-year cycle that begins during this period. You may develop a greater interest and knowledge related to family history and expand your activities and contacts with family members. You may seek a grander, larger residence or build additions to your present home. You may also become involved in the sale of domestic furnishings or real estate.

Any new venture that you begin or transactions related to the purchase or sale of a home or domestic property are successful when *favorable* aspects are made to natal planets from Jupiter as it transits your fourth house.

Unfavorable aspects made to natal planets from Jupiter as it transits your fourth house can mean the loss of your personal growth and independence within the family circle and negative prospects for a family-owned business or a new venture.

JUPITER TRANSIT HOUSE FIVE

Your capacity for enjoyment is enhanced and overindulgence is almost impossible to avoid unless you are particularly strong-willed or current circumstances impose the necessary restrictions. There is no guarantee of the lottery-winning good fortune that you might expect. There is, however, the desire to live the good life and the feeling that prosperity is within easy reach. As a result, you may purchase more luxury items, take more expensive vacations, and buy fancier or more expensive clothes. Your imagination and creativity increase, but to what end you apply them depends on your interests and circumstances. You may, for example, be inspired to develop artistic talents as a hobby. Relationships and contacts with children may be expanded. Romance can blossom, or, in its wider application, can enhance the quality of your life in general. You are more willing to take risks, and, for the most part, you should emerge on the winning side of chances you take.

You can be a great success when *favorable* aspects are made to natal planets from Jupiter as it transits your fifth house. If your work or career is of a creative nature, show off your ideas and imagination. This is a good period for matters related to your child's education.

You may suffer the unhappy consequences of pleasurable pursuits and other self-indulgent habits when *unfavorable* aspects are made to natal planets from Jupiter as it transits your fifth house.

JUPITER TRANSIT HOUSE SIX

The nature and scope of your work and daily responsibilities expand during this period. Your work may require more travel or advanced training may become necessary. You may hire others to work for you at this time and your relationships with co-workers will expand or increase. There is a possibility (which you may want to avoid) that you will inflate the importance of your job or become overly impressed with your performance of required tasks—an impression that may not necessarily be shared by others. Although there is certainly an excellent chance that your work will be recognized and handsomely rewarded, it would be a mistake to take your job or any aspect of it for granted. The potential of this period includes acquiring a pet or increasing your activities involving a pet, which can mean the breeding of such animals. Although there is no guarantee that you will actually pursue it, your interest concerning health and physical fitness may increase. Do not believe that your physical health will be protected.

If circumstances require you to seek medical care or advice while *favorable* aspects are made to natal planets from Jupiter as it transits your sixth house, you will find excellent physicians or other health-care professionals to help you. This is a good time to seek employment or to begin a new job or work project.

Do not expect generosity from co-workers or increased prosperity from your work when *unfavorable* aspects are made to natal planets from Jupiter as it transits your sixth house.

JUPITER TRANSIT HOUSE SEVEN

This is not a period to work or spend a lot of time alone and out of touch. Since it is through other people that you are most likely to succeed, there are benefits to be gained from increased interactions. Other people, especially a partner or ally, can be a source of stimulation, broader knowledge, and new experiences for you. The outlook is just as potentially prosperous for new unions you establish. The focus of your activities extends to consultations, legal matters, contract negotiations, and your efforts to gain the assistance or cooperation of others.

The status and circumstances of a current partnership and other alliances as well as joint ventures are greatly enhanced when *favorable* aspects are made to natal planets from Jupiter as it transits your seventh house.

Avoid the tendency to take others (especially a partner) for granted, to exaggerate the prospects or status of a relationship or joint venture, to overestimate the assistance or cooperation you may receive, and your ability to impress others when *unfavorable* aspects are made to natal planets from Jupiter as it transits your seventh house.

JUPITER TRANSIT HOUSE EIGHT

Joint income, investments, taxes, insurance, collection of debts, and the settlement of estate matters are areas affected by current circumstances. The outcome of this period is tricky to predict since it includes the potential for increased assets through luck or association with the right people as well as the potential for diminished assets through overestimation and extravagance.

If a marriage or other joint venture occurs when *favorable* aspects are made to natal planets from Jupiter as it transits your eighth house, the indication is for greater prosperity as a result of the union. You may be released from a debt or given additional resources. Requests for financial assistance are likely to be favored. Progress and the growth of knowledge are easier to achieve with respect to analysis, investigation, or research. Enjoyment is felt on a much deeper level, and it springs as much from psychological satisfaction as physical gratification. Greater sexual enjoyment is a potential but the broader possibility includes gaining a deeper understanding of the nature and purpose of sex as well as other forces of nature.

Extravagance or overextension can deplete your joint income or inheritance when *unfavorable* aspects are made to natal planets from Jupiter as it transits your eighth house.

JUPITER TRANSIT HOUSE NINE

This is likely to be an interesting and fortunate period that includes many potential areas for success and personal growth. People and circumstances you encounter may give you the chance or inspiration to broaden your intellectual horizons through higher education, advanced training, study or the use of foreign languages, or long-distance travel. You may develop a desire to expand your spiritual awareness, political interests, and cultural appreciation. Greater opportunities for success are possible if you are involved in writing, publishing, arts and entertainment (especially theater and dance), finance and investment, advertising, or promotion.

Favorable aspects made to natal planets from Jupiter as it transits your ninth house can mean success in games of chance, but remember it only takes one lottery ticket, one horse, or one team to make you a winner. The health or job prospects of a parent or in-law may be improved. You will be favored in most decisions made by others.

An increased tendency for overestimation and exaggeration may lead to intellectual arrogance, name-dropping, and shameless social climbing when *unfavorable* aspects are made to natal planets from Jupiter as it transits your ninth house. During this time, you will not be favored by court decisions or succeed with educational or political ambitions.

JUPITER TRANSIT HOUSE TEN

A greater feeling of optimism inspires you to expand your personal ambitions, and the prospects for the future seem much brighter. Those with money or influence may come along to encourage your desire to further your career and other long-range goals, so it is a good time to aggressively go after what you want and to unreservedly promote yourself and your interests, Family members may be given special promotions or recognition, and it is through their success that your own reputation and status are enhanced. During this period, you may receive recognition or rewards. It is even possible to receive recognition or rewards that you really have not earned. At first, it may seem a stroke of good fortune to carry off a prize or gain an exalted position with no strings attached. In reality, however, the very lack of accountability or merit poses a danger that what has been gained so easily can be as easily lost.

Your public reputation is enhanced when *favorable* aspects are made to natal planets from Jupiter as it transits your tenth house, so don't waste a minute if you are given some public forum in which to express your ideas and opinions or to demonstrate your skills. This is also one of the best times to initiate any important changes in your life.

When *unfavorable* aspects are made to natal planets from Jupiter as it transits your tenth house, do not let yourself be misguided by false promises or put much faith in those who have failed you before just because they happen to take a different approach this time around.

JUPITER TRANSIT HOUSE ELEVEN

All that you do may not have fortunate consequences or immediately bring the happiness and satisfaction you envisioned, but what happens during this period—even in situations you think are failures—may prove more and more providential as time goes on. Friendships increase and relationships with current friends are expanded; the same may be true with regard to children in your life. Your participation in organizations may increase or become more beneficial to you. The increased energy and enthusiasm you are likely to feel can engender the desire to broaden the ways and means that bring you happiness.

Friends may provide the means to your good fortune when *favorable* aspects are made to natal planets from Jupiter as it transits your eleventh house. Success is also likely to come if you place a larger emphasis on the role you play in the lives of others and understand that there is a need for more personal freedom within those associations.

Too much of a good thing can bring troublesome consequences and ruin close relationships when *unfavorable* aspects are made to natal planets from Jupiter as it transits your eleventh house. Friends may be tempted to overstate their monetary status or exaggerate the possibilities of some venture. Remain cautious if you do not want to emerge from this period with less of a friendship and a smaller bank account.

JUPITER TRANSIT HOUSE TWELVE

Benefits you accrue or gains you make during this period may be hidden, or at least not obvious to others. This can include such situations as being given a raise in salary for certain efforts, but not the title or recognition that should have accompanied the raise. Other potentials include improvement in the job or health of a family member, or your own generosity in helping those who are in trouble.

Positive potentials when *favorable* aspects are made to natal planets from Jupiter as it transits your twelfth house include developing inner strength and power through expanding your psychic energy and intuitive ability and overcoming your hidden fears and worries. During this period, if you need help, it is likely to arrive just in time to save the day, and it may come from hidden or unexpected sources.

The adverse possibilities when *unfavorable* aspects are made to natal planets from Jupiter as it transits your twelfth house include indulging in self-pity, laboring under the burden of unnecessary guilt, or using guilt as a weapon to get others to do what you want.

SATURN THROUGH PLUTO

The transits of the slower-moving planets (Saturn through Pluto) in your natal houses must be thought of as long-term periods when other influences occur that can sometimes emphasize the conditions associated with a particular transit and sometimes temporarily mask them. Other significant factors that contribute to the way you react and ultimately to the way things turn out include your age, maturity, and past experiences. Each planet is associated with a different task or goal by means of which you can achieve a higher level of personal evolution and growth. Saturn is associated with achieving the wisdom of experience and maturity through correct actions, patience, determination, and hard work. Uranus is associated with achieving flexibility and independence by adapting to conditions you can neither manipulate nor control, conditions in which you are expected to understand and express your individuality while remaining an integral member of a team or group (which includes marriage, family, and community). Neptune means working in the dark, dealing with unknown and unknowable forces, and seeking the reality of unreality—all of which are necessary to achieve greater spirituality, heightened awareness, and increased sensitivity. Pluto's transits are associated with intense concentration and focus, the ultimate purpose of which is to bring about a transformation to satisfy a karmic responsibility. During the various periods of Pluto's transits, you may be transformed by the circumstances you experience and still not recognize that it is your karma that has been at work. No matter, the result in this lifetime is dramatic and effective enough to change your course (if it is necessary) to one aligned with your destiny.

Transit Saturn Through Natal Houses

Saturn Transit House One

During this period, you are constantly confronted with yourself. Look in the mirror and ask yourself who is responsible for your physical appearance, your personality, and your self-image. After you get through blaming your childhood and whatever people and other situations come to mind, you arrive at the moment of truth, which is that ultimately you are the one who must be accountable. You are the one who must seek to understand and correct a poor self-image or whatever other personal problems you have. If you have failed to maintain your health and fitness in the past, circumstances will cause you to regret it now. Whatever situations occur these days, they are going to require your personal attention. Do things yourself and make your own decisions. The highest reward for correct actions and healthier habits will be your emergence from this time as a more mature, productive individual with a definite focus on your personal goals and development. When Saturn transits your first house, you may worry too much, and contributing to this problem is the likelihood that you will take on extra responsibilities. Be prepared for the fact that if you gain something valuable, it will not be gained without some personal sacrifice. Take one day at a time, be moderate, and stay calm—or you will spoil the impressive progress it is possible to make.

SATURN TRANSIT HOUSE TWO

Circumstances cause you to question what is important versus what is not important, and the biggest threat you may face is the loss of something you truly value. You may not lose money during this period but if your income increases, it is because you have worked hard or been willing to make some other sacrifice to obtain it. Your behavior and attitude when it comes to handling money are a big consideration when Saturn transits your second house. Have you placed too much emphasis on money and material assets at the expense of more important things? Have you wasted or irresponsibly managed money? Have you used money as the means to escape other responsibilities? If you have neglected relationships, you may be threatened with their loss. Your willingness to take corrective action and develop a better attitude and perspective regarding finances will be tested. Even more importantly, you will be challenged either to establish or defend clearly defined priorities and unassailable values. Another possible scenario you may experience is a situation in which you do not lack money or purchasing power, but you lack the desire to shop, or what you want to purchase is unavailable or unappealing.

SATURN TRANSIT HOUSE THREE

It is difficult to get around in your neighborhood or your ability to get beyond your immediate environment is restricted when Saturn transits your third house. Circumstances conspire to point out inadequacies in the methods you use; your inability to express, organize, or think through ideas and opinions; and your lack of basic information or skills. Such deficiencies may have developed as a result of past neglect or an indifferent attitude on your part. Responsibilities related to relatives, neighbors, and those with whom you deal on a daily basis can become tedious or your contacts with them become troublesome or restricted. Travel and daily transportation can be frustrating. If you have not routinely maintained vehicles, they must be repaired or replaced. The same is true if you have failed to properly care for communications equipment, computers, appliances, and other machinery you rely on. The test of this period is your willingness to develop better attitudes and behavior toward gathering information, exchanging ideas and opinions, learning new things, and acquiring new skills. It is wise to remember that part of the test is overcoming obstacles. When one way is blocked, you must find another path. When one method fails, you must devise a new one. Meetings and discussions must have structure and purpose. Allocation of time and activities must be more organized and efficient. Although this period is filled with potential restrictions and limitations, you can learn how and when to get things done—leaving you with more free time.

SATURN TRANSIT HOUSE FOUR

You may become discouraged or disappointed with your home, domestic arrangements, or family relationships. You resent the attempt of family members to restrict or impede your progress, and they will be just as antagonistic toward your interference. You may be required to accept additional responsibilities for family members or with regard to your home. Childhood conditioning may be emphasized, and if you have negative attitudes and behavior that resulted from such conditioning, you have a responsibility to confront and overcome them. If you want to achieve the next level of personal growth and experience (along with the rewards that come with it), your sacrifice and efforts should be focused on improving family ties, establishing a healthy domestic environment, and gaining understanding and acceptance of yourself and your background. When Saturn transits your fourth house, it marks the completion of one phase and the beginning of another. Circumstances will prevent you from being successful in new situations if you have failed to complete unfinished business. If you are reluctant to move on with your life or fail to realize that it is time, circumstances may force you to do so.

SATURN TRANSIT HOUSE FIVE

It may be difficult to enjoy life, especially since the pursuit of pleasure will invariably be accompanied by responsibilities when Saturn transits your fifth house. You may have additional responsibilities for children or problems regarding them demand resolution. Children may regard you as too severe or inflexible, or you may suffer estrangement from them. Children are apt to be conceived at this time if your age and circumstances are appropriate. Although this period implies the possibility of long-lasting, stable romance, it also suggests that a serious emotional commitment must accompany such a relationship or it will not last. Destructive habits and overindulgence in the past may cause great difficulties for which you must now pay the price. Social activities may be either nonexistent or so consuming that you are prevented from concentrating on other important matters. Another focus of this period may be the development, use, or abuse of artistic and creative talents. Risk-taking—whether the risk is physical, economic, or emotional—is only to be embarked upon with the greatest of caution and maturity. The failure or inability to adopt this approach is likely to end in severe loss. What you must seek are stronger, more stable relationships, a better sense of how to control selfish desires, and a more mature and successful approach to enjoying every aspect of life.

SATURN TRANSIT HOUSE SIX

Your work and health are the main targets of this period. Work means your daily tasks and responsibilities, whether you take care of home and family or have a job outside the home. Work-related responsibilities are apt to increase. Routine schedules, endless details, and tasks may become boring and tedious when Saturn transits your sixth house. Loss of employment and other disappointments or difficulties related to work occur, your working environment is restrictive, and relationships with co-workers are burdensome. Problems demand resolution and appropriate changes. The emphasis on health does not mean that you will experience illness, but this period will reflect any past disregard you had for maintaining good health and physical fitness. Chronic illness is apt to flare up, and it would not be unusual to suffer physical distress as a result of overwork, strain, and emotional burdens. Correct actions include becoming more organized and structured, finding better methods to make your tasks easier to accomplish, and, as a result, you may gain increased income and recognition for your hard work. If you realize the importance of routine medical and dental examinations and you start eating a healthy diet and getting appropriate exercise, the ultimate payoff is that you can add happier, healthier years to your life.

Saturn Transit House Seven

Circumstances during this period will emphasize how you interact with other people and how others tend to view you (as opposed to the image you try to project). One potential, for example, is that people tend to look upon you as an authority figure. They may also see you as more austere, inflexible, or unapproachable than you actually are. The greatest focus, however, targets your partnerships, alliances, and joint ventures. Your partner may be burdened with responsibilities or suffer ill health. Should you and those involved with you harbor disappointment or seriously diverging opinions and goals, the relationship will suffer when Saturn transits your seventh house. The relationship may even be terminated if compromise or agreement cannot be reached. On the other hand, a longer-lasting, more stable marriage or other alliance may emerge if difficulties are surmounted and commitments are strengthened. Marriage or partnership that is undertaken at this time suggests the possibility that the union may be forged from the pressure of responsibility or as a matter of expediency. This description seems to predict an unhappy and restricted association, but this is not necessarily the total picture. It is possible for the participants to gain great satisfaction and valuable experience from the association if they make an effort to do so. Legal matters are not apt to be conducted in an easy atmosphere or find a swift conclusion, and the same is true for contract negotiations. Although gaining cooperation from others is certainly possible, it will not be granted freely and the additional responsibilities you are required to accept in exchange for such help may not be worth it.

Saturn Transit House Eight

Values are imposed on you. They are the values of others and not necessarily in agreement with your own. During this period you are required to acknowledge (and accept) not only the existence of these values but also the reason for their existence. Joint income or whatever assets and status you have gained through marriage, business partnerships, or inheritance; investments or property you own or manage for others; and finances related to debt or the collection of debt are the areas in which you are expected to demonstrate responsibility and take mature actions. The tax collector will cast his long shadow if there has been careless attention paid to such matters or deliberate attempts to evade or mislead him in the past. Sexual encounters that take place at this time (particularly if this is your first experience) may not necessarily be devoid of romance but they have more of a serious nature or have more of a profound or lasting effect than if they occurred at other times. When Saturn transits your eighth house, death is apt to be another focus. It does not imply your own demise or even that of a family member or friend. Some aspect of death, however remote it occurs from your own circle, may come along to remind you of the need to value life. This is also likely to be a period of personal evaluation with regard to being more resourceful and more willing to use whatever skills and abilities you possess to contribute to your own independence, financial and otherwise. If you are forced to understand and handle the responsibility of debts, monetary assets, and material and nonmaterial resources at this time, do these things willingly and well. It is the key to your future security.

SATURN TRANSIT HOUSE NINE

When Saturn transits your ninth house, the emphasis is on broadening your intellectual horizons and reaching out for new experiences. You may be required to confront past disappointment, failure, or neglect in these areas. You can more seriously participate in cultural pursuits and religious or political groups, as well as undertake an education or specialized training (or get a second chance if circumstances prevented you from doing so at an earlier time). A second marriage, in-laws, and a court decision are areas that may impose a burden of responsibility. Long-distance travel may be delayed or circumstances surrounding such travel may require more organization or involve restrictions. You may become concerned with the job and health of a parent and the loss or failure of a boss or other authority figure. Responsibilities and restrictions increase concerning foreign people, foreign trade, education, computers, publishing, broadcasting, promotion, advertising, and direct-mail activities.

SATURN TRANSIT HOUSE TEN

You are likely to get what you have worked for and the recognition or increased status you deserve. However, what you gain will correspondingly be accompanied by additional responsibilities when Saturn transits your tenth house. If you have not established long-range goals and gained no perception of what your ultimate destiny should be, circumstances will generate either the need or desire to take a more responsible attitude toward your direction in life. Although you can and should seek the wisdom and guidance of others, letting them make decisions for you is a mistake. Do not be tempted to blame others for failure or wrong actions on your part. You may find consolation in doing so, but the people and circumstances that surround you during this period will not allow you to cast any blame except on yourself. This is especially true if you have abused a position of trust or authority. By accepting the consequences of your actions and taking charge of your life, you achieve the experience and maturity that place you on a higher level where true success and fulfillment are now possible.

SATURN TRANSIT HOUSE ELEVEN

During this period, you become concerned with your own happiness. Happiness is such an individual perception that your age, maturity, and past experiences are significant factors in the way you assess your satisfaction with a career or other long-range goals and the role you play in the lives of other people. Perhaps more painful than anything else that happens when Saturn transits your eleventh house is confronting the issue of what you actually derive from being someone's child, lover, spouse, parent, friend, business associate, or fellow club member. As these various roles come under your increasing scrutiny, a strain is to be expected in the relationships and activities that are not making you happy. Your happiness is not the only consideration. Saturn's associated lessons of restriction, responsibility, and maturity suggest that being part of a group is important and that your talents and skills must not be directed inward but directed outward through others. A lack of friends in the past can engender the need to establish friendships. If it is a case of having many friends, you may realize that these associations lack the qualities of affection and commitment that accompany fewer but more meaningful friendships. Friendship is only one example. The same circumstances may attach themselves to any of your relationships. You may have to take responsibility for a child who is not biologically yours or become more responsible as a member of an organization or group effort. The answers you need are not found by searching within yourself, but by understanding your place in the community.

SATURN TRANSIT HOUSE TWELVE

You will confront that which is deliberately or inadvertently, consciously or subconsciously hidden from others. When Saturn transits your twelfth house, you must face your fears and worries, resolve issues from the past that continue to weaken your happiness and productivity, and deal responsibly with loss and disappointment. If you have taken refuge in self-pity and unnecessary guilt in the past, you now have the responsibility to rid yourself of these and other hidden and destructive habits. Confinement or other restrictions may be imposed upon you or on those for whom you are responsible. This is not a period in which you can expect others to notice or applaud your struggles and successes. These are private affairs and meant to be handled on that level. Significant inner strength and understanding are gained and you emerge better prepared to deal with present and future circumstances. You may be required to assist a family member with a serious health- or work-related difficulty. One of the most positive potentials suggests that you will be rewarded for whatever previous sacrifice and deprivation you sustained or lonely confinement you endured in order to achieve an important goal.

TRANSIT URANUS THROUGH NATAL HOUSES

URANUS TRANSIT HOUSE ONE

The general focus when Uranus transits your first house involves significant and sometimes unanticipated changes in your personality, self-image, and even your physical appearance. You may start to think of yourself as somehow different than everyone else. People who come into your life at this time as well as situations you never expected to encounter can cause you to seek or to unexpectedly discover a unique concept of yourself or a side of your personality that you had not realized you possessed. You may actively seek to express your newfound self. Personal freedom becomes increasingly important during this period, and you may engage in rebellious acts or take other steps to assure yourself that you are independent. Your need for independence does not necessarily exclude marriage or other partnerships if they do not prevent you from expressing yourself as an individual. You are less predictable, more restless, and perhaps more unstable as you try to establish a compatible mix of old and new elements within yourself. Since your physical body is associated with the first house, unexpected illness can develop and more cautious actions are necessary to offset the higher potential for accidents and injury, especially to the head and face.

URANUS TRANSIT HOUSE TWO

Your financial status is likely to undergo some changes and perhaps even a complete reversal. Unreliable circumstances surround income and finances when Uranus transits your second house, and potential circumstances include both the gain and the loss of income. Your expenditures may change as new or unanticipated situations develop. Such potential for change makes this a difficult time to take monetary risks or take your income for granted. On the other hand, there is also the potential that unlooked-for or unimagined circumstances may reverse a negative cash flow. The loss of money in one area may force you to find a way to make it up in another, which may not be such a bad thing. During this period, you may experience monetary gain or loss through friends and groups to which you belong. Financial independence is a key factor in what you can or should try to achieve, but money and material wealth are not the only focus. During this period, your values are also vulnerable to some revisions. An important relationship that is lost or a new one that is made can motivate you to establish new values and abandon old priorities.

URANUS TRANSIT HOUSE THREE

You can expect to encounter people or circumstances that cause your ideas and methods to change when Uranus transits your third house. But that may be the only thing you can expect since it is a time of unpredictable situations. Greater independence of thought and self-expression becomes a new or more powerful focus. A flood of new ideas and information flows through your mind. Your mechanical or technological skills and methods may be used in new ways, or circumstances may demand or inspire you to develop new skills in order to keep pace with your present needs. The amount of travel you do or the pattern of your daily transportation may be altered. There is even the possibility that your general mobility—that is, how you physically get from one place to another—may change in some unusual or unexpected way. Contacts with siblings and neighbors are also a target for change as they move into or away from your immediate environment. Your normal activities, meetings, and discussions can take on a radically new character as will the type of people with whom you interact. Motivation for the things you say and do is more apt to be (at least initially) your reaction to the decisions and actions of others than the result of your own inclinations. During this lengthy period, there is the danger of accidents and other ill-timed situations, but there is also the potential for experiencing dramatic success in the promotion of your ideas or the application of new skills and information that you acquire.

URANUS TRANSIT HOUSE FOUR

Current living arrangements should be viewed as temporary since unstable circumstances and unpredictable developments related to your home, domestic environment, and family relationships are likely to occur. By 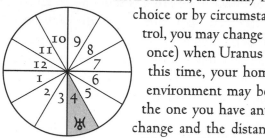 choice or by circumstances over which you have no control, you may change your residence (perhaps more than once) when Uranus transits your fourth house. During this time, your home or the nature of your domestic environment may be highly unusual or different than the one you have anticipated. Family relationships can change and the distance between you and other family members may be altered geographically, emotionally, or in other ways. Circumstances may require you to seek more independence from family ties and responsibilities and be more independent within the family group. Your family circle may be extended to include people who are not relatives. Long-term personal cycles of activity and endeavor can abruptly begin, come to an end, or change in some totally unexpected way.

URANUS TRANSIT HOUSE FIVE

When Uranus transits your fifth house, there is potential for dramatic change in certain areas, one of which involves romance. You may, for instance, suddenly break off with a romantic partner, unexpectedly begin a new romance, or form a romantic attachment with someone 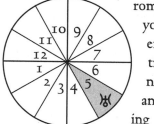 you never expected to be involved with. You may encounter unusual or nontraditional romantic situations or partners. Circumstances over which you have no control may have a great impact on your attitudes and activities concerning the pursuit of pleasure, risk-taking adventures, and speculation. Your present status regarding children and your ideas, attitudes, and relationships that involve children may be significantly altered, which includes the possibility of separation from them. Also vulnerable to the same unpredictable turn of events is your social life. There may be sudden periods of increased social activities and interest as well as periods when there are circumstances that prevent you from socializing or a total lack of anything going on. Your imagination and artistic and creative talents are other target areas, their use and development being carried off in some new direction by unpredictable circumstances. You may develop a preference for unorthodox or avant-garde trends in entertainment, art, music, or design.

URANUS TRANSIT HOUSE SIX

Whether you are employed outside the home or occupied with domestic tasks and responsibilities, your work is subject to adjustment, change, and unstable circumstances. You are likely to change jobs and work habits or initiate a change in your employment to achieve greater independence. It is possible that you may be fired or offered new employment during this period. A new job may not turn out to be what you expected or what those who employ you expected since events may occur that no one can control. The unstable circumstances when Uranus transits your sixth house are disruptive but not necessarily of a negative character. The loss of a job may force you to seek another that may be better. There is the potential that your work at this time may be of an unusual or nontraditional nature or you may find yourself working with people who are different or unusual in some way. Activities and relationships with those who work for or with you are also subject to change and separation. Another major focus is related to health, which means that your physical status is as vulnerable to unpredictable developments and new patterns as your work. Your ideas concerning health undergo some radical revisions, and you may seek or be introduced to unorthodox or alternative health and physical fitness methods.

URANUS TRANSIT HOUSE SEVEN

You may encounter some strange or unusual people during this period, and dealing with other people in general is an unpredictable state of affairs. When Uranus transits your seventh house, there is no telling exactly what out-of-the-ordinary situations you will encounter with others, especially if your job or other activities require you to deal with the public. This is a time of sudden developments and unexpected actions with regard to the status of marriage and other partnerships, alliances, and joint ventures. These associations may suddenly or unexpectedly begin, come to an end, or undergo significant change. If you are involved in a partnership, each of you must retain your individuality while remaining part of the team. Other potentials include an alliance with someone who is an unusual or unexpected partner. The circumstances or terms of a partnership or joint venture that occurs at this time should be regarded as temporary and it may be an unusual or unorthodox arrangement. Circumstances, that in all probability are not under your control, may require that you cooperate with others or make it necessary for you to seek cooperation, and either condition may be of an unusual or unanticipated nature. The terms and status of formal contracts and other legal matters during this lengthy period may be changed and even reversed. Separation from a partner or allies is a potential but so is the prospect of taking these associations in stimulating new directions.

URANUS TRANSIT HOUSE EIGHT

This is a period when you are not likely to get what you want or perhaps what you expect. You must take what you can get—and if you are not good at knowing how to take or knowing what you need, there may be problems. When Uranus transits your eighth house, unstable circumstances can come along that will affect the status of joint income and property, the payment of debts that you owe, collection of debts and benefits owed to you, insurance matters, taxes, legacies, and assets that you manage for others. Changes and reversals occur, but they may reflect gain as well as loss. The key to your future is gaining independence during this period. For this reason, it is necessary and to your distinct advantage to become more self-reliant and resourceful and to achieve a clear sense of self-worth. The reason you will need to establish self-worth or financial independence at this time is as unpredictable as the circumstances that bring it about. An unexpected brush with death or a medical emergency may cause you to take on some radically new perspectives.

Uranus Transit House Nine

You may decide to continue your education or take advanced training or else such activities may be abruptly terminated. You may become involved with travel abroad or with those of another race or culture. Other unsta-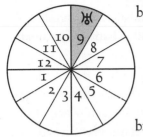ble and unpredictable circumstances when Uranus transits your ninth house are associated with a second marriage, in-laws, and the job or health of a parent. If you are involved with court decisions at this time, they will tend to have unexpected or unusual outcomes, or they may be reversed. The current status of writing, publishing, broadcasting, advertising, marketing, religious and political ideas and activities is targeted for change. Your thinking becomes more independent and original, or at least represents a departure from the past. This can be a highly stimulating time. Disruptions and the unstable nature of situations may be difficult to handle when they occur, but they may also provide the provocation you need to broaden your understanding and to experiment with alternative ideas and methods. If you travel, some caution is necessary since the potential for unexpected developments also includes accidents. However, while avoiding situations that put you unnecessarily at risk, you should nevertheless seek to get away from your immediate environment to explore new areas and meet new people.

Uranus Transit House Ten

Life is not likely to be uneventful when Uranus transits your tenth house. Some of the strongest potential circumstances are a change in career, a significant alteration in life-style, or a major new direction in goals. These 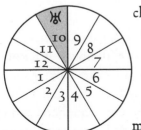changes may be part of a natural progression in your life or a way of achieving more independence concerning your future. The need for independence notwithstanding, you may not really have the initiative or a totally free choice because a key element implied by this period is outside forces over which you have no control. This means that a change that occurs may be triggered not by you but as a result of the fallout from events that happen to other people or as a result of the decisions others make. Disruptions that occur may include separation from home, family members, or those who represent authority.

URANUS TRANSIT HOUSE ELEVEN

Do you have definite ideas about what or who makes you a happy and productive person? This is a period when those ideas may dramatically change. The unstable and unpredictable circumstances when Uranus transits your eleventh house may bring separation from those in your personal network of family, friends, and associates, or they may alter the role you play in each other's lives. Unexpected or sudden developments may change the way you view your association and increase your desire to make the role you play more stimulating. This period focuses on participation in groups which means that as you seek more independence of thought and expression, you are, at the same time, challenged to find ways to attain your goals as you work with, through, and for others—not an easy thing for some people to accomplish. How easily you can do so will determine the degree to which you are troubled by the inevitable disruptions and changes that occur. New associations may suddenly begin while old ones may abruptly come to an end. If you were once content to be a loner, circumstances may cause you to seek the friendship of others. If you have many friends, circumstances may now cause you to be content with the company of very few friends. There may be highly unusual or unorthodox relationships waiting for you, and they may be of a nature or with people you might never have thought possible or imagined.

URANUS TRANSIT HOUSE TWELVE

Change, disruption, unanticipated events, and the issue of personal independence are the potentials to consider when Uranus transits your twelfth house. It is not a certainty that you will be aware that independence is what you are looking for, but in fact it is that quest that can cause you to break away from the burdens of the past and to confront subconscious resentments, secret fears, childhood conditioning, past failures, and disappointments. During this period, your past comes back in unexpected ways or at unexpected times. Delving into your past and examining your subconscious motivations and attitudes produces totally unexpected results. That which you have deliberately hidden from others and, in some cases, even from yourself may suddenly be revealed and must be dealt with openly. It would not be unusual to develop interests in the occult, the interpretation of dreams, the subconscious, and psychic energy. An inner independence is what you can accomplish by overcoming inner struggles. Circumstances may unexpectedly cause you to be confined or isolated for health, work, or other reasons, or they may require you to assist a family member who unexpectedly experiences a serious work- or health-related difficulty. There is potential for involvement in secret societies or becoming a witness or confidant in the circumspect activities of a friend.

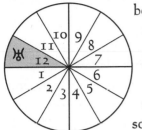

TRANSIT NEPTUNE THROUGH NATAL HOUSES

NEPTUNE TRANSIT HOUSE ONE

An increasing sense of abandonment and self-pity and the gradual erosion of self-image are some of the possible manifestations you may exhibit during this period. Such negative potentials can be devastating to the young and inexperienced, but if you have attained maturity and a healthy self-image by the time Neptune transits your first house, you may be better equipped to sidestep negative circumstances (real or imagined) that threaten to weaken your self-esteem. Whether or not it is deliberate on your part, you can project an image of helplessness, confusion, mystery, glamor, or a combination of these qualities. Others are attracted to you for reasons they may not quite understand or be able to describe. Your personal goals may be achieved simply because others find you so appealing, or, if there are unfortunate circumstances, your personal quests may fail for reasons that are obscure or unknown. As your spiritual and artistic awareness increases, you are or can become more

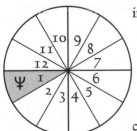

sensitive and inspired as well as inspiring. Although you may lose sight of reality and practicality from time to time during this lengthy period, you may gain keener instincts and intuition.

NEPTUNE TRANSIT HOUSE TWO

Strong priorities, unassailable values, and unwavering principles are difficult to establish or maintain during transit Neptune's long sojourn through your second house. As always, there are potentially positive as well as negative circumstances, but it is not always easy to distinguish between them. Situations can be so disappointing or negative that your values are compromised or undermined. Income and material assets, which are another major focus of this period, can be adversely affected as a result of bad investments, unwise extravagance, or the loss of earning ability. Circumstances may cause you to become confused or unable to judge what or whom is important in your life. Your values need not suffer since your experiences during this long period may cause you to realize that there are other things that are more important than money and material advantages. Positive potentials include your awareness of the possibility for bankruptcy and other financial disasters and your avoidance of people and situations that can cause such disasters. You may become more intuitive or inspired in the management of income and in finding ways to increase it. Money may be derived from work or other situations that involve such areas as religion, photography, dance, charitable foundations, penal institutions, and commercial enterprises that involve drugs, alcohol, oil and gasoline, marine equipment, or footwear.

NEPTUNE TRANSIT HOUSE THREE

When Neptune transits your third house, previous ideas and methods are infiltrated by new ideas and information, but this is not necessarily a bad thing. The positive potential includes the prospect of developing greater inspiration and intuition, especially in your ability to communicate your ideas and use information, ideas, and methods. You may become interested in or involved with boats and other water vehicles, and, when traveling, you may choose this mode of transportation. The negative potentials of this period are vagueness, misunderstanding, and mistakes that can undermine many of your efforts because facts and reality have little chance of surfacing long enough to correct inaccuracy and misjudgment. If you do not possess common sense, practicality, and careful judgment, admit it and seek the help of those who can guide you through confusing circumstances. Contacts with neighbors and siblings can become more compassionate, spiritual, or clairvoyantly close, and in the case of unfortunate circumstances, these relationships can become afflicted with mistrust, fear, and hatred. During this long phase, your neighborhood may, on the one hand, experience flooding and gas leaks or become infiltrated by drug dealers or other criminal activities, while, on the other hand, it may become the site for a church, charitable foundation, hospital, or a business such as a drugstore, liquor store, or marine supply store.

NEPTUNE TRANSIT HOUSE FOUR

More caution than may seem necessary should be used if you are involved in the sale or purchase of real estate or domestic items when Neptune transits your fourth house. Although there is certainly the possibility that keener intuition and instincts will produce successful results in such transactions, there is also the chance that confusion or deception can infiltrate the information and activities surrounding them. A parent (or parental figure) may suffer from drugs or alcohol, be involved in some mystery or scandal, or become more clairvoyant or spiritual. Home can become a strange or unreal place or it can be a true spiritual retreat depending on the circumstances. Unfortunate circumstances can bring disappointment and loss or sow the seeds of mistrust that undermine family bonds. Favorable situations can provide an atmosphere that creates more compassionate relationships, higher family ideals, and greater spirituality. You may discover something of your family's hidden past, assuming, of course, that there is any scandal or mystery to be found. It may be a time when you are tempted to disguise or deny a less than ideal family background. One of the mundane possibilities involves water connected with your home, but this can mean moving to an oceanside residence as well as a flood in your basement or a leak in your roof. Dangerous chemicals should not be used or kept at home during this period.

NEPTUNE TRANSIT HOUSE FIVE

The cliche that "love is blind" has no truer application than if love occurs when Neptune transits your fifth house. Romance can turn into a disheartening waste of time or bring you to new heights of inspiration and joy. If you have children, your relationship with them can be negatively affected by circumstances that bring disillusionment and disappointment or enhanced by positive circumstances that create more intuitive, spiritual bonds. You may adopt a child, suffer the loss of a child, or be forced by adverse circumstances to abandon one. Your imagination and creative talents may be enhanced, but whether using them leads to impressive artistic achievements or merely pleasant diversions will depend on other factors. Self-indulgence and gambling can become truly destructive if prudent limitations are not in place. The worst circumstances can occur when you fail to see the danger in physical risks, the foolhardiness in monetary risks, and the dire consequences of carelessly abandoning yourself to the pursuit of whatever temptations come along. The best of circumstances include not only the attainment of pleasure but also an increased awareness and appreciation of enjoyment, humor, and imagination.

NEPTUNE TRANSIT HOUSE SIX

When Neptune transits your sixth house, an element of uncertainty or confusion, perhaps even secrecy or mystery, creeps into the performance of your tasks and daily responsibilities whether they are related to a job or carried out at home or in other capacities. Your job description may be vague or misunderstood by you, by your employer, and by those who know you well but are not quite sure exactly what you do for a living. This potential is the reason why it is important to understand clearly what is expected of you, especially if you take on a new job or work assignment during this period. The same kind of clarification is also necessary if you employ others. Your work may involve confidential information, covert activities, bankruptcy, or scandal. Those who work for or with you may be involved in illegal or secret activities. At some point during the lengthy period of Neptune's transit, the potentials of your employment may include work related to footwear (sales, design, or distribution), maritime industries, gas or oil, pharmaceuticals, the penal system, charitable institutions, dance, religion, or photography. Your health and physical fitness represent another major sixth-house focus. Unfortunately, the same specter of unknown or mysterious conditions associated with Neptune makes illness difficult to diagnose or treat. This is a dangerous time in which to experiment with drugs, medicine, or alcohol since you may have adverse reactions. You may also be the victim of bogus health or diet systems. On the positive side, there is potential for health benefits from water therapy, spiritual guidance, and meditation. In the best of circumstances, you may be fortunate enough to find just the right medicine or health-care professional.

NEPTUNE TRANSIT HOUSE SEVEN

The feedback you get from others may not be truthful or clear-sighted when Neptune transits your seventh house. This does not mean other people automatically form a negative impression of you, but their impressions are liable to be distorted or inaccurate. You are in a difficult position trying to correct the negative image some people may have of you or trying to live up to the impossible standards of those who insist on seeing you in some idealistic way. There is no guarantee that you will have any clearer notion of other people than they have of you. A certain risk is involved in choosing a marriage or business partner and engaging in other joint ventures during this period. Ideals and expectations may be too high. Partnerships and cooperative efforts are plagued by misunderstanding, paralyzed by confusion, and undermined by distrust. Counterbalance the insidious grip of uncertainty and confusion with strong commitment, and forestall the erosion of mistrust with total honesty. There is much that is worthwhile to be gained. The positive prospects suggest that marriage and other close alliances may become more spiritual, intuitive, and sensitive. Confusion and deception can leave their marks on contracts and other legal agreements, while the positive potential includes negotiations, agreements, and joint ventures that succeed as a result of inspired actions or intuition, or perhaps for reasons no one can identify.

NEPTUNE TRANSIT HOUSE EIGHT

The potential circumstances associated with Neptune's transit in your eighth house imply the need to be independent with a realistic sense of whether or not you are a resourceful, problem-solving person. There are reasons for this. You may be dealing with confusing, undermining, or even deliberately deceptive situations concerning the values, income, and other material assets of a marriage or business partner. It is also possible that such troubling circumstances can impact not just the status of joint income, but also obscure the reality of such important matters as taxes, insurance, debts, or inheritance. Remaining alert and fully informed in these areas and seeking the advice of those who are qualified and trustworthy may save you from grief. Fortunate possibilities include the fact that you may not experience any financial problems. Another potential is that a partner's income, investments, or tax and insurance benefits are connected with Neptune-ruled areas such as gas, oil, drugs, alcohol, maritime industries, dance, footwear, charitable foundations, and disabilities. This is a period when it is possible for you to accept the values of others (especially those of a partner) in the belief that these values are better than your own—and this may in fact be the case, at least in the most positive circumstances. Ideals, motivation, behavior, and other factors involved in sexual encounters or issues dealing with sex are vulnerable to misconceptions or confusion, or they can benefit from heightened sensitivity and more intuitive understanding.

NEPTUNE TRANSIT HOUSE NINE

Where the ninth house is concerned, you are (or should be) reaching beyond your immediate environment in order to gain a greater understanding of the world, seeking new experiences, and meeting new people. But when Neptune is the transit that is involved with your ninth house, caution is necessary. Your thoughts and writings may take a more spiritual direction, you may become more philosophical in your approach, or you may become more vague or confused. In matters related to a second marriage, writing, publishing, advertising, long-distance travel, and people of another culture or race, you are sailing in tricky waters and will have to navigate a safe course to avoid being trapped by fanatic ideas, misplaced idealism, and unrealistic schemes. If you are involved in a court decision or any kind of formal decision during this lengthy period, it may be impossible to say how or why a verdict was determined. The job or health of a parent or in-law may be jeopardized by drugs, alcohol, illegal activities, or an illness that is difficult to diagnose or treat. Spiritual guidance, inspiration, imagination, and other creative talents are some of the assets that are available to further your goals.

Neptune Transit House Ten

There is the danger of scandal or notoriety attached to your reputation when Neptune transits your tenth house. If you hold a public or highly visible executive position, greater care must accompany your choice of companions as well as the situations in which you allow yourself to become involved. Circumstances can bring uncertainty about the directions your life is taking or increased feelings that your current direction has no meaning or purpose. Relationships with a parent, supervisors, and people with influence or authority are apt to be confusing and vulnerable to misunderstanding and disillusionment. On the positive side, your public image may become more inspirational, glamorous, or alluring and your ambitions become more idealistic, spiritual, and altruistic.

Neptune Transit House Eleven

The most basic issue that may ultimately emerge from the period when Neptune transits your eleventh house is the attainment of something or someone that makes you happy. Because this is such a lengthy period, you may not always realize that achieving your goals and aspirations is at the core of all circumstances.

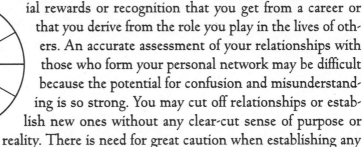

You may become disillusioned by the lack of adequate material rewards or recognition that you get from a career or that you derive from the role you play in the lives of others. An accurate assessment of your relationships with those who form your personal network may be difficult because the potential for confusion and misunderstanding is so strong. You may cut off relationships or establish new ones without any clear-cut sense of purpose or reality. There is need for great caution when establishing any new association during this period. Those who come into your life are more apt to need your help than to be in positions to help you, and they may take unfair advantage of your friendship or association. You may attract the downtrodden and disadvantaged or those with great artistry and spirituality. On the positive side, there is potential that your relationships can reach remarkable spiritual and intuitive, perhaps clairvoyant levels.

Neptune Transit House Twelve

You may develop a much deeper interest in the occult and the paranormal and attempt to reach higher levels of spiritual understanding and inner growth. The negative circumstances to avoid include the tendency to engage in such destructive emotions as self-pity, guilt, inadequacy, and fear. Other unfortunate possibilities include your failure to recognize danger and your inability to detect those who may wish you harm. While there is always the chance that you will escape loss, injury, victimization, and perilous situations, the potential for experiencing these things is a reason to have the ready advice and guidance of more than one trusted ally. When Neptune transits your twelfth house, discussions about inner fear or worry may be unproductive since you may not have a clear sense of exactly what the trouble is, or those who try to help you may be unable to understand the problem. A better use of your time during this period may be to concentrate on the positive potential, which is the gaining of inner spirituality and psychic growth. In the most positive instances, your instincts and intuition may be so heightened that they reach the level of ESP. By choice or circumstances, you may lead a more confined or isolated existence or become more involved with those who do.

TRANSIT PLUTO THROUGH NATAL HOUSES

PLUTO TRANSIT HOUSE ONE

Pluto's transit covers a period of many years and the character of its circumstances has a powerful impact on you. Because of the long duration of Pluto's transit in the first house, its effect occurs on a gradual basis and may only be witnessed when other circumstances and influences highlight your personality and behavior. Your needs and goals are strictly personal and have little to do with your family and others close to you. You may not necessarily neglect your family, but, for the most part, it is primarily your own goals that dominate your time and attention. You consciously or subconsciously seek control and a more powerful image. You are likely to take a vigorous and dedicated approach to improving yourself. The type of self-improvement you choose will depend on many factors, but it will be in areas where your background and experiences have caused you to feel the weakest and most vulnerable. It may mean pursing higher education or advanced training, developing a more dynamic personality, projecting a stronger image, engaging in physical fitness, or undergoing cosmetic surgery and other treatments to enhance your appearance and boost your confidence. Events during this long period are apt to be sobering and your reaction is to retreat more and more within yourself, sometimes to the point of isolation. You find it difficult to accept advice or be led by others and end up handling situations alone and doing things your way. What you are unable to control, you are likely to ignore. The more you are aware of the personal power that is possible to achieve, the more you will be able to use it to your own advantage. Remarkable personal accomplishments can result from the intense physical energy and focus you can generate.

PLUTO TRANSIT HOUSE TWO

Being totally honest about what you want gives you a much better chance of actually getting it when Pluto transits your second house. There is no escape from this truthful revelation because it will come out one way or another. Your attitudes and behavior about what is important and valuable are significantly affected by the circumstances you experience. The real key to this period is to understand the rightful place money and status have in life: to realize that you cannot truly own anything and that whatever you are given or whatever you take must be returned in some form. That philosophical lesson may, however, take second place to efforts to increase your income and develop your social or professional status. Living in a society that is overwhelmingly materialistic makes it almost impossible to avoid concern with achieving social status and other advantages that accompany wealth. The issue is whether money and material possessions control you or you control them. Unfortunate consequences result from using money or status as a wedge to manipulate others or allowing yourself to be used in such a manner. You should not go overboard and neglect financial matters or start believing that money is inherently evil. In the proper scheme of things, this can be an excellent period to learn how to conserve, invest, and increase your income and assets. Pluto's involvement in your second house is not itself an indication that money, material possessions, or anything of value (which includes relationships) will be gained or lost. However, the regenerative nature of the circumstances associated with Pluto indicates the potential that you may lose everything, start all over again, and ultimately regain what was lost.

PLUTO TRANSIT HOUSE THREE

Others find it difficult to hide anything from you. Situations may arise that compel you to seek information about individuals even to the point of covert actions and invasion of privacy. Such efforts may get you the data you are after, but they can have a devastating impact on your relationships with those whose privacy you abuse. In the circumstances that develop when Pluto transits your third house, you do not deal with trivialities and routine matters may take on a much greater significance. Your ideas and self-expression become more serious and intense. You become more observant and seek more control in your immediate environment. The places that you go and the people with whom you associate on a daily basis are gradually brought into sharper focus, and you may develop greater interest and participation in community affairs. You seek greater understanding and control of the methods and products that you use to communicate, to take care of paperwork, and to accomplish your business and personal transactions. One result may be that you become more deeply involved with computers, communications equipment, sales techniques and with the development of your mechanical or design skills. Circumstances during this long phase may establish a karmic or psychological link (which can be of a positive or negative nature) with a sibling or neighbor, or some dramatic event that they experience will have a significant impact on your life as well as theirs.

PLUTO TRANSIT HOUSE FOUR

Circumstances may force you to make a complete break with the past, but not before it has been confronted and dealt with openly and honestly. This includes coping with destructive childhood conditioning that may be adversely affecting your present behavior and attitudes. When Pluto transits your fourth house, it is unlikely that issues and events that have been buried will stay buried. Your status within the family is a likely focus of attention. If you feel your position is or has been one of weakness or vulnerability, you will (or should) attempt to strengthen it. This process may mean that family ties are either broken or become more powerful and close. For you, home must now be a place that reflects your personal influence and control, either literally or figuratively. Renovation and repair of your home or property may be part of the way you deal with the past or are forced to deal with it at this time. Control of family property and resources may become an issue of intense interest. One potential is that a parent or elderly relative may experience some significant transition which, in turn, will have a deep impact on your life. At some point before this period ends, circumstances will require you to make a new start. No matter what the reasons are that cause it to happen, a new beginning can be the means as well as the result of achieving control of how, where, and with whom you choose to live.

PLUTO TRANSIT HOUSE FIVE

You are in a long period of transition related to children and romantic partners, to the development and use of creative talents, and to the pursuit of pleasure when Pluto transits your fifth house. Throughout the years of this phase of life, you become more intense and focused as constructive and destructive situations come along. These situations give you the ultimate choice in the kind of impact that children and romantic partners have on you and you on them. Negative potentials include the tendency to manipulate and control them, to view them only as extensions of your own influence and identity, or to allow them to treat you in similar fashion. The positive prospects for these relationships are circumstances in which you establish more powerful bonds. A significant transition or event experienced by a child or romantic partner may further impact and change your own outlook and perspective. The emphasis on creative and artistic talents, if you possess such skills, means that circumstances demand a much deeper understanding, wiser application, and greater efforts to develop your true potential. The pursuit of pleasure and the desire to enjoy life can be intense, but how you deal with putting these matters in proper perspective depends on your past attitudes and experiences.

PLUTO TRANSIT HOUSE SIX

When Pluto transits your sixth house, your attitude toward work and daily responsibilities becomes more intense and serious. You develop an increasing need to have some control or influence over your work which may or may not extend to your working environment. As a result, you may find yourself engaged in power struggles with those who work for or with you. Because this period is so long, it would not be unusual for your job and responsibilities to change, but some tasks or jobs associated with Pluto may come your way—including work that involves renovation and repair, breeding of animals, death, conservation and distribution of resources, research and development, or investigative projects. No matter what your job may be, one of the issues you must confront involves your willingness to be of service to others. If service is not associated with your work, then conditions may arise that require you to extend yourself to help or to guide others. Another area in which you may experience a major transition concerns your behavior and attitude toward health and physical fitness. If you have generally been neglectful or abusive of your body, it is not unlikely that you will suffer the consequences by gradually developing corresponding physical complaints. Even if past abuse has not been the case or physical complaints do not arise, it is to your advantage during this time to gain greater control over your body through proper diet and exercise as well as through preventive medical attention and check-ups.

PLUTO TRANSIT HOUSE SEVEN

Circumstances during this period force you to be brutally honest about what you want and need from other people; it is all or nothing at all. If you are involved in a marriage and either you or your partner is not totally committed, you may abandon the alliance rather than accept such a half-way status. Consciously or subconsciously, you may view all partnerships and cooperative efforts as a means of gaining greater personal power. Alliances and joint ventures that fail to give you increased status and influence or that interfere with your being able to achieve such things are likely to be terminated. When Pluto transits your seventh house, you may seek to manipulate or gain control in partnerships or you may be used in the same manner by a more powerful partner. Even healthy relationships may flounder when one of the partners becomes more emotionally isolated (or, in some cases, physically remote) as a means of escaping the real or imagined control that the other partner has. A partner may experience a traumatic event or other significant transition and its impact will change both of you and, consequently, the relationship. But this does not have to be a bad situation. In the long run, the relationship may improve. The positive potential suggests that you can establish and nurture extremely powerful alliances that benefit everyone concerned. There are karmic links to work out and increased power to be gained through cooperation and the realization that you must use others as well as allow yourself to be used—but in equal measure.

PLUTO TRANSIT HOUSE EIGHT

A common characteristic in many of the circumstances associated with Pluto is that you are forced to give up one thing to gain another, and this is especially true when Pluto transits your eighth house. Transitions that you undergo during this period are akin to death and rebirth. They are serious and life-changing. At some point a more powerful monetary or social position may be achieved through marriage and other close alliances, inheritance, and tax or insurance benefits—but if any of these potentials comes to pass, you are likely to pay a very high price for whatever you have gained. One possibility is that you must now accommodate the values and principles of a partner or other people even though their values and priorities may not agree with your own. Joint income and family assets may be gained or lost, but circumstances will show that your worth cannot be measured by such things, and the power you seek transcends material wealth. What will matter most is the realization that your resourcefulness, skills, and talent can give you independence and strength. Debts are a significant issue. Money and other material assets that you receive as well as assistance and favors that you are granted are debts that must be repaid. But there are different kinds of debts to consider. The eighth house is a strong position for transit Pluto, and, even if you have no awareness of it, the circumstances you experience during this period represent karmic debts. By choice or circumstance, you will be forced to question your motives and behavior as well as to analyze the motives and behavior of those who have had or still have a great deal of influence over you. Gaining personal power and greater control is the object of this period, and there is no better place to start than by gaining a deeper understanding of yourself.

PLUTO TRANSIT HOUSE NINE

The old saying that knowledge is power will become increasingly true if you make the effort to extend the boundaries and depth of your knowledge and experiences when Pluto transits your ninth house. Your interest in foreign lands and cultures may become more serious and involved, and if you should travel abroad, your thinking and ideas will be deeply affected by experiences in other lands and among people of a different culture or race. Your attitude and activities related to higher education, cultural pursuits, and religious or spiritual growth become more intense and serious. If you lacked the means or the willingness to expand the depth of your knowledge and experience in the past, you seek to correct this vulnerability now. Furthermore, if you cannot or do not wish to pursue a formal education, you have the drive to read and study on your own. If you write, teach, or are occupied in some other area of communication, you develop an ability to present your ideas and information in much greater depth, and, in turn, others will tend to regard them as more profound. The negative potentials include the possibility of developing fanatic ideas or becoming obsessed with gaining information or using it as a weapon to manipulate or gain some type of control. Those related to you by marriage may experience a transition, and a significant change in the job or health of a parent will have an impact on your life. A second marriage (or circumstances related to a second marriage), in-laws, the judicial system or court decisions, publishing, writing, broadcasting, advertising, politics, and foreign travel are all areas that can potentially become the means by which you achieve greater spiritual and intellectual power.

PLUTO TRANSIT HOUSE TEN

Focus and determination fuel a relentless pursuit of a career or other important ambition. You resent and resist anyone who attempts to exert control over your future. If you allow others to make important decisions for you or put yourself in a position where you are forced to allow others to make decisions regarding your future, you will regret it by the time this long period has ended. If you have not established definite directions in life by the time Pluto transits your tenth house, circumstances will occur in which you will no doubt learn the importance of doing so. If you fail to take charge of your life, no matter how clear the need to do so becomes, the events and people you encounter will conspire to force you to make changes — some of which you may come to regret. Drifting along in the same pattern year after year will not be acceptable. One of the potentials is that a parent, employer, or guardian may undergo a transition as a result of some traumatic event or significant development, and this has a deep impact on your future. The choices you make, voluntarily or otherwise, are not likely to be easy or trivial. You will not gain something without giving up something else. One of the consequences may be an intense struggle to accommodate the demands of home and family while pursuing your personal ambitions. No matter how dedicated you are to personal privacy and the family circle, this is a public period in your life: a time when you are thrust into the public arena, when your attitudes and actions are observed, and when you may be perceived as a person of power and influence.

PLUTO TRANSIT HOUSE ELEVEN

The focus of this period can only be viewed through the lens of total honesty. During this long phase in your life, you will not be able to escape from admitting what and who you want and need to be happy. You will gradually develop a deeper, more serious concern with the rewards that you derive from your work and other efforts, and your relationships with others will take on greater significance. The potential of Pluto always includes being of service to others and, in this instance, it specifically relates to friends and organizations. There is also the possibility of finding karmic ties with a child who is not your biological offspring. There is happiness to be gained when Pluto transits your eleventh house, but it must come through others, through the role that you play in the lives of others. If you are a member of organizations, you will seek a more powerful position within them or use your memberships to enhance your position in other areas. You may seek to manipulate or control relationships or to retreat from those in which you are the one who is manipulated. Recognizing that you need to be part of something outside of yourself, you may establish a network of relationships that help you become happier and more successful.

PLUTO TRANSIT HOUSE TWELVE

Power and control, the prominent factors associated with Pluto, are hidden when Pluto transits your twelfth house. This can mean secret activities. It can mean that your resources (monetary assets, confidential information) or the political, economic, or other kinds of control you have over others may be hidden. You may be able to overcome the people or situations that have victimized you, but if you are guilty of such destructive behavior, it will be you who must face the consequences. Self-pity, guilt, and denial are emotional mechanisms that will not work. The true objective of this period involves the power and control within yourself. To seek inner power and control—to develop it and to use it—is a difficult, even courageous quest that cannot be achieved without serious determination and honest self-reflection. You may not be able to voice your disappointments and failures to others, but you will have to confront them within yourself. You must analyze inner resentments, fears, worries, and issues from the past that should have been long forgotten but that continue to adversely affect your behavior and attitudes. Isolation may become a way of life, whether you physically inhabit a remote place or simply retreat within yourself. Confinement and restrictions, mental as well as physical, are important concerns that you need to confront. Part of this period's karmic lesson, however, is not so much to abolish limitations and restrictions (though that may become a necessity at some point) as it is to understand and control how you deal with them. Do not expect others to recognize or applaud your inner struggles, for these are private battles and must be handled on that level. The answers you seek are buried within yourself. Circumstances throughout this long period will provide ways for you to help yourself. You may, for example, investigate dream analysis and study other psychological techniques to understand how your subconscious reveals itself on a conscious level. You may develop your intuitive powers and psychic energy. Yet another path to gaining inner power is through helping others, and in the bargain coming to the realization that true charity is the purest form of compassion, and that compassion is never burdened by the expectation of personal gain or recognition.

Chapter Twelve

Transits in the Natal Chart: The Art of Prediction

O nce you master its main concepts, the only way to learn astrology is by studying as many horoscopes as possible. The natal charts of your family and friends are limited in number, so you should also study the charts of famous people. Books that feature such charts are listed in the bibliography. Analyzing the horoscopes of public personalities is even more meaningful if you take the time to read their biographies. Studying their behavior, attitudes, and personal traits as well as details about the era in which they lived or the social, economic, and cultural backgrounds from which they came, considerably broadens your understanding of astrology, history, and psychology.

Previous chapters described the kinds of potential circumstances that are associated with the transiting planets and in this chapter those descriptions will be applied to four natal charts. A similar sequence was followed in *The Instant Horoscope Reader*; in the final chapter of that book, natal interpretations presented in previous chapters were applied to the natal charts of four famous people: Theodore Bundy, Grace Kelly, Mata Hari, and Theodore Roosevelt. You will meet them again in this, the final chapter of *The Instant Horoscope Predictor*. If you have not read the natal interpretations and biographical accounts for Ted Bundy, Grace Kelly, Mata Hari, and Theodore Roosevelt in the earlier book, you will find it very helpful to do so as a supplement to what is presented here. Knowing the personality and character of an individual is important if we are to derive an accurate interpretation of the transiting planets in his or her horoscope. When a horoscope is presented for study, the source of birth data must always be cited. The sources of the birth data for the people I have discussed are listed in Appendix C and the biographies are listed in the bibliography. Some of the astrological interpretations that I include in this chapter are in italics to indicate that they are taken directly from material in previous chapters of this book. In the many cases where I have not done so, I urge readers to refer to previous chapters to refresh their memories as to the interpretation for specific aspects.

There are various ways to analyze the transiting planets as they move through a natal chart, including some very complicated methods that are not appropriate to this book. There is, however, a general method that pulls together the basic astrological concepts to yield significantly accurate and detailed predictions. Part of this method is simply to interpret the natal house positions in which the transiting planets appear. The other part involves more work but is not difficult to understand. Every natal chart has its own internal dynamics which are determined by the aspects between the natal planets. When the internal energy of a natal conjunction, sextile, square, trine, or opposition is triggered by the outer dynamics of transiting planets, that internal energy is released and the individual responds in some way to the circumstances in which he finds himself. The kind of circumstances he encounters are indicated by the external dynamics of whatever aspects are being made by the transiting planets.

Figure 12.1 shows a chart that features a natal Cancer-Capricorn opposition between Mars and Venus in Cancer and Moon in Capricorn. The series of examples (a-h) indicates various points that are triggered by aspects made to the natal planets from Saturn as it transits the twelve signs. Two points are activated when transit Saturn in Aries forms a square to the natal planets in Cancer as well as a square to the natal Moon in Capricorn (Example a). Two similar points are activated from the other side when Saturn initiates the squares as it transits Libra (Example b). Squares suggest circumstances that cause frustration, disappointment, and anger that result in actions that attempt to relieve stress. Two points are triggered when transit Saturn in Cancer conjoins natal Venus and Mars and opposes natal Moon in Capricorn (Example c), and two similar points are sparked when transit Saturn conjoins the Moon in Capricorn while opposing natal Venus and Mars in Cancer (Example d). Although conjunctions signify powerful energy, the kind of situations they indicate can be either harmonious or discordant in nature. Oppositions are associated with problematical situations that cannot be overcome, and the energy that is released compels actions that attempt to compensate for whatever cannot be obtained or changed. Harmonious points are activated when the transit of Saturn in Taurus (Example e) or Virgo (Example f) trines natal Moon in Capricorn and sextiles natal Venus and Mars in

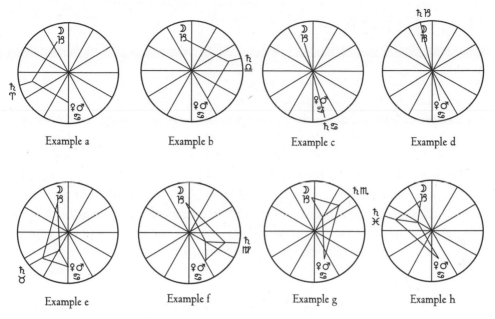

Example a   Example b   Example c   Example d

Example e   Example f   Example g   Example h

Figure 12.1: Transit Examples

Cancer. Similar harmonies are set in motion when transit Saturn in Scorpio (Example g) or Pisces (Example h) trines natal Venus and Mars in Cancer and sextiles natal Moon in Capricorn. The inherent promise of a trine is fortunate, or successful circumstances occur with little or no effort. A sextile offers the potential of an opportunity that, if taken advantage of, will lead to some victory or reward.

Keep in mind that aspects describe the harmonious or discordant dynamics of potential circumstances, but they do not imply with any certainty what the outcome will be. Just as there are good and bad situations that can occur when transits initiate squares and oppositions, there are good and bad situations that can occur when the transits form trines and sextiles to the planets in a natal chart. The good fortune indicated by a trine may mean circumstances that allow someone to get away with murder, and the unfortunate situation indicated by a square or opposition may cause an individual to work hard enough to achieve success. What an individual will do or what happens to him as a result of circumstances depends, among other things, on the kind of behavior and attitudes he has developed. This is why it is so necessary to understand with whom you are dealing when interpreting the transits in their horoscope.

TED BUNDY

A young woman walks alone. She would not picture herself the victim of a man who looked like Ted Bundy or imagine being attacked by someone who is physically handicapped. And, indeed, she will not be frightened by the appearance of an ill-clothed, evil-looking brute. What she does see is a young man walking toward her—a good-looking man, the kind she would like to date. He is on crutches (the result of a skiing accident he will tell her) and it is obvious that he is struggling when several books he carries fall to the ground. As he makes an awkward attempt to pick them up, he smiles and asks her to help him carry the books just around the corner to where his car is parked. She feels no alarm or hesitation at the spontaneous request. She is never seen alive again. A young woman asleep in her bed might dream of an attractive lover who looks like Ted Bundy. But she will never wake to see the real Ted who sneaks into her room carrying a log which he uses to savagely crush her skull.

The life that was to become an evil odyssey bringing horror and death to more than thirty young women and unimaginable pain to their families began in Burlington, Vermont, on November 24, 1946, at 10:35 PM EST. Planetary patterns in Ted's natal chart that indicated potential violence in his nature were the opposition between his natal planets in Gemini and Sagittarius and the square between his natal planets in Leo and Scorpio. Many people born with similar planetary configurations in their horoscope do not turn out to be like Ted Bundy—a strong reminder of how important it is to include a person's heredity and background as integral factors when interpreting their chart.

Ted's defense team asked Dorothy Otnow Lewis, a professor at the New York University Medical Center, to evaluate him. In testimony based on her evaluation of Ted and interviews she conducted with his relatives, Lewis makes it clear that rage and mental imbalance existed in his maternal grandparents. Recounting this testimony in her book, Ann Rule added, "The fact that Ted was damaged early on comes out in a most-telling incident that Dr. Lewis related in Ted's December 1987 competency hearing. It occurred when Ted was three years old. His Aunt Julia, then about fifteen, awakened from a nap to find that her body was surrounded by knives. Someone had placed them around her as she slept. ... she looked up to see her three-year-old nephew. The adorable, elfin Ted Bundy stood by her bed, grinning at her. Three years old."[1]

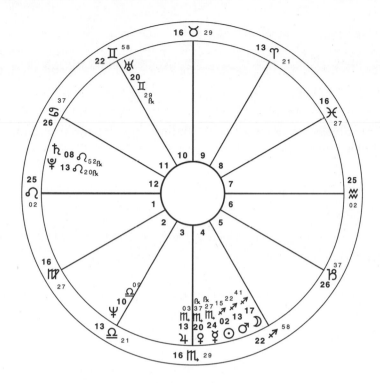

Figure 12.2: Ted Bundy's Natal Chart

Although we are aware of his abnormal behavior patterns as we study Ted's chart, these tendencies must be put into the context of a life that also included many ordinary activities as well as some extraordinary achievements. What were some of the aspects and positions of the transiting planets that indicated circumstances in which he could achieve great success, generously help others, find love, perform unspeakable acts of violence, and, ultimately, be put to death in the electric chair? Study the stress points in the internal dynamics of Ted's natal chart (see Figure 12.2). His natal square between Mercury-Venus-Jupiter in Scorpio and Saturn-Pluto in Leo, for example, is triggered when transits in Aquarius square the natal planets in Scorpio and oppose the natal planets in Leo. When the transits move into Gemini, they set off the natal Gemini-Sagittarius opposition as they oppose natal Sun, Mars, and Moon and conjoin natal Uranus. While in Gemini, the transits also sextile the natal Saturn-Pluto conjunction in Leo and trine natal Neptune in Libra. One of Ted Bundy's strongest characteristics was

323

the innate need to control and manipulate; the result, he admitted, of having a very low opinion of himself. He was easily inhibited by people that he viewed as superior. To him, superior people meant those with wealth and social position, two things he equated with power and control. He said killing someone was what gave him the ultimate kind of control. How does an urge of such insane and malignant magnitude develop? Determining the answer starts with the outer planets since their long-term transits establish periods in his life of significant length and influence.

1961–1965

In the summer of 1954, when Ted was seven years old, transit Pluto began a long and crucial period in his first house where it remained until he was almost twenty. Transit Pluto in a first-house position indicates circumstances that encourage the development of a personality and self-image strongly marked by the urge for power and control. In 1961, transit Pluto in the first house was joined by transit Uranus, increasing the potential for problems as the unpredictable environment associated with Uranus started to have an impact on fifteen-year-old Ted who, by this time, had a well-developed inclination to control and manipulate. In discussions with writers Stephen Michaud and Hugh Aynesworth, Ted recalled his frustration at no longer being able to control his environment: "In junior high, everything was fine. ... Nothing that I can recall happened that summer before my sophomore year to stunt me or otherwise hinder my progress. But I got to high school and I didn't make *any* progress. How can I say it? I'm at a loss to describe it even now."[2]

As sure as Ted was about wanting to be in control, he was equally unsure and vague about himself: a symptom that is indicated by Neptune's transit in his third house. In addition to the house positions of Pluto, Neptune, and Uranus, the aspects formed by these and other transits to his natal planets from 1961 to 1965 contribute clues to many of the situations he experienced and later described. During his sophomore year, transit Saturn in Aquarius activated his natal Leo-Scorpio square as it opposed natal Saturn, an indication that circumstances provide *little or no room for real freedom or actual progress*. From Virgo, transit Uranus triggered his natal Gemini-Sagittarius opposition with a square to his natal Sun, implying that his biggest frustration was *not being able to control or manipulate situations*. Transit Neptune in Scorpio, already triggering his natal Leo-Scorpio square, initiated the first of a series of squares it would make to natal

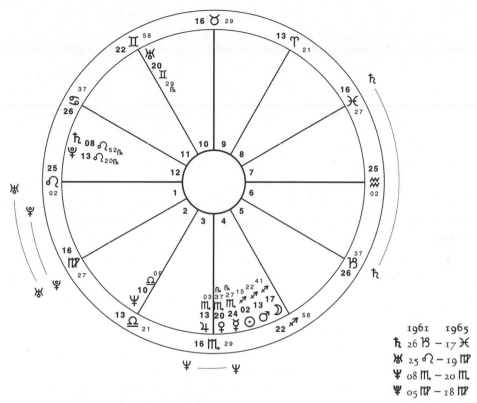

Figure 12.3: Ted Bundy's 1961–1965 Transits

Pluto: the potential for yet another loss of control real or imagined, *just when you think, for instance, that you have gained mastery over something, it may suddenly fall apart or elude you.* By April 1963, transit Saturn in Aquarius squared natal Venus, an aspect repeated the following summer and in January 1964. The restrictive conditions associated with Saturn that affected Ted's social life and inclinations (natal Venus) are well documented in his own words: "In my earlier schooling, it seemed like there was no problem in learning what the appropriate social behaviors were. It just seemed that I reached a wall, as it were, in high school. It never crossed my mind to see a counselor. I didn't think anything was wrong, necessarily. I wasn't sure what was wrong and what was right. ... Emotionally and socially, something stunted my progress in high school."[3]

In 1964 and 1965, transit Uranus and transit Pluto in Virgo sextiled Ted's natal Jupiter, an implication of opportunity. Uranus suggests increased popularity in groups and Pluto promises a more powerful image. Ted revealed how much of an opportunist he was as he discussed his interest in politics and sports (two areas that fall within the province of natal Jupiter). In high school, Ted worked as a volunteer in a local political race, an enjoyable experience and opportunity that led six years later to working for the Republican gubernatorial candidate Don Evans. "Politics gave me the opportunity to be close to people. ... To be socially involved with them. ... In my younger years, I was, as I've said before, socially unskilled. ... But politics gave me a lot. It gave me a direction and an education in a lot of things tangential to politics—things I needed to know."[4] Although he did not participate in team sports (a situation in which he was not in control), he did benefit from being a good skier (a situation in which he was in control). "Oddly enough, it was through my deep interest in skiing that I became involved in the most socially minded and socially active people in my class."[5]

Ted began his junior year when transit Pluto in Virgo squared his natal Mars, an implication of situations in which *your competitive spirit and aggressiveness increase*, with the additional promise that *increased competitiveness can be a good thing if it helps you to accomplish some worthwhile goal you might not otherwise have tackled*. Ted was, in fact, an excellent student, urged on by the aggressive energy indicated by transit Pluto's square to his natal Mars and by the academic success that came from his efforts (natal Mars is part of the natal Leo-Sagittarius trine in his chart). A troubling situation was indicated by transit Neptune in Scorpio. Ted had good looks, academic success, and opportunities to make friends. Why did he think of himself as a failure? Analyzing the low self-esteem in his youth, Ted remarked, "When people were genuinely interested in me, I seldom picked up on it. Simply, I just didn't appreciate my worth."[6] This is a good example of the false or confused impressions a person can get when transit Neptune conjoins natal Jupiter and natal Venus.

1965–1970

Between 1965 and 1970, Uranus and Pluto occupied Ted's natal second house, transit Neptune was in the fourth, and Saturn's transit in Pisces, Aries, and Taurus took it through his natal eighth and ninth houses and into the tenth. Beginning in his tenth house, the faster transit of Jupiter covered six natal houses

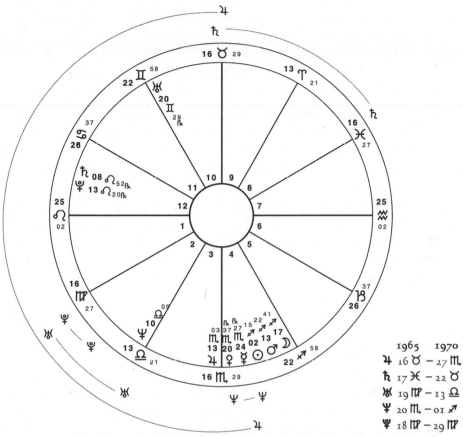

Figure 12.4: Ted Bundy's 1965–1970 Transits

putting that planet in the fourth house by the end of 1970. During these years, Ted was in and out of several universities, had two serious romantic relationships, and worked for the Republican Party in Seattle. In September 1965, he started college on a scholarship to the University of Puget Sound, but in 1966, with transit Jupiter in Cancer trine natal Mercury and Venus, he transferred to a program of intensive Chinese at the University of Washington. The fortunate circumstances of Jupiter's trine to Mercury indicates his enthusiasm for foreign languages as well as potential for *broadening your intellectual horizons, ... and success in higher education.* The trine to natal Venus promises that *if it is romance you seek, it is romance you will find.* Experiencing the reality of these fortunate potentials, he earned high grades in the Asian Studies program in which he had enrolled, and in the spring of 1967, he met a woman who was the epitome of his dreams. The problem with trines, as well as the optimism associated with Jupiter, is that success can disappear as quickly as it appeared. In 1968, his girlfriend broke off their relationship and Ted was floundering so badly in his studies that he dropped out of school. His love life and academic performance may have suffered, but his ego was well served by the success of his political activities in the spring of 1968 as transit Saturn in Aries in his natal ninth house triggered the natal Mars-Pluto trine. He was appointed Seattle chairman and assistant state chairman of the Majority for Rockefeller, and he was rewarded for his work with a trip to Miami for the convention. By the end of the year, his candidate had lost the election, and Ted was in a slump with no productive activities or success to bolster his ego.

The transits of Mars in 1969 and 1970 give some clues as to what happened next. Born out of wedlock and adopted by his stepfather, Ted never knew his real father. Transit Mars conjoin his natal Jupiter in January 1969 suggested that *work or physical efforts may be for or concerned with your father*, and it was to learn more about his father that he took a trip early in 1969. Transit Mars entered his fourth house (one's childhood and family background) in January, appropriately indicating his urge to go back to Philadelphia where he had spent the first few years of his life. Relating the incident to Ann Rule, he told her "I went back east in 1969. I needed to prove it to myself, to know for sure. I traced my birth to Vermont, and I went to the city hall, and I looked at the records. It wasn't difficult; I just asked for my birth certificate under my mother's name—and there it was."[7]

Over the summer, Ted moved back to Seattle; during the last week in September, shortly after transit Mars entered his fifth house (romance), Ted met Liz, a woman who almost immediately came to love and believe in him. "It wasn't three months after he met Liz that they began to discuss marriage. They took out a license and talked to her relatives about using their home for the ceremony."[8] (This doesn't seem surprising since by this time transit Mars was in Ted's seventh house of marriage.) The marriage plans were soon called off, however, although the relationship continued. Since 1968, transit Pluto had been sextiling Ted's natal Mercury, suggesting *opportunities that involve education, psychology*. The last of Pluto's sextiles in June of 1970 inaugurated Ted's return to school, this time with a major in psychology. His choice of study did turn out to be a fortunate opportunity that enabled him to get his life back on track. "In a psychology curriculum, Ted seemed to have found his niche. ... The boy who had seemed to be without direction or plans now became an honors student."[9] A letter, written by one of his former psychology professors recommending him for Law School, praised Ted's academic work in psychology, adding that "Mr. Bundy has become intensely interested in studying psychological variables which influence jury decisions."[10] In view of what was to come, this letter provides either a glimpse of Ted's prophetic sense of his destiny or, more likely, a view of his cunning, self-protective nature. At the end of 1970, transit Neptune began a series of conjunctions with Ted's natal Sun, one of the potentials being confusion in the matter of his ego. Ted admitted that his choice of psychology as a major "was probably an outgrowth of my confusion about myself."[11]

1971–1973

For Ted, 1971 began with transit Neptune as well as transit Jupiter in Sagittarius conjoin his natal Sun. The potential for heightened sensitivity and involvement with charitable causes was evidenced by Ted's work at the Seattle Crisis Clinic where he was a paid work-study student. Ann Rule, who was one of his coworkers, describes a sensitive and caring Ted who patiently listened to the woes of drug users, alcoholics, and would-be suicides who telephoned the clinic for help. The last conjunction of transit Neptune with his natal Sun covered June and October in 1972. The association of transit Neptune with work at the Crisis Clinic gave way to involvement in situations with other Neptunian implications when, after graduation, Ted went to work for the Committee to Re-Elect Washington's Republican Governor. His job was to travel around the state and monitor the speeches of the opposing candidate. He would sometimes wear a false mustache, a masquerade he enjoyed: "I just mingled with the crowds and nobody knew who I was."[12] One highlight was on September 2, when Ted became one of the first people to traverse the North Cascade Highway. Driving Governor Evans and other dignitaries, he led a parade of cars over the sixty-four-mile route across the mountains.

Ted applied to Law School at the University of Utah in 1973. Although his LSAT scores were low and they had previously turned him down, his excellent grades at the University of Washington and letters of recommendation from his former professors plus the newly reelected Governor turned the tide in his favor, and he was accepted. In spite of this academic coup, Ted did not go to Utah in September, a choice that still remains a mystery. According to Ann Rule, it may

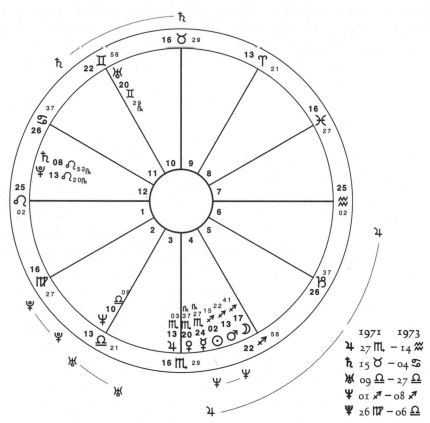

Figure 12.5: Ted Bundy's 1971–1973 Transits

have been because he was awarded such an excellent political job in April 1973. At the time, transit Jupiter was in his natal sixth house, which brings the potential for fortunate employment. "His $1,000 a month salary was more money than he'd ever made. The 'perks' that came with the job were something that a man who had struggled for money and recognition most of his life could revel in: the use of a Select Credit Card issued to the Republican Party, attendance at meetings with the 'big boys,' and occasional use of a flashy car. There was statewide travel with all expenses paid."[13] He did attend Law School that September but it was night classes at the University of Puget Sound. Ted appeared to have the brains and ambition of a young man on his way to a successful career. No one who knew him—not his college professors who were impressed with his excellent work in psychology; not the people in politics who were impressed with his excellent work for the Republican Party; not his coworker Ann Rule who would end up writing a book about him; not Liz, the woman who loved him and believed they would marry one day; not even his mother—suspected that he was living a secret life, a ghastly and brutal existence. None of them were prepared for what they would learn about the real Ted Bundy.

THE KILLINGS

In a desperate attempt to stay his execution, Ted eventually confessed to killing thirty young women, beginning with a hitchhiker he picked up in Olympia, Washington, in May 1973. There is strong evidence to suggest there were more than thirty victims and the first one may have been a young girl who disappeared from her home in the early morning hours of August 31, 1961. Speaking of himself in the third person (a method used by writers Michaud and Aynesworth to get him to talk about the murders), Ted related how the crimes occurred in two phases: "At first he was an amateur, impulsive killer. The girl in Olympia, for example, was a whim murder committed with his bare hands. He wouldn't kill that way again ... 'until Florida.' His prime, which he also calls his 'predator' phase, is the second period, beginning about the time of Linda Healy's murder. Ted began seeking victims equal to his skills, women 'worthy,' in another of his terms, to be hunted."[14] Linda Healy's murder took place on January 31, 1974.

Whatever the actual pattern of his violence had been until 1973, it grew increasingly malignant in that year and became a frenzy of madness throughout 1974 and 1975 until he was arrested for the first time on August 6, 1975. He escaped from prison in Colorado twice. His first escape, on June 7, 1977, was brief and he was recaptured June 13. His second escape lasted longer and was to have profoundly tragic consequences for five more young women who would be murdered or maimed before he was arrested in Florida on February 15, 1978. A brief description of transit Mars, between the time of the first killing in May 1973 (my speculation is on or around May 13) and the day he was arrested in 1978, provides evidence of the violence in his natal Gemini-Sagittarius opposition and Leo-Scorpio square when these aspects were triggered by Mars and were actualized in Ted's inclinations and behavior. In May 1973, the transit of Mars (not shown in chart), the indicator of physical actions, was in early Pisces beginning to trigger his natal Gemini-Sagittarius opposition. Throughout the period of his murders, transit Mars

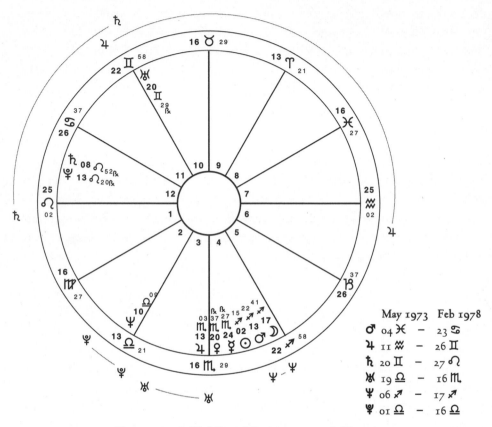

Figure 12.6: Ted Bundy's 1973–1978 Transits

	May 1973		Feb 1978
♂	04 ♓	–	23 ♋
♃	11 ♒	–	26 ♊
♄	20 ♊	–	27 ♌
♅	19 ♎	–	16 ♏
♆	06 ♐	–	17 ♐
♇	01 ♎	–	16 ♎

Mars completed one cycle through his natal chart, returning to Pisces in April 1975. Beginning another cycle, it moved through Pisces, Aries, and Taurus. When transit Mars reached early Gemini opposing his natal Sun, it coincided with Ted's first arrest on August 6. A few years later in his twelfth house of hidden activity and confinement and tucked between natal Saturn and Pluto in Leo, transit Mars activated his natal Leo-Scorpio square when Ted escaped from jail for the second time on December 31, 1977. The easygoing circumstances of a trine (from transit Mars in Cancer to his natal Mercury) when he was arrested the following February indicated he may have been careless enough to think he would not be caught.

Transit Jupiter in Aquarius was activating his natal Leo-Scorpio square in May 1973. At least half of Ted's victims were killed as transit Jupiter made its way through Pisces touching off the Gemini-Sagittarius opposition along the way. When transit Jupiter passed out of Pisces and through Aries, which trined his natal planets in Leo and Sagittarius, he continued to elude detection. Jupiter was still in Aries when he was arrested in August 1975, but it had passed the last trine to his natal Moon. At the time he escaped from prison, Jupiter was retrograde in Gemini triggering his natal opposition, which is where it was when he killed the three girls in Florida before being recaptured. Conjoined natal Uranus in May 1973, transit Saturn was part of the natal opposition. By the end of the year, Saturn passed into Cancer where it was, with a few exceptions, when most of his victims were murdered. When Ted was arrested the first time, transit Saturn sat squarely on the cusp of his twelfth house (confinement). When he escaped from jail, transit Saturn in his first house brought the potential of circumstances that required Ted to take responsibility for his actions: dim prospects for an escaped prisoner. In Scorpio between 1973 and 1975, transit Uranus triggered the natal Leo-Scorpio square. The unpredictable circumstances as well as the issue of personal freedom associated with transit Uranus were demonstrated by Ted's unexpected jail breaks. At the time of the first escape, transit Uranus at 8° Scorpio squared natal Saturn and, the second time, it was just shy of his fourth-house cusp. When he was recaptured in February, Uranus was on his fourth-house cusp, signifying the end of one cycle and the beginning of another.

During the period of the murders, transit Neptune was part of Ted's natal Gemini-Sagittarius opposition as it hovered between 6°-11° Sagittarius trine natal Saturn. Potential circumstances indicated *you may not be aware of how you managed to succeed*, and Ted's own description not only fits the influence of Neptune but also the kind of atmosphere associated with a trine: "... there were times when I think he ... he almost felt as if he were immune from detection. Not in a mystical or a spiritual sense or anything, but ... that on occasion he felt like he could walk through doors. He didn't feel like he was, uh, invisible or anything like that. But at times he felt ... nothing could go wrong. The boldness [was] probably a result of not being rational. Of just being moved by the situation— not really thinking it out clearly, and not even seeing risks. ... Only in retrospect would he wonder how he managed to succeed in spite of some of those rash and bold acts."[15] Neptune, still a part of his Gemini-Sagittarius opposition, conjoined his natal Moon at the time of his later killings and final arrest. Many people thought because he was so bright and skilled at manipulating people, Ted could have started over and never been caught. Ted's explanation for his capture is a

classic case of the power of Neptune's circumstances to disintegrate and undermine (which, in this case, turned out to be a good thing) his emotions (natal
Moon): "I felt overwhelmed by things. I felt out of control. I felt I couldn't manipulate, if that's the word, the environment around me. I couldn't get hold of the
things I needed to get hold of. I couldn't get a job. I didn't do the things that I
should have done. I knew what I had to do and I didn't do it. It just boggles my
mind. I failed miserably. I did everything I shouldn't have done. You have to
remember, I was on the run, so I couldn't truly be myself. If I was truly shrewd
and in control of myself, I would not have done the things that I did, which were
terribly stupid."[16]

The slow transit of Pluto in Libra sextiled Ted's Sun in 1973 and natal Saturn in 1974 and 1975. Sextiles present opportunity and there is no doubt he was
an opportunist. When asked if his murders were planned, his answer was no:
"What we're talking about here is just opportunity, ... In other words, the girls
simply had been in the wrong place at the wrong time."[17] He did pick up some of
his victims as hitchhikers, always a dangerous situation for any woman foolhardy
enough to do it, but many of the girls were asleep in their own beds when they
were attacked, which makes it hard to think of them as being in the wrong place
at the wrong time. Ted (again, speaking of himself in the third person) supplied
the answer when he described the abduction and murder of Linda Healy: "He
had seen the house before ... and for one reason or another had been attracted to
its occupants. Then one evening, just being in the mood, so to speak, he checked
out the house [and] found out the front door was open. He thought about it.
What kind of opportunity that offered. And returned to the house later and
entered the house and explored it. ... he went around the house and found a particular bedroom door that he opened—really hit and miss. Not knowing who or
what, not looking for any particular individual. And that would be the opportunity. This was late at night. And presumably everybody would be asleep."[18]

The casual oversight of leaving a door unlocked cost Linda Healy her life.
The same oversight would cost many of his other victims their lives, including
the Chi Omega coeds he killed in Florida. The circumstances of transit Pluto
indicated the opportunity for Ted to commit murder, and when he was electro-
cuted in Florida on January 24, 1989, it was Pluto, at the door of his fourth
house, that signaled the end of a life filled with dark and terrible karma.

GRACE KELLY

Judith Quine, one of Grace Kelly's bridesmaids and author of a best-selling book about their long friendship, recalls that Grace was an astrology buff. "... Grace decided to use her fascination with the stars to buffer the shock she felt at turning forty. ... Bilingual invitations were mailed around the world. They read like horoscopes for those born under Grace's birth sign."[19] Born in Philadelphia on November 12, 1929, at 5:31 AM EST, Grace had Sun, Mercury, Mars, and Ascendant in Scorpio. Aspects in her natal chart include a T-Square with Pisces Moon square Jupiter in Gemini opposed Saturn in Sagittarius. Natal Venus in Libra shares a trine with natal Jupiter in Gemini, a square with natal Pluto in Cancer, and a sextile with Saturn in Sagittarius.

The most prominent pattern is a Grand Trine containing Sun, Mercury, and Mars in Scorpio; Moon in Pisces; and Pluto in Cancer. We can associate this Grand Trine with Grace's success in masking the great contradictions in her life.

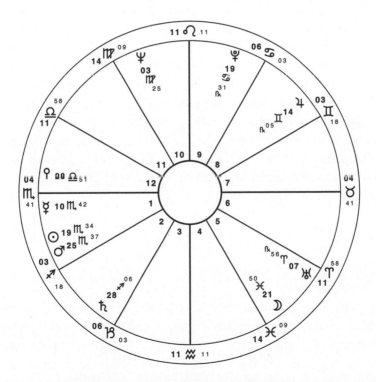

Figure 12.7: Grace Kelly's Natal Chart

Pluto's involvement with the Grand Trine serves as one example of how this aspect worked. Pluto represents power and control, and the circumstances that influence a person's identification with power and control are described by the natal house Pluto occupies. When Grace was born, Pluto landed in the ninth house of her natal chart and transit Pluto continued on through the ninth house until she was sixteen years old. The ninth-house position of both natal and transit Pluto implied that power and control would involve religion, cultural pursuits, politics, higher education, or foreign countries. Young Grace understood power and control through "an all-embracing and quite unshakable faith in the Catholic religion and its relevance to every detail of her life."[20] Led down the path of least resistance by the easygoing nature of natal Pluto's Grand Trine position, Grace did not challenge or rebel against her religion's strict rules of conduct.

But natal Pluto is square natal Venus in the twelfth house (hidden activity), indicating obedience and proper behavior were obstacles to be overcome, especially when it came to romantic escapades (Venus). They were not formidable obstacles to Grace. She willingly complied with whatever she was told to do, but when no one was looking she did whatever she wanted. Her sexual inclinations were not inhibited by the religious instructions she received regarding modesty, abstinence, and adultery. On the other hand, her activities in the bedroom did not prevent Grace from attending Mass every Sunday. Her sexual liaisons with married men were never publicly revealed to her personal or professional disadvantage: another potential of her Grand Trine. The transits that passed through her natal chart recorded a life of beauty, wealth, accomplishments, and worthwhile endeavors. But it was also a life of emotional frustration and unrealized potential.

1946–1949

In the fall of 1945, Grace turned sixteen as transit Pluto entered her tenth house where it remained until 1965. The potential of transit Pluto's tenth-house position fits every biographical description of Grace Kelly. *Focus and determination fuel a relentless pursuit of a career or other important ambition. You resent and resist anyone who attempts to exert control over your future. If you allow others to make important decisions for you or put yourself in a position where you are forced to allow others to make decisions regarding your future, you will regret it by the time this long period has ended. ...*

One of the consequences may be an intense struggle to accommodate the demands of home and family while pursuing your personal ambitions.

When it came to her career, Grace Kelly was driven and purposeful, but, in her private life, she was dominated by her parents and, after her marriage, by her husband. In later years she had deep regrets about having given up control of her life. Between 1946 and 1949, however, she had other obstacles to overcome: "Flat-chested, overweight, and wearing glasses. 'Grace was not really known as a beauty queen in those days,' remembers 'Butch' Jim McAllister, who knew Grace down in Ocean City, New Jersey, where the Kellys had a summer home. As Grace's mother crisply put it, 'She was nobody's Princess Charming.'"[21] Furthermore, when Grace was between fourteen and sixteen, her mother recalled she was nothing but a "giggly somebody with a high, nasal voice. She always had had

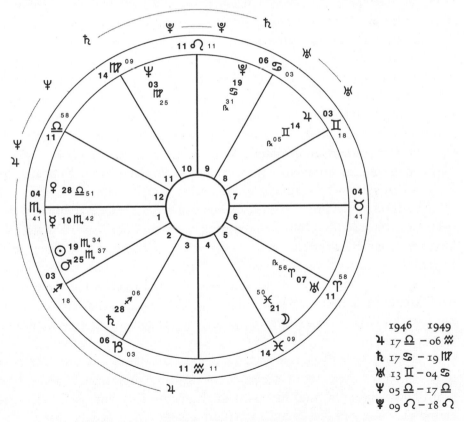

Figure 12.8: Grace Kelly's 1946–1949 Transits

337

trouble with her nose. ... That gave her the peculiar voice. Her enjoyment of food gave her a little extra weight. And she had been nearsighted for several years, which made it necessary for her to wear glasses."[22]

Long after she had grown into a beautiful woman and become Her Serene Royal Highness, Princess of Monaco, Grace still felt the ache of those painful years and her crippling shyness. The three-year period of transit Pluto square first-house natal Mercury (1944–1947) can be associated with circumstances that cause eye and nose problems. A square from transit Saturn in Cancer to natal Venus in 1946, and Saturn's square from Leo to natal Mercury and natal Sun in 1947 added the potential for loss of confidence. Whatever Grace felt about her shyness or gawky appearance was internalized as she pursued her goals. By the end of 1946, transit Jupiter in Scorpio began a series of conjunctions with her natal Sun—the potential of which includes several situations Grace experienced: greater enjoyment of food (causing weight gain), increased interest in acting and the theater, and greater self-confidence.

As transit Jupiter made a final conjunction with natal Sun on August 20, 1947, its fortunate potential was actualized. Grace applied for entrance to the American Academy of Dramatic Arts in New York and was told that enrollment was closed. With the help of a family friend (and because she was the niece of playwright George Kelly), Grace managed to get an audition. Getting the coveted audition was one thing, doing it well enough to get accepted was another. The handwritten audition book of the American Academy of the Dramatic Arts records that Grace Patricia Kelly of Philadelphia appeared in front of Emil F. Diestel, director of admissions, on August 20, 1947. Grace's audition performance convinced Diestel of her promising talent and she was admitted. Not long after completing the Academy's two-year course, Grace got her first part on Broadway, making her theatrical debut on November 14, 1949. Transit Jupiter at 27° Capricorn square natal Venus in Libra, transit Saturn at 17° Virgo square natal Jupiter in Gemini, and transit Pluto at 18° Scorpio square natal Sun did not favor success for this enterprise. The play soon closed and Grace did not work again in the theater for two years. Squares, however, do not mean failure, especially for people like Grace with the attitude that if one way does not work, they will try another. As the decade of the '50's began, transit Uranus in her ninth house (broadcasting) indicated an alternative path and, in Cancer, triggering the energy of her Grand Trine, Uranus also indicated success (Jupiter rules the theater and Uranus rules television).

1950–1955

Grace appeared in dozens of television shows. "Television," wrote Robert Lacey, "was where Grace Kelly learned the basics of her craft as a working actress."[23] As 1950 moved into 1951, she continued to work steadily but television was not Grace's objective. She wanted to be a movie star and she also wanted more work on the stage.

In the summer of 1951, with transit Jupiter in her sixth house bringing potential for fortunate employment, both goals were achieved. She got an offer from the prestigious Elitch Gardens stock company in Colorado and, while working with them, she received a telegram telling her to report to Hollywood on August 28 for a role opposite Gary Cooper in *High Noon*. This was Grace Kelly's

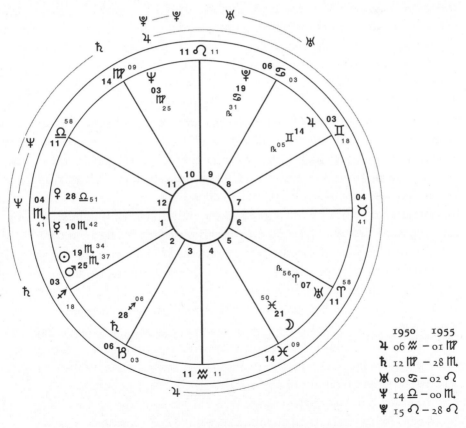

Figure 12.9: Grace Kelly's 1950–1955 Transits

first major step toward becoming a star. In 1952, transit Uranus in Cancer in her ninth house (foreign travel) made its way toward natal Pluto trine natal Sun and Grace went to Africa for a small role in Mogambo, starring Clark Gable and Ava Gardner. When the film was released the following year, Look magazine named Grace as the best actress of 1953 and she was also nominated for an Academy Award. As transit Uranus continued to stimulate her Grand Trine, another of its fortunate potentials turned out to be Alfred Hitchcock. He first cast her in Dial M for Murder and, then, in an even better role in Rear Window. Released in August 1954, Rear Window sparked the fantastic rise in Grace's career. Robert Lacey describes it as "the first of the classic and inimitable Grace Kelly movies, stirring up the special magic that was hers and hers alone."[24]

The Grand Trine in Grace's chart was occupied at the time by transit Jupiter and transit Uranus in Cancer. Apart from the aspects they make to the planets in a natal chart, the aspects that transits make between themselves are meaningful. Grace's success in Hollywood offers an excellent example of the potential of aspects made between transit Saturn and transit Pluto, two planets that signify a strong element of conservatism in society. When Grace began her career at the Academy of Dramatic Arts, transit Saturn conjoined transit Pluto in Leo. By the time she was a major film star, transit Saturn in Scorpio was square transit Pluto in Leo. Robert Lacey puts the reality of the transit Saturn-Pluto potential into perfect context: "Grace Kelly struck a timely chord. ... She was the very opposite of the sweater girls. 'We are sick of flamboyant, bouncy, flashy sex,' wrote Edward Linn in Saga magazine. 'Grace Kelly is all the more exciting for her quality of restraint.' With her cool good looks and restrained public style, Grace appeared to be virginity personified—the very essence of pedigree and purity."[25]

The turning point of Grace's career was 1954, but some of the transits indicated that not everything in her life was so successful. As she began filming Dial M For Murder in the fall of 1953, transit Pluto in Leo initiated a series of squares to natal Mars (men in her life) that lasted through the summer of 1955. Grace had love affairs with Bing Crosby and Oleg Cassini and similar relationships with Ray Milland and William Holden, both of whom were married. All these relationships ended by 1955, but not without emotional pain and, in the case of the married men, the threat of ruinous scandal.

On March 30, 1955, when Grace won an Academy Award for Country Girl, the transits in her chart reveal an interesting set of contradictions. Transit Sun at 9° Aries conjoined natal Uranus in her fifth house indicated the focus on artistic achievements. Winning the award was indicated by her Grand Trine fully occupied with transits of the Moon at 14° Cancer, Jupiter at 20° Cancer, Uranus at 23° Cancer, Mercury at 19° Pisces, and Saturn at 20° Scorpio. In contrast to the array of fortunate aspects, there were others that were less promising. Transit Pluto in the tenth house squared natal Mars, transit Mars in her seventh house opposed transit Saturn along with natal Sun and Mars in Scorpio. Transit Neptune conjoined natal Venus brought added glamor but also the possibility of illusion. The combined transits of Pluto, Saturn (even though it was involved in her Grand Trine), Mars, and Neptune suggested that in spite of winning an Oscar, something was amiss in her life. Robert Lacey writes, "It was the small hours of the morning by the time that Grace got back to her bungalow in the Bel Air Hotel. She was all alone, with only her Oscar for company. ... She lay down on the bed, she later remembered, and looked across the room at the statuette that represented so much effort and hope and sacrifice, the culmination of her life and work to that point. 'There we were,' she recalled, ' just the two of us. It was terrible. It was the loneliest moment of my life.' "[26]

According to James Spada, the absence of a lover or a husband was not the only cause of Grace's pain: "For months Grace's father had been making less than gallant comments about his daughter's success. At one point he had said, 'Peggy's the family extrovert. Just between us, I've always thought her the daughter with the most on the ball.' He expressed 'bewilderment' at Grace's stardom, saying, 'I thought it would be Peggy. Anything that Grace could do Peggy could always do better.' Grace had been deeply hurt by her father's insensitivity; it was bad enough to make comments like that privately, but to make them to reporters seemed to Grace in her more resentful moments cruelly calculated attempts to keep her in her place. No amount of success, it seemed, could shake her father's low opinion of her. Winning the Academy Award ... would finally, she had hoped, bring her the paternal approval she so craved. But it was not to be. To a reporter, in a comment wired to every newspaper across the country, Kelly expressed amazement at Grace's accomplishment: 'I can't believe it. I simply can't believe Grace won.' "[27]

Less than a month later, Grace attended the Cannes Film Festival as head of the Hollywood delegation, a trip that would mark another important turning point for her. Part of the official duties that had been arranged included a photo opportunity in which Grace would be introduced to Prince Rainier of Monaco. One of the significant aspects that occurred the day Grace and Rainier met was a

Full Moon. A Full Moon is a natural turning point and also a time when people have more of a tendency to lose their tempers, to feel hungrier than usual, and to be more emotional. When the Full Moon's position occurs in your first house, your body retains more water and you may not look your best or feel like being charming. The Full Moon at 15° Scorpio on May 6, 1955, was in Grace's first house, putting the transit Sun in her seventh house (marriage). Transit Mars in Grace's eighth house, opposed natal Saturn and square natal Moon, suggested delays and other frustrations. Waking up later than she planned gave her day a bad start, and when she plugged in her hair dryer, there was no power (unknown to her, the electrical workers had called a strike). With a wet head and wearing a dress that made her "look like a pear" (it was the only unwrinkled dress she had), Grace jumped into the car with her entourage for the trip to Monaco. On the way, they were hit from behind by the car carrying the photographers, causing them to lose time. The group was already late as they approached Monaco, but Grace complained that she was hungry so another stop was made to pick up a sandwich, which she ate as they raced to the palace. As it turned out, their late arrival did not matter since the prince was still having a leisurely lunch with guests at his villa down the coast. The further delay did nothing to improve Grace's mood since she had to get back to Cannes for an early evening reception. "It was a definitely testy Miss Kelly who finally shook hands with Prince Rainier III of Monaco shortly after four o'clock on that May afternoon."[28] For all that went wrong, there were some astrological indications that something was right. Transit Venus at 14° Aries, in Grace's fifth house (romance), was sextile natal Jupiter. Sextile is opportunity and natal Jupiter's potential in the eighth house (joint income) meant that opportunity might lead to an increased economic and social position through marriage.

1956–1965

The potential opportunity of transit Venus sextile natal Jupiter that occurred on the day of their first meeting became reality when transit Venus conjoined natal Jupiter in Gemini the following spring. On April 18 and 19, Monaco was overflowing with people who had come from all over the world to witness and record the spectacular wedding between the American movie star and the Prince of Monaco. Transit Venus in the eighth house conjoin Jupiter brought Grace an exalted economic and social status to be sure, but natal Jupiter is part of the natal

T-Square that, in her chart, involved her father's low opinion of her achievements and lack of paternal love she felt so keenly all of her life. Transit Venus
(the marriage) triggering the T-Square had as dismal a potential for her relationship with her husband as it had for her relationship with her father. Rainier
came to treat her artistic achievements with scorn, and the marriage would not
be the loving and romantic experience Grace envisioned. As befits the occasion,
transit Jupiter and transit Pluto in Leo were in her tenth house. For the Civil
Ceremony at 11:10 AM CET on April 18, 1956, the transit Moon was at 4° Leo
in Grace's ninth house, an indication of making her home in a foreign country.
For the church service the next morning at 10:30 AM CET, the transit Moon had
moved to 17° Leo conjoining transit Jupiter at 21° Leo and transit Uranus at 26°

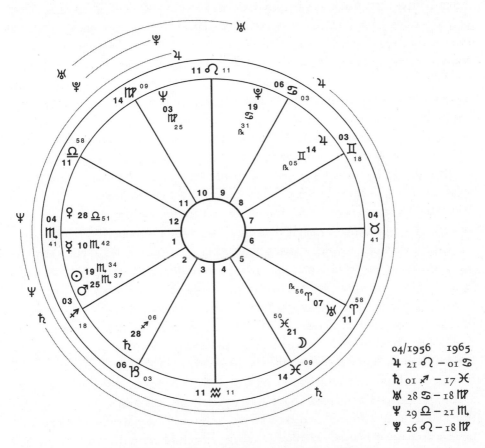

Figure 12.10: Grace Kelly's 1956–1965 Transits

Leo. The natal T-Square representing Grace's emotional problems with her father was triggered in 1960 by transit Jupiter. Among other things, Jupiter rules the father or father figure in a natal chart. On June 20, 1960, the transit of Jupiter at 28° Sagittarius conjoined natal Saturn and opposed transit Venus and natal Jupiter in Grace's eighth house (death), coinciding with her father's death. Between 1956 and 1965, Grace provided Monaco with three royal heirs: Princess Caroline on January 23, 1957, Prince Albert on March 14, 1958, and Princess Stephanie on February 1, 1965.

1966–1976

After Princess Stephanie was born, Grace tried to have other children. The series of oppositions Uranus started to make to her natal Moon in 1966 meant that carrying a child to full term was an unlikely prospect. When the opposition between transit Uranus and natal Moon occurred in July 1967, its potential was revealed as Grace was attending the World's Fair in Montreal. "At the age of thirty-seven, she was pregnant again, expecting her fourth child the following January, and according to the official announcement, she was 'very happy and very well.' Rupert Allan was in the party, masterminding a hectic program of engagements, when, unexpectedly one evening, he was summoned to Grace's and Rainier's hotel suite. As he arrived, Grace was being loaded onto a stretcher under the supervision of two solemn-looking doctors. Her pregnancy had gone very badly wrong. ... The operation that Grace underwent ... brought an end to her sixth pregnancy in eleven years. ... The doctors told her there could be no more pregnancies."[29]

There were other major transits of note between 1966 and 1976. Describing a trip she took to meet Grace in the early '70's, Judith Quine wrote: "From a distance, I read numerous quotes in the press that revealed a woman who was becoming increasingly more conservative. The statements I read in the newspapers or in articles or interviews with her began to reveal zealous criticism of nearly every facet of modern-day life."[30] At the end of 1969, transit Pluto began a series of squares to natal Saturn, the last of which was in September 1971. Recall that aspects between transit Pluto and transit Saturn indicated the rising conservatism in society that helped Grace achieve her fame as a movie star. Now, with transit Pluto square natal Saturn, she was echoing that potential in herself: "I believe Grace was mortally terrified of raising her children in the world that raged about her. ... It was the only period during her lifetime when I thought of her, in

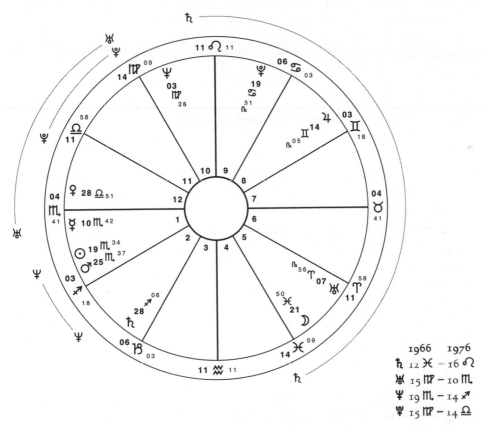

Figure 12.11: Grace Kelly's 1966–1976 Transits

the vernacular of the day, as uptight. She made countless public statements opposing the new sexual freedom, relaxed dress codes, and nudity and violence in films. Those were elements of the new world she opposed and had every right to speak about. But she also shrank her curiosity about the world of ideas. She lost her will to examine and clung closely to her will to condemn."[31]

In addition to transit Pluto's aspects to natal Saturn, the potential of other transits can be associated with Grace's conservatism, her fear regarding her children, and her inflexibility and need for control. Fear and rigidity are the province of transit Saturn. In 1970 and 1971, transit Saturn in Taurus opposed her Scorpio planets and, moving into Gemini, it squared natal Neptune in Virgo in her tenth house (indication that part of her fear concerned her public reputation). By

July 1972, transit Saturn was firmly entrenched in her T-Square, where it remained to trigger that unhappy aspect through the spring of 1974. The potential of transit Saturn square natal Moon in May and June 1973 included emotional restrictions, anger, resentment, and problems related to children. Potential collided with reality when Grace's daughter Caroline returned home after graduation in 1973. From that point, the formerly close relationship that had existed between mother and daughter changed with dramatic swiftness. "Caroline's rebellion against the strictures under which she was raised ... was conducted in public, and that mortified Grace. ... what could photographs of Caroline smoking, drinking, nightclubbing, and sunbathing nude with a boyfriend say about her upbringing, and about her parents? ... Caroline's behavior was a body blow and a source of numbing embarrassment."[32]

For the next three years, Caroline became increasingly more independent, willful, and wild, but she was not the only one who experienced dramatic personal changes. By the end of 1975, Grace herself began to change as Uranus moved into her first house where it would stay until her death in 1982. The interpretation of transit Uranus in the first house is accurately descriptive: *significant and sometimes unanticipated changes in your personality, self-image, and even your physical appearance [occur]*. Almost every year from 1956 onward, the Grimaldi's Christmas card was a family portrait. Through the years the annual card pictured new babies who became children and then finally grew into young adults. The cards showed different trends in fashions and an aging Prince Rainier with hair that gradually turned gray and then became white. "Only Grace is the constant: tight, slender, blonde, and smiling, looking even better in her early forties than she did at eighteen—until 1976, when startlingly, in just a matter of a year or so, the rose is blown. ... Suddenly the geography of Grace's face was changing. Her features were shifting, in an insidious continental drift."[33] In a conversation with her friend Judith Quine, Grace revealed an accurate picture of first-house transit Uranus. Saying it was not so much the physical changes that bothered her, Grace complained that it was "more an attitude, a feeling or an unexpected set of responses ... I find I'm not as patient as I used to be. ... It's a kind of selfishness. I get rather testy and demanding for my own sake in a way I've never been before. I feel a bit mean and I don't like it."[34]

1976–1982

Many transiting aspects accompanied the notable events in Grace's life between 1976 and 1982. Two significant developments were her growing independence and her determination to find outlets for her creative talents. In 1976, transit Jupiter was in Taurus. In early Gemini by 1977, Jupiter squared natal Neptune (films, dance, unrealistic aspirations) in her tenth house (career, public reputation) and then triggered her natal Gemini-Sagittarius-Pisces T-Square (frustrations) as it passed through her eighth house. Eighth-house matters include death and transformation, sexual desire, and the use of talent and skills as a measure of independence and resourcefulness. No matter what sign happens to be on the eighth-house cusp of a particular chart (Gemini in Grace's case), there is a Scorpio character to the circumstances that occur when transits pass through this house. Jupiter is associated with independence, journalism, art, and other cultural pursuits. Transit Jupiter in Gemini was also trine natal Venus in Libra in the twelfth house. Venus represents flowers, romance, and artistic activities while the twelfth house involves secret activities, disappointment, escape mechanisms, and charitable actions.

All these aspects involving transit Jupiter in Taurus and Gemini can be incorporated into the pattern of aspects and circumstances of Grace's life. In 1976, Grace was offered either of the leading roles in *The Turning Point*. This movie was about ballet and would have been an ideal vehicle for Grace who had always wanted to be a dancer. The offer was extremely tempting but her husband would not consider the possibility. Transit Jupiter in Taurus in her seventh house (marriage) opposed natal Sun (her ego) and natal Mars (men in her life as well as her physical work). The opposition suggested circumstances that cannot be changed. Crushed with disappointment, she was forced to turn down the opportunity.

As a struggling young actress, Grace had the attitude that if one way did not work, she would try another. This same attitude was true of the middle-aged Grace: "… she had to become involved in projects of her own, activities that brought her creative fulfillment and took her mind off her problems and responsibilities. Or, she feared, she would go mad. The first of these grew out of an earlier escape mechanism—Grace's habit of walking and collecting flowers for hours among the footpaths of Monaco's hills."[35] A friend introduced her to the art of pressed flower design and it became Grace's new obsession.

As transit Jupiter moved into Cancer and began to trigger her Grand Trine, creating pressed flower arrangements was only the beginning of a more enjoyable and creatively satisfying phase. In 1976, she met Robert Dornhelm, a young film director who came to Monaco to work on a documentary about Russia's Imperial Ballet School which Grace had agreed to narrate. There was an immediate rapport between Grace and Robert, and it soon developed into a close and stimulating relationship. According to Lacey's account, Dornhelm never minced his words with Grace: "All that time and energy that you devote to arranging dead, withered flowers .... Isn't that the metaphor of your life?"[36] Lacey also writes that the question of Grace's relationship with Robert Dornhelm (which was almost certainly a romantic one) "is complicated by the fact that he was by no means the only younger man with whom she consorted in her later years. There was quite a list."[37]

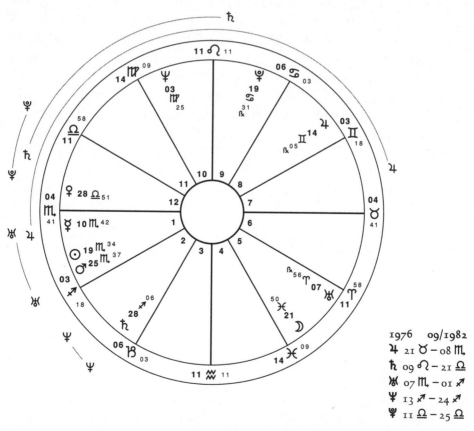

Figure 12.12: Grace Kelly's 1976–1982 Transits

In Grace's second house, transit Neptune (disintegration of values and priorities) began 1976 by setting off the natal T-Square with a series of oppositions to natal Jupiter through the fall of 1977. As it moved through Sagittarius, transit Neptune triggered the natal T-Square again with a series of squares to natal Moon between the end of 1979 and November 1981. Neptune is associated with drugs and alcohol, confusion and illusion. Natal Jupiter and natal Moon indicate a tendency to go overboard emotionally and in other ways. The astrological interpretation of transit Neptune's involvement in her T-Square strongly suggested that circumstances would undermine certain areas of Grace's life, an interpretation described in reality by James Spada: "But although Grace could get drunk with the best of them, her friends didn't start to worry about her drinking until the mid-1970's, when it seemed to them that she was drinking too much and for the wrong reasons. Clearly she was 'letting herself go.' ... By the mid-1970's she no longer bothered to stop drinking to control her weight. 'What's the point?' she asked her friend Fleur Cowles. The result was that Grace put on a great deal of weight. ... Grace's drinking worried her friends all the more because when she was drunk, she would become careless about her actions and appearance and, even worse, mindless of her personal safety. For Grace to behave irresponsibly, even at a carefree party, was so out of character for her that her friends became deeply concerned."[38]

The best overall description of Grace's final years is found in the interpretation of transit Uranus and transit Pluto. The first-house position of transit Uranus suggests that *people who come into your life at this time as well as situations you never expected to encounter can cause you to seek or to unexpectedly discover a unique concept of yourself or a side of your personality that you had not realized you possessed. You may actively seek to express your newfound self. Personal freedom becomes increasingly important during this period, and you may engage in rebellious acts or take other steps to assure yourself that you are independent. Your need for independence does not necessarily exclude marriage or other partnerships if they do not prevent you from expressing yourself as an individual. You are less predictable, more restless, and perhaps more unstable as you try to establish a compatible mix of old and new elements within yourself.* " 'Dornhelm was quite often around when I was going out with Caroline,' remembers Philippe Junot, who started dating Grace's elder daughter in 1976. 'There was never any sign of Rainier. He was leading his own life down in Monaco, while Grace was leading hers up in Paris. Sometimes we would all go out together as two couples—Caroline with me and Grace with Dornhelm. I do not know if they were lovers, but let me put it this way, I would be very surprised if they were not.' "[39]

The twelfth-house transit of Pluto indicates secret activities. "Whenever Grace suspected that press photographers might be around, she took care to hide her young escorts in a group of miscellaneous companions."[40] *You may be able to overcome the people or situations that have victimized you, but if you are guilty of such destructive behavior, it will be you who must face the consequences.* Grace was finding ways to escape the restricting influence of her royal status and the pain of an indifferent husband, but when she attempted to restrict her daughter's social and romantic activities, she met with failure and public embarrassment. *You may not be able to voice your disappointments and failures to others, but you will have to confront them within yourself. Part of this period's karmic lesson, however, is not so much to abolish limitations and restrictions (though that may become a necessity at some point) as it is to understand and control how you deal with them. Do not expect others to recognize or applaud your inner struggles, for these are private battles and must be handled on that level. The answers you seek are buried within yourself. Circumstances throughout this long period will provide ways for you to help yourself.*

The young men Grace cultivated "offered no real escape from the ultimate issues. How could she go on hiding behind her famous front when some of the most important components of that front were crumbling? Grace had spent her entire life pleasing others—her father, her mother, her husband, her children, the world as a whole that wanted her to be Princess Grace, and her church, which had taught her from her earliest days that the way to happiness lay through sacrifice to the higher cause. ... the dutiful princess did come to realize that there was a sense in which there could be no higher cause than herself."[41]

As the decade of the '80's began, the restlessness and activity associated with first-house transit Uranus continued to be evident as Grace pursued her artistic ambitions and philanthropic endeavors on many fronts and with many travels back and forth between the United States and Europe. Transit Uranus in the first house includes a more ominous prospect than restlessness, however. *Unexpected illness can develop and more cautious actions are necessary to offset the higher potential for accidents and injury, especially to the head and face.* The fact that transit Uranus conjoined natal Mercury, Sun, and especially Mars in the first house added much weight to this grim potential.

Appropriately, the timing mechanism was transit Mars. Natally as well as by transit, Mars rules the head and is also associated with cars and (when adversely aspected) with accidents, especially accidents that injure the face and head. On January 1, 1982, the transit of Mars at 7° Libra opposed Grace's natal Uranus (planetary ruler of her fourth house and indication of the end of a cycle). Grace caught a cold. Mars made a second opposition to natal Uranus in April and a third opposition in the middle of June before moving into her twelfth house. Did Mars passing through the twelfth house hide the symptoms of a brain lesion? Mars began to transit her first house in August and, at the end of August, Grace and Rainier flew to Norway. "Grace had been complaining of headaches that summer—and she had cried off some dinner parties uncharacteristically—and during the voyage the pains had got worse."[42]

Her health may have seemed the least likely of her problems to Grace as she became involved in a raging battle with her daughter Stephanie. Spoiled and out of control, Stephanie announced she no longer wished to attend the Institute of Fashion Design in Paris and that she wanted to be with her boyfriend and learn to race cars. Meanwhile, the cold that had plagued Grace since the start of the year had grown worse. When Robert Dornhelm arrived to visit Grace at Roc Agel on September 10, he found her complaining about it and other difficulties that she could not seem to handle: "Robert was accustomed to seeing her make an effort to pull herself out of her doldrums, so he was astonished to find Grace so depressed and unhappy that she seemed unable to conquer her gloom."[43] Grace had planned to take Stephanie back to Monaco on Monday morning and, glad to escape an atmosphere which was rancid and tense, Robert left Roc Agel on Sunday, September 12.

Speaking to her friend Gwen Robyns on the phone late Sunday night, Grace complained that her headaches had returned (transit Mars conjoined her natal Mars). The next morning, as she drove her daughter down the steep and winding mountain road, Grace suffered a brain lesion. The car plunged over an embankment, finally coming to rest upside down on a pile of rocks below. Although her child's life was spared, the fortunate potential of natal Mars conjoin transit Mars at 25° Scorpio in her Grand Trine did not include circumstances that would save Grace. She died the following evening at 10:30 PM CED.

MATA HARI

In fiction and in reality the mysterious world of espionage is largely populated by men. When women are mentioned, there is very often a reference to Mata Hari, a name universally synonymous with female spy.

Mata Hari was real, but her reputation was and is surrounded by a great deal of fiction. She deliberately cloaked herself with an aura of mystery and glamor, and, in death, her name became legendary. Who was this dangerous criminal Mata Hari that was executed by a French firing squad in a field outside Paris just after dawn on October 15, 1917? The Paris newspapers reported that she was buried in Vincennes, but when curiosity seekers flocked to the newly dug grave, they found it empty. Immediately, rumors circulated that she had not died, that she had won her freedom by throwing open her coat revealing her naked body, that she had been saved by a lover who had ridden through the firing line and

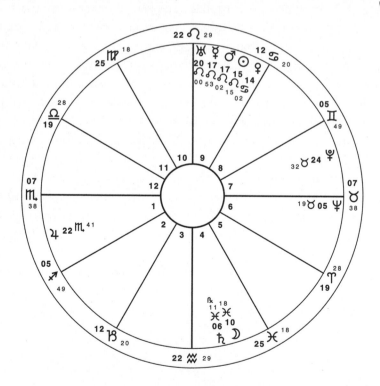

Figure 12.13: Mata Hari's Natal Chart

snatched her away at the last minute. The truth was less fantastic. When no one stepped forward to claim her body, Mata Hari was delivered to the University of Paris for dissection.

Forty-one years before her finale on the dissection table in Paris, Mata Hari's life had begun in another land and another century. She was born Margaretha Geertruida Zelle in Leeuwarden, Holland, on August 7, 1876. There is a discrepancy concerning the time of birth which makes her natal chart controversial. Sources quote English astrologer Chryss Craswell for a birth time of 1:00 PM LMT and Douglas Lannark of Copenhagen for a birth time of 12:34 PM LMT. The later time puts Venus in the eighth house; otherwise, all the natal planets remain in the same houses, the Ascendant is still Scorpio, and the aspects between the planets are the same in charts cast for either birth time. The chart I use is cast for 12:34 PM but I encourage readers as I encourage my students, to explore the possibilities of using the other birth time. One of the dominant planetary patterns in the natal chart is a T-Square that includes Sun, Mercury, Mars, and Uranus in Leo square the opposition between Jupiter in Scorpio and Pluto in Taurus. There is also a Grand Trine in water that involves Moon and Saturn in Pisces, Venus in Cancer, and Jupiter in Scorpio. Note that transits in Scorpio trigger the Grand Trine but they also square her natal planets in Leo which triggers the natal T-Square. Transits in Sagittarius trine natal planets in Leo but square the natal Saturn-Moon conjunction in Pisces. Anything gained will also have difficulty associated with it. The important periods in Margaretha's life can be described through her roles as wife and mother, as exotic dancer and courtesan, and, finally, as international spy. She was an impetuous adventurer, greedy for all that life could provide and bold enough to risk everything to get what she wanted.

1889–1896

Margaretha, or M'greet as she was familiarly called, was born into a prosperous family and for the first thirteen years of her life received the education and privileges of wealth. However, the family's life-style abruptly ended in 1889 when her father became bankrupt and abandoned his wife and children.

Where were the transiting planets that signaled such a drastic change? One of the most important transits at that time (as it would be throughout her life) was Pluto. In July 1889, when M'greet's father left his family, transit Pluto at 5° Gemini had begun its journey through her eighth house where it would remain until her death in 1917. Starting in 1889, the circumstances and events she experienced for the rest of her life can all be described in part by the potential of Pluto's eighth-house transit. *Transitions that you undergo during this period are akin to death and rebirth. They are serious and life-changing. At some point a more powerful monetary or social position may be achieved through marriage and other close alliances, inheritance, and tax or insurance benefits—but if any of these potentials comes to pass, you are likely to pay a very high price for whatever you have gained. One possibility is that you must now accommodate the values and principles of a partner or other people even though their values and priorities may not agree with your own. Joint income and family assets may be gained or lost, but circumstances will show that your worth cannot be measured by such things, and the power you seek transcends material wealth. What will matter most is the realization that your resourcefulness, skills, and talent can give you independence and strength.*

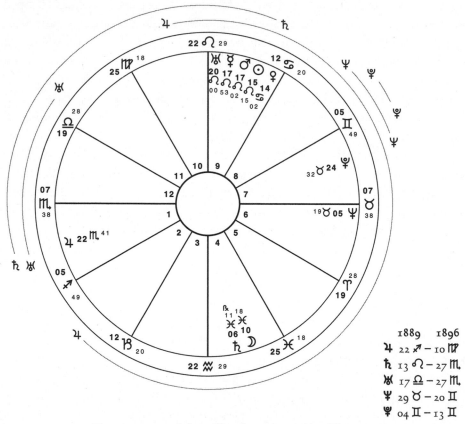

Figure 12.14: Mata Hari's 1889–1896 Transits

Transit Saturn was also part of the picture. In 1888 and 1889, transit Saturn conjoining her natal planets in Leo activated her natal T-Square. In July 1889, it made a final conjunction with natal Uranus, the potential of which is the restriction of freedom, and, for M'greet, it was the freedom that had come from wealth. Squaring the natal opposition between Jupiter and Pluto at the end of July, Saturn began its journey through her tenth house (the father) which suggested M'greet's involvement with her father would continue to be restricted and surrounded by burdens.

After M'greet's father left, she and her mother and three brothers moved out of their grand home into another section of town not far from the railroad station and the cattle market, in a section far less lovely than the one she had left. "The canal they faced sent up odors of stagnation and decay. It seemed to M'greet that all the hallways smelled of boiled vegetables and insecticide and that her mother had grown smaller, as if shrunken into herself with grief and shame. ... [M'greet] walked in thick, ugly boots along the grimy corridors. Toward childhood's end. The true end came somewhat later: the day that her mother died. [Entering Virgo, transit Saturn in her tenth house began to form oppositions to her Saturn-Moon conjunction in 1890 adding the potential for more sorrow and deprivation as well as separation from the mother. Saturn's final opposition to her natal Moon occurred May 12, 1891.] She had been ailing for over a year, but it was hard to tell whether she suffered from their near poverty, her husband's legal separation from his family, the shame of being thus abandoned in a society in which conformity, domesticity, and fidelity were extolled, or whether it was mere physical illness that brought her to her grave. Johannes and M'greet, being older, could see their mother becoming more feeble and silent each day. They watched helplessly as she faded from their life, uncomplaining, discreet as a cat that knows it is doomed. Until one day in May she simply did not rise from her bed. And they knew from the way she lay there that she was dead."[44]

At the time of her mother's death, May 10, 1891, transit Neptune had joined transit Pluto in Gemini square her natal Saturn-Moon conjunction. The potential of a square implies obstacles, disappointments, and other frustrations. The homelessness and inability to find a stable environment that M'greet experienced after her mother's death are examples of the disintegrating and confusing circumstances associated with transit Neptune. She went for a time to live with her godfather, and, when that did not work out, she was sent to a school to train as a kindergarten teacher. But this too was not a suitable arrangement. She was restless and disliked the boring routine. When the headmaster became more interested in her than in her work, a scandal erupted. Leaving the school in disgrace, she was sent to stay with an uncle in Amsterdam.

Also outlining her circumstances was transit Uranus which had entered her first house in the summer of 1892 triggering her Grand Trine. For M'greet the implication associated with transit Uranus was restlessness, a growing tendency in the coming years to think of herself as unique and different, and a craving for a more stimulating environment in which she could operate. By 1895, she was of marriageable age with no foreseeable career or means of support, but the series of trines between transit Uranus and her natal Venus held the potential for just the kind of change she was hoping for. *Interactions include exciting and unusual people, any one of whom may turn out to be a new business or marriage partner. ... During the stimulating and favorable, if somewhat unpredictable, period when transit Uranus trines your natal Venus, your social life and activities include an element of the unexpected or unusual. ... Staying home alone or in isolated spots reduces the favorable odds. You cannot control or bring about the circumstances of your good fortune since they are apt to hinge on the actions or decisions made by others, but you can attract good fortune by putting yourself in social or public situations among many different people. Be willing to try new experiences and to travel to new and exotic places.* Possibly as a result of feeling pressure from her relatives to whom she was a financial burden, M'greet started to read the matrimonial ads in newspapers. None of them interested her until she read, "Officer on home leave from Dutch East Indies would like to meet girl of pleasant character—object matrimony."[45] This sounded exciting and exotic to the imaginative young girl and she responded immediately. Captain Rudolph MacLeod, an officer who had arrived home after sixteen years in the Dutch colonies, replied to M'greet's note and the couple arranged to meet at the *Rijksmuseum* in Amsterdam.

The day they met (March 30, 1895), transit Venus, planet of romance and marriage, at 7° Taurus was on the cusp of her seventh house (marriage). Transit Mercury (communication, newspapers) indicated how they met, and, at 12° Pisces, it conjoined her Pisces Moon in her fourth house (a new beginning) and trined natal Venus (love and marriage) in Cancer. Only six days after their meeting, Captain MacLeod asked M'greet to be his wife. Events often occur quickly when transit Uranus is involved, and as it made its final trine to natal Venus the following July, they were married. However, any transit that triggered her Grand Trine from

Scorpio also triggered her natal T-Square, so transit Uranus square her natal planets in Leo was also a factor, and it implied chaotic, unstable circumstances.

The reality of this potential was evident almost immediately after M'greet received her exciting marriage proposal. "Their engagement should have been a blissful period, but it was, in fact, full of tribulations. Rudolph had another attack of rheumatism, so severe this time that his sister Louise had to write the letters to his fiancee."[46] M'greet did not help matters by telling Rudolph she was an orphan, "being loath to produce an impoverished traveling salesman living in a decrepit part of town as her progenitor."[47] When she learned that she could not legally marry without parental consent, she had to admit that Adam Zelle was alive and well. The couple's haste also produced alarmed reactions. "There were also raised eyebrows on both sides to contend with when they announced they would marry in July, only three months after their already shockingly swift engagement."[48]

On July 11, Margaretha Geertruida Zelle became Margaretha MacLeod, but her new role in life would not lead to the freedom and adventure she anticipated, for now transit Saturn in her first house pointed to increased restrictions rather than increased freedom. This unhappy prospect became reality during 1895 and 1896 as transit Saturn squared her natal planets in Leo. Hovering in the background were transit Pluto's discouraging squares to her natal Moon which also cast a dark shadow on the new bride: *your ability to overcome depression or disappointment will be tested, as well as your determination to fulfill your desires and make your dreams come true.* "The honeymoon was soon over. ... Rudolph was visibly irritated by men's attentions to his young wife. ... It seemed to him that she encouraged their advances, and he began to make violent scenes."[49] When they returned home, the couple stayed with his sister and M'greet was "full of bitter feelings. Her aging, widowed sister-in-law seemed to resent her youth, her looks, her brother's desire for a woman who had answered a matrimonial ad. Rudolph had actually not abandoned any of his bachelor ways. He often stayed out late at night, offering no explanation for his whereabouts."[50] M'greet spent long, lonely evenings at home, and, often when her husband returned, he was drunk and full of rage. In 1896, a new responsibility and restriction occurred with pregnancy and the birth of her son at the end of January 1897.

1897–1904

In the spring of 1897, as transit Mars in her fourth house conjoined natal Moon (her home), Rudolph announced they would be moving to the East Indies. M'greet was thrilled. To her, the region was a new and exciting place, "a garden of earthly delights .... She began to picture herself in this island paradise, clothed in splendid native robes, striding among exotic fauna and unknown flowers. ... She could hardly wait for their journey to begin."[51] M'greet, Rudolph, and their baby son Norman departed for the Dutch colonies on the first day in May with transit Mars trine her natal Venus in the ninth house (foreign countries). According to biographer Erika Ostrovsky, M'greet bloomed in her new environment like the exotic flowers that surrounded her. Astrology suggested this was only a superficial appearance, made possible no doubt by her youth and a natural

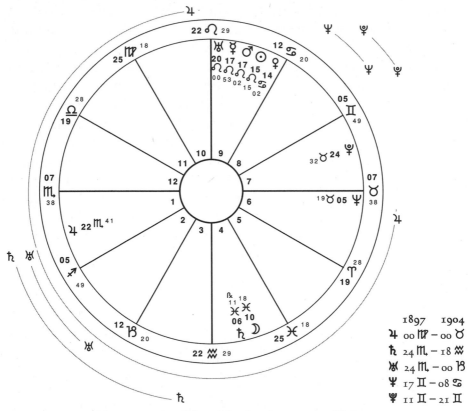

Figure 12.15: Mata Hari's 1897–1904 Transits

358

Leo exuberance that is willing to overlook the unhappiness of a situation if it is exciting enough.

The MacLeods settled into their island home and, as transit Saturn in Sagittarius initiated a series of squares to her natal Moon implying restriction, M'greet became pregnant again, giving birth on May 2, 1898 to a daughter whom they called Non. Her husband's criticism and abuse grew worse. "Margaretha's description of her husband's violence is consistent with the rage revealed in his letters. ... His harsh letters condemning Margaretha for her stupidity also bear the hallmarks of an abuser."[52]

Between the end of 1898 and mid-November 1900, transit Uranus, close on the heels of transit Saturn, moved into M'greet's second house (money and values) and initiated a series of squares to natal Saturn-Moon conjunction in Pisces. *When transit Uranus squares your natal Saturn, an event or situation creates a generation gap. There is a threat to the status of seniority or authority. These potentials are not likely to be caused by you so much as they are by the actions or decisions made by other people.* The potential of Uranus square Saturn was evident in biographical accounts that described a strict Victorian husband who insisted on absolute authority within his family and a youthful wife who thought of nothing but spending money on dresses and other material possessions. M'greet wrote to her friends: "My husband won't get me any dresses because he's afraid I will be too beautiful .... It's intolerable. Meanwhile the young lieutenants pursue me and are in love with me. It's difficult for me to behave in a way which will give my husband no cause for reproaches."[53] For his part, Rudolph depicted M'greet as "'an uncaring, unkempt slattern with a passion for material acquisition and no maternal feelings.' However, read in the light of his comments and his criticisms, her greatest crime was her refusal to live up to his rigid expectations."[54]

No unhappiness Rudolph and M'greet caused each other can be measured against the heart-numbing catastrophe that befell them on June 27, 1899, when their children were poisoned by one of the servants. The doctor that was summoned managed to save their baby daughter but it was too late to save their young son. "A few days later, one of the children's nurses caught cholera and on her deathbed confessed that she had been forced by a soldier to poison the family's food. But it was only Norman who ate enough of the tainted rice to be fatally stricken. ... The soldier, who was under MacLeod's command, sought revenge for disciplinary measures taken against him. Rumors among the Dutch colonists, however, said the soldier was the nurse's lover, whom MacLeod had caught and beaten. Others said that MacLeod had attempted to seduce the nurse and the soldier had poisoned the children in revenge."[55]

The long-term transit of Uranus square her natal Saturn-Moon conjunction and a twelfth-house transit of Jupiter in Scorpio opposing natal Neptune in Taurus were in position, but they did not pinpoint the day when the tragedy occurred. Natal Neptune in the sixth house (household servants) opposed by transit Jupiter in the twelfth house (hidden enemies) occurred four times between the end of 1898 and September 1899 which meant its potential for treacherous servants covered that period of time. The transit that revealed the possibility of harmful circumstances on June 27 was Mars in her tenth house opposed the natal Saturn-Moon conjunction in Pisces. The fourth house position of her Saturn-Moon conjunction indicated problems could occur in her home and involve members of her family, especially her children (natal Moon afflicted by transit Mars and natal Neptune—ruler of her fifth house of children— afflicted by transit Jupiter). Transit Mars represents male figures, which, in this case, includes her husband and her son. Her husband's actions precipitated the event and her son was the victim.

As the new century began, there was little for the MacLeods to celebrate. Transit Uranus began to square M'greet's natal Moon, a potential of danger to her health and a violent or unpredictable home life. In March, the possibility of illness was given added weight when transit Jupiter joined transit Uranus in Sagittarius to square her natal Moon. Accounts indicate that in mid-March M'greet contracted typhoid fever and it was exactly then that transit Mars (which is associated with fever) conjoined her natal Moon.

In October, as transit Uranus made the final square to her natal Moon, her husband retired from the army and the couple moved to a small mountain village in Java. There is no telling if M'greet found a way to enjoy the last two months of 1900 with transit Jupiter in Sagittarius trine her natal planets in Leo. In the spring of 1901, transit Jupiter joined transit Saturn in Capricorn to oppose her natal Venus (marriage, love, harmony, cooperation), suggesting that any happiness she may have had would have been short-lived. "Rudolph became increasingly abusive to his wife and on 27 May 1901 Adam Zelle received a petition in Amsterdam from a Batavian justice official asking him to witness Margaretha MacLeod's petition for divorce on the grounds of maltreatment."[56] On May 27, transit Moon in Libra squared natal Venus in Cancer and transit Mars at 6° Virgo opposed natal Moon. On August 3, 1901, M'greet sent her father a letter in which she complained that "Rudolph could no longer control himself during his attacks of rage; he had recently threatened to kill her, waved a loaded revolver in front of her and spat in her face."[57] On August 3, transit Mars in Libra squared natal Venus and transit Venus at 5° Virgo opposed her natal Moon. Helped along by the faster transit of Mars, the Jupiter-Saturn transit opposing natal Venus dominated her natal chart for the rest of the year, and MacLeod's behavior continued to deteriorate. Between January and March of 1902, transits of the Sun, Mercury, Venus, and Mars were focused on her fourth house (home) when M'greet, Rudolph, and their daughter Non left the East Indies and returned to Holland.

Bleak though her marriage and life in the East Indies had been, transit Pluto represented the potential for more hopeful circumstances. From mid-summer of 1896 until the spring of 1907, transit Pluto in Gemini was involved in an eleven-year series of sextiles to her natal planets in Leo. The reality of how transit Pluto's potential worked out in M'greet's life provides an excellent understanding of how the dynamics of sextiles can be associated with opportunity. Pluto's sextile to her Sun promised an opportunity that would help her *revitalize something that has been lost, or to make a new start. Opportunities may also lead to resolving (or getting out of) relationships and situations where your ego cannot grow or is being stifled, and bring a chance to strike out on your own.* Pluto's sextile to natal Mars suggested ultimate benefits involving *areas related to your job or work, to physical activities, and to male relationships.* Pluto's sextile to Mercury implied a *chance to develop and make advantageous use of ideas, methods, and ... skills.* Her sojourn in the East Indies provided M'greet, who already spoke Dutch, German, English, and French, with the opportunity to learn Javanese and acquire extensive knowledge of the Hindu epics and Javanese dances performed according to Hindu traditions that had been transmitted to Java from India. Taking advantage of this opportunity would one day help M'greet turn her life around. When transit Pluto began to sextile natal Uranus in 1904, it was time for M'greet to take advantage of all that she had learned and experienced. But as she sailed for home in 1902, she still had to endure the next few years when transit Saturn would enter Aquarius to oppose her natal planets in Leo, aspects that held few immediate prospects for freedom, independence, and success.

Life become intolerable between 1902 and 1904 as first Jupiter and then Saturn in Aquarius opposed her natal planets in Leo. Her husband left and eventually took custody of their daughter since M'greet had no means of providing for her child's welfare. She attempted to go to Paris to find work in 1903 but failed and was forced to return to live with her husband's relatives throughout 1904. "It was in the winter that she thought she had reached the bottom rung of the ladder, and despair. She was exiled in the desolate province of North Brabant, watched over by Rudolph's relatives like a dangerous criminal. If she complained, he jeeringly offered to let her enter a convent as an alternative and threatened her with lawsuit if she made the slightest move."[58] Transit Saturn completed a last opposition to her Leo planets and entered her fourth house (new beginnings) in January 1905. "Penniless, childless, unknown, unskilled, at the end of her youth and virtually at the end of her strength as well, she landed in Paris once more."[59] This time things would be different.

1905–1914

As Pluto continued the last sextiles to her natal Mercury and natal Uranus in 1905 and 1906, it marked the potential for conditions that would give M'greet the opportunity to use what she had learned in the East Indies. Society was becoming fascinated with the mysterious Orient, helped along as it was by the writers of the day who described its exotic landscape, strange practices, and sensual women. The time was perfect for M'greet to reinvent herself as Mata Hari, the Hindu dancer. Gone was her married name and her troubled past. Mata Hari was becoming a "woman whose past was merely another prop in her own personal theatre, altered, like her name, to fit the current scene."[60]

But this is a story best told through transit Neptune. Transit Uranus in Scorpio had triggered her Grand Trine when she began her career as wife and mother. Now it would be the transit of Neptune in Cancer triggering her Grand Trine that marked her new career. The *Musee Guimet* in Paris had begun as a private collection of art objects and documents of the wealthy industrialist Emile Guimet. Eventually it had become an excellent library and served as a study center for orientalists. On the evening of March 13, 1906, the second floor of the library had been transformed into a Hindu temple and, as the audience sat and waited, "sounds of a strange music were heard. ... In the mysterious light there appeared a silhouette of a woman. ... A golden collar round her throat and several strings of pearls on her arms and legs ... almost naked, she began to 'dance.' Her undulating body floated with infinite grace among the disarray of veils and the intoxicating odor of perfumes. Her look contained all the *fauve* languor of a true Oriental."[61] Few who knew M'greet would have recognized her as the utterly captivating "Mata Hari, Hindu dancer, who had 'come to honor the museum and the Parisians with the dances of the Devadasis and present the sacred art of expressing, by harmonious gestures, the far-off mysteries of vanished cults.' "[62] Her audience was thrilled. Taking her bows, Mata Hari further awed the spectators by explaining her dance in English, German, Dutch, and Javanese. With her new name, a new life had begun. "Her luck," as biographer Ostrovsky writes, "appeared to have turned. In the space of one night, she had become the sensation of the season."[63]

Where were the transits on this auspicious night? Having set the stage, so to speak, transit Neptune trine natal Saturn was part of the background. The transits that evening included transit Sun (ruler of her tenth house of public reputation) at 22° Pisces trine transit Mars conjoined natal Jupiter in her first house at 22° Scorpio (which, in turn, is trine her tenth-house cusp or Midheaven). At 5° Taurus, transit Venus (with transit Jupiter not far behind) conjoined natal Neptune, an aspect we can associate with her successful illusion of glamor and mystery.

Throughout the following decade transit Neptune (which rules dancing) trined natal Saturn and natal Moon, conjoined Venus, and ultimately trined natal Jupiter at the outer edge of her Grand Trine, and Mata Hari enjoyed fantastic success. Transit Neptune's trine to natal Saturn promised increased recognition for her hard work as well as help from elderly people. It was older men who advised and helped her get started, and such men would thereafter be a constant fixture in her life. Transit Neptune's trine to her natal Moon can be associated with the illusion and mystery that would surround her and create the legend that is still associated with her name. Neptune's conjunction with Venus no doubt helped her dancing career, but Venus is also the planet of social behavior, romance, and values, so we may associate this aspect with her role as *demimonde* which she began shortly after her fame started to spread, bringing her in contact with many influential and wealthy men. "With her sights set on power, Mata Hari followed in the tradition of many grand Parisian courtesans, combining a stage career with a highly public private life. These sexual liaisons attempted to satisfy mutual interests; husbands maintained an active erotic life ... while the courtesan enjoyed her financial independence, social prestige and perhaps even a degree of political power."[64]

Transit Neptune began to inhabit her ninth house in 1906 where it would remain until her death. Since Neptune is such a slow-moving planet, there are people who will never experience its transit in their ninth house, and those who do will relate to what happens to them from their own background and perspective. As for Mata Hari, the potential of circumstances associated with transit Neptune in the ninth house perfectly describes the environment in which she was operating between 1906 and 1917, when she was executed as a spy: *you are (or should be) reaching beyond your immediate environment in order to gain a greater understanding of the world, seeking new experiences, and meeting new people. But when Neptune is the transit that is involved with your Ninth house, caution is necessary. In matters related to ... long-distance travel, and people of another culture or race, you are sailing in tricky waters and will have to navigate a safe course to avoid being trapped by fanatic ideas, misplaced idealism, and unrealistic schemes. If you are involved in a court decision or any kind of formal decision during this lengthy period, it may be impossible to say how or why a verdict was determined.*

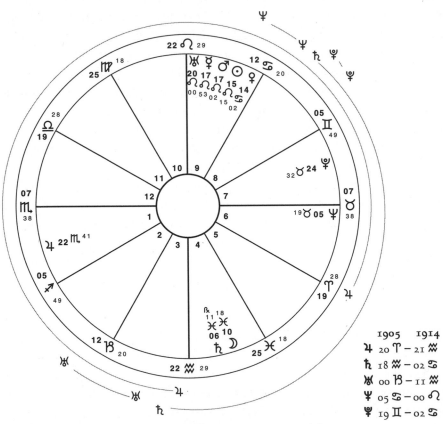

Figure 12.16: Mata Hari's 1905–1914 Transits

There were, of course, other interesting transits that characterized her life as she embarked on her successful career. One of them was transit Saturn. In 1906, Mata Hari left France to conquer Spain and was greeted in that country with wild enthusiasm. She gloried in the acclaim she received wherever she traveled, but the real M'greet Zelle MacLeod did not succeed nearly as well offstage as she did in the spotlight. She often wore a look of great sadness, and one of the well-known portrait painters of the day who knew her was quoted as saying that he could not recall ever seeing Mata Hari smile. Her private state of mind at this time is suggested by transit Saturn conjoined her natal Moon. Biographical descriptions reveal the discouraging lack of emotional satisfaction associated with a transit Saturn-natal Moon conjunction. "Despite her vanquished rivals; despite entering her second triumphant season; despite having launched—if not a thousand ships—dozens of news items, she appeared pensive and somewhat melancholy offstage. Her mind was certainly preoccupied with the part of her life that, to her audiences, remained unseen: Rudolph had succeeded in getting a divorce, with all the 'wrongs' on her side ('debauchery'...'adultery') and had almost instantly remarried, a woman almost thirty years younger than he; Non had already been sent to live with another family, obviously at her stepmother's request, a bitter lot as she remembered from her own past; her father had published a book that was supposedly her biography, which had been countered by a hostile exposé from the pen of Rudolph's lawyer, both cashing in on her fame, or infamy."[65]

At the end of 1907, transit Uranus entered her natal third house, the potential of which provides another dimension of Mata Hari's existence: *Circumstances may demand or inspire you to develop new skills in order to keep pace with your present needs.* The reality was that whenever the public seemed to lose interest in her, it forced Mata Hari to invent another fantasy. She danced with a large snake, she appeared on horseback, she danced in a Spanish *tableau vivant*, and she danced in virginal laced gowns.

Between 1908 and 1911, Mata Hari continued to keep herself before the public with varying degrees of success. The wealthy banker Xavier Rousseau financed a house and furniture for her, she wore the latest fashions, and she stayed in the finest hotels wherever she traveled. Rousseau was by no means her only lover. Mata Hari had a particular taste for lovers of high military rank whom she pursued with the greatest determination, sowing at the same time the seeds of her own destruction.

As the years passed, it was natural that her age would begin to work against her as well as her lavish spending habits. At the end of 1911, Rousseau's bank failed and the rent on her villa and other debts remained unpaid. Mata Hari continued to drift from one place to another, always in the company of wealthy and influential people. By 1913, she was getting fewer and fewer bookings. Although she had many admirers, her fame rested chiefly on the fact that the carefully orchestrated movements she claimed represented mystical sacred rites allowed sophisticated society to applaud and appreciate as "art" the unspoken thrill of watching her dance in the nude. It was not long before theaters were full of her imitators. She was never ranked as a professional artist, and her dalliances with men rich and important enough to help her achieve her ambitions prevented her from being accepted into respectable society. Thus, when she would need a champion, when it was literally a matter of life or death, there was no one to take up her cause.

1914–1917

In 1913 and 1914, she tried to revive her fading career and turned to her friend Emile Guimet for help. He contacted a friend in Berlin who managed to secure an engagement for her. The French had grown cold toward her art and M'greet, remembering how enthusiastically German audiences had always received her, was happy to leave for Berlin where she was scheduled to appear September 1, 1914. Although M'greet would be leaving her French lovers behind, Berlin would not be a difficult transition since she had already established liaisons in Germany with men such as the German Foreign Minister, Herr von Jagow. "She had won him over when he was still the chief of the German police and had visited the theater in which she performed, ostensibly to censor her costumes, only to succumb to her spell."[66] Looking forward to a triumphal return to the stage, Mata Hari prepared to head for Berlin.

Unstable political situations in the Balkan countries made Europe a dangerous place in the summer of 1914. While visiting Bosnia to attend a military review, the Austrian heir to the throne, Archduke Ferdinand, and his wife were assassinated in the streets of Sarajevo on June 28. This outrage made Austria determined to make war on Serbia, causing an unprecedented domino effect. If Austria made war on Serbia, Russia was determined to make war on Austria. If Russia made war on Austria, Germany was prepared to make war on Russia. If

Germany made war on Russia, France was determined to make war on Germany. And no one knew what the British government might do.

Patriotic fever in Germany had reached fever pitch and Serbia, Latvia, and Herzegovina crowded the newspaper headlines in July when Mata Hari arrived in Berlin. Dining with Foreign Minister Von Jagow on July 31, Mata Hari noted his obvious preoccupation. At five o'clock, the Kaiser had declared general mobilization and that night Jagow sent a telegram to his ambassador in Paris to please keep France quiet for the time being. On August 3, war was declared and the German populace was elated. Von Jagow asked Mata Hari to drive with him in his official car, accompanied by an escort of mounted police. "They went from one end of the city to the other, to the railroad station from which trains left for the front, to all the public gatherings. She felt that she shared a triumphal chariot, as though she were his consort. The crowds that cheered the representative of war seemed to be cheering her also. Playing Venus to his Mars, she enjoyed the sense of glory, the power of the voices raised in unison, the heady sensation of victory."[67]

This was the kind of public appearance that Mata Hari truly enjoyed, but it was one that would have ominous implications for her three years later. As a result of the declaration of war, the theater where she was to perform was closed. On August 6, she attempted to return to Paris but was refused entry into France because she was a foreigner. Forced to return to Berlin, she found that her bank account was blocked because she was considered a French resident. Eventually, a Dutch compatriot bought her a ticket and she returned to Holland.

Mata Hari was settled into a small house in The Hague and was trying to adjust to a Dutch provincial life that she found tedious and boring when transit Uranus began to oppose her Leo planets in the summer of 1915. As we noted at the time of M'greet's engagement and marriage, events tend to happen quickly and unexpectedly when transit Uranus is involved. Increasingly restless with her life in The Hague, M'greet longed to return to France, but she did not expect nor could she have imagined that in two years she would end up on a dissecting table in Paris. For a woman accustomed to the excitement of the stage and the intrigues of society, the opposition between transit Uranus and her Sun suggested circumstances in which her ego would urge her to seek greater stimulation and recognition. Transit Uranus opposing her Mercury suggested the potential for turbulent confrontations and discussions and that travel was risky. The opposition between transit Uranus and natal Mars implied careless actions and associations with men could be perilous. Transit Uranus opposed natal Uranus describes a period *when* generations clash. You may be as unwilling to give up the unique qualities that belong to your age group as another generation is to give up their special character. There is little meeting of the minds (or tastes).

The reality of this aspect can be seen in the consequences of Mata Hari's attempt to return to her old life at a time when the mood in society was turned against such performers and courtesans were considered untrustworthy women capable of consorting with the enemy. In December, Mata Hari returned to France to retrieve her possessions that had been placed in storage. She briefly renewed some of her former acquaintances, packed the things she wished to keep, and returned home. But not for long. With reckless abandon she continued to invite her doom by returning once again to France as transit Uranus opposed her Leo planets in the spring of 1916. The potential of circumstances

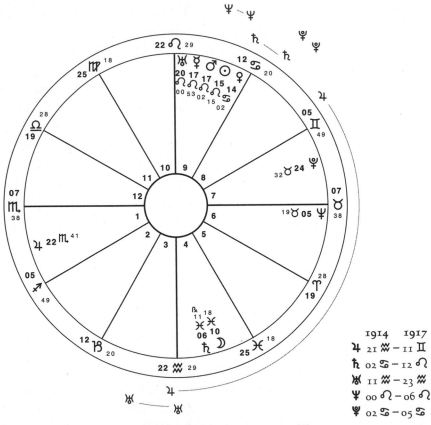

Figure 12.17: Mata Hari's 1914–1917 Transits

(whether good or bad) associated with transit Uranus are those in which you are not the one in control and in which you will be unable to manipulate the outcome. By this time, the British military authorities had listed her as an undesirable and warned the French of their suspicions. Mata Hari, however, continued to keep a highly public profile. According to one biographer, she was determined to control every situation, but according to the position of transit Uranus in her natal chart, it was the very last thing she should have been trying to do. Arriving in Paris June 16, she was followed by two inspectors from the Deuxieme Bureau. On this day, her natal Moon (ruler of her ninth house of foreign countries) was squared by transit Mercury at 10° Gemini in her eighth house and opposed by transit Mars at 9° Virgo in her tenth house.

Captain Georges Ladoux, head of the French office of military espionage, sent the inspectors who followed Mata Hari, and between June 1916 and January 1917, they filed regular reports of her visitors, telephone calls, mail, and other activities including a suspicious number of male visitors, mostly officers. Reading these reports, it occurred to Ladoux that Mata Hari might be useful as a French agent. The transit of Uranus opposing her Mercury and Mars makes his meetings with Mata Hari and subsequent events interesting occasions to note. "In Ladoux's memoirs, he vividly recalls their first meeting in August 1916. With hindsight, he claimed to have suspected Mata Hari was a German agent from the start and hiring her as a double-agent was an effective trap. ... But according to Mata Hari, this initial discussion with Ladoux about working for the French was entirely unexpected."[68]

They met for a second interview in September to discuss her services, but several days later Ladoux must have started to regret his decision when "with marvelous indiscretion, two days later Mata Hari sent Ladoux a letter through the post asking for an advance to buy dresses she would need to lure Von Bissing [the German officer commanding the Belgian occupation]."[69] Ladoux told Mata Hari to go back to Holland and wait for further instructions. Returning to The Hague via Spain and England, she ran into trouble when the ship docked at Falmouth. Mistaken for another woman who was known to the MI5 (British Intelligence) as a German agent from Hamburg, Mata Hari was taken to Scotland Yard for interviews with Sir Basil Thompson, Assistant Metropolitan Police Commissioner of Scotland Yard and head of the Special Branch. "Suddenly Mata Hari announced that she had something important to say. She was a spy, yes, but for the French, not the Germans. She had had two interviews with Captain Georges

Ladoux, Thompson's counterpart in Paris, so there was no need for this interro-gation. As a rule, agents did not divulge their identity, even to the allies, but since Mata Hari faced such serious charges she gambled that the truth would set her free."[70] Thompson sent an inquiry to Paris asking if Ladoux had hired her. In reply, Ladoux admitted nothing but advised that Mata Hari be sent back to Spain where she would no doubt reveal her connection with the Germans.

Ladoux did more than just send a telegram to Thompson. "He not only denied to the Dutch legation in Paris that he had hired her as an agent but encouraged suspicions about her working for the Germans. Mata Hari from now on would be regarded as an enemy agent and nothing more; the plan to have her seduce von Bissing was off."[71] Knowing nothing of this development, Mata Hari arrived in Madrid December 11 and wrote to Ladoux for instructions. When he failed to respond, she plotted her own course and contacted the German envoy in Madrid, Major Arnold Kalle. Later, she stated that she went to his home, they chatted, and then they made love. She claimed that she told him she was working for the Germans only to gain his trust.

The next day, Mata Hari met the French military attaché responsible for French espionage in Spain, Colonel Joseph Denvignes and told him of her meet-ing with Kalle. Throughout December, she continued to have amorous meetings with Kalle, and he fed her worthless news that she took at face value. She received no word from Ladoux and finally headed for Paris on January 2 where she expected to get a large payment for her services. When she arrived, two of Ladoux's inspectors followed her cab to the hotel. At first Ladoux refused to see her, and when they met January 7, he immediately reproached Mata Hari for openly visiting the French embassy in Madrid. She related the information she had learned from Kalle but Ladoux was unimpressed and said he would pay her nothing. "She had fallen into a trap. She had no money to return to Holland and, anyway, could not leave without official permission from the French .... her plan to make a fortune from espionage had failed."[72]

Mata Hari was desperate to return to The Hague but Ladoux was playing for time. When she had arrived in Paris he reported the British suspicions about Margaretha Zelle, aka Mata Hari, to Captain Pierre Bouchardon, chief investi-gating officer of the military tribunal. On February 13, five inspectors and the police commissioner came to her hotel and told Mata Hari they had orders for her arrest. "The woman Zelle, Margaretha, known as Mata Hari, ... is accused of espionage, complicity and intelligence with the enemy, in an effort to assist them in their operations."[73] She was taken directly to Bouchardon's office in the Palais de Justice and from there to Saint-Lazare prison where she would be interrogated for five months. Between the time she was arrested and her trial in July, transit Saturn entered Taurus and began to square her natal Neptune. This aspect describes an accurate potential for how the proceedings would go. *Be wary of false hopes or false promises .... It is wise to be mindful that some deception or disillusionment in your general circumstances is possible .... Imposing reality and structure on ideas and situations that are incompatible or severely discouraged by such limitations will not work.* The reality was that throughout the long period of interrogation, Mata Hari was convinced she would be rescued. However, even her own government's attempts to intervene met with indifference.

She increasingly turned to her Oriental fantasies for comfort. "But neither Mata Hari's identification with this imaginary 'Orient' nor her tireless campaign against Bouchardon's charges could have any effect. She had become the victim of her success."[74] As the transit of Neptune had warned, there was grave danger from fanatic ideas. A great paranoia concerning spies swept through France during World War I. In August 1915, a Mademoiselle Lallart was condemned to death, and the following February another woman was accused of espionage and consigned to the firing squad. Although capital punishment in France had ended in 1887, the execution of female spies was carried on with particular fanaticism. Many claims were made that Mata Hari was not a spy, that she was merely a scapegoat, and that the French had no direct evidence to convict her of such activities. On July 24–25, her trial took place appropriately enough with the transits of the Sun, Mercury, Saturn, and Neptune in her ninth house (court decisions) and with transit Uranus exactly on the cusp of her fourth house signaling a new beginning. But what kind of new beginning? On July 25, Mata Hari was sentenced to die, an order that was duly carried out October 15, 1917.

THEODORE ROOSEVELT

Most people recognize the name Theodore Roosevelt. At least they know he was President of the United States, and those who visit the Black Hills of South Dakota will surely be reminded of his role in history as they gaze at the face of Teddy Roosevelt in the impressive company of Lincoln, Washington, and Jefferson memorialized on Mount Rushmore. His sixty-foot high image is a more appropriate symbol for Teddy Roosevelt than many of the tourists who look at it realize. Possessed of a nearly photographic memory, unlimited intellectual curiosity, indomitable courage, and irrepressible humor, he was the author of thirtyeight books, winner of the Nobel Peace Prize, and a dedicated husband and father. He was, indeed, a man who seems bigger than life. If ever a man lived to the fullest extent of his potential and exemplified the Scorpio ability to rebound physically, mentally, and emotionally, it was Theodore Roosevelt.

The Roosevelt family's common ancestor Nicholas had two sons, Johannes and Jacob. Jacob's line settled along the Hudson River and were known as the Hyde Park Roosevelts. Descendants of Johannes Roosevelt settled in Manhattan and Long Island. They were known as the Oyster Bay Roosevelts, and, in time, they produced Theodore Roosevelt. The two branches of this large family often intermingled. Eleanor Roosevelt, the daughter of Theodore Roosevelt's tragic brother Elliot, would one day be given in marriage by her Uncle Teddy (who at the time was President of the United States) to a member of the Hyde Park branch of the family, Franklin Delano Roosevelt. But this was still in the future on October 27, 1858, as Martha Bulloch Roosevelt, known to the family as Mittie, gave birth to an eight-and-a-half-pound boy whom they named Theodore.

Theodore Roosevelt's chart contains many difficult dynamics. When astrology students see squares and oppositions in a natal chart, they tend to think the harsh circumstances that these aspects imply will prevent an individual from being productive, happy, and successful. In TR's natal chart there are two T-Squares, one in mutable signs with Neptune in Pisces square the opposition between Jupiter in Gemini and Venus in Sagittarius, and the other in fixed signs with Saturn in Leo square the opposition between Sun and Mercury in Scorpio opposed Pluto in Taurus. There is also an opposition between the Moon in Cancer and Mars in Capricorn. On the plus side, there is a trine between the Moon and Neptune and a trine between Saturn and Venus, but the chart unmistakably indicates that life for this individual will be difficult. Theodore Roosevelt was

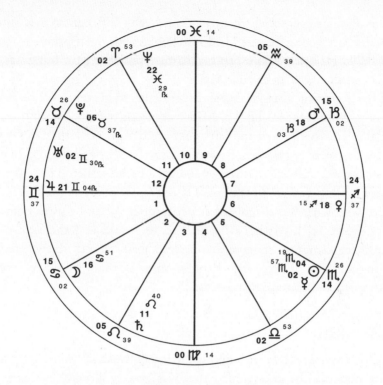

Figure 12.18: Theodore Roosevelt's Natal Chart

always engaged in a struggle of some kind and more than once he was plunged into the darkness of inconsolable grief. He confronted problems head on and, in turn, extracted every last ounce of happiness.

TR's battles began when he developed severe bronchial asthma at around three years of age. Often forced to sleep sitting up, he was haunted by the nightmare of waking in the dark gasping for breath. He also suffered from nervous diarrhea that debilitated him for days at a time. Family correspondence and his own diaries, which he began to keep as a child, are full of accounts of his illnesses. TR had very poor eyesight. When it was finally discovered and he received his first pair of glasses, his improved vision seemed a miracle to him. To strengthen his body, he began a program of constant exercise and other physical activities when he was about twelve years old that would exhaust most adults. He continued to keep such a strenuous physical pace that years later, during a medical examination, his doctor warned that he had actually weakened his heart by his aggressive

373

exertions (a diagnosis to which he paid no heed). TR had an avid interest in nature and as a young boy he filled notebooks with descriptions of birds and other wildlife. He became an expert taxidermist, preserving the hundreds of birds and other small creatures he collected.

At the beginning of 1876, transit Saturn entered his tenth house signaling a period of increased responsibilities, serious decisions regarding his future, and the potential for restrictions or burdens connected with his father. That fall, TR began his first year at Harvard. By September 1877, he had decided to pursue a career in science, a choice that was encouraged by his father. The two enjoyed a close relationship and, in December, TR was upset by news that his father had collapsed with what was diagnosed as peritonitis. When he went home for the holidays, however, his father's health had improved and the family enjoyed Christmas together. Returning to Cambridge shortly after the New Year, TR was beginning a period of profound changes. Some of them would require all the inner strength and courage he possessed.

1878–1885

TR began the winter term with his customary enthusiasm, something he would not have done had he known his father was gravely ill with agonizing, swiftly spreading cancer. On February 9, as he studied for his semiannual examinations, a telegram arrived telling him to come home immediately. With an anxious heart he traveled through the night, but when he reached New York the next morning, he was too late. "None of the Roosevelts, least of all Theodore himself, could have foreseen how shattered he would be by the premature loss of his father. 'He was everything to me'—so much so that it seemed, for a while, as if the boy could not survive without him. Like a fledgling shoved too soon from the bough, he tumbled nakedly through the air; some of his diary entries are not so much expressions of sorrow as squawks of fright. They give the impression of a sensitivity so extreme it verges on mental imbalance."[75] When his father died, transit Saturn in his tenth house (its implications were mentioned above) at 19° Pisces triggered his mutable T-Square. Transit Neptune at 4° Taurus opposed his natal Sun (the father), was indicative of his being unaware of his father's condition. Transit Mars conjoined natal Pluto at 6° Taurus activated his fixed-sign T-Square. Transit Jupiter (the father) and transit Mercury (indicating the bad news he received) were to be found in his eighth house (death and transition). After the funeral, TR resumed his studies with intense fervor as he struggled to overcome his private grief. When his classes were over, he went to Oyster Bay for the summer, relentlessly putting the same tireless exertion into physical activities as he had put into his studies. When he returned to school in September 1878, the pain of his loss was slowly healing and he was able to begin the new term with a lighter heart: a potential of the Libra transits of the Sun, Mercury, and more importantly (as we shall see) Venus and Mars in his fifth house.

In need of diversion and relaxation, he accepted a few social invitations, one of which was to visit the home of his friend Dick Saltonstall. On October 18, the two men rode the six miles in Dick's buggy out to Chestnut Hill. Adjoining the Saltonstall property was the home of George Cabot Lee who was related by marriage to Dick. His seventeen-year-old daughter Alice Lee was a close companion of Dick's sister Rose. That evening, TR met both girls and throughout the weekend enjoyed their company. He visited Chestnut Hill several times and by Thanksgiving he was passionately in love with Alice. Prior to meeting Alice Lee, he had been close to his childhood friend Edith Carow, but the romance had stalled the previous summer when they had a falling out. After TR met Alice, Edith was out of his thoughts. The evening they were introduced (October 18), Venus at 13° Libra and Mars at 15° Libra in his fifth house (romance) trined natal Jupiter, ruler of his seventh house (marriage). Transit Venus and Mars activated the natal Moon and Mars opposition implying there would be problems. TR launched a campaign to win the hand of the fair Alice. However, since his heart's delight was so young, it was not going to happen very quickly. His overtures were discouraged (although not totally rejected) and he suffered through 1879 in unrequited love. Finally, on January 25, 1880, Alice consented to be his wife. On that date, the transit Moon in Cancer touched off the opposition between natal Moon and Mars, the same position it had occupied the October evening that the couple first met. Mr. Lee officially announced his daughter's engagement on Valentine's day, a date on which TR's natal Moon-Mars opposition was activated by the transit Moon in Aries and transit Venus at 18° Capricorn conjoined natal Mars. In a few short years, that Valentine's Day would become a date that was painful to recall.

As marvelous as the impending marriage was for TR, he had launched another project that was also very important. During the winter of 1879-1880, with transit Jupiter in Pisces trine his Sun and Mercury, he began writing *The Naval War of 1812*. One area associated with Jupiter is publishing, and, in turn, the Neptune-ruled sign of Pisces is associated with the sea and consequently with the navy. Natal Mercury rules his chart (Gemini rising) as well as writing and intellectual pursuits, while natal Sun rules his third house (writing). The potential of Jupiter's trine favored success for this project.

On October 27, 1880, TR and Alice Lee were married. Transit Jupiter at 11° Aries formed a Grand Trine with natal Saturn in Leo and natal Venus in Sagittarius. However, it also triggered his natal Moon-Mars opposition. They soon took up residence in New York City where TR started law classes and became involved in local politics. Since he and Alice were prominent members of society, their social life kept them busy nearly every evening. Between all his comings and goings, TR still managed to squeeze enough time to keep researching and writing his book, efforts his young wife may not have appreciated. An anecdote

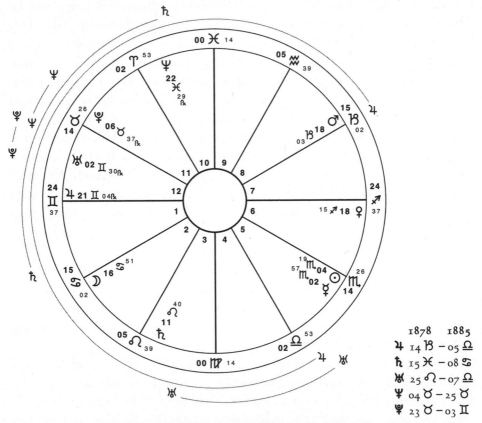

Figure 12.19: Theodore Roosevelt's 1878–1885 Transits

attributed to biographer and friend Owen Wister describes this period: "It is the pre-dinner hour; Theodore, standing on one leg at the bookcases in his New York house, is sketching a diagram for *The Naval War of 1812*. In rushes Alice, exclaiming in a plaintive drawl, 'We're dining out in twenty minutes, and Teddy's drawing little ships!' "[76]

Throughout 1880 and 1881, TR became increasingly involved in the Twenty-first District Republican Association. The men with whom he fraternized were not from his wealthy and privileged background but he studiously set out to cultivate them: "... some instinct told him that if he desired raw political power—and from this winter on, for the rest of his life, he never ceased to desire it—he must start on the shop floor, learn to work those greasy levers one by one."[77] Such circumspect desire is described in part by transit Pluto in his twelfth house. In 1881, transit Neptune entered his twelfth house, adding other potentials—the possibility of hidden enemies and situations of which he would be unaware—to the pattern of events. The most prominent transit was Uranus entering his fourth house (new beginnings) shortly after his father's death in 1878, where it remained until 1885. This meant that he could not predict the permanence or the outcome of any new enterprise. It also meant a period of unexpected events and changes, the reality of which included meeting and falling in love with Alice Lee, law classes taking the place of the science career he had planned, and his interest in the law being soon set aside in favor of politics.

By October and November 1881, TR was a regular participant in the Twenty-first District as they were preparing to return an assemblyman to Albany. Eager to help defeat the previous year's delegate, William Trimble, the hand-picked candidate of party boss Jake Hess, TR worked hard on behalf of independent delegates. At the preconvention meeting on October 24, he gave an impassioned speech against renominating Trimble. Unknown to TR, one of the more powerful party members by the name of Joe Murray strongly disagreed with Hess about Trimble and had been quietly gathering enough support so that now he and not Hess could choose the candidate. This is why, in due course, TR unexpectedly found himself taken aside by Joe Murray and asked if he would accept the nomination. Although he was unsure of Murray's motives, TR accepted, and at the Assembly Convention on October 28, he received the nomination. Election day, November 9, was another date with the transit Moon in Cancer and it was part of a Grand Trine that involved transit Mars at 15° Cancer conjoin his natal Moon, transit Sun at 17° Scorpio in his sixth house (a new job), and natal Neptune in Pisces in his tenth house (public reputation). The Grand Trine's potential for success reflected three factors that helped TR win. The first was favorable press coverage, the second was that his district was solidly Republican, and the third was that he came from a well respected, prominent family while the only thing recommending the Democratic opponent was his recent removal as director of a lunatic asylum.

Assemblyman Theodore Roosevelt, age twenty-three and the youngest man in the Legislature, took up his duties in Albany on January 3, 1882 (another date with transit Moon in Cancer) where he quickly became "something of an angrily buzzing fly in the Republican ointment."[78] Success was suggested by a trine between transit Uranus (ruler of his ninth house of political interests) and natal Mars (ruler of his eleventh house of hopes and aspirations) that inaugurated his political birth. Transit Uranus implies the unexpected, and certainly no member of the Assembly in 1882 expected the feisty freshman in their midst to one day occupy the White House. Tom Arnold, who had been Speaker of the House when Roosevelt was born, cynically assessed Republican strength in the House as "sixty and one-half members."[79]

TR had more to consider, however, than political adventures and aspirations. In June 1882, with transit Neptune trine natal Mars, *The Naval War of 1812* was published. (Neptune rules the sea and Mars is associated with war.) "Reviewers were almost unanimous in their praise of its scholarship, sweep, and originality. It was recognized on both sides of the Atlantic as 'the last word on the subject,' and a classic of naval history."[80] By the end of 1882, transit Jupiter was the one to watch as it went back and forth over his Ascendant and into his first house, an implication of increased prestige and influence. At the Republican Assembly caucus on January 1, 1883, Isaac Hunt nominated Theodore Roosevelt for Speaker. "The nomination was approved by acclamation, and Roosevelt could congratulate himself on a political ascent without parallel in American history."[81] The problem was that the Democrats controlled the House so Roosevelt had to be satisfied with the position of Minority Leader.

When transit Jupiter trined natal Sun and Mercury in his fifth house (children) in May, an unparalleled personal event occurred and Alice became pregnant. As transit Jupiter moved into his natal Moon-Mars opposition in July, it coincided with a serious health setback for TR. "This time he became so ill that, looking back on the summer of 1883, he described the whole period as 'a nightmare.' ... By the beginning of August he was, if not fully recovered, at least well enough to retire to Oyster Bay."[82] As transit Jupiter reached Leo and triggered his natal fixed-sign T-Square during the last months of 1883, TR was campaigning hard to be renominated for Speaker of the House. But there was serious opposition within his party and ultimately the position went to another candidate. He was upset at losing the nomination "and by the added annoyance of drawing the second-last seat in the House, on the extreme back row of the northern tier."[83]

The transits of Pluto, Neptune, and Saturn in his twelfth house pointed to less obvious forms of power. This potential became reality as 1884 got under way and he began to realize that "far from being weakened by failure, he was now a more potent political force than ever."[84] The circumstances of loss described by the major transits in his twelfth house held a far more ominous potential than his failure to be nominated as Speaker. On February 13, he received a telegram informing him of his daughter's birth. This message was followed by a second one directing him to come home immediately. In a grim reenactment of his homeward journey prior to his father's death, TR departed Albany. He arrived home that night to find his mother dying of typhoid fever and Alice dying from Brights disease, an illness that had gone undetected during her pregnancy. On February 14, Valentine's day, his mother Mittie passed away in the early morning hours and Alice followed her to the grave that afternoon. In addition to the potential of the transits in his twelfth house and the unexpectedness of events associated with transit Uranus, we find transit Mars conjoin natal Saturn (ruler of his eighth house) activating his fixed-sign T-Square. Transit Mercury in his eighth house, as it was when his father died, indicated the bad news he received. Mercury is not only the ruler of his chart with Gemini on the Ascendant, but also rules the fourth house which points to home and family.

None of these transits, troublesome though they seem, could have been used to predict the two-fold tragedy that occurred. As he had done when his father died, TR absorbed his private grief and, on February 18, he returned to Albany to lose himself in work. In April he was elected delegate-at-large from New York at the State Republican Convention. "Although Roosevelt was reported to be 'beaming with smiles' on his return to the Capitol, he was still privately tortured with sorrow. ...'You could not mention the fact that his wife and mother had been taken away ... you could see at once that it was a grief too deep.' There were signs that the pain inside him was increasing, rather than diminishing, due no doubt to its too cruel suppression."[85] The rest of 1884 and a large part of 1885 were devoted to political activities and a number of long sojourns in the Bad Lands of what was then called the Dakota Territory. He bought cattle and land and began to build Elkhorn Ranch (now part of the Theodore Roosevelt National Park in the southwest corner of North Dakota). In October 1885, just after returning to New York from one of his trips out West, transit Uranus entered his fifth house (romance) and, by design or coincidence, he happened to run into his old friend Edith Carow. Uranus is a harbinger of swiftly moving events, and the following month, TR proposed marriage. Societal conventions would frown on an engagement so soon after Alice's death, so they decided to keep their intentions secret for another year. As 1886 drew near, it marked the beginning of a new life with Edith at his side.

1886–1896

Transit Jupiter divided the time between November 1885 and December 1886 in TR's fourth house (new beginnings) and fifth house (romance, social activities, and creative projects). Jupiter's fourth-house association was his new life with Edith. Its fifth-house potential is described by his mood after they became secretly engaged. "Unable to tear himself away from Edith, Roosevelt remained in the East for a 'purely society winter,' as he called it, of dinners, balls, and the Opera. At the height of the season, through January and February 1886, he was going out every other night."[86] In January, TR's friend Henry Cabot Lodge came to New York to visit. Hearing that Henry was writing a life of George Washington as part of an American Statesman book series, TR expressed interest in doing something similar. Lodge arranged for him to receive a commission to write an American Statesman book. In mid-March, with transit Jupiter (retrograde) back in his fourth house, he traveled West to check on Elkhorn Ranch and his cattle, his 'backwoods babies' as he called them.

The potential of transit Jupiter can be associated with the circumstances that enabled TR to put his life back together, but transit Saturn was also in the picture. At the end of July 1886, Saturn entered his second house (money) to conjoin natal Moon (indicating the possibility of expenditures motivated by emotional need or that involve home or family) and oppose natal Mars in his eighth house (inheritance, debts) suggesting a period of increased responsibility in these areas. Saturn indicates worry, restrictions, and lack of enthusiasm, all of which began to occur. "The hot August days dragged on. Plagued by a recurrent 'caged wolf feeling,' Roosevelt also began to worry about Dakota's continuing drought."[87] In spite of his newfound happiness with Edith, he appeared to be under considerable strain that summer. The memory of Alice inspired guilt over his intentions to remarry. He was heard pacing the floor at night groaning over and over again, "I have no constancy! I have no constancy!"[88] Worry over his lack of faithfulness to Alice was an impediment that soon disappeared, but learning Saturn's lesson of monetary prudence would not be so easy. Saving money was never one of TR's strong points. After Alice's death, his single status hardly warranted building one home, let alone two. Nevertheless, he built a home (Sagamore Hill) in Oyster Bay that cost him $45,000 and he invested $85,000, virtually half his patrimony, in the Elkhorn Ranch and its cattle. If it failed, he would be in serious financial difficulty. Returning East in October, he tarried long enough to lose his bid for mayor in the New York City elections before leaving for England and marriage to Edith.

On the morning of December 2, TR and Edith were wed in a private ceremony and they soon embarked on a European tour, a period which Edith in later years recalled as the most romantic time in her life. Romantic it may have been, but transit Saturn's potential in her husband's natal chart suggested there was also a strong element of sober practicality that overshadowed the honeymooners. In Florence, they began to receive disturbing reports that the Bad Lands had suffered the worst blizzards in frontier history and thousands of cattle, already weakened by the summer drought, had been wiped out. When the newlyweds returned to the United States at the end of March, TR headed for Elkhorn to see for himself what, if anything, was left of his investment. "He already had a fairly accurate idea. Or rather, Edith had. That level-headed lady knew that her husband, whatever his other talents, was a financial imbecile. Soon after the wedding she had gone over his affairs with him and discovered that, on the basis of last year's figures alone, they should 'think very seriously of closing Sagamore Hill.'... Clearly, if they were to rear their family at Oyster Bay, they would have to 'cut down tremendously along the whole line.' Roosevelt must learn to live within his income for a change, and begin to pay off his debts. He must sell his enormously expensive hunting horse, grow his own crops and fodder (for Sagamore Hill was a potentially profitable farm), and stop running the house as a summer resort for friends with large appetites, and thirsts to match."[89]

Riding out to Elkhorn Ranch, the barren land he passed was much worse than TR had feared. It was clear that his losses were crippling and any optimism about recovering part of his investment vanished. The fiscal responsibility associated with transit Saturn in the second house was demonstrated by the circumstances in which TR found himself. But another facet of Saturn's potential is having (or developing) the ability to put monetary matters in perspective. This is the plus side and it is accurately interpreted by his attitude. "Although his Dakota venture had impoverished him, he was nevertheless rich in nonmonetary dividends. He had gone West sickly, foppish, and racked with personal despair; during his time there he had built a massive body, repaired his soul, and learned to live on equal terms with men poorer and rougher than himself. ... These men, in turn, had found him to be the leader they craved in that lawless land, a superior being, who, paradoxically, did not make them feel inferior. They loved him so much they would follow him anywhere, to death if necessary—as some eventually did. They and their kind, multiplied seven millionfold across the country, became his natural constituency. 'If it had not been for my years in North Dakota,' he said long

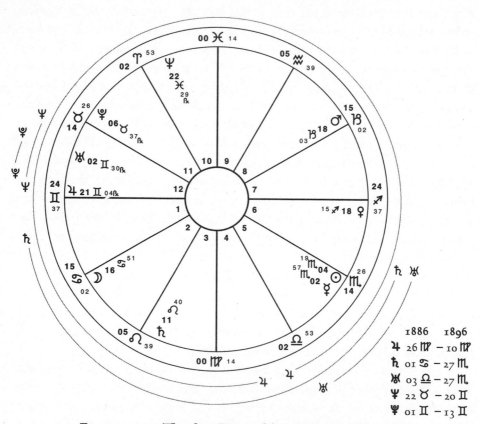

Figure 12.20: Theodore Roosevelt's 1886–1896 Transits

	1886	1896
♃	26 ♍ –	10 ♍
♄	01 ♋ –	27 ♏
♅	03 ♎ –	27 ♏
♆	22 ♉ –	20 ♊
♇	01 ♊ –	13 ♊

afterward, 'I never would have become President of the United States.' "[90] TR set-tled his accounts as best he could for the time being and returned East to decide what to do next. There was not much hope on the political horizon with the Democratic President Grover Cleveland firmly entrenched in the White House, but perhaps Henry Cabot Lodge could get him another book to write.

From January through December 1887, the transits of Saturn and Jupiter dominated his chart. As TR, Edith (who was pregnant), and little Alice (who since birth had been cared for by his sister) settled into Sagamore Hill, transit Saturn, in Cancer conjoined natal Moon and opposed natal Mars, continued to suggest heavy responsibilities regarding money and his increasing family. Because of their financial constraints, they had few guests but this gave Alice and her father more time to become reacquainted. Softening Saturn's potential was tran-sit Jupiter in Scorpio conjoin natal Mercury (September 4) and natal Sun (Sep-tember 11). One of its happy benefits occurred when Edith gave birth to a baby boy on September 12.

Even though transit Jupiter in the early degrees of Scorpio activated his fixed-sign T-Square, once it entered his sixth house (work) it activated the natal Moon-Neptune trine. For some time TR had been thinking about writing a history of the conquest of the North American continent, and with transit Jupiter auguring the potential for success, he began to write *The Winning of the West*. However, transit Saturn in Leo was now square natal Sun and Mercury suggesting obstacles and delays. Throughout 1888, progress on the book was extremely slow, and he did not finish it until April 1, 1889. Jupiter's beneficence was exhibited when the book was released in the fall to overwhelmingly favorable reviews. The two-vol-ume first printing quickly sold out. But during the two years it took to finish the book project, other significant developments had occurred.

When TR started his book in the fall of 1887, Jupiter's transit in his sixth house promised favorable employment and the work he really wanted was to get back into politics. The election in 1887 (in which he had played a significant role) put Republican candidate Benjamin Harrison in the White House and now TR hoped for a presidential appointment. However, when Henry Cabot Lodge tried to secure a job for him in the new administration, it became apparent that TR's steamroller personality and reputation for aggressive reform were working against him. Officials voiced their misgivings because they knew Mr. Roosevelt could not be controlled and, if he were given a highly visible and sensitive gov-ernment position, they could never be sure what he might do.

Lodge continued to press his case directly with President Harrison but here, too, he met with reluctance. "Eventually he [Harrison] thought of a dusty sinecure that paid little, and promised less in terms of real political power. Ambitious men invariably turned it down; if Roosevelt was crazy enough to want it, he might be crazy enough to make something of it."[91] Lodge hurried to New York to inform TR that Harrison was willing to appoint him as a Civil Service Commissioner at a salary of $3,500 per year. "He doubted, however, that his friend would want the post. Such a pittance could only plunge him deeper into financial difficulties; bureaucratic entanglements would interfere with his upcoming book contracts; besides, the work was bound to make him unpopular, for everybody in Washington was heartily sick of the subject of Civil Service Reform. Roosevelt accepted at once."[92]

The last thing the Administration and Congress wanted was to have an active Civil Service Commission. This was, of course, the very first objective of newly appointed Commissioner Roosevelt when he began his job May 13, 1889. Transit Mars at 2° Gemini conjoin natal Uranus emphasized the potential for his aggressive, nontraditional approach. Transit Jupiter at 7° Capricorn in his seventh house (partners, allies, those with whom you cooperate) trine natal Pluto (power and control) was an indication of how much he would dominate the three-man Civil Service Commission. The potential of transit Neptune conjoin natal Uranus best describes the reality of what occurred during the six years of his tenure: *When transit Neptune conjoins your natal Uranus, confusion, disorientation or unrealistic expectations arise to cause certain changes in society. Ideals and spiritual goals conflict with technical and economic considerations and almost anything can happen. Eventually, of course, this conflict can mean significant changes in how things get done.*

As TR's idealism clashed with the more practical self-serving interests of the members of Congress, there was plenty of confusion, disorientation, and unrealistic expectations as well as continuous cries for his removal and tactics to circumvent him that transcended party lines. Nothing hindered for one moment TR's unflinching efforts to seek out and expose those responsible for fraud and favoritism in government: "Roosevelt kept the Civil Service Commission, which had dozed comfortably in a wing of the old City Hall on Judiciary Square, in a constant state of turmoil. Swooping down without warning upon far-flung outposts of his empire, he investigated rumors of fraud, held hearings, issued reports, made speeches, and wrote magazine articles to dramatize the cause of reform."[93] When the Democrat Grover Cleveland was reelected in 1892, Roosevelt expected to be replaced, but he was not. TR stayed in his post and the battles he fought for reform under Cleveland were essentially the same as those he had fought under Harrison. "There were the same 'mean, sneaky little acts of petty spoilsmongering' in government; the same looting of Federal offices across the nation, which Roosevelt combated with his usual weapons of publicity and aggressive investigation; the same plea for extra funds and extra staff ... the same fiery reports and five-thousand-word letters bombarding members of Congress."[94] By 1893, he began to talk about stepping down and the following year, "an increasing restlessness through the spring and summer of 1894 is palpable in his correspondence."[95]

In his private life, TR constantly worried about money and he was also vexed by a serious problem with his brother Elliott. His brother, who suffered from epilepsy, was slowly ruining his life with alcohol. More than once TR tried to get him on the road to recovery but with little success. On August 13, 1894, he received a telegram that Elliott was very ill. "Roosevelt, desk-bound in Washington, did not respond: he knew from experience that Elliott would not let any members of the family come near him. There had been many such messages in recent months, 'He can't be helped, and he must simply be let go his own gait.' The following day [August 14] Elliott, racked with delirium tremens, tried to jump out of the window of his house, suffered a final epileptic fit, and died."[96] Relevant transits in TR's chart on August 14 include Mercury (ruler of his fourth house, home and family) at 4° Leo at the door of his third house (siblings) and square natal Sun, ruler of his third house. Transit Uranus at 11° Scorpio squared his third-house Saturn, ruler of his eighth house (death and transition).

Weary of the Civil Service Commission, TR was drawn back to New York City with an invitation to run for mayor in October. He would have been delighted to do so had it not been for the strenuous objections of his wife. Although he was obliged to turn down the mayoral race, transit Uranus entering his sixth house of work in 1894 suggested job changes. Returning to Washington in 1895, he continued to take an active interest in the reform administration of New York's new mayor, William Strong. In March, he let it be known that he would like to be appointed one of the four New York City Police Commissioners. He received word that this could be arranged and, on April 17, the appointment was confirmed. Looking forward to the challenges that awaited him in New York, TR could look back with pride on his accomplishments in Washington: "A total of 26,000 jobs were removed from the category of political plum and placed under the merit system, and new tests for applicants were devised."[97] He had given the Civil Service Commission an influence it had never had and he gained the admiration of the American people for having taken on the spoilsmen.

On May 8, 1895, TR bounded up the stairs of police headquarters ready to tackle the new job with his usual aggressiveness and dedication. "'Where are our offices?' demanded Roosevelt of the startled police officers. 'Where is the Board Room? What do we do first?' Making his way to the second floor, he found the outgoing board waiting, stiff, formal, and dignified, for their successors. Quickly dispensing with ceremony, Roosevelt shook hands, called a meeting of the new Police Board, and had himself elected its president."[98]

Predictably, his tenure as Police Commissioner was controversial and combative. "Over the next two years, Roosevelt was the delight of newspaper cartoonists and reporters, the pride of reformers, and the despair of Tammany Hall, crooked policemen, and saloonkeepers. Often, he was at odds with his own party and his colleagues on the Police Board."[99] As Police Commissioner, his accomplishments were impressive. During the less than two years he spent on the Police Board, he "established a sense of professionalism heretofore unknown to the department and made a seeping series of changes, reforms, and innovations that outlasted his tenure."[100] On the day he began his job (May 8), one indication of how things would go was transit Jupiter at 4° Cancer in his first house trine natal Sun. The promise of transit Jupiter is increased influence, and, in this case, it also pointed to the amount of favorable press coverage (ruled by Jupiter) that he was able to generate. "Out-of-town newspapers were unanimous in their praise for New York's vigorous new police commissioner. Residents of other cities troubled with the same problems were impressed by his performance, and Roosevelt's image as a reformer took firm hold on the public imagination. Lodge began to see the presidency as a possibility for his friend."[101]

As much as TR was able to achieve, it was not accomplished without acrimonious, sometimes embarrassing situations. There were continual difficulties with his colleagues on the Police Board and, by the summer of 1896, he was becoming dissatisfied with his job. The Republican nomination of William McKinley in June 1896 turned TR's thoughts back to Washington. Although McKinley was not his first choice as a candidate, he worked hard to help get him elected, and, in the process, ingratiate himself with McKinley and McKinley's campaign chairman, Mark Hanna. When McKinley was elected by an overwhelming plurality, TR began once again to hope for a presidential appointment. This time he wanted to be Assistant Secretary of the Navy.

1897–1900

Henry Cabot Lodge attempted to negotiate the appointment for TR, but McKinley, like Benjamin Harrison before him, was worried about TR's unpredictable and bellicose temperament. Various friends put in a good word for TR throughout the winter of 1897, but there were others who voiced objections to his naval appointment, not the least of which was Secretary of the Navy, John Long, who feared that if Roosevelt became his assistant, he would try to take over. TR continued to agitate for the position, sending letters and assurances to those who had expressed concerns. In early April, Lodge informed him that the President was sending his name to the Senate for confirmation as Assistant Secretary of the Navy.

Transit Jupiter entered his fourth house (new beginnings) as TR took up his duties in the Navy Department on April 19. He quickly proved his usefulness to Naval Secretary John Long. After his first meeting with Roosevelt, Long noted in his diary "best man for the job." Secretary Long was a capable administrator but saw no reason to strain himself "to master the details of warship design, engines, armor plate, guns, or dry docks. 'What is the need of my making a dropsical tub of any lobe of my brain,' he noted, 'when I have right at hand a man possessed with more knowledge than I could acquire.' "[102] For his part, TR was more than happy to assume the burden. The paint on the walls of his new office was barely dry before he embarked on an aggressive campaign to expand the fleet. "He had a smattering of knowledge about the navy's affairs and the enthusiasm of the dedicated amateur. He was delighted to spend long hours discussing the intricacies of ship construction and armament with his staff and wrote articles and gave speeches propagandizing for a strong navy. Before long, he was popping up everywhere to inspect ships and store stations, and the hulking figure with the flashing teeth became familiar to everyone. ... Gossip had it that officers waited until Long was away—which was often—and brought problems to Assistant Secretary Roosevelt for final resolution."[103]

Within the first week of his arrival, he inserted four separate warnings of potential trouble in Cuba into a report the President had ordered on fleet preparedness. TR advocated annexing Hawaii and throwing Spain out of the Caribbean. His first public address at the Naval War College in Newport, Rhode Island, in which he emphasized the need for more ships, was a triumph. It was printed in most major newspapers and unanimously praised. Even President McKinley admitted that Roosevelt was right.

As summer approached, Secretary Long left for a vacation in Massachusetts to avoid the stifling heat in Washington. He was, of course, greatly encouraged to do this by his able assistant. As Acting Secretary, TR managed to gain the ear of the President and present to him a Cuban war plan. In addition, TR told the President that at the first sign of trouble he intended to enlist in the Army. The President promised he would give him the opportunity to serve. One of the longer-term transits during 1897 and 1898 was Neptune conjoining natal Jupiter and crossing the Ascendant into his first house. Transit Neptune also opposed natal Venus which, as we will see, meant encountering problems, but on one level at least the transit Neptune-natal Jupiter conjunction marked a period when Roosevelt gained political backing for his plans and, ultimately, the fame that would catapult him into the White House. "And so the year ended with a crescendo of praise for Assistant Secretary Theodore Roosevelt, who was now recognized to be one of the best-informed and most influential men in Washington."[104]

Early in 1898, Edith became very ill with typhoid fever and little Ted suffered from a strange nervous condition. This situation was the reality of transit Neptune opposed natal Venus (his marriage partner) ruler of his fifth house (children). The fact that Neptune was involved suggested the potential for misdiagnosis or difficulty in finding a problem at all. Edith's so-called typhoid fever eventually ended with an operation to remove a tumor, and the five different physicians that examined young Ted were unable to determine the cause of his illness. TR also learned he had personal tax problems in New York. But even as family physicians and accountants were pressed into service, Roosevelt's mind was constantly on Cuba. Secretary Long proposed to McKinley that the battleship Maine should be sent to Havana as "an act of friendly courtesy." TR restlessly awaited news of a disturbance, but reports indicated that the Cuban capital was quiet and peaceful.

On the evening of February 15, passengers steaming into Havana's harbor on the liner *City of Washington* admired the *Maine*'s sleek white beauty from four hundred yards away. After dark the passengers went below decks for dinner while over on the *Maine*, Captain Sigsbee was in his cabin writing a letter to his wife. Hearing the melancholy sound of taps, he put down his pen and listened. As the last note faded away, he looked at his watch and noted that the time was 9:40 PM. He was putting his letter in an envelope when the explosion came. "Groping his way on deck, Sigsbee found the forward part of his ship was shattered and rapidly sinking into the mud. Casualties were heavy—266 of the 354 officers and men on board were killed."[105] In Washington, President McKinley as well as Secretary Long were awakened and given the news. The question of who was responsible for the calamity has never been determined. It could have been the Spaniards or it could have been the work of Cuban revolutionaries hoping to provoke a war with Spain. It also could have been an accident, a theory that in later years gained more credence. The President cautioned Americans to keep an open mind until an investigation could be conducted. Assistant Naval Secretary Roosevelt had no doubt, however, that the finger of guilt pointed to Spain.

On the morning of February 25, Secretary Long, feeling unwell with various aches and pains and worn out from a bout with insomnia, went home. Acting Secretary Roosevelt lost no time in jumping into the power vacuum caused by Long's absence. He sent a message to Commodore George Dewey in Hong Kong to keep his ships full of coal: "In the event declaration [of] war Spain, your duty will be to see that the Spanish Squadron does not leave the Asiatic coast."[106] TR sent similar messages to squadron commanders all over the world. To make sure that coal was available, TR authorized the Navy's coal-buying agents to purchase maximum stocks. He also ordered supplies of ammunition and guns. "He even sent demands to both Houses of Congress for legislation authorizing the unlimited recruitment of seamen."[107] In a single afternoon, TR placed the Navy "in a state of such readiness it had not known since the Civil War."[108] Early in March, preliminary reports from the divers examining the wreck of the *Maine* confirmed that the explosion could have been caused by a mine. In response, the President asked Joseph Cannon of the House Appropriations Committee for $50 million saying, "I must have money to get ready for war. I am doing everything possible to prevent war, but it must come, and we are not prepared for war."[109] The request was granted with no dissenting vote. Roosevelt reviewed all available warships with Long and was given responsibility for purchasing any available vessel that could be converted to a cruiser.

While carrying out his duties in the Navy Department, he continued to ask for a place in the battle lines. McKinley finally sent his declaration of war to Congress on April 11. At 3:00 in the morning, Congress voted to endorse the President's declaration of war. Resigning his naval post, TR immediately received permission to raise a regiment of U.S. Cavalry volunteers and train them in San Antonio. The newspapers began calling his regiment "Teddy's Terrors," "Teddy's Cowboy Contingent," and other names, but the nickname that stuck was "Roosevelt's Rough Riders."

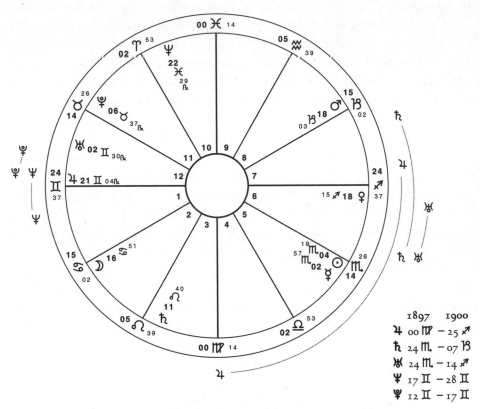

Figure 12.21: Theodore Roosevelt's 1897–1900 Transits

On April 24, as TR was busy in Washington processing thousands of applications for his cavalry regiment, Commodore Dewey received the orders from Secretary Long that he had been expecting since Roosevelt had alerted him at the end of February. On May 1, news was heard of Dewey's spectacular naval victory. "In seven hours of stately maneuvers off Manila, George Dewey had destroyed Spain's Asiatic Squadron. Almost every enemy ship was sunk, deserted, or in flames; not one American life had been lost, in contrast to 381 Spanish casualties. The victorious Commodore (who was promptly promoted to Rear-Admiral) modestly ascribed his success to 'the ceaseless routine of hard work and preparation' demanded of him by the Navy Department."[110]

Roosevelt reported to Camp Wood on May 15 to begin training his men and, by May 29, the Rough Riders struck camp, ready for action. Seven trains carrying the regiment and twelve hundred horses and mules inched its way south, depositing them near Tampa, Florida, on June 2. They would spend another twelve days of waiting around for something to happen. Late in the afternoon on June 14, they finally sailed out of Tampa Bay on the Yucatan bound for Cuba. Transit Moon and transit Mars conjoin his natal Pluto suggested the fierce intensity with which TR approached the task ahead. Between the day they left and July 1 when they fought the battle of San Juan Hill (which Theodore called "the greatest day of my life"), transit Mars sextiled natal Moon and transit Jupiter moved from 0° to 2° Libra which trined natal Uranus. In turn, Jupiter rules his seventh house (open enemies) and Uranus rules his ninth house (foreigners). For his bravery in capturing San Juan Hill, Major General Joseph Wheeler, commander of the army's regular cavalry division, recommended TR for the Medal of Honor.

When the skirmish was over, each day that passed became more hazardous for the men, many of whom had caught yellow fever, to remain in Cuba. TR wrote a letter criticizing the War Department for not moving faster to bring the army home. Then he leaked the letter to the press. President McKinley and Secretary of War Russell Alger were angered by the criticism, especially since they had already made arrangements to set up a camp for the returning army at Montauk Point, Long Island. Several days later, when Alger ordered the men home, it looked as though it had been TR who had forced the action. In revenge, Alger made sure Theodore never received the Medal of Honor: "It was, as Edith wrote later, 'one of the bitterest disappointment of his life.' "[111] His private disappointment aside, it didn't matter whether the government recognized his heroism because the newspapers were having a field day glorifying his exploits and making TR an American hero.

Once back in civilian life, TR predictably returned to politics, and in the fall he became New York's Republican gubernatorial candidate. On November 8, 1898, Theodore was elected Governor of New York. The transit Moon in Virgo in his fourth house (another new beginning) was part of a Grand Trine that included natal Pluto and natal Mars. Transit Neptune perched on his Ascendant and transit Sun at 16° Scorpio were trined natal Moon in Cancer and natal Neptune in Pisces in his tenth house (public reputation). His term as governor has been described: "Roosevelt proved to be a good governor.... As chief executive of the most important state in the Union, he had to deal with the complex problems of an urban-industrial society and exhibited a mixture of imagination, pragmatism, and shrewdness. ... New York assumed some of the early characteristics of a progressive state government. Fearing radicalism on the one hand and the excesses of the great corporations and trusts on the other, Roosevelt saw himself as a mediator, or honest broker, between these contending forces who had the interests of all Americans in mind."[112]

Throughout 1899, TR aggressively pursued his usual reform and altruistic legislation which embittered many of New York's most powerful politicians, especially those who were directly in his line of fire. No matter how they contrived to cover their tracks in illegal schemes and profiteering, TR was there to expose them. His enemies were no doubt on the edge of contriving a means for his demise when fate gave them an alternative. On November 21, 1899, McKinley's Vice President Garret Hobart died, clearing the way for TR's enemies to get him elected as Vice President and out of New York.

Theodore, however, had no intention of running for Vice President. In his mind it was a powerless position. Elected as a delegate-at-large to the Republican National Convention, he left for Philadelphia still protesting that he did not want nor would he seek the Vice Presidential nomination. The convention on June 19, 1900, became a convoluted twist of agendas that involved New York politicians who wanted to get rid of their troublesome governor at all costs and Roosevelt's genuine friends and admirers who also wanted him nominated as Vice-President. McKinley and Roosevelt were nominated—TR casting the convention's only vote against himself. "On November 6, 1900, the Republican party won its greatest victory since the triumph of Grant in 1872. ... the Vice President-elect was entitled to much of the credit."[113]

1901–1909

When Vice President-elect Roosevelt was inaugurated on March 4, 1901, the transit Moon at 6° Virgo was in his fourth house (another new beginning) trine natal Pluto, ruler of his sixth house (work). The fact that transit Mercury in his tenth house was retrograde provided a clue that something about the event could change. This is by no means a hard and fast rule concerning retrograde Mercury, but nevertheless a good one to remember. In the fall of 1904, the President and Vice President took a tour of the country, and, on September 6, Roosevelt was in Vermont while McKinley was touring the Pan American Exposition in Buffalo, New York. As TR was getting ready for a reception, the telephone rang. Answering it, he was told the President had been shot, and although the extent of his wounds was not yet determined, the Vice President was requested to come to Buffalo. Four days after the shooting, TR was advised that it was no longer necessary to stay with the recuperating McKinley, and he left to join his family in the Adirondacks. A few days later, McKinley suddenly took a turn for the worse. Urgent messages were sent once again directing TR to come to Buffalo. On September 14, the President's breathing grew labored and, at 2:15 AM, he died. At 3:00 PM that afternoon, Theodore Roosevelt was sworn into office. At age forty-two, he was the youngest president in American history.

The most singular transit was Pluto conjoined natal Jupiter and opposed natal Venus. Unlike the transit of Neptune in that position in 1898, the potential of transit Pluto opposed natal Venus did not coincide with personal difficulties. It did, however, indicate that legal matters (his oath of office) are *not lighthearted or pleasurable*. An even more revealing description of his presidential life was the potential of transit Pluto conjoined natal Jupiter indicating that *political ambitions are the likely areas through which you seek to attain greater power and influence. Your father or his influence may have a subtle and significant karmic role in what happens at this time.* The emphasis on the father is interesting. As TR signed letters and other documents on September 23, 1901—his first day in the White House—he realized it was his father's birthday. He regarded this as an omen that all would be well, "I feel my father's hand on my shoulder, as if there were a special blessing over the life I am to lead here."[114] That evening he dined in the White House with his sisters and their husbands. It was the custom of the White House to present each male guest with a boutonniere when the coffee was served after dinner. Holding the yellow saffonia rose he was given, TR replied, "'Isn't that strange!' he exclaimed. 'This is the rose we all connect with our father.' "[115]

It is impossible to recount every incident of Theodore's presidency, so instead, I will choose a few highlights and invite readers to go to the history books to examine his seven-year tenure in more detail. One activity for which Theodore Roosevelt is well known involves his role as trustbuster. The trouble began when the Northern Securities Company was launched November 12, 1901, as the result of attempts by E. H. Harriman of the Union Pacific Railroad and James J. Hill of the Great Northern Railroad to win a route to Chicago. J. P. Morgan settled the resulting clash between Harriman and Hill by bringing the two men together in the spirit of common cause. From this meeting, the Northern Securities Company was created to control the Northern Pacific, the Great

Northern, and the Burlington Quincy Railroad, which was the ideal connection for the other two railroads to Chicago.

The public at this time was already upset with the growing number of large holding companies that held virtual monopolies. When Northern Securities was formed, the enormous public outcry that followed provided exactly the opportunity Roosevelt needed to go into action. Without discussing anything with his Cabinet, TR secretly ordered Attorney General Philander Knox to bring suit to dissolve the company. Later he explained that his cloak-and-dagger method had been necessary to prevent disaster in the stock market, but part of his reason was no doubt simply to avoid those who would have tried to dissuade him from taking such action. It was two years before the courts unraveled the Northern Securities case. In the meantime, the majority of opinions were that when the case reached

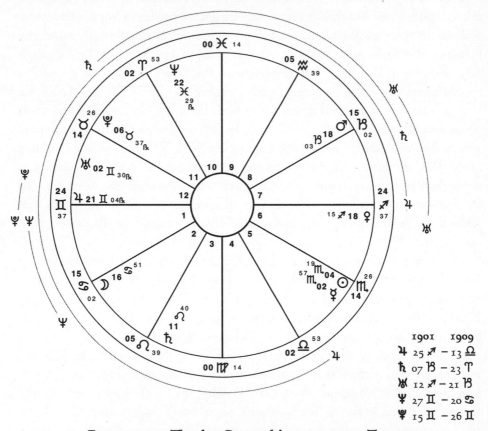

Figure 12.22: Theodore Roosevelt's 1901–1909 Transits

the Supreme Court, the justices would rebuff the President. These opinions were wrong. On March 14, 1904, the Supreme Court upheld a lower-court ruling that dissolved the company—and Theodore's reputation as a trustbuster was made. The relevant transit when TR secretly ordered the suit brought against Northern Securities was Jupiter at 2° Aquarius trine his twelfth house (hidden activity, secrets) natal Uranus, ruler of his ninth house (court decisions, political activities). This suggested the successful outcome which eventually occurred on March 14, 1904—a day when transits of the Moon, Venus, and Saturn in Aquarius in his ninth house (court decisions) trined natal Jupiter and his Ascendant.

With transit Pluto at 21° Gemini conjoined his natal Jupiter, the election on November 8, 1904, put TR in the White House, this time on his own merits. In the coming years transit Pluto continued to be a major delineator as it moved back and forth over natal Jupiter across his Ascendant and entered his first house, an indication of increased desire for power and control. There is no question that TR's identification with increased power was personal but it also figured strongly in the role he envisioned for the United States. His aim was to transform the United States from "a provincial nation on the fringes of global affairs into a world power."[116]

On November 8, 1904, when TR was elected, his Jupiter-Venus opposition was activated by a T-Square that involved transit Mars in Virgo square the opposition between transit Pluto conjoined natal Jupiter in Gemini and natal Venus in Sagittarius. The potential of these aspects could easily be used to describe his foreign policy. "'More and more,' he declared, 'the increasing interdependence and complexity of international and political and economic relations render it incumbent on all civilized and orderly powers to insist on the proper policing of the world.'"[117] The T-Square suggests aggressive tactics that sometimes earned him widespread condemnation as it did for his involvement in Panama, and sometimes worked to his advantage as it did for his successful efforts to end the war between Russia and Japan. In the first instance, TR encouraged Panama to wrest its independence from Colombia on November 3, 1903. Fortunately, the revolution turned out to be a peaceful coup and within hours Washington recognized the newly independent Republic of Panama. In return, a treaty was signed giving the United States control of a ten-mile zone across the Isthmus where TR intended to build the canal. "No action during Roosevelt's presidency aroused greater controversy among his contemporaries and later generations than the methods used to 'take' Panama—or reveals more about the workings of his mind.

Personal ambition, intense patriotism, and firm belief in the leadership of the 'superior' nations guided him throughout the adventure."[118]

In the second instance, the Russo-Japanese war involved a cardinal point of TR's foreign policy, which was to maintain a balance of power. The war that broke out in 1904 involved Russian interests in Manchuria and Japanese desire to control Korea; the main issue being which country would dominate the Far East. TR became concerned that no matter who was victorious, the war would set a precedent for a possible future clash over U.S. interests in the Pacific. He set about to negotiate a peace that would restore a balance of power. When he failed in his efforts to involve the Kaiser and other European heads of state in the peace process, he seized the initiative himself. A meeting of peace delegates from Russia and Japan was arranged in August 1904 at Portsmouth naval yard in New Hampshire. When the talks broke down, TR drafted a compromise himself and eventually the peace agreement was signed. Because of his role in achieving this treaty, TR became the first American to receive the Nobel Peace Prize.

Transit Pluto implies more than the struggle for power and control, it also involves the use and development of natural resources. TR began a revolution in conservation that added 150 million acres to the country's public lands. "...Roosevelt dealt with environmental issues with statesmanship and administrative skill as well as moral fervor. In his seven and a half years in the presidency, he impressed upon the nation the importance of preserving natural resources for future generations. The concept of conservation was broadened to include not only forests and wildlife, but coal and mineral lands, oil reserves, and power sites. Government land reserves were increased from 45 million acres in 1901 to 195 million acres in 1909. During the Roosevelt years, thirty irrigation projects were started, including some of the nation's largest dams; Grand Canyon and Niagara Falls were among the eighteen protected national monuments, and five new national parks and fifty-one wildlife refuges were established. These were to be Theodore Roosevelt's great legacy to the American people."[119]

As the end of Theodore's presidency drew to a close, the whole family regretted his rash pledge on the night of his election victory in 1904 not to seek another term. However, there was nothing to be done about it, and, on March 4, 1909, as William Howard Taft recited the words of the presidential oath, it signaled the end of Theodore Roosevelt's reign.

Ephemeris

How To Use the Ephemeris

Using the ephemeris to look up the planetary positions for a given date is very simple. The twenty-four hour clock is used so there are no AM or PM designations for the times given in the ephemeris. The list below will be helpful if you are not used to seeing the time designated in this way.

00:00 is 12:00 AM GMT (Midnight)	12:00 is 12:00 PM GMT (Noon)
01:00 is 01:00 AM GMT	13:00 is 01:00 PM GMT
02:00 is 02:00 AM GMT	14:00 is 02:00 PM GMT
03:00 is 03:00 AM GMT	15:00 is 03:00 PM GMT
04:00 is 04:00 AM GMT	16:00 is 04:00 PM GMT
05:00 is 05:00 AM GMT	17:00 is 05:00 PM GMT
06:00 is 06:00 AM GMT	18:00 is 06:00 PM GMT
07:00 is 07:00 AM GMT	19:00 is 07:00 PM GMT
08:00 is 08:00 AM GMT	20:00 is 08:00 PM GMT
09:00 is 09:00 AM GMT	21:00 is 09:00 PM GMT
10:00 is 10:00 AM GMT	22:00 is 10:00 PM GMT
11:00 is 11:00 PM GMT	23:00 is 11:00 PM GMT

The positions are given from the date and time a planet enters a sign until it enters the next sign. As an example, let's use a date of November 26, 1944. In the ephemeris, turn to the year 1944 and list the positions of the Sun and planets for November 26, 1944.

- The Sun was in Sagittarius between November 22 at 10:07 GMT and the time it entered Capricorn at 23:15 GMT on December 21.
  This tells us that on November 26 the Sun was in Sagittarius ... ☉ ♐
- Mercury was in Sagittarius between November 10 at 11:10 GMT and the time it entered Capricorn at 15:29 GMT December 1.
  This tells us that on November 26 Mercury was in Sagittarius ... ☿ ♐
- Venus was in Capricorn between November 16 at 07:21 GMT and the time it entered Aquarius at 04:44 GMT December 11.
  This tells us that on November 26 Venus was in Capricorn ... ♀ ♑
- Mars was in Sagittarius after November 25 at 16:15 GMT.
  This tells us that on November 26 Mars was in Sagittarius ... ♂ ♐
- Jupiter was in Virgo after July 26 at 01:33 GMT.
  This tells us that on November 26 Jupiter was in Virgo ... ♃ ♍
- Saturn was in Cancer after June 20 at 07:48 GMT.
  This tells us that on November 26 Saturn was in Cancer ... ♄ ♋
- Uranus was in Gemini the entire year.
  This tells us that on November 26 Uranus was in Gemini ... ♅ ♊
- Neptune was in Libra the entire year.
  This tells us that on November 26 Neptune was in Libra ... ♆ ♎
- Pluto was in Leo the entire year.
  This tells us that on November 26 Pluto was in Leo ... ♇ ♌

Using this method, look up planetary positions for any date. Certain dates are marked with R or D to indicate the beginning (R) and the end (D) of retrograde motion. Retrograde motion is the apparent backward movement of a planet, as viewed from Earth, due to its position in relation to the Earth. Thus a planet may appear to slow down and move backward. An example is found on the facing page. On April 3, 1944, Mercury entered Taurus. Mercury began to retrograde (move backward) on April 22 at 15° Taurus, and on May 15 it resumed its forward motion at 6° Taurus.

1944

Sun

♒ Jan 21 04:08	♈ Mar 20 17:47	♊ May 21 04:52	♌ Jul 22 23:58	♎ Sep 23 04:04	♐ Nov 22 10:07
♓ Feb 19 18:27	♉ Apr 20 05:16	♋ Jun 21 13:04	♍ Aug 23 06:48	♏ Oct 23 12:58	♑ Dec 21 23:15

Mercury

Jan 1 25♑
D Jan 19 9♑
♒ Feb 12 14:20
♓ Mar 3 02:51
♈ Mar 19 07:43
♉ Apr 3 17:32
R Apr 22 15♉
D May 15 6♉
♊ Jun 11 11:49
♋ Jun 27 03:39
♌ Jul 11 07:36
♍ Jul 28 23:13
R Aug 24 21♍
D Sep 16 8♍
♎ Oct 5 03:27
♏ Oct 22 11:33
♐ Nov 10 11:10
♑ Dec 1 15:29
R Dec 13 8♑
♐ Dec 23 23:31

Venus

Jan 1 27♏
♐ Jan 3 04:44
♑ Jan 28 03:12
♒ Feb 21 16:39
♓ Mar 17 02:45
♈ Apr 10 12:08
♉ May 4 22:04
♊ May 29 08:40
♋ Jun 22 19:13
♌ Jul 17 04:48
♍ Aug 10 13:14
♎ Sep 3 21:18
♏ Sep 28 06:12
♐ Oct 22 17:05
♑ Nov 16 07:21
♒ Dec 11 04:44

Mars

Jan 1 5♊
D Jan 10 5♊
♋ Mar 28 10:00
♌ May 22 14:15
♍ Jul 12 02:59
♎ Aug 29 00:30
♏ Oct 13 12:12
♐ Nov 25 16:15

Jupiter

Jan 1 26♌
D Apr 13 17♌
♍ Jul 26 01:33

Saturn

Jan 1 21♊
D Feb 20 19♊
♋ Jun 20 07:40
R Oct 23 10♋

Uranus

Jan 1 5♊
D Feb 12 4♊
R Sep 18 13♊

Neptune

Jan 1 4♎
R Jan 6 4♎
D Jun 12 1♎

Pluto

Jan 1 8♌
D Apr 18 6♌
R Nov 11 10♌

1945

Sun

♒ Jan 20 09:53	♈ Mar 20 23:37	♊ May 21 10:39	♌ Jul 23 05:47	♎ Sep 23 09:52	♐ Nov 22 15:55
♓ Feb 19 00:15	♉ Apr 20 11:06	♋ Jun 21 18:52	♍ Aug 23 12:38	♏ Oct 23 18:45	♑ Dec 22 05:04

Mercury

Jan 1 22♐
D Jan 2 23♐
♑ Jan 14 02:47
♒ Feb 5 09:21
♓ Feb 23 11:24
♈ Mar 11 06:49
R Apr 3 27♈
D Apr 27 16♈
♉ May 16 15:03
♊ Jun 4 10:28
♋ Jun 18 12:27
♌ Jul 3 15:40
♍ Jul 26 14:54
R Aug 6 4♍
♌ Aug 17 08:37
D Aug 30 22♌
♍ Sep 10 07:25
♎ Sep 27 12:08
♏ Oct 15 00:22
♐ Nov 3 23:19
R Nov 27 23♐
D Dec 17 6♐

Venus

Jan 1 24♒
♓ Jan 5 10:10
♈ Feb 2 08:08
♉ Mar 11 10:56
R Mar 25 3♉
♈ Apr 7 19:42
D May 6 17♈
♉ Jun 4 22:59
♊ Jul 7 16:22
♋ Aug 4 10:57
♌ Aug 30 13:04
♍ Sep 24 16:06
♎ Oct 19 04:09
♏ Nov 12 07:06
♐ Dec 6 05:22
♑ Dec 30 01:55

Mars

Jan 1 26♐
♑ Jan 5 19:01
♒ Feb 14 10:03
♓ Mar 25 03:47
♈ May 2 20:37
♉ Jun 11 12:09
♊ Jul 23 09:03
♋ Sep 7 21:01
♌ Nov 11 21:28
R Dec 4 3♌
♋ Dec 26 14:53

Jupiter

Jan 1 27♍
R Jan 12 27♍
D May 14 17♍
♎ Aug 25 06:18

Saturn

Jan 1 7♋
D Mar 5 3♋
R Nov 6 24♋

Uranus

Jan 1 9♊
D Feb 15 9♊
R Sep 23 17♊

Neptune

Jan 1 6♎
R Jan 7 6♎
D Jun 14 3♎

Pluto

Jan 1 9♌
D Apr 20 7♌
R Nov 13 11♌

1946

Sun

♒ Jan 20 15:45	♈ Mar 21 05:31	♊ May 21 16:31	♌ Jul 23 11:37
♎ Sep 23 15:45	♐ Nov 22 21:49		
♓ Feb 19 06:07	♉ Apr 20 16:59	♋ Jun 22 00:43	♍ Aug 23 18:27
♏ Oct 24 00:39	♑ Dec 22 10:55		

Mercury

Jan 1 18♐	♌ Jun 27 18:55
♑ Jan 9 14:15	R Jul 19 17♌
♒ Jan 29 07:25	D Aug 12 4♌
♓ Feb 15 15:44	♍ Sep 3 16:24
♈ Mar 4 09:22	♎ Sep 19 14:35
R Mar 16 10♈	♏ Oct 7 21:17
♓ Apr 1 17:56	♐ Oct 30 11:22
D Apr 9 26♓	R Nov 11 7♐
♈ Apr 16 14:53	♏ Nov 20 20:08
♉ May 11 14:28	D Dec 1 20♏
♊ May 27 04:11	♐ Dec 13 00:10
♋ Jun 10 01:51	

Venus

Jan 1 2♑	♍ Jul 13 19:25
♒ Jan 22 22:28	♎ Aug 9 08:38
♓ Feb 15 20:11	♏ Sep 7 00:22
♈ Mar 11 20:31	♐ Oct 16 11:15
♉ Apr 5 01:00	R Oct 28 2♐
♊ Apr 29 10:57	♏ Nov 8 08:25
♋ May 24 03:38	D Dec 8 17♏
♌ Jun 18 05:00	

Mars

Jan 1 28♋	
D Feb 21 14♋	
♌ Apr 22 19:35	
♍ Jun 20 08:33	
♎ Aug 9 13:22	
♏ Sep 24 16:29	
♐ Nov 6 18:23	
♑ Dec 17 10:53	

Jupiter

Jan 1 24♎	
R Feb 11 27♎	
D Jun 14 17♎	
♏ Sep 25 10:07	

Saturn

Jan 1 22♋
D Mar 20 17♋
♌ Aug 2 15:19
R Nov 20 8♌

Uranus

Jan 1 14♊
D Feb 20 13♊
R Sep 27 21♊

Neptune

Jan 1 8♎
R Jan 10 8♎
D Jun 17 5♎

Pluto

Jan 1 11♌
D Apr 22 9♌
R Nov 15 13♌

1947

Sun

♒ Jan 20 21:35	♈ Mar 21 11:15	♊ May 21 22:08	♌ Jul 23 17:13
♎ Sep 23 21:29	♐ Nov 23 03:39		
♓ Feb 19 11:55	♉ Apr 20 22:39	♋ Jun 22 06:19	♍ Aug 24 00:08
♏ Oct 24 06:27	♑ Dec 22 16:44		

Mercury

Jan 1 26♐	R Jul 1 27♋
♑ Jan 3 01:43	D Jul 25 17♋
♒ Jan 21 21:05	♌ Aug 10 17:47
♓ Feb 8 01:48	♍ Aug 26 14:49
R Feb 27 23♓	♎ Sep 11 20:49
D Mar 22 9♓	♏ Oct 1 15:27
♈ Apr 16 04:50	R Oct 25 20♏
♉ May 4 05:57	D Nov 15 5♏
♊ May 18 13:32	♐ Dec 7 12:30
♋ Jun 2 13:48	♑ Dec 26 23:17

Venus

Jan 1 26♏	♋ Jul 8 13:29
♐ Jan 5 16:49	♌ Aug 2 01:06
♑ Feb 6 05:40	♍ Aug 26 08:17
♒ Mar 5 05:08	♎ Sep 19 12:01
♓ Mar 30 22:14	♏ Oct 13 13:49
♈ Apr 25 03:03	♐ Nov 6 14:58
♉ May 20 02:06	♑ Nov 30 16:22
♊ Jun 13 21:34	♒ Dec 24 19:10

Mars

Jan 1 11♑	
♒ Jan 25 11:44	
♓ Mar 4 16:46	
♈ Apr 11 23:02	
♉ May 21 03:46	
♊ Jul 1 03:37	
♋ Aug 13 21:41	
♌ Oct 1 02:45	
♍ Dec 1 12:06	

Jupiter

Jan 1 20♏	
R Mar 14 27♏	
D Jul 15 17♏	
♐ Oct 24 02:22	

Saturn

Jan 1 7♌
D Apr 3 1♌
R Dec 4 22♌

Uranus

Jan 1 18♊
D Feb 25 17♊
R Oct 2 26♊

Neptune

Jan 1 10♎
R Jan 12 10♎
D Jun 19 8♎

Pluto

Jan 1 12♌
D Apr 23 10♌
R Nov 16 14♌

1948

Sun

| ♒ Jan 21 03:20 | ♈ Mar 20 16:57 | ♊ May 21 03:58 | ♌ Jul 22 23:07 | ♎ Sep 23 03:22 | ♐ Nov 22 09:28 |
| ♓ Feb 19 17:37 | ♉ Apr 20 04:26 | ♋ Jun 21 12:10 | ♍ Aug 23 06:01 | ♏ Oct 23 12:18 | ♑ Dec 21 22:32 |

Mercury

Jan 1 7 ♑	D Jul 5 28 ♊
♒ Jan 14 10:07	♋ Jul 11 20:40
♓ Feb 2 01:17	♌ Aug 2 13:54
R Feb 11 6 ♓	♍ Aug 17 08:41
♒ Feb 20 11:06	♎ Sep 3 15:41
D Mar 4 22 ♒	♏ Sep 27 06:58
♓ Mar 18 08:10	R Oct 8 4 ♏
♈ Apr 9 02:31	♎ Oct 17 03:23
♉ Apr 25 01:37	D Oct 28 19 ♎
♊ May 9 04:30	♏ Nov 10 02:37
♋ May 28 11:00	♐ Nov 29 15:08
R Jun 11 7 ♋	♑ Dec 18 16:47
♊ Jun 28 18:03	

Venus

Jan 1 8 ♒	D Jul 16 24 ♊
♓ Jan 18 02:13	♋ Aug 3 02:22
♈ Feb 11 18:49	♌ Sep 8 13:37
♉ Mar 8 06:58	♍ Oct 6 12:24
♊ Apr 4 12:39	♎ Nov 1 06:43
♋ May 7 08:27	♏ Nov 26 00:54
R Jun 3 11 ♋	♐ Dec 20 07:27
♊ Jun 29 08:00	

Mars

Jan 1 7 ♍
R Jan 8 7 ♍
♌ Feb 12 10:39
D Mar 29 18 ♌
♍ May 18 21:00
♎ Jul 17 05:31
♏ Sep 3 13:51
♐ Oct 17 05:49
♑ Nov 26 21:55

Jupiter

Jan 1 15 ♐
R Apr 15 28 ♐
D Aug 16 19 ♐
♑ Nov 15 09:47

Saturn

Jan 1 21 ♌
D Apr 17 15 ♌
♍ Sep 19 05:36
R Dec 17 6 ♍

Uranus

Jan 1 23 ♊
D Feb 29 22 ♊
♋ Aug 30 13:37
R Oct 6 0 ♋
♊ Nov 12 14:43

Neptune

Jan 1 12 ♎
R Jan 14 12 ♎
D Jun 21 10 ♎

Pluto

Jan 1 14 ♌
D Apr 24 12 ♌
R Nov 17 16 ♌

1949

Sun

| ♒ Jan 20 09:08 | ♈ Mar 20 22:47 | ♊ May 21 09:48 | ♌ Jul 23 04:53 | ♎ Sep 23 09:03 | ♐ Nov 22 15:14 |
| ♓ Feb 18 23:27 | ♉ Apr 20 10:14 | ♋ Jun 21 18:00 | ♍ Aug 23 11:44 | ♏ Oct 23 18:00 | ♑ Dec 22 04:22 |

Mercury

Jan 1 21 ♑	♋ Jul 10 03:01
♒ Jan 0 08:53	♌ Jul 25 08:18
R Jan 24 20 ♒	♍ Aug 9 09:02
D Feb 14 5 ♒	♎ Aug 28 15:43
♓ Mar 14 09:57	R Sep 21 18 ♎
♈ Apr 1 16:04	D Oct 12 3 ♎
♉ Apr 16 14:55	♏ Nov 3 18:58
♊ May 2 01:51	♐ Nov 22 09:06
R May 23 17 ♊	♑ Dec 11 13:35
D Jun 16 8 ♊	

Venus

Jan 1 14 ♐	♌ Jul 1 23:39
♑ Jan 13 09:00	♍ Jul 26 15:43
♒ Feb 6 09:05	♎ Aug 20 12:37
♓ Mar 2 09:39	♏ Sep 14 17:10
♈ Mar 26 11:54	♐ Oct 10 10:15
♉ Apr 19 16:44	♑ Nov 6 04:52
♊ May 14 00:26	♒ Dec 6 06:08
♋ Jun 7 10:48	

Mars

Jan 1 27 ♑
♒ Jan 4 17:49
♓ Feb 11 18:05
♈ Mar 21 21:58
♉ Apr 30 02:32
♊ Jun 10 00:49
♋ Jul 23 05:56
♌ Sep 7 04:49
♍ Oct 27 01:00
♎ Dec 26 05:25

Jupiter

Jan 1 10 ♑
♒ Apr 12 17:43
R May 20 2 ♒
♑ Jun 27 20:02
D Sep 18 22 ♑
♒ Nov 30 19:38

Saturn

Jan 1 5 ♍
♌ Apr 3 00:03
D May 1 29 ♌
♍ May 29 14:02
R Dec 30 19 ♍

Uranus

Jan 1 28 ♊
D Mar 5 26 ♊
♋ Jun 10 02:58
R Oct 11 5 ♋

Neptune

Jan 1 15 ♎
R Jan 16 15 ♎
D Jun 23 12 ♎

Pluto

Jan 1 16 ♌
D Apr 26 14 ♌
R Nov 19 18 ♌

1950

Sun

| ♒ Jan 20 15:00 | ♈ Mar 21 04:34 | ♊ May 21 15:27 | ♌ Jul 23 10:30 | ♎ Sep 23 14:43 | ♐ Nov 22 21:00 |
| ♓ Feb 19 05:17 | ♉ Apr 20 15:59 | ♋ Jun 21 23:37 | ♍ Aug 23 17:22 | ♏ Oct 23 23:43 | ♑ Dec 22 10:11 |

Mercury

Jan 1 29♑
♒ Jan 1 12:51
R Jan 8 5♒
♑ Jan 15 07:36
D Jan 29 18♑
♒ Feb 14 19:27
♓ Mar 7 21:57
♈ Mar 24 15:52
♉ Apr 8 11:11
R May 3 27♉
D May 27 17♉
♊ Jun 14 14:32

♋ Jul 2 14:59
♌ Jul 16 17:10
♍ Aug 2 02:57
♎ Aug 27 14:07
R Sep 4 2♎
♍ Sep 10 19:30
D Sep 26 17♍
♎ Oct 9 14:39
♏ Oct 27 10:34
♐ Nov 15 03:08
♑ Dec 5 01:43
R Dec 23 19♑

Venus

Jan 1 16♒
R Jan 10 18♒
D Feb 20 3♒
♓ Apr 6 15:05
♈ May 5 19:16
♉ Jun 1 14:17
♊ Jun 27 10:43

♋ Jul 22 17:47
♌ Aug 16 14:17
♍ Sep 10 01:37
♎ Oct 4 05:52
♏ Oct 28 05:33
♐ Nov 21 03:02
♑ Dec 14 23:54

Mars

Jan 1 2♎
R Feb 12 11♎
♍ Mar 28 11:30
D May 3 21♍
♎ Jun 11 20:39
♏ Aug 10 16:46
♐ Sep 25 19:53
♑ Nov 6 06:31
♒ Dec 15 08:52

Jupiter

Jan 1 6♒
♓ Apr 15 08:25
R Jun 27 7♓
♒ Sep 15 03:53
D Oct 24 27♒
♓ Dec 1 18:49

Saturn

Jan 1 19♍
D May 15 12♍
♎ Nov 20 17:24

Uranus

Jan 1 2♋
D Mar 9 0♋
R Oct 16 9♋

Neptune

Jan 1 17♎
R Jan 18 17♎
D Jun 26 14♎

Pluto

Jan 1 17♌
D Apr 28 15♌
R Nov 21 19♌

1951

Sun

| ♒ Jan 20 20:52 | ♈ Mar 21 10:25 | ♊ May 21 21:15 | ♌ Jul 23 16:22 | ♎ Sep 23 20:39 | ♐ Nov 23 02:53 |
| ♓ Feb 19 11:10 | ♉ Apr 20 21:46 | ♋ Jun 22 05:25 | ♍ Aug 23 23:17 | ♏ Oct 24 05:38 | ♑ Dec 22 16:01 |

Mercury

Jan 1 11♑
D Jan 12 2♑
♒ Feb 9 17:52
♓ Feb 28 13:03
♈ Mar 16 11:53
♉ Apr 2 02:52
R Apr 14 7♉
♈ May 1 20:04
D May 8 28♈
♉ May 15 02:40
♊ Jun 9 08:37
♋ Jun 24 03:13

♌ Jul 8 13:37
♍ Jul 27 15:06
R Aug 17 14♍
D Sep 9 2♍
♎ Oct 2 14:25
♏ Oct 19 21:45
♐ Nov 8 04:53
♑ Dec 1 19:56
R Dec 7 2♑
♐ Dec 12 12:40
D Dec 27 16♐

Venus

Jan 1 21♑
♒ Jan 7 21:08
♓ Jan 31 20:13
♈ Feb 24 23:25
♉ Mar 21 10:06
♊ Apr 15 08:33
♋ May 11 01:42

♌ Jun 7 05:13
♍ Jul 8 04:56
R Aug 13 18♍
D Sep 25 2♍
♎ Nov 9 18:47
♏ Dec 8 00:19

Mars

Jan 1 13♒
♓ Jan 22 13:05
♈ Mar 1 22:01
♉ Apr 10 09:39
♊ May 21 15:28
♋ Jul 3 23:42
♌ Aug 18 10:52
♍ Oct 5 00:21
♎ Nov 24 06:21

Jupiter

Jan 1 4♓
♈ Apr 21 14:35
R Aug 4 14♈
D Nov 30 4♈

Saturn

Jan 1 2♎
R Jan 12 2♎
♍ Mar 7 11:37
D May 29 25♍
♎ Aug 13 17:11

Uranus

Jan 1 7♋
D Mar 14 5♋
R Oct 20 13♋

Neptune

Jan 1 19♎
R Jan 21 19♎
D Jun 28 16♎

Pluto

Jan 1 19♌
D Apr 30 17♌
R Nov 23 21♌

1952

Sun

♒ Jan 21 02:39	♈ Mar 20 16:11	♊ May 21 03:01	♌ Jul 22 22:06	♎ Sep 23 02:22	♐ Nov 22 08:35
♓ Feb 19 16:56	♉ Apr 20 03:34	♋ Jun 21 11:11	♍ Aug 23 05:01	♏ Oct 23 11:21	♑ Dec 21 21:43

Mercury

Jan 1 18 ♐	♌ Jun 30 10:28
♑ Jan 13 06:36	R Jul 29 27 ♌
♒ Feb 3 01:43	D Aug 22 15 ♌
♓ Feb 20 18:57	♍ Sep 7 12:02
♈ Mar 7 17:01	♎ Sep 23 18:46
R Mar 26 20 ♈	♏ Oct 11 13:02
D Apr 19 8 ♈	♐ Nov 1 05:22
♉ May 14 14:32	R Nov 20 16 ♐
♊ May 31 15:25	D Dec 10 0 ♐
♋ Jun 14 12:22	

Venus

Jan 1 27 ♏	♋ Jun 22 05:45
♐ Jan 2 18:45	♌ Jul 16 15:22
♑ Jan 27 15:59	♍ Aug 9 23:57
♒ Feb 21 04:43	♎ Sep 3 08:16
♓ Mar 16 14:16	♏ Sep 27 17:34
♈ Apr 9 23:15	♐ Oct 22 04:58
♉ May 4 08:53	♑ Nov 15 19:57
♊ May 28 19:17	♒ Dec 10 18:27

Mars

Jan 1 20 ♎	
♏ Jan 20 01:45	
R Mar 25 18 ♏	
D Jun 10 0 ♏	
♐ Aug 27 18:45	
♑ Oct 12 04:47	
♒ Nov 21 19:36	
♓ Dec 30 21:36	

Jupiter

Jan 1 5 ♈
♉ Apr 28 20:56
R Sep 9 20 ♉

Saturn

Jan 1 14 ♎
R Jan 24 14 ♎
D Jun 10 8 ♎

Uranus

Jan 1 12 ♋
D Mar 18 9 ♋
R Oct 24 18 ♋

Neptune

Jan 1 21 ♎
R Jan 23 21 ♎
D Jun 30 18 ♎

Pluto

Jan 1 21 ♌
D Apr 30 19 ♌
R Nov 24 23 ♌

1953

Sun

♒ Jan 20 08:21	♈ Mar 20 22:01	♊ May 21 08:52	♌ Jul 23 03:50	♎ Sep 23 08:06	♐ Nov 22 14:20
♓ Feb 18 22:42	♉ Apr 20 09:24	♋ Jun 21 16:58	♍ Aug 23 10:45	♏ Oct 23 17:06	♑ Dec 22 03:30

Mercury

Jan 1 21 ♐	R Jul 11 8 ♌
♑ Jan 6 13:26	♋ Jul 28 13:51
♒ Jan 25 19:07	D Aug 4 28 ♋
♓ Feb 11 23:55	♌ Aug 11 14:27
♈ Mar 2 19:42	♍ Aug 30 22:51
R Mar 9 2 ♈	♎ Sep 15 21:43
♓ Mar 15 21:21	♏ Oct 4 16:39
D Apr 1 20 ♓	♐ Oct 31 15:27
♈ Apr 17 16:45	R Nov 3 29 ♏
♉ May 8 06:18	♏ Nov 7 00:17
♊ May 23 03:59	D Nov 23 14 ♏
♋ Jun 6 08:19	♐ Dec 10 14:51
♌ Jun 26 11:06	♑ Dec 30 17:15

Venus

Jan 1 24 ♒	♊ Jul 7 10:27
♓ Jan 5 11:13	♋ Aug 4 01:05
♈ Feb 2 05:57	♌ Aug 30 01:31
♉ Mar 14 18:37	♍ Sep 24 03:45
R Mar 23 1 ♉	♎ Oct 18 15:25
♈ Mar 31 05:20	♏ Nov 11 18:12
D May 4 14 ♈	♐ Dec 5 16:23
♉ Jun 5 10:30	♑ Dec 29 12:52

Mars

Jan 1 0 ♓
♈ Feb 8 00:58
♉ Mar 20 06:49
♊ May 1 06:02
♋ Jun 14 03:45
♌ Jul 29 19:17
♍ Sep 14 17:54
♎ Nov 1 14:16
♏ Dec 20 11:18

Jupiter

Jan 1 11 ♉
D Jan 5 10 ♉
♊ May 9 15:53
R Oct 15 26 ♊

Saturn

Jan 1 26 ♎
R Feb 5 27 ♎
D Jun 23 20 ♎
♏ Oct 22 15:52

Uranus

Jan 1 16 ♋
D Mar 22 14 ♋
R Oct 29 23 ♋

Neptune

Jan 1 23 ♎
R Jan 25 23 ♎
D Jul 2 21 ♎

Pluto

Jan 1 22 ♌
D May 2 20 ♌
R Nov 26 25 ♌

1954

Sun

♒ Jan 20 14:12	♈ Mar 21 03:53	♊ May 21 14:46	♌ Jul 23 09:43	♎ Sep 23 13:55	♐ Nov 22 20:15
♓ Feb 19 04:32	♉ Apr 20 15:19	♋ Jun 21 22:52	♍ Aug 23 16:33	♏ Oct 23 22:57	♑ Dec 22 09:24

Mercury

Jan 1 1♑	♌ Aug 7 14:43
♒ Jan 18 07:42	♍ Aug 22 17:41
♓ Feb 4 17:56	♎ Sep 8 08:14
R Feb 20 16♓	♏ Sep 29 03:45
D Mar 14 2♓	R Oct 18 13♏
♈ Apr 13 11:36	♎ Nov 4 12:26
♉ Apr 30 11:27	D Nov 7 28♎
♊ May 14 13:55	♏ Nov 11 10:13
♋ May 30 16:17	♐ Dec 4 07:01
R Jun 23 18♋	♑ Dec 23 12:10
D Jul 17 10♋	

Venus

Jan 1 3♑	♍ Jul 13 08:44
♒ Jan 22 09:21	♎ Aug 9 00:35
♓ Feb 15 07:02	♏ Sep 6 23:28
♈ Mar 11 07:22	♐ Oct 23 21:41
♉ Apr 4 11:55	R Oct 25 0♐
♊ Apr 28 22:02	♏ Oct 27 11:06
♋ May 23 15:02	D Dec 5 14♏
♌ Jun 17 17:05	

Mars

Jan 1 6♏	
♐ Feb 9 19:28	
♑ Apr 12 16:58	
R May 23 9♑	
♐ Jul 3 07:39	
D Jul 29 25♐	
♑ Aug 24 12:45	
♒ Oct 21 11:55	
♓ Dec 4 07:51	

Jupiter

Jan 1 19♊
D Feb 10 16♊
♋ May 24 05:38
R Nov 17 29♋

Saturn

Jan 1 7♏
R Feb 17 9♏
D Jul 6 2♏

Uranus

Jan 1 21♋
D Mar 27 18♋
R Nov 3 27♋

Neptune

Jan 1 25♎
R Jan 27 26♎
D Jul 5 23♎

Pluto

Jan 1 24♌
D May 4 22♌
R Nov 28 26♌

1955

Sun

♒ Jan 20 20:04	♈ Mar 21 09:39	♊ May 21 20:28	♌ Jul 23 15:24	♎ Sep 23 19:40	♐ Nov 23 02:00
♓ Feb 19 10:22	♉ Apr 20 21:00	♋ Jun 22 04:33	♍ Aug 23 22:19	♏ Oct 24 04:43	♑ Dec 22 15:10

Mercury

Jan 1 13♑	♋ Jul 13 14:53
♒ Jan 10 23:14	♌ Jul 30 17:21
R Feb 3 0♓	♍ Aug 14 13:07
D Feb 25 15♒	♎ Sep 1 12:07
♓ Mar 17 20:51	R Oct 1 28♎
♈ Apr 6 16:13	D Oct 22 12♎
♉ Apr 22 03:00	♏ Nov 8 07:03
♊ May 6 13:06	♐ Nov 27 04:36
R Jun 3 28♊	♑ Dec 16 06:05
D Jun 27 20♊	

Venus

Jan 1 25♏	♋ Jul 8 00:15
♐ Jan 6 06:48	♌ Aug 1 11:41
♑ Feb 6 01:12	♍ Aug 25 18:51
♒ Mar 4 20:19	♎ Sep 18 22:40
♓ Mar 30 11:32	♏ Oct 13 00:38
♈ Apr 24 15:16	♐ Nov 6 01:59
♉ May 19 13:36	♑ Nov 30 03:39
♊ Jun 13 08:37	♒ Dec 24 06:49

Mars

Jan 1 19♓
♈ Jan 15 04:38
♉ Feb 26 10:31
♊ Apr 10 23:13
♋ May 26 00:52
♌ Jul 11 09:21
♍ Aug 27 10:07
♎ Oct 13 11:15
♏ Nov 29 01:25

Jupiter

Jan 1 26♋
D Mar 16 19♋
♌ Jun 13 01:00
♍ Nov 17 05:31
R Dec 18 1♍

Saturn

Jan 1 18♏
R Mar 1 21♏
D Jul 19 14♏

Uranus

Jan 1 26♋
D Apr 1 23♋
♌ Aug 24 17:14
R Nov 8 2♌

Neptune

Jan 1 28♎
R Jan 29 28♎
D Jul 7 25♎
♏ Dec 24 14:59

Pluto

Jan 1 26♌
D May 6 24♌
R Dec 1 28♌

1956

Sun

| ♒ Jan 21 01:50 | ♈ Mar 20 15:22 | ♊ May 21 02:16 | ♌ Jul 22 21:22 | ♎ Sep 23 01:35 | ♐ Nov 22 07:49 |
| ♓ Feb 19 16:07 | ♉ Apr 20 02:46 | ♋ Jun 21 10:28 | ♍ Aug 23 04:15 | ♏ Oct 23 10:33 | ♑ Dec 21 20:58 |

Mercury

Jan 1 24♑	♋ Jul 6 19:11
♒ Jan 4 09:18	♌ Jul 21 05:33
R Jan 18 14♒	♍ Aug 5 19:05
♑ Feb 2 12:09	♎ Aug 26 13:33
D Feb 8 27♑	R Sep 13 12♎
♒ Feb 15 06:03	♍ Sep 29 20:45
♓ Mar 11 10:30	D Oct 5 26♍
♈ Mar 28 22:48	♎ Oct 11 07:42
♉ Apr 12 17:06	♏ Oct 31 08:16
♊ Apr 29 23:20	♐ Nov 18 21:41
R May 14 9♊	♑ Dec 8 07:07
D Jun 7 29♉	

Venus

Jan 1 9♒	D Jul 13 22♊
♓ Jan 17 14:19	♋ Aug 4 10:00
♈ Feb 11 07:47	♌ Sep 8 09:21
♉ Mar 7 21:32	♍ Oct 6 03:12
♊ Apr 4 07:26	♎ Oct 31 19:39
♋ May 8 02:27	♏ Nov 25 13:00
R May 31 9♋	♐ Dec 19 19:05
♊ Jun 23 11:42	

Mars

| Jan 1 21♏ |
| ♐ Jan 14 02:23 |
| ♑ Feb 28 19:51 |
| ♒ Apr 14 23:43 |
| ♓ Jun 3 07:29 |
| R Aug 10 23♓ |
| D Oct 10 13♓ |
| ♈ Dec 6 10:44 |

Jupiter

| Jan 1 1♍ |
| ♌ Jan 18 01:17 |
| D Apr 17 21♌ |
| ♍ Jul 7 19:33 |
| ♎ Dec 13 02:43 |

Saturn

| Jan 1 28♏ |
| ♐ Jan 12 19:05 |
| R Mar 12 2♐ |
| ♏ May 14 02:52 |
| D Jul 30 26♏ |

Uranus

| Jan 1 1♌ |
| ♋ Jan 28 01:54 |
| D Apr 5 28♋ |
| ♌ Jun 10 00:55 |
| R Nov 12 6♌ |

Neptune

| Jan 1 0♏ |
| R Feb 1 0♏ |
| ♎ Mar 12 02:15 |
| D Jul 9 27♎ |
| ♏ Oct 19 09:04 |

Pluto

| Jan 1 28♌ |
| D May 7 26♌ |
| ♍ Oct 20 05:33 |
| R Dec 2 0♍ |

1957

Sun

| ♒ Jan 20 07:37 | ♈ Mar 20 21:15 | ♊ May 21 08:10 | ♌ Jul 23 03:15 | ♎ Sep 23 07:26 | ♐ Nov 22 13:37 |
| ♓ Feb 18 21:57 | ♉ Apr 20 08:39 | ♋ Jun 21 16:21 | ♍ Aug 23 10:07 | ♏ Oct 23 16:24 | ♑ Dec 22 02:49 |

Mercury

Jan 1 28♑	♌ Jul 12 19:50
R Jan 1 27♑	♍ Jul 30 02:05
D Jan 21 12♑	R Aug 27 24♍
♒ Feb 12 14:30	D Sep 19 11♍
♓ Mar 4 11:32	♎ Oct 6 11:05
♈ Mar 20 19:47	♏ Oct 23 20:47
♉ Apr 4 23:41	♐ Nov 11 18:00
R Apr 25 18♉	♑ Dec 2 11:16
D May 19 9♉	R Dec 16 11♑
♊ Jun 12 13:40	♐ Dec 28 17:43
♋ Jun 28 17:10	

Venus

Jan 1 15♐	♌ Jul 1 10:43
♑ Jan 12 20:21	♍ Jul 26 03:09
♒ Feb 5 20:15	♎ Aug 20 00:43
♓ Mar 1 20:39	♏ Sep 14 06:20
♈ Mar 25 22:46	♐ Oct 10 01:15
♉ Apr 19 03:29	♑ Nov 5 23:46
♊ May 13 11:10	♒ Dec 6 15:27
♋ Jun 6 21:36	

Mars

| Jan 1 13♈ |
| ♉ Jan 28 14:09 |
| ♊ Mar 17 21:35 |
| ♋ May 4 15:25 |
| ♌ Jun 21 12:22 |
| ♍ Aug 8 05:30 |
| ♎ Sep 24 04:31 |
| ♏ Nov 8 20:59 |
| ♐ Dec 23 01:29 |

Jupiter

| Jan 1 1♎ |
| R Jan 16 1♎ |
| ♍ Feb 19 15:10 |
| D May 19 21♍ |
| ♎ Aug 7 02:20 |

Saturn

| Jan 1 9♐ |
| R Mar 24 14♐ |
| D Aug 11 7♐ |

Uranus

| Jan 1 5♌ |
| D Apr 10 2♌ |
| R Nov 17 11♌ |

Neptune

| Jan 1 2♏ |
| R Feb 2 2♏ |
| ♎ Jun 15 20:22 |
| D Jul 11 29♎ |
| ♏ Aug 6 08:07 |

Pluto

| Jan 1 0♍ |
| ♌ Jan 15 03:45 |
| D May 9 27♌ |
| ♍ Aug 19 03:26 |
| R Dec 4 2♍ |

1958

Sun

♒ Jan 20 13:29	♈ Mar 21 03:05	♊ May 21 13:52	♌ Jul 23 08:53	♎ Sep 23 13:11	♐ Nov 22 19:30
♓ Feb 19 03:48	♉ Apr 20 14:28	♋ Jun 21 22:00	♍ Aug 23 15:48	♏ Oct 23 22:12	♑ Dec 22 08:39

Mercury

Jan 1 27♐	♋ Jun 20 02:18
D Jan 5 25♐	♌ Jul 4 23:58
♑ Jan 14 09:55	♍ Jul 26 10:09
♒ Feb 6 15:21	R Aug 9 7♍
♓ Feb 24 21:45	♌ Aug 23 14:34
♈ Mar 12 17:27	D Sep 2 24♌
♉ Apr 2 20:37	♍ Sep 11 01:00
R Apr 6 0♉	♎ Sep 28 22:45
♈ Apr 10 13:45	♏ Oct 16 08:55
D Apr 30 19♈	♐ Nov 5 02:22
♉ May 17 02:31	R Nov 30 25♐
♊ Jun 5 21:07	D Dec 20 9♐

Venus

Jan 1 15♒	♋ Jul 22 05:27
R Jan 8 16♒	♌ Aug 16 01:30
D Feb 18 0♒	♍ Sep 9 12:37
♓ Apr 6 15:53	♎ Oct 3 16:45
♈ May 5 11:57	♏ Oct 27 16:27
♉ Jun 1 04:07	♐ Nov 20 13:58
♊ Jun 26 23:08	♑ Dec 14 10:54

Mars

Jan 1 6♐	
♑ Feb 3 18:48	
♒ Mar 17 07:06	
♓ Apr 27 02:11	
♈ Jun 7 06:07	
♉ Jul 21 07:08	
♊ Sep 21 06:29	
R Oct 10 2♊	
♉ Oct 28 22:38	
D Dec 20 16♉	

Jupiter

Jan 1 28♎	
♏ Jan 13 12:36	
R Feb 15 1♏	
♎ Mar 20 19:21	
D Jun 19 21♎	
♏ Sep 7 08:44	

Saturn

Jan 1 19♐
R Apr 4 25♐
D Aug 24 19♐

Uranus

Jan 1 10♌
D Apr 15 7♌
R Nov 22 16♌

Neptune

Jan 1 4♏
R Feb 5 4♏
D Jul 14 2♏

Pluto

Jan 1 2♍
♌ Apr 11 19:28
D May 11 29♌
♍ Jun 10 15:30
R Dec 6 4♍

1959

Sun

♒ Jan 20 19:20	♈ Mar 21 08:55	♊ May 21 19:43	♌ Jul 23 14:47	♎ Sep 23 19:11	♐ Nov 23 01:30
♓ Feb 19 09:39	♉ Apr 20 20:16	♋ Jun 22 03:51	♍ Aug 23 21:45	♏ Oct 24 04:14	♑ Dec 22 14:37

Mercury

Jan 1 18♐	R Jul 22 20♌
♑ Jan 10 16:52	D Aug 15 7♌
♒ Jan 30 15:41	♍ Sep 5 02:38
♓ Feb 17 02:12	♎ Sep 21 01:19
♈ Mar 5 11:51	♏ Oct 9 04:07
R Mar 19 13♈	♐ Oct 31 00:55
D Apr 12 29♓	R Nov 14 10♐
♉ May 12 19:46	♏ Nov 25 11:47
♊ May 28 17:37	D Dec 3 22♏
♋ Jun 11 14:15	♐ Dec 13 15:39
♌ Jun 28 16:32	

Venus

Jan 1 22♑	♍ Jul 8 12:14
♒ Jan 7 08:15	R Aug 10 16♍
♓ Jan 31 07:26	♌ Sep 20 01:07
♈ Feb 24 10:52	D Sep 22 29♌
♉ Mar 20 21:54	♍ Sep 25 10:12
♊ Apr 14 21:06	♎ Nov 9 18:10
♋ May 10 15:45	♏ Dec 7 16:42
♌ Jun 6 22:47	

Mars

Jan 1 17♉	
♊ Feb 10 13:39	
♋ Apr 10 09:45	
♌ Jun 1 02:31	
♍ Jul 20 11:11	
♎ Sep 5 22:54	
♏ Oct 21 09:45	
♐ Dec 3 18:17	

Jupiter

Jan 1 23♏	
♐ Feb 10 13:24	
R Mar 18 1♐	
♏ Apr 24 14:34	
D Jul 20 22♏	
♐ Oct 5 14:25	

Saturn

Jan 1 29♐
♑ Jan 5 13:36
R Apr 16 7♑
D Sep 5 0♑

Uranus

Jan 1 15♌
D Apr 20 12♌
R Nov 27 21♌

Neptune

Jan 1 6♏
R Feb 7 6♏
D Jul 16 4♏

Pluto

Jan 1 4♍
D May 13 1♍
R Dec 8 6♍

1960

Sun

♒ Jan 21 01:11   ♈ Mar 20 14:42   ♊ May 21 01:32   ♌ Jul 22 20:37   ♎ Sep 23 01:00   ♐ Nov 22 07:17

♓ Feb 19 15:26   ♉ Apr 20 02:05   ♋ Jun 21 09:43   ♍ Aug 23 03:35   ♏ Oct 23 10:02   ♑ Dec 21 20:25

Mercury

Jan 1 24♐	R Jul 3 0♌	
♑ Jan 4 08:24	♋ Jul 6 01:37	
♒ Jan 23 06:18	D Jul 27 20♋	
♓ Feb 9 10:12	♌ Aug 10 18:07	
R Mar 1 25♓	♍ Aug 27 03:15	
D Mar 24 12♓	♎ Sep 12 06:32	
♈ Apr 16 02:53	♏ Oct 1 17:20	
♉ May 4 16:52	R Oct 27 23♏	
♊ May 19 03:26	D Nov 16 7♏	
♋ Jun 2 20:46	♐ Dec 7 17:34	
♌ Jul 1 02:44	♑ Dec 27 07:21	

Venus

Jan 1 28♏	♋ Jun 21 16:34
♐ Jan 2 08:43	♌ Jul 16 02:12
♑ Jan 27 04:46	♍ Aug 9 10:54
♒ Feb 20 16:47	♎ Sep 2 19:30
♓ Mar 16 01:53	♏ Sep 27 05:12
♈ Apr 9 10:31	♐ Oct 21 17:09
♉ May 3 19:54	♑ Nov 15 08:54
♊ May 28 06:12	♒ Dec 10 08:34

Mars

Jan 1 20♐
♑ Jan 14 05:01
♒ Feb 23 04:16
♓ Apr 2 06:21
♈ May 11 07:14
♉ Jun 20 09:05
♊ Aug 2 04:30
♋ Sep 21 04:22
R Nov 20 18♋

Jupiter

Jan 1 18♐
♑ Mar 1 12:49
R Apr 20 3♑
♐ Jun 10 03:04
D Aug 20 23♐
♑ Oct 26 02:42

Saturn

Jan 1 9♑
R Apr 27 18♑
D Sep 15 11♑

Uranus

Jan 1 20♌
D Apr 24 16♌
R Dec 1 25♌

Neptune

Jan 1 8♏
R Feb 10 9♏
D Jul 18 6♏

Pluto

Jan 1 6♍
D May 15 3♍
R Dec 10 8♍

1961

Sun

♒ Jan 20 07:02   ♈ Mar 20 20:33   ♊ May 21 07:23   ♌ Jul 23 02:24   ♎ Sep 23 06:44   ♐ Nov 22 13:07

♓ Feb 18 21:18   ♉ Apr 20 07:54   ♋ Jun 21 15:30   ♍ Aug 23 09:20   ♏ Oct 23 15:47   ♑ Dec 22 02:18

Mercury

Jan 1 7♑	D Jul 8 1♋
♒ Jan 14 19:03	♌ Aug 4 01:15
♓ Feb 1 21:08	♍ Aug 18 20:55
R Feb 12 9♓	♎ Sep 4 22:13
♒ Feb 24 20:31	♏ Sep 27 12:22
D Mar 6 25♒	R Oct 10 7♏
♓ Mar 18 10:08	♎ Oct 22 02:39
♈ Apr 10 09:25	D Oct 31 21♎
♉ Apr 26 14:34	♏ Nov 11 00:35
♊ May 10 16:37	♐ Nov 30 22:53
♋ May 28 17:22	♑ Dec 20 01:03
R Jun 14 10♋	

Venus

Jan 1 25♒	♋ Aug 3 15:24
♓ Jan 5 03:35	♌ Aug 29 14:15
♈ Feb 2 04:52	♍ Sep 23 15:43
R Mar 20 29♈	♎ Oct 18 02:59
D May 2 12♈	♏ Nov 11 05:34
♉ Jun 5 19:26	♐ Dec 5 03:40
♊ Jul 7 04:31	♑ Dec 29 00:06

Mars

Jan 1 8♋
♊ Feb 4 22:21
D Feb 6 0♊
♋ Feb 7 05:19
♌ May 6 01:11
♍ Jun 28 23:46
♎ Aug 17 00:41
♏ Oct 1 20:04
♐ Nov 13 21:53
♑ Dec 24 17:50

Jupiter

Jan 1 14♑
♒ Mar 15 07:03
R May 25 7♒
♑ Aug 12 11:15
D Sep 23 27♑
♒ Nov 4 01:05

Saturn

Jan 1 19♑
R May 9 29♑
D Sep 27 23♑

Uranus

Jan 1 25♌
D Apr 29 21♌
♍ Nov 1 15:05
R Dec 6 0♍

Neptune

Jan 1 10♏
R Feb 11 11♏
D Jul 20 8♏

Pluto

Jan 1 8♍
D May 17 5♍
R Dec 12 10♍

1962

Sun

♒ Jan 20 12:58	♈ Mar 21 02:29	♊ May 21 13:15	♌ Jul 23 08:18	♎ Sep 23 12:39	♐ Nov 22 19:04
♓ Feb 19 03:15	♉ Apr 20 13:50	♋ Jun 21 21:23	♍ Aug 23 15:14	♏ Oct 23 21:43	♑ Dec 22 08:16

Mercury

Jan 1 19♑	♋ Jul 11 07:21
♒ Jan 7 15:06	♌ Jul 26 18:48
R Jan 27 23♒	♍ Aug 10 19:30
D Feb 17 7♒	♎ Aug 29 15:41
♓ Mar 15 11:42	R Sep 24 21♎
♈ Apr 3 02:28	D Oct 15 5♎
♉ Apr 18 04:12	♏ Nov 5 02:20
♊ May 3 05:42	♐ Nov 23 17:29
R May 26 20♊	♑ Dec 12 20:56
D Jun 19 11♊	

Venus

Jan 1 3♑	♌ Jun 17 05:32
♒ Jan 21 20:32	♍ Jul 12 22:34
♓ Feb 14 18:08	♎ Aug 8 17:16
♈ Mar 10 18:27	♏ Sep 7 00:13
♉ Apr 3 23:04	R Oct 23 27♏
♊ Apr 28 09:22	D Dec 3 12♏
♋ May 23 02:44	

Mars

Jan 1 5♑	
♒ Feb 1 23:12	
♓ Mar 12 08:05	
♈ Apr 19 17:05	
♉ May 28 23:58	
♊ Jul 9 03:55	
♋ Aug 22 11:41	
♌ Oct 11 23:51	
R Dec 26 24♌	

Jupiter

Jan 1 10♒	
♓ Mar 25 21:23	
R Jul 2 12♓	
D Oct 29 2♓	

Saturn

Jan 1 29♑
♒ Jan 3 18:29
R May 21 11♒
D Oct 9 4♒

Uranus

Jan 1 0♍
♌ Jan 10 06:24
D May 4 26♌
♍ Aug 10 00:57
R Dec 11 5♍

Neptune

Jan 1 12♏
R Feb 13 13♏
D Jul 23 10♏

Pluto

Jan 1 10♍
D May 19 7♍
R Dec 14 12♍

1963

Sun

♒ Jan 20 18:55	♈ Mar 21 08:20	♊ May 21 18:59	♌ Jul 23 13:59	♎ Sep 23 18:25	♐ Nov 23 00:50
♓ Feb 19 09:10	♉ Apr 20 19:36	♋ Jun 22 03:04	♍ Aug 23 20:59	♏ Oct 24 03:30	♑ Dec 22 14:02

Mercury

Jan 1 28♑	♊ Jun 14 22:52
♒ Jan 2 01:49	♋ Jul 4 02:54
R Jan 11 7♒	♌ Jul 18 06:17
♑ Jan 20 04:53	♍ Aug 3 09:26
D Feb 1 20♑	♎ Aug 26 20:54
♒ Feb 15 10:09	R Sep 6 5♎
♓ Mar 9 05:34	♍ Sep 16 20:46
♈ Mar 26 03:48	D Sep 29 19♍
♉ Apr 9 21:59	♎ Oct 10 16:33
♊ May 3 05:01	♏ Oct 28 19:54
R May 6 0♊	♐ Nov 16 11:08
♉ May 10 20:44	♑ Dec 6 05:12
D May 30 21♉	R Dec 26 21♑

Venus

Jan 1 25♏	♋ Jul 7 11:16
♐ Jan 6 17:38	♌ Jul 31 22:37
♑ Feb 5 20:34	♍ Aug 25 05:47
♒ Mar 4 11:38	♎ Sep 18 09:44
♓ Mar 30 01:00	♏ Oct 12 11:50
♈ Apr 24 03:41	♐ Nov 5 13:25
♉ May 19 01:21	♑ Nov 29 15:20
♊ Jun 12 19:55	♒ Dec 23 18:49

Mars

Jan 1 24♌	
D Mar 16 5♌	
♍ Jun 3 06:21	
♎ Jul 27 04:07	
♏ Sep 12 09:00	
♐ Oct 25 17:28	
♑ Dec 5 08:59	

Jupiter

Jan 1 9♓	
♈ Apr 4 03:19	
R Aug 9 19♈	
D Dec 5 9♈	

Saturn

Jan 1 9♒
R Jun 3 23♒
D Oct 21 16♒

Uranus

Jan 1 5♍
D May 9 1♍
R Dec 16 10♍

Neptune

Jan 1 15♏
R Feb 16 15♏
D Jul 25 12♏

Pluto

Jan 1 12♍
D May 21 9♍
R Dec 17 14♍

1964

Sun

♒ Jan 21 00:42	♈ Mar 20 14:10	♊ May 21 00:49	♌ Jul 22 19:52	♎ Sep 23 00:18	♐ Nov 22 06:39
♓ Feb 19 14:58	♉ Apr 20 01:27	♋ Jun 21 08:57	♍ Aug 23 02:52	♏ Oct 23 09:22	♑ Dec 21 19:50

Mercury

Jan 1 18♑	♍ Jul 27 11:37
D Jan 15 5♑	R Aug 19 17♍
♒ Feb 10 21:37	D Sep 11 4♍
♓ Feb 29 22:44	♎ Oct 3 00:22
♈ Mar 16 23:49	♏ Oct 20 07:15
♉ Apr 2 00:34	♐ Nov 8 11:01
R Apr 16 10♉	♑ Nov 30 19:15
D May 10 1♉	R Dec 9 4♑
♊ Jun 9 15:55	D Dec 29 19♐
♋ Jun 24 17:17	
♌ Jul 9 00:27	

Venus

Jan 1 10♒	D Jul 11 20♊
♓ Jan 17 02:51	♋ Aug 5 08:58
♈ Feb 10 21:08	♌ Sep 8 04:52
♉ Mar 7 12:39	♍ Oct 5 18:09
♊ Apr 4 03:05	♎ Oct 31 08:54
♋ May 9 03:21	♏ Nov 25 01:25
R May 29 6♋	♐ Dec 19 07:01
♊ Jun 17 18:20	

Mars

Jan 1 20♑
♒ Jan 13 06:10
♓ Feb 20 07:30
♈ Mar 29 11:20
♉ May 7 14:42
♊ Jun 17 11:40
♋ Jul 30 18:27
♌ Sep 15 05:24
♍ Nov 6 03:22

Jupiter

Jan 1 10♈
♉ Apr 12 07:06
R Sep 14 26♉

Saturn

Jan 1 20♒
♓ Mar 24 03:26
R Jun 15 5♓
♒ Sep 16 22:03
D Nov 1 28♒

Uranus

Jan 1 9♍
D May 13 5♍
R Dec 20 14♍

Neptune

Jan 1 17♏
R Feb 18 17♏
D Jul 27 15♏

Pluto

Jan 1 14♍
D May 22 11♍
R Dec 18 16♍

1965

Sun

♒ Jan 20 06:28	♈ Mar 20 20:02	♊ May 21 06:47	♌ Jul 23 01:45	♎ Sep 23 06:04	♐ Nov 22 12:27
♓ Feb 18 20:46	♉ Apr 20 07:24	♋ Jun 21 14:53	♍ Aug 23 08:39	♏ Oct 23 15:08	♑ Dec 22 01:40

Mercury

Jan 1 20♐	♍ Jul 31 09:40
♑ Jan 13 02:50	R Aug 1 0♍
♒ Feb 3 09:04	♌ Aug 3 09:36
♓ Feb 21 05:37	D Aug 25 17♌
♈ Mar 9 02:35	♍ Sep 8 17:13
R Mar 29 23♈	♎ Sep 25 05:47
D Apr 22 11♈	♏ Oct 12 21:06
♉ May 15 13:12	♐ Nov 2 05:50
♊ Jun 2 03:37	R Nov 23 19♐
♋ Jun 16 01:56	D Dec 12 2♐
♌ Jul 1 15:53	

Venus

Jan 1 15♐	♌ Jun 30 21:58
♑ Jan 12 07:59	♍ Jul 25 14:49
♒ Feb 5 07:43	♎ Aug 19 13:04
♓ Mar 1 07:56	♏ Sep 13 19:48
♈ Mar 25 09:53	♐ Oct 9 16:45
♉ Apr 18 14:31	♑ Nov 5 19:35
♊ May 12 22:08	♒ Dec 7 04:39
♋ Jun 6 08:38	

Mars

Jan 1 23♍
R Jan 28 28♍
D Apr 19 8♍
♎ Jun 29 00:50
♏ Aug 20 12:00
♐ Oct 4 06:38
♑ Nov 14 07:12
♒ Dec 23 05:34

Jupiter

Jan 1 16♉
D Jan 10 16♉
♊ Apr 22 15:15
♋ Sep 21 06:51
R Oct 19 1♋
♊ Nov 17 02:55

Saturn

Jan 1 1♓
R Jun 28 17♓
D Nov 14 10♓

Uranus

Jan 1 14♍
D May 18 10♍
R Dec 25 19♍

Neptune

Jan 1 19♏
R Feb 20 20♏
D Jul 29 17♏

Pluto

Jan 1 16♍
D May 25 13♍
R Dec 21 18♍

1966

Sun

♒ Jan 20 12:21	♈ Mar 21 01:52	♊ May 21 12:32	♌ Jul 23 07:22	♎ Sep 23 11:42	♐ Nov 22 18:14
♓ Feb 19 02:38	♉ Apr 20 13:11	♋ Jun 21 20:34	♍ Aug 23 14:16	♏ Oct 23 20:51	♑ Dec 22 07:28

Mercury

Jan 1 20♐	♌ Jun 26 18:43
♑ Jan 7 18:29	R Jul 14 12♌
♒ Jan 27 04:16	D Aug 7 0♌
♓ Feb 13 10:17	♍ Sep 1 10:35
♈ Mar 3 02:45	♎ Sep 17 08:18
R Mar 12 6♈	♏ Oct 5 22:01
♓ Mar 22 02:17	♐ Oct 30 07:36
D Apr 4 22♓	R Nov 6 3♐
♈ Apr 17 21:18	♏ Nov 13 03:12
♉ May 9 14:50	D Nov 26 16♏
♊ May 24 17:59	♐ Dec 11 15:28
♋ Jun 7 19:20	

Venus

Jan 1 13♒	♊ Jun 26 11:37
R Jan 5 13♒	♋ Jul 21 17:10
♑ Feb 6 12:47	♌ Aug 15 12:45
D Feb 15 28♑	♍ Sep 8 23:39
♒ Feb 25 11:04	♎ Oct 3 03:44
♓ Apr 6 15:48	♏ Oct 27 03:27
♈ May 5 04:31	♐ Nov 20 01:06
♉ May 31 17:59	♑ Dec 13 22:07

Mars

Jan 1 6♒
♓ Jan 30 07:04
♈ Mar 9 12:55
♉ Apr 17 20:37
♊ May 28 22:02
♋ Jul 11 03:13
♌ Aug 25 15:45
♍ Oct 12 18:36
♎ Dec 4 00:57

Jupiter

Jan 1 24♊
D Feb 15 21♊
♋ May 5 15:26
♌ Sep 27 13:37
R Nov 21 4♌

Saturn

Jan 1 12♓
R Jul 11 29♓
D Nov 26 22♓

Uranus

Jan 1 19♍
D May 23 15♍
R Dec 30 24♍

Neptune

Jan 1 21♏
R Feb 22 22♏
D Aug 1 19♏

Pluto

Jan 1 18♍
D May 27 15♍
R Dec 23 20♍

1967

Sun

♒ Jan 20 18:07	♈ Mar 21 07:36	♊ May 21 18:19	♌ Jul 23 13:16	♎ Sep 23 17:38	♐ Nov 23 00:05
♓ Feb 19 08:23	♉ Apr 20 18:55	♋ Jun 22 02:23	♍ Aug 23 20:13	♏ Oct 24 02:44	♑ Dec 22 13:17

Mercury

Jan 1 29♐	R Jun 26 21♋
♑ Jan 1 00:49	D Jul 20 13♋
♒ Jan 19 17:06	♌ Aug 8 22:21
♓ Feb 6 00:57	♍ Aug 24 06:17
R Feb 23 18♓	♎ Sep 9 16:49
D Mar 17 5♓	♏ Sep 30 01:31
♈ Apr 14 14:29	R Oct 21 16♏
♉ May 1 23:35	D Nov 10 1♏
♊ May 16 03:25	♐ Dec 5 13:43
♋ May 31 18:08	♑ Dec 24 20:35

Venus

Jan 1 22♑	♍ Jul 8 22:17
♒ Jan 6 19:33	R Aug 8 13♍
♓ Jan 30 18:51	♌ Sep 9 11:41
♈ Feb 23 22:29	D Sep 20 27♌
♉ Mar 20 09:55	♍ Oct 1 18:13
♊ Apr 14 09:53	♎ Nov 9 16:31
♋ May 10 06:05	♏ Dec 7 08:49
♌ Jun 6 16:52	

Mars

Jan 1 14♎
♏ Feb 12 12:22
R Mar 8 3♏
♎ Mar 31 06:17
D May 26 14♎
♏ Jul 19 22:54
♐ Sep 10 01:32
♑ Oct 23 01:59
♒ Dec 1 20:01

Jupiter

Jan 1 1♌
♋ Jan 16 02:01
D Mar 21 24♋
♌ May 23 08:47
♍ Oct 19 11:23
R Dec 22 5♍

Saturn

Jan 1 24♓
♈ Mar 3 20:18
R Jul 25 12♈
D Dec 9 5♈

Uranus

Jan 1 24♍
D May 28 20♍

Neptune

Jan 1 23♏
R Feb 24 24♏
D Aug 3 21♏

Pluto

Jan 1 20♍
D May 29 17♍
R Dec 26 22♍

1968

Sun

♒ Jan 20 23:55	♈ Mar 20 13:21	♊ May 21 00:04	♌ Jul 22 19:07	♎ Sep 22 23:25	♐ Nov 22 05:46
♓ Feb 19 14:10	♉ Apr 20 00:40	♋ Jun 21 08:13	♍ Aug 23 02:01	♏ Oct 23 08:29	♑ Dec 21 18:59

Mercury

Jan 1 11 ♑	D Jun 30 23 ♊
♒ Jan 12 07:15	♋ Jul 13 00:46
♓ Feb 1 12:44	♌ Jul 31 06:10
R Feb 6 2 ♓	♍ Aug 15 00:45
♒ Feb 11 18:22	♎ Sep 1 16:48
D Feb 28 17 ♒	♏ Sep 28 14:54
♓ Mar 17 14:43	R Oct 3 0 ♏
♈ Apr 7 01:05	♎ Oct 8 00:00
♉ Apr 22 16:17	D Oct 24 15 ♎
♊ May 6 23:12	♏ Nov 8 10:57
♋ May 29 21:41	♐ Nov 27 12:45
R Jun 6 2 ♋	♑ Dec 16 14:10
♊ Jun 13 22:47	

Venus

Jan 1 28 ♏	♋ Jun 21 03:22
♐ Jan 1 22:39	♌ Jul 15 13:00
♑ Jan 26 17:35	♍ Aug 8 21:49
♒ Feb 20 04:54	♎ Sep 2 06:40
♓ Mar 15 13:31	♏ Sep 26 16:44
♈ Apr 8 21:47	♐ Oct 21 05:13
♉ May 3 06:55	♑ Nov 14 21:43
♊ May 27 17:02	♒ Dec 9 22:37

Mars

Jan 1 23 ♒	
♓ Jan 9 09:44	
♈ Feb 17 03:14	
♉ Mar 27 23:41	
♊ May 8 14:12	
♋ Jun 21 05:00	
♌ Aug 5 17:02	
♍ Sep 21 18:32	
♎ Nov 9 06:05	
♏ Dec 29 21:58	

Jupiter

Jan 1 5 ♍
♌ Feb 27 02:12
D Apr 21 25 ♌
♍ Jun 15 15:23
♎ Nov 15 22:57

Saturn

Jan 1 6 ♈
R Aug 7 25 ♈
D Dec 21 18 ♈

Uranus

Jan 1 29 ♍
R Jan 4 29 ♍
D Jun 2 25 ♍
♎ Sep 28 16:25

Neptune

Jan 1 25 ♏
R Feb 27 26 ♏
D Aug 5 23 ♏

Pluto

Jan 1 22 ♍
D May 31 20 ♍
R Dec 27 25 ♍

1969

Sun

♒ Jan 20 05:38	♈ Mar 20 19:07	♊ May 21 05:49	♌ Jul 23 00:47	♎ Sep 23 05:07	♐ Nov 22 11:30
♓ Feb 18 19:54	♉ Apr 20 06:25	♋ Jun 21 13:54	♍ Aug 23 07:44	♏ Oct 23 14:10	♑ Dec 22 00:43

Mercury

Jan 1 24 ♑	♌ Jul 22 19:11
♒ Jan 4 12:18	♍ Aug 7 04:24
R Jan 20 16 ♒	♎ Aug 27 06:54
D Feb 10 0 ♒	R Sep 16 14 ♎
♓ Mar 12 15:18	♍ Oct 7 04:48
♈ Mar 30 09:57	D Oct 8 29 ♍
♉ Apr 14 05:59	♎ Oct 9 18:18
♊ Apr 30 15:39	♏ Nov 1 16:53
R May 17 12 ♊	♐ Nov 20 06:00
D Jun 10 3 ♊	♑ Dec 9 13:20
♋ Jul 8 03:41	

Venus

Jan 1 25 ♒	♋ Aug 3 05:25
♓ Jan 4 20:09	♌ Aug 29 02:44
♈ Feb 2 04:48	♍ Sep 23 03:23
R Mar 18 26 ♈	♎ Oct 17 14:16
D Apr 29 10 ♈	♏ Nov 10 16:39
♉ Jun 6 01:48	♐ Dec 4 14:39
♊ Jul 6 22:02	♑ Dec 28 11:02

Mars

Jan 1 1 ♏
♐ Feb 25 06:07
R Apr 27 17 ♐
D Jul 8 1 ♐
♑ Sep 21 06:36
♒ Nov 4 18:46
♓ Dec 15 14:16

Jupiter

Jan 1 5 ♎
R Jan 20 6 ♎
♍ Mar 30 21:13
D May 23 26 ♍
♎ Jul 15 13:43
♏ Dec 16 15:44

Saturn

Jan 1 18 ♈
♉ Apr 29 21:20
R Aug 21 8 ♉

Uranus

Jan 1 3 ♎
R Jan 8 4 ♎
♍ May 20 19:27
D Jun 7 29 ♍
♎ Jun 24 12:00

Neptune

Jan 1 27 ♏
R Feb 28 28 ♏
D Aug 7 25 ♏

Pluto

Jan 1 25 ♍
D Jun 2 22 ♍
R Dec 30 27 ♍

1970

Sun
♒ Jan 20 11:23	♈ Mar 21 00:55	♊ May 21 11:37
♓ Feb 19 01:42	♉ Apr 20 12:14	♋ Jun 21 19:42

♌ Jul 23 06:36	♎ Sep 23 11:00	♐ Nov 22 17:25
♍ Aug 23 13:33	♏ Oct 23 20:07	♑ Dec 22 06:38

Mercury
Jan 1 29♑	♋ Jun 30 06:21
R Jan 4 0♒	♌ Jul 14 08:04
D Jan 24 13♑	♍ Jul 31 05:38
♒ Feb 13 13:12	R Aug 30 28♍
♓ Mar 5 20:04	D Sep 22 13♍
♈ Mar 22 07:58	♎ Oct 7 17:55
♉ Apr 6 07:35	♏ Oct 25 06:18
R Apr 28 22♉	♐ Nov 13 01:14
D May 22 12♉	♑ Dec 3 10:14
♊ Jun 13 12:47	R Dec 19 14♑

Venus
Jan 1 4♑	♌ Jun 16 17:50
♒ Jan 21 07:27	♍ Jul 12 12:18
♓ Feb 14 05:04	♎ Aug 8 10:01
♈ Mar 10 05:23	♏ Sep 7 01:53
♉ Apr 3 10:05	R Oct 20 25♏
♊ Apr 27 20:33	D Nov 30 9♏
♋ May 22 14:18	

Mars
Jan 1 12♓	
♈ Jan 24 21:23	
♉ Mar 7 01:28	
♊ Apr 18 18:59	
♋ Jun 2 06:50	
♌ Jul 18 06:40	
♍ Sep 3 04:53	
♎ Oct 20 10:54	
♏ Dec 6 16:25	

Jupiter
Jan 1 2♏	
R Feb 19 5♏	
♎ Apr 30 07:07	
D Jun 23 26♎	
♏ Aug 15 17:45	

Saturn
Jan 1 2♉
D Jan 3 2♉
R Sep 4 22♉

Uranus
Jan 1 8♎
R Jan 13 8♎
D Jun 12 4♎

Neptune
Jan 1 29♏
♐ Jan 4 18:42
R Mar 3 0♐
♏ May 3 02:50
D Aug 10 28♏

Pluto
Jan 1 27♍
D Jun 5 24♍

1971

Sun
♒ Jan 20 17:15	♈ Mar 21 06:41	♊ May 21 17:16
♓ Feb 19 07:30	♉ Apr 20 17:57	♋ Jun 22 01:20

♌ Jul 23 12:15	♎ Sep 23 16:45	♐ Nov 22 23:14
♍ Aug 23 19:13	♏ Oct 24 01:52	♑ Dec 22 12:23

Mercury
Jan 1 1♑	♋ Jun 21 16:26
♐ Jan 3 00:35	♌ Jul 6 08:50
D Jan 8 28♐	♍ Jul 26 16:50
♑ Jan 14 02:24	R Aug 12 10♍
♒ Feb 7 20:54	♌ Aug 29 20:42
♓ Feb 26 07:57	D Sep 5 27♌
♈ Mar 14 04:52	♍ Sep 11 06:26
♉ Apr 1 14:37	♎ Sep 30 09:21
R Apr 9 3♉	♏ Oct 17 17:41
♈ Apr 18 21:42	♐ Nov 6 06:54
D May 3 22♈	R Dec 3 28♐
♉ May 17 04:04	D Dec 22 12♐
♊ Jun 7 06:40	

Venus
Jan 1 24♏	♋ Jul 6 22:02
♐ Jan 7 01:01	♌ Jul 31 09:15
♑ Feb 5 14:57	♍ Aug 24 16:25
♒ Mar 4 02:24	♎ Sep 17 20:27
♓ Mar 29 14:04	♏ Oct 11 22:43
♈ Apr 23 15:46	♐ Nov 5 00:29
♉ May 18 12:47	♑ Nov 29 02:39
♊ Jun 12 06:57	♒ Dec 23 06:29

Mars
Jan 1 16♏	
♐ Jan 23 01:32	
♑ Mar 12 10:04	
♒ May 3 21:00	
R Jul 11 21♒	
D Sep 9 12♒	
♓ Nov 6 12:37	
♈ Dec 26 18:05	

Jupiter
Jan 1 27♏	
♐ Jan 14 08:10	
R Mar 23 6♐	
♏ Jun 5 03:32	
D Jul 24 26♏	
♐ Sep 11 14:21	

Saturn
Jan 1 15♉
D Jan 17 15♉
♊ Jun 18 15:38
R Sep 19 6♊

Uranus
Jan 1 13♎
R Jan 18 13♎
D Jun 17 9♎

Neptune
Jan 1 1♐
R Mar 5 3♐
D Aug 12 0♐

Pluto
Jan 1 29♍
R Jan 1 29♍
D Jun 7 26♍
♎ Oct 5 06:15

1972

Sun

♒ Jan 20 22:59 ♈ Mar 20 12:22 ♊ May 20 23:01 ♌ Jul 22 18:03 ♎ Sep 22 22:32 ♐ Nov 22 05:00

♓ Feb 19 13:11 ♉ Apr 19 23:38 ♋ Jun 21 07:07 ♍ Aug 23 01:03 ♏ Oct 23 07:40 ♑ Dec 21 18:12

Mercury

  Jan 1 17♐   R Jul 24 22♌

♑ Jan 11 18:27   D Aug 17 10♌

♒ Jan 31 23:40   ♍ Sep 5 11:35

♓ Feb 18 12:53   ♎ Sep 21 22:12

♈ Mar 5 16:49   ♏ Oct 9 11:13

R Mar 21 15♈   ♐ Oct 30 19:51

D Apr 14 3♈   R Nov 15 12♐

♉ May 12 23:38   ♏ Nov 29 07:03

♊ May 29 06:45   D Dec 5 25♏

♋ Jun 12 02:45   ♐ Dec 12 22:33

♌ Jun 28 16:51

Venus

  Jan 1 10♒   D Jul 9 18♊

♓ Jan 16 14:59   ♋ Aug 6 01:32

♈ Feb 10 10:08   ♌ Sep 7 23:27

♉ Mar 7 03:26   ♍ Oct 5 08:34

♊ Apr 3 22:52   ♎ Oct 30 21:40

♋ May 10 13:56   ♏ Nov 24 13:23

R May 27 4♋   ♐ Dec 18 18:32

♊ Jun 11 20:02

Mars

  Jan 1 3♈

♉ Feb 10 14:09

♊ Mar 27 04:36

♋ May 12 13:21

♌ Jun 28 16:14

♍ Aug 15 01:01

♎ Sep 30 23:22

♏ Nov 15 22:11

♐ Dec 30 16:11

Jupiter

  Jan 1 22♐

♑ Feb 6 18:39

R Apr 25 8♑

♐ Jul 24 19:21

D Aug 25 28♐

♑ Sep 25 16:22

Saturn

  Jan 1 0♊

♉ Jan 10 05:55

D Jan 31 29♉

♊ Feb 21 13:37

R Oct 2 20♊

Uranus

  Jan 1 18♎

R Jan 23 18♎

D Jun 21 14♎

Neptune

  Jan 1 4♐

R Mar 7 5♐

D Aug 14 2♐

Pluto

  Jan 1 2♎

R Jan 4 2♎

♍ Apr 17 09:59

D Jun 9 29♍

♎ Jul 30 11:18

1973

Sun

♒ Jan 20 04:48 ♈ Mar 20 18:12 ♊ May 21 04:54 ♌ Jul 22 23:56 ♎ Sep 23 04:21 ♐ Nov 22 10:52

♓ Feb 18 19:01 ♉ Apr 20 05:30 ♋ Jun 21 13:02 ♍ Aug 23 06:52 ♏ Oct 23 13:29 ♑ Dec 22 00:05

Mercury

  Jan 1 24♐   R Jul 6 3♌

♑ Jan 4 14:41   ♋ Jul 16 08:13

♒ Jan 23 15:21   D Jul 30 23♋

♓ Feb 9 19:25   ♌ Aug 11 12:12

R Mar 4 28♓   ♍ Aug 28 15:19

D Mar 27 15♓   ♎ Sep 13 16:14

♈ Apr 16 20:59   ♏ Oct 2 20:14

♉ May 6 02:45   R Oct 30 25♏

♊ May 20 17:22   D Nov 19 10♏

♋ Jun 4 04:24   ♐ Dec 8 21:32

♌ Jun 27 07:08   ♑ Dec 28 15:15

Venus

  Jan 1 16♐   ♌ Jun 30 09:56

♑ Jan 11 19:14   ♍ Jul 25 02:14

♒ Feb 4 18:44   ♎ Aug 19 01:10

♓ Feb 28 18:46   ♏ Sep 13 09:04

♈ Mar 24 20:35   ♐ Oct 9 08:06

♉ Apr 18 01:07   ♑ Nov 5 15:37

♊ May 12 08:44   ♒ Dec 7 21:37

♋ Jun 5 19:22

Mars

  Jan 1 0♐

♑ Feb 12 05:47

♒ Mar 26 21:05

♓ May 8 04:06

♈ Jun 20 21:08

♉ Aug 12 15:09

R Sep 19 8♉

♈ Oct 29 23:09

D Nov 26 25♈

♉ Dec 24 07:28

Jupiter

  Jan 1 17♑

♒ Feb 23 08:52

R May 30 12♒

D Sep 28 2♒

Saturn

  Jan 1 15♊

D Feb 13 13♊

♋ Aug 1 22:19

R Oct 17 4♋

Uranus

  Jan 1 22♎

R Jan 27 23♎

D Jun 26 18♎

Neptune

  Jan 1 6♐

R Mar 9 7♐

D Aug 16 4♐

Pluto

  Jan 1 4♎

R Jan 6 4♎

D Jun 11 1♎

1974

Sun

♒ Jan 20 10:45	♈ Mar 21 00:05	♊ May 21 10:37	♌ Jul 23 05:33	♎ Sep 23 10:01	♐ Nov 22 16:37
♓ Feb 19 00:58	♉ Apr 20 11:19	♋ Jun 21 18:41	♍ Aug 23 12:30	♏ Oct 23 10:11	♑ Dec 22 05:55

Mercury

Jan 1 5 ♑	D Jul 12 5 ♋
♒ Jan 16 03:53	♌ Aug 5 11:42
♓ Feb 2 22:17	♍ Aug 20 09:03
R Feb 15 11 ♓	♎ Sep 6 06:00
♒ Mar 2 17:52	♏ Sep 27 23:46
D Mar 9 27 ♒	R Oct 13 9 ♏
♓ Mar 17 21:05	♎ Oct 26 23:04
♈ Apr 11 15:12	D Nov 3 24 ♎
♉ Apr 28 03:06	♏ Nov 11 15:49
♊ May 12 04:51	♐ Dec 2 06:17
♋ May 29 08:02	♑ Dec 21 09:16
R Jun 17 13 ♋	

Venus

Jan 1 11 ♒	♊ Jun 25 23:43
R Jan 3 11 ♒	♋ Jul 21 04:34
♑ Jan 29 20:11	♌ Aug 14 23:47
D Feb 13 25 ♑	♍ Sep 8 10:29
♒ Feb 28 14:08	♎ Oct 2 14:29
♓ Apr 6 14:09	♏ Oct 26 14:14
♈ May 4 20:19	♐ Nov 19 11:57
♉ May 31 07:20	♑ Dec 13 09:04

Mars

Jan 1 2 ♉
♊ Feb 27 10:13
♋ Apr 20 08:22
♌ Jun 9 01:05
♍ Jul 27 14:07
♎ Sep 12 19:10
♏ Oct 28 07:03
♐ Dec 10 22:26

Jupiter

Jan 1 14 ♒
♓ Mar 8 11:01
R Jul 7 17 ♓
D Nov 3 7 ♓

Saturn

Jan 1 0 ♋
♊ Jan 7 20:11
D Feb 27 27 ♊
♋ Apr 18 22:42
R Oct 31 18 ♋

Uranus

Jan 1 27 ♎
R Feb 1 27 ♎
D Jul 2 23 ♎
♏ Nov 21 10:30

Neptune

Jan 1 8 ♐
R Mar 12 9 ♐
D Aug 19 6 ♐

Pluto

Jan 1 6 ♎
R Jan 9 6 ♎
D Jun 14 4 ♎

1975

Sun

♒ Jan 20 16:34	♈ Mar 21 05:56	♊ May 21 16:25	♌ Jul 23 11:25	♎ Sep 23 16:00	♐ Nov 22 22:33
♓ Feb 19 06:48	♉ Apr 20 17:07	♋ Jun 22 00:28	♍ Aug 23 18:27	♏ Oct 24 01:09	♑ Dec 22 11:47

Mercury

Jan 1 16 ♑	♋ Jul 12 08:55
♒ Jan 8 22:03	♌ Jul 28 08:07
R Jan 30 26 ♒	♍ Aug 12 06:12
D Feb 20 10 ♒	♎ Aug 30 17:14
♓ Mar 16 11:50	R Sep 26 23 ♎
♈ Apr 4 12:26	D Oct 18 8 ♎
♉ Apr 19 17:18	♏ Nov 6 09:01
♊ May 4 11:57	♐ Nov 25 01:48
R May 29 23 ♊	♑ Dec 14 04:07
D Jun 22 15 ♊	

Venus

Jan 1 23 ♑	♍ Jul 9 11:13
♒ Jan 6 06:38	R Aug 6 11 ♍
♓ Jan 30 06:02	♌ Sep 2 15:01
♈ Feb 23 09:52	D Sep 18 25 ♌
♉ Mar 19 21:42	♍ Oct 4 05:37
♊ Apr 13 22:25	♎ Nov 9 13:55
♋ May 9 20:14	♏ Dec 7 00:31
♌ Jun 6 11:00	

Mars

Jan 1 14 ♐
♑ Jan 21 18:45
♒ Mar 3 05:28
♓ Apr 11 19:10
♈ May 21 08:08
♉ Jul 1 04:02
♊ Aug 14 20:40
♋ Oct 17 09:20
R Nov 6 2 ♋
♊ Nov 25 18:31

Jupiter

Jan 1 13 ♓
♈ Mar 18 16:34
R Aug 14 24 ♈
D Dec 10 14 ♈

Saturn

Jan 1 15 ♋
D Mar 14 11 ♋
♌ Sep 17 05:10
R Nov 14 2 ♌

Uranus

Jan 1 1 ♏
R Feb 6 2 ♏
♎ May 1 17:18
D Jul 7 28 ♎
♏ Sep 8 06:24

Neptune

Jan 1 10 ♐
R Mar 14 11 ♐
D Aug 21 9 ♐

Pluto

Jan 1 9 ♎
R Jan 11 9 ♎
D Jun 17 6 ♎

1976

Sun

♒ Jan 20 22:26	♈ Mar 20 11:4/	♊ May 20 22:19	♌ Jul 22 17:18
♓ Feb 19 12:40	♉ Apr 19 22:59	♋ Jun 21 06:22	♍ Aug 23 00:20

♎ Sep 22 21:49	♐ Nov 22 04:22
♏ Oct 23 06:59	♑ Dec 21 17:36

Mercury

Jan 1 27♑	♊ Jun 13 18:52
♒ Jan 2 19:54	♋ Jul 4 14:22
R Jan 14 10♒	♌ Jul 18 19:37
♑ Jan 25 01:14	♍ Aug 3 16:37
D Feb 3 23♑	♎ Aug 25 21:06
♒ Feb 15 19:16	R Sep 8 7♎
♓ Mar 9 12:05	♍ Sep 21 07:10
♈ Mar 26 15:39	D Oct 1 22 ♍
♉ Apr 10 09:29	♎ Oct 10 14:47
♊ Apr 29 23:38	♏ Oct 29 04:53
R May 9 3♊	♐ Nov 16 19:02
♉ May 19 19:05	♑ Dec 6 09:21
D Jun 2 24♉	R Dec 28 24♑

Venus

Jan 1 29♏	♋ Jun 20 13:56
♐ Jan 1 12:18	♌ Jul 14 23:37
♑ Jan 26 06:09	♍ Aug 8 08:37
♒ Feb 19 16:50	♎ Sep 1 17:45
♓ Mar 15 00:59	♏ Sep 26 04:15
♈ Apr 8 08:55	♐ Oct 20 17:19
♉ May 2 17:46	♑ Nov 14 10:38
♊ May 27 03:43	♒ Dec 9 12:51

Mars

Jan 1 17♊	
D Jan 20 14♊	
♌ Mar 18 13:24	
♌ May 16 11:18	
♍ Jul 6 23:30	
♎ Aug 24 05:59	
♏ Oct 8 20:21	
♐ Nov 20 23:55	

Jupiter

Jan 1 15♈
♉ Mar 26 10:40
♊ Aug 23 11:36
R Sep 19 1♊
♉ Oct 16 19:13

Saturn

Jan 1 1♌
♋ Jan 14 12:13
D Mar 27 26♋
♌ Jun 5 06:02
R Nov 27 16♌

Uranus

Jan 1 6♏
R Feb 10 7♏
D Jul 11 3♏

Neptune

Jan 1 12♐
R Mar 15 13♐
D Aug 23 11♐

Pluto

Jan 1 11♎
R Jan 14 11♎
D Jun 18 8♎

1977

Sun

♒ Jan 20 04:14	♈ Mar 20 17:41	♊ May 21 04:12	♌ Jul 22 23:04
♓ Feb 18 18:30	♉ Apr 20 04:55	♋ Jun 21 12:13	♍ Aug 23 06:01

♎ Sep 23 03:31	♐ Nov 22 10:07
♏ Oct 23 12:43	♑ Dec 21 23:23

Mercury

Jan 1 22♑	♍ Jul 28 10:15
D Jan 17 8♑	R Aug 22 20♍
♒ Feb 11 00:03	D Sep 14 7♍
♓ Mar 2 08:12	♎ Oct 4 09:22
♈ Mar 18 11:56	♏ Oct 21 16:22
♉ Apr 3 02:27	♐ Nov 9 17:22
R Apr 20 13♉	♑ Dec 1 06:45
D May 13 4♉	R Dec 12 7♑
♊ Jun 10 21:20	♐ Dec 21 07:15
♋ Jun 26 07:07	D Dec 31 21♐
♌ Jul 10 11:58	

Venus

Jan 1 26♒	♋ Aug 2 19:13
♓ Jan 4 13:04	♌ Aug 28 15:06
♈ Feb 2 05:57	♍ Sep 22 15:05
R Mar 16 24♈	♎ Oct 17 01:38
D Apr 27 8♈	♏ Nov 10 03:52
♉ Jun 6 06:04	♐ Dec 4 01:49
♊ Jul 6 15:04	♑ Dec 27 22:09

Mars

Jan 1 29♐
♑ Jan 1 00:43
♒ Feb 9 12:01
♓ Mar 20 02:24
♈ Apr 27 15:47
♉ Jun 6 03:00
♊ Jul 17 15:05
♋ Sep 1 00:17
♌ Oct 26 18:46
R Dec 12 11♌

Jupiter

Jan 1 21♉
D Jan 15 21♉
♊ Apr 3 15:50
♋ Aug 20 13:39
R Oct 24 6♋
♊ Dec 30 21:52

Saturn

Jan 1 15♌
D Apr 11 9♌
♍ Nov 17 03:59
R Dec 11 0♍

Uranus

Jan 1 10♏
R Feb 14 11♏
D Jul 16 7♏

Neptune

Jan 1 14♐
R Mar 18 16♐
D Aug 25 13♐

Pluto

Jan 1 14♎
R Jan 16 14♎
D Jun 21 11♎

1978

Sun

♒ Jan 20 10:05	♈ Mar 20 23:33	♊ May 21 10:07	♌ Jul 23 04:58	♎ Sep 23 09:27	♐ Nov 22 16:07
♓ Feb 19 00:22	♉ Apr 20 10:49	♋ Jun 21 18:08	♍ Aug 23 11:57	♏ Oct 23 18:41	♑ Dec 22 05:23

Mercury

Jan 1 21 ♐	♍ Jul 27 06:21
♑ Jan 13 20:20	R Aug 4 3 ♍
♒ Feb 4 15:54	♌ Aug 13 07:11
♓ Feb 22 16:11	D Aug 28 20 ♌
♈ Mar 10 12:08	♍ Sep 9 19:27
R Apr 1 25 ♈	♎ Sep 26 16:42
D Apr 25 14 ♈	♏ Oct 14 05:35
♉ May 16 08:19	♐ Nov 3 07:43
♊ Jun 3 15:27	R Nov 25 21 ♐
♋ Jun 17 15:49	D Dec 15 5 ♐
♌ Jul 2 22:30	

Venus

Jan 1 5 ♑	♌ Jun 16 06:21
♒ Jan 20 18:30	♍ Jul 12 02:16
♓ Feb 13 16:07	♎ Aug 8 03:09
♈ Mar 9 16:29	♏ Sep 7 05:07
♉ Apr 2 21:14	R Oct 18 22 ♏
♊ Apr 27 07:52	D Nov 28 7 ♏
♋ May 22 02:04	

Mars

Jan 1 8 ♌	
♋ Jan 26 02:12	
D Mar 2 22 ♋	
♌ Apr 10 19:07	
♍ Jun 14 02:43	
♎ Aug 4 09:03	
♏ Sep 19 20:51	
♐ Nov 2 01:19	
♑ Dec 12 17:33	

Jupiter

Jan 1 29 ♊	
D Feb 20 26 ♊	
♋ Apr 12 01:34	
♌ Sep 5 09:28	
R Nov 25 9 ♌	

Saturn

Jan 1 0 ♍	
♌ Jan 4 22:09	
D Apr 25 23 ♌	
♍ Jul 26 13:15	
R Dec 24 13 ♍	

Uranus

Jan 1 15 ♏	
R Feb 19 16 ♏	
D Jul 21 12 ♏	

Neptune

Jan 1 16 ♐	
R Mar 20 18 ♐	
D Aug 28 15 ♐	

Pluto

Jan 1 16 ♎	
R Jan 19 16 ♎	
D Jun 24 13 ♎	

1979

Sun

♒ Jan 20 16:03	♈ Mar 21 05:23	♊ May 21 15:54	♌ Jul 23 10:49	♎ Sep 23 15:17	♐ Nov 22 21:54
♓ Feb 19 06:16	♉ Apr 20 16:36	♋ Jun 21 23:57	♍ Aug 23 17:46	♏ Oct 24 00:28	♑ Dec 22 11:11

Mercury

Jan 1 19 ♐	♌ Jun 27 10:01
♑ Jan 8 22:45	R Jul 17 15 ♌
♒ Jan 28 12:51	D Aug 11 3 ♌
♓ Feb 14 20:40	♍ Sep 2 21:28
♈ Mar 3 21:24	♎ Sep 18 18:59
R Mar 15 8 ♈	♏ Oct 7 03:58
♓ Mar 28 10:40	♐ Oct 30 07:04
D Apr 7 25 ♓	R Nov 9 6 ♐
♈ Apr 17 12:44	♏ Nov 18 03:05
♉ May 10 22:06	D Nov 29 18 ♏
♊ May 26 07:44	♐ Dec 12 13:35
♋ Jun 9 06:27	

Venus

Jan 1 24 ♏	♋ Jul 6 09:01
♐ Jan 7 06:42	♌ Jul 30 20:07
♑ Feb 5 09:16	♍ Aug 24 03:16
♒ Mar 3 17:18	♎ Sep 17 07:22
♓ Mar 29 03:20	♏ Oct 11 09:47
♈ Apr 23 04:05	♐ Nov 4 11:49
♉ May 18 00:29	♑ Nov 28 14:16
♊ Jun 11 18:13	♒ Dec 22 18:30

Mars

Jan 1 14 ♑	
♒ Jan 20 17:07	
♓ Feb 27 20:29	
♈ Apr 7 01:12	
♉ May 16 04:32	
♊ Jun 26 01:53	
♋ Aug 8 13:28	
♌ Sep 24 21:16	
♍ Nov 19 21:29	

Jupiter

Jan 1 6 ♌	
♋ Feb 28 20:56	
D Mar 26 29 ♋	
♌ Apr 20 10:40	
♍ Sep 29 10:57	
R Dec 26 10 ♍	

Saturn

Jan 1 13 ♍	
D May 9 7 ♍	

Uranus

Jan 1 19 ♏	
R Feb 24 20 ♏	
D Jul 26 16 ♏	

Neptune

Jan 1 18 ♐	
R Mar 23 20 ♐	
D Aug 30 17 ♐	

Pluto

Jan 1 19 ♎	
R Jan 21 19 ♎	
D Jun 27 16 ♎	

1980

Sun

♒ Jan 20 21:49	♈ Mar 20 11:10
♓ Feb 19 12:01	♉ Apr 19 22:23

♊ May 20 21:43	♌ Jul 22 16:43
♋ Jun 21 05:47	♍ Aug 22 23:40

♎ Sep 22 21:09	♐ Nov 22 03.41
♏ Oct 23 06:18	♑ Dec 21 16:55

Mercury

Jan 1 27 ♐	R Jun 28 25 ♋
♑ Jan 2 08:02	D Jul 22 16 ♋
♒ Jan 21 02:18	♌ Aug 9 03:16
♓ Feb 7 08:15	♍ Aug 24 18:45
R Feb 26 21 ♓	♎ Sep 10 02:13
D Mar 19 8 ♓	♏ Sep 30 01:09
♈ Apr 14 15:53	R Oct 23 19 ♏
♉ May 2 10:52	D Nov 12 3 ♏
♊ May 16 17:07	♐ Dec 5 19:47
♋ May 31 22:28	♑ Dec 25 04:46

Venus

Jan 1 11 ♒	D Jul 6 16 ♊
♓ Jan 16 03:34	♋ Aug 6 14:25
♈ Feb 9 23:39	♌ Sep 7 17:54
♉ Mar 6 18:55	♍ Oct 4 23:06
♊ Apr 3 19:50	♎ Oct 30 10:36
♋ May 12 20:56	♏ Nov 24 01:34
R May 24 2 ♋	♐ Dec 18 06:21
♊ Jun 5 05:33	

Mars

Jan 1 13 ♍
R Jan 16 15 ♍
♌ Mar 11 20:36
D Apr 6 25 ♌
♍ May 4 02:52
♎ Jul 10 18:03
♏ Aug 29 05:53
♐ Oct 12 06:29
♑ Nov 22 01:34
♒ Dec 30 22:23

Jupiter

Jan 1 10 ♍
D Apr 26 0 ♍
♎ Oct 27 10:19

Saturn

Jan 1 26 ♍
R Jan 6 27 ♍
D May 22 20 ♍
♎ Sep 21 12:00

Uranus

Jan 1 24 ♏
R Feb 29 25 ♏
D Jul 30 21 ♏

Neptune

Jan 1 20 ♐
R Mar 24 22 ♐
D Aug 31 19 ♐

Pluto

Jan 1 21 ♎
R Jan 24 21 ♎
D Jun 28 18 ♎

1981

Sun

♒ Jan 20 03:36	♈ Mar 20 17:00
♓ Feb 18 17:51	♉ Apr 20 04:15

♊ May 21 03:37	♌ Jul 22 22:36
♋ Jun 21 11:41	♍ Aug 23 05:36

♎ Sep 23 03:03	♐ Nov 22 09:35
♏ Oct 23 12:12	♑ Dec 21 22:50

Mercury

Jan 1 10 ♑	D Jul 3 26 ♊
♒ Jan 12 15:50	♋ Jul 12 21:15
♓ Jan 31 17:18	♌ Aug 1 18:30
R Feb 8 5 ♓	♍ Aug 16 12:47
♒ Feb 16 08:06	♎ Sep 2 22:25
D Mar 2 20 ♒	♏ Sep 27 10:54
♓ Mar 18 04:22	R Oct 6 3 ♏
♈ Apr 8 09:10	♎ Oct 14 01:55
♉ Apr 24 05:31	D Oct 27 17 ♎
♊ May 8 09:38	♏ Nov 9 13:12
♋ May 28 16:58	♐ Nov 28 20:50
R Jun 9 5 ♋	♑ Dec 17 22:21
♊ Jun 22 23:01	

Venus

Jan 1 17 ♐	♌ Jun 29 20:18
♑ Jan 11 06:48	♍ Jul 24 14:04
♒ Feb 4 06:08	♎ Aug 18 13:45
♓ Feb 28 06:01	♏ Sep 12 22:51
♈ Mar 24 07:43	♐ Oct 9 00:03
♉ Apr 17 12:08	♑ Nov 5 12:39
♊ May 11 19:47	♒ Dec 8 20:51
♋ Jun 5 06:29	R Dec 31 8 ♒

Mars

Jan 1 0 ♒
♓ Feb 6 22:45
♈ Mar 17 02:35
♉ Apr 25 07:19
♊ Jun 5 05:25
♋ Jul 18 08:56
♌ Sep 2 01:49
♍ Oct 21 01:45
♎ Dec 16 00:10

Jupiter

Jan 1 9 ♎
R Jan 24 10 ♎
D May 27 0 ♎
♏ Nov 27 02:14

Saturn

Jan 1 9 ♎
R Jan 18 9 ♎
D Jun 5 2 ♎

Uranus

Jan 1 28 ♏
♐ Feb 17 14:22
R Mar 5 0 ♐
♏ Mar 20 18:32
D Aug 4 26 ♏
♐ Nov 16 13:09

Neptune

Jan 1 23 ♐
R Mar 27 24 ♐
D Sep 3 22 ♐

Pluto

Jan 1 24 ♎
R Jan 26 24 ♎
D Jul 1 21 ♎

1982

Sun
♒ Jan 20 09:30　♈ Mar 20 22:54　♊ May 21 09:22　♌ Jul 23 04:13　♎ Sep 23 08:45　♐ Nov 22 15:22
♓ Feb 18 23:45　♉ Apr 20 10:06　♋ Jun 21 17:21　♍ Aug 23 11:15　♏ Oct 23 17:58　♑ Dec 22 04:37

Mercury
Jan 1 22♑
♒ Jan 5 16:47
R Jan 23 19♒
D Feb 13 3♒
♓ Mar 13 19:02
♈ Mar 31 21:03
♉ Apr 15 18:47
♊ May 1 13:33
R May 21 15♊
D Jun 13 6♊
♋ Jul 9 11:24
♌ Jul 24 08:49
♍ Aug 8 14:07
♎ Aug 28 03:30
R Sep 19 17♎
D Oct 11 1♎
♏ Nov 3 01:07
♐ Nov 21 14:27
♑ Dec 10 20:10

Venus
Jan 1 8♒
♑ Jan 23 03:21
D Feb 10 23♑
♒ Mar 2 11:18
♓ Apr 6 12:15
♈ May 4 12:24
♉ May 30 21:01
♊ Jun 25 12:13
♋ Jul 20 16:21
♌ Aug 14 11:09
♍ Sep 7 21:38
♎ Oct 2 01:33
♏ Oct 26 01:20
♐ Nov 18 23:07
♑ Dec 12 20:18

Mars
Jan 1 7♎
R Feb 20 19♎
D May 11 29♍
♏ Aug 3 11:52
♐ Sep 20 01:30
♑ Oct 31 22:55
♒ Dec 10 06:08

Jupiter
Jan 1 6♏
R Feb 24 10♏
D Jun 27 0♏
♐ Dec 26 01:45

Saturn
Jan 1 21♎
R Jan 31 22♎
D Jun 18 15♎
♏ Nov 29 11:34

Uranus
Jan 1 2♐
R Mar 9 4♐
D Aug 9 0♐

Neptune
Jan 1 25♐
R Mar 29 27♐
D Sep 5 24♐

Pluto
Jan 1 26♎
R Jan 29 26♎
D Jul 4 24♎

1983

Sun
♒ Jan 20 15:18　♈ Mar 21 04:37　♊ May 21 15:05　♌ Jul 23 10:04　♎ Sep 23 14:42　♐ Nov 22 21:20
♓ Feb 19 05:31　♉ Apr 20 15:49　♋ Jun 21 23:08　♍ Aug 23 17:07　♏ Oct 23 23:56　♑ Dec 22 10:31

Mercury
Jan 1 29♑
♒ Jan 1 13:12
R Jan 7 3♒
♑ Jan 12 07:04
D Jan 27 16♑
♒ Feb 14 09:30
♓ Mar 7 04:29
♈ Mar 23 20:11
♉ Apr 7 17:00
R May 1 25♉
D May 25 15♉
♊ Jun 14 08:06
♋ Jul 1 19:21
♌ Jul 15 21:03
♍ Aug 1 10:26
♎ Aug 29 04:01
R Sep 2 0♎
♍ Sep 6 02:44
D Sep 24 15♍
♎ Oct 8 23:17
♏ Oct 26 15:47
♐ Nov 14 08:57
♑ Dec 4 11:21
R Dec 22 17♑

Venus
Jan 1 24♑
♒ Jan 5 17:57
♓ Jan 29 17:30
♈ Feb 22 21:34
♉ Mar 19 09:50
♊ Apr 13 11:24
♋ May 9 10:57
♌ Jun 6 06:08
♍ Jul 10 05:22
R Aug 3 9♍
♌ Aug 27 11:44
D Sep 15 23♌
♍ Oct 5 19:37
♎ Nov 9 10:52
♏ Dec 6 16:15

Mars
Jan 1 16♒
♓ Jan 17 13:06
♈ Feb 25 00:12
♉ Apr 5 14:01
♊ May 16 21:42
♋ Jun 29 06:54
♌ Aug 13 16:55
♍ Sep 30 00:10
♎ Nov 18 10:28

Jupiter
Jan 1 1♐
R Mar 27 10♐
D Jul 29 1♐

Saturn
Jan 1 2♏
R Feb 12 4♏
♎ May 6 17:30
D Jul 1 27♎
♏ Aug 24 12:18

Uranus
Jan 1 6♐
R Mar 14 9♐
D Aug 14 5♐

Neptune
Jan 1 27♐
R Apr 1 29♐
D Sep 8 26♐

Pluto
Jan 1 29♎
R Feb 1 29♎
D Jul 7 26♎
♏ Nov 5 21:25

1984

Sun

♒ Jan 20 21:06	♈ Mar 20 10:23	♊ May 20 20:56	♌ Jul 22 15:54	♎ Sep 22 20:30	♐ Nov 22 03:07
♓ Feb 19 11:16	♉ Apr 19 21:36	♋ Jun 21 04:59	♍ Aug 22 22:56	♏ Oct 23 05:42	♑ Dec 21 16:22

Mercury

Jan 1 7♑	♌ Jul 6 19:04
D Jan 11 1♑	♍ Jul 26 06:52
♒ Feb 9 01:48	R Aug 14 13♍
♓ Feb 27 18:03	D Sep 7 0♍
♈ Mar 14 16:23	♎ Sep 30 19:38
♉ Mar 31 20:46	♏ Oct 18 03:07
R Apr 11 6♉	♐ Nov 6 12:06
♈ Apr 25 12:01	♑ Dec 1 15:46
D May 5 26♈	R Dec 4 0♑
♉ May 15 12:40	♐ Dec 7 22:32
♊ Jun 7 15:46	D Dec 24 14♐
♋ Jun 22 06:38	

Venus

Jan 1 29♏	♋ Jun 20 00:49
♐ Jan 1 02:01	♌ Jul 14 10:31
♑ Jan 25 18:50	♍ Aug 7 19:40
♒ Feb 19 04:52	♎ Sep 1 05:07
♓ Mar 14 12:36	♏ Sep 25 16:02
♈ Apr 7 20:13	♐ Oct 20 05:40
♉ May 2 04:52	♑ Nov 13 23:51
♊ May 26 14:39	♒ Dec 9 03:25

Mars

Jan 1 24♎
♏ Jan 11 03:18
R Apr 5 28♏
D Jun 19 11♏
♐ Aug 17 19:54
♑ Oct 5 06:01
♒ Nov 15 18:09
♓ Dec 25 06:39

Jupiter

Jan 1 25♐
♑ Jan 19 15:00
R Apr 29 12♑
D Aug 29 3♑

Saturn

Jan 1 13♏
R Feb 24 16♏
D Jul 13 9♏

Uranus

Jan 1 11♐
R Mar 18 13♐
D Aug 18 9♐

Neptune

Jan 1 29♐
♑ Jan 19 01:33
R Apr 2 1♑
♐ Jun 23 03:12
D Sep 9 28♐
♑ Nov 21 11:27

Pluto

Jan 1 1♏
R Feb 4 2♏
♎ May 18 13:36
D Jul 9 29♎
♏ Aug 28 05:16

1985

Sun

♒ Jan 20 02:58	♈ Mar 20 16:13	♊ May 21 02:42	♌ Jul 22 21:36	♎ Sep 23 02:07	♐ Nov 22 08:49
♓ Feb 18 17:08	♉ Apr 20 03:24	♋ Jun 21 10:44	♍ Aug 23 04:34	♏ Oct 23 11:19	♑ Dec 21 22:06

Mercury

Jan 1 18♐	R Jul 28 25♌
♑ Jan 11 18:31	D Aug 20 13♌
♒ Feb 1 07:47	♍ Sep 6 19:33
♓ Feb 18 23:50	♎ Sep 22 23:16
♈ Mar 7 00:22	♏ Oct 10 18:43
R Mar 24 18♈	♐ Oct 31 16:52
D Apr 17 6♈	R Nov 18 15♐
♉ May 14 02:15	♏ Dec 4 20:08
♊ May 30 19:46	D Dec 8 28♏
♋ Jun 13 16:13	♐ Dec 12 11:17
♌ Jun 29 19:33	

Venus

Jan 1 26♒	♋ Aug 2 09:04
♓ Jan 4 06:27	♌ Aug 28 03:36
♈ Feb 2 08:34	♍ Sep 22 02:52
R Mar 13 22♈	♎ Oct 16 13:04
D Apr 25 6♈	♏ Nov 9 15:08
♉ Jun 6 08:52	♐ Dec 3 13:00
♊ Jul 6 07:58	♑ Dec 27 09:18

Mars

Jan 1 5♓
♈ Feb 2 17:15
♉ Mar 15 05:05
♊ Apr 26 09:07
♋ Jun 9 10:39
♌ Jul 25 04:00
♍ Sep 10 01:27
♎ Oct 27 15:07
♏ Dec 14 18:51

Jupiter

Jan 1 21♑
♒ Feb 6 15:02
R Jun 4 16♒
D Oct 3 7♒

Saturn

Jan 1 24♏
R Mar 7 28♏
D Jul 25 21♏
♐ Nov 17 02:28

Uranus

Jan 1 15♐
R Mar 22 17♐
D Aug 23 13♐

Neptune

Jan 1 1♑
R Apr 5 3♑
D Sep 12 0♑

Pluto

Jan 1 4♏
R Feb 6 4♏
D Jul 12 1♏

1986

Sun

| ♒ Jan 20 08:45 | ♈ Mar 20 22:03 | ♊ May 21 08:28 | ♌ Jul 23 03:23 | ♎ Sep 23 07:59 | ♐ Nov 22 14:44 |
| ♓ Feb 18 22:57 | ♉ Apr 20 09:12 | ♋ Jun 21 16:30 | ♍ Aug 23 10:26 | ♏ Oct 23 17:15 | ♑ Dec 22 04:03 |

Mercury

Jan 1 22 ♐	♌ Jun 26 14:08
♑ Jan 5 20:45	R Jul 9 6 ♌
♒ Jan 25 00:39	♋ Jul 23 21:50
♓ Feb 11 05:22	D Aug 3 26 ♋
♈ Mar 3 07:04	♌ Aug 11 22:05
R Mar 7 1 ♈	♍ Aug 30 03:32
♓ Mar 11 17:15	♎ Sep 15 02:31
D Mar 30 18 ♓	♏ Oct 4 00:19
♈ Apr 17 12:26	R Nov 2 28 ♏
♉ May 7 12:37	D Nov 22 13 ♏
♊ May 22 07:27	♐ Dec 10 00:25
♋ Jun 5 14:10	♑ Dec 29 23:12

Venus

Jan 1 5 ♑	♌ Jun 15 18:52
♒ Jan 20 05:37	♍ Jul 11 16:25
♓ Feb 13 03:10	♎ Aug 7 20:45
♈ Mar 9 03:31	♏ Sep 7 10:10
♉ Apr 2 08:19	R Oct 15 20 ♏
♊ Apr 26 19:09	D Nov 26 4 ♏
♋ May 21 13:46	

Mars

| Jan 1 10 ♏ |
| ♐ Feb 2 06:22 |
| ♑ Mar 28 03:31 |
| R Jun 8 23 ♑ |
| D Aug 12 11 ♑ |
| ♒ Oct 9 00:34 |
| ♓ Nov 26 02:37 |

Jupiter

| Jan 1 18 ♒ |
| ♓ Feb 20 15:28 |
| R Jul 12 22 ♓ |
| D Nov 8 12 ♓ |

Saturn

| Jan 1 5 ♐ |
| R Mar 19 9 ♐ |
| D Aug 7 3 ♐ |

Uranus

| Jan 1 19 ♐ |
| R Mar 27 22 ♐ |
| D Aug 27 18 ♐ |

Neptune

| Jan 1 3 ♑ |
| R Apr 7 5 ♑ |
| D Sep 14 3 ♑ |

Pluto

| Jan 1 6 ♏ |
| R Feb 8 7 ♏ |
| D Jul 15 4 ♏ |

1987

Sun

| ♒ Jan 20 14:41 | ♈ Mar 21 03:53 | ♊ May 21 14:12 | ♌ Jul 23 09:06 | ♎ Sep 23 13:46 | ♐ Nov 22 20:29 |
| ♓ Feb 19 04:52 | ♉ Apr 20 14:59 | ♋ Jun 21 22:11 | ♍ Aug 23 16:09 | ♏ Oct 23 23:00 | ♑ Dec 22 09:45 |

Mercury

Jan 1 3 ♑	D Jul 15 8 ♋
♒ Jan 17 13:08	♌ Aug 6 21:27
♓ Feb 4 03:02	♍ Aug 21 21:38
R Feb 18 14 ♓	♎ Sep 7 13:47
♒ Mar 11 19:27	♏ Sep 28 17:32
♒ Mar 12 20:22	R Oct 16 12 ♏
D Mar 12 0 ♓	♎ Nov 1 02:14
♈ Apr 12 20:12	D Nov 6 27 ♎
♉ Apr 29 15:43	♏ Nov 11 20:52
♊ May 13 17:52	♐ Dec 3 13:32
♋ May 30 04:13	♑ Dec 22 17:39
R Jun 21 16 ♋	

Venus

Jan 1 24 ♏	♋ Jul 5 19:50
♐ Jan 7 10:22	♌ Jul 30 06:48
♑ Feb 5 03:02	♍ Aug 23 13:59
♒ Mar 3 07:55	♎ Sep 16 18:13
♓ Mar 28 16:22	♏ Oct 10 20:49
♈ Apr 22 16:08	♐ Nov 3 23:02
♉ May 17 11:56	♑ Nov 28 01:49
♊ Jun 11 05:15	♒ Dec 22 06:24

Mars

| Jan 1 24 ♓ |
| ♈ Jan 8 12:20 |
| ♉ Feb 20 14:53 |
| ♊ Apr 5 16:44 |
| ♋ May 21 03:07 |
| ♌ Jul 6 16:50 |
| ♍ Aug 22 19:50 |
| ♎ Oct 8 19:26 |
| ♏ Nov 24 03:15 |

Jupiter

| Jan 1 17 ♓ |
| ♈ Mar 2 18:36 |
| R Aug 19 29 ♈ |
| D Dec 15 19 ♈ |

Saturn

| Jan 1 15 ♐ |
| R Mar 31 21 ♐ |
| D Aug 19 14 ♐ |

Uranus

| Jan 1 23 ♐ |
| R Apr 1 26 ♐ |
| D Sep 1 22 ♐ |

Neptune

| Jan 1 5 ♑ |
| R Apr 10 8 ♑ |
| D Sep 17 5 ♑ |

Pluto

| Jan 1 9 ♏ |
| R Feb 11 9 ♏ |
| D Jul 18 7 ♏ |

1988

Sun

♒ Jan 20 20:25	♈ Mar 20 09:40	♊ May 20 19:58	♌ Jul 22 14:53	♎ Sep 22 19:30	♐ Nov 22 02:11
♓ Feb 19 10:36	♉ Apr 19 20:46	♋ Jun 21 03:59	♍ Aug 22 21:55	♏ Oct 23 04:45	♑ Dec 21 15:26

Mercury

Jan 1 14♑	♋ Jul 12 06:22
♒ Jan 10 05:24	♌ Jul 28 21:18
R Feb 2 28♒	♍ Aug 12 17:31
D Feb 23 13♒	♎ Aug 30 20:09
♓ Mar 16 10:09	R Sep 28 26♎
♈ Apr 4 22:03	D Oct 20 11♎
♉ Apr 20 06:45	♏ Nov 6 14:58
♊ May 4 19:52	♐ Nov 25 10:06
R May 31 26♊	♑ Dec 14 11:53
D Jun 24 18♊	

Venus

Jan 1 12♒	D Jul 4 13♊
♓ Jan 15 16:02	♋ Aug 6 23:27
♈ Feb 9 13:06	♌ Sep 7 11:37
♉ Mar 6 10:26	♍ Oct 4 13:13
♊ Apr 3 17:16	♎ Oct 29 23:18
♋ May 17 17:07	♏ Nov 23 13:32
R May 22 0♋	♐ Dec 17 17:55
♊ May 27 06:35	

Mars

Jan 1 24♏
♐ Jan 8 15:20
♑ Feb 22 10:07
♒ Apr 6 21:38
♓ May 22 07:19
♈ Jul 13 19:54
R Aug 26 11♈
♓ Oct 24 03:27
D Oct 28 29♓
♈ Nov 1 08:23

Jupiter

Jan 1 20♈
♉ Mar 8 15:54
♊ Jul 22 00:46
R Sep 24 6♊
♉ Nov 30 19:46

Saturn

Jan 1 25♐
♑ Feb 14 00:05
R Apr 11 2♑
♐ Jun 10 05:11
D Aug 30 25♐
♑ Nov 12 09:32

Uranus

Jan 1 27♐
♑ Feb 15 02:22
R Apr 4 1♑
♐ May 27 00:17
D Sep 5 27♐
♑ Dec 2 16:59

Neptune

Jan 1 7♑
R Apr 11 10♑
D Sep 18 7♑

Pluto

Jan 1 11♏
R Feb 14 12♏
D Jul 20 9♏

1989

Sun

♒ Jan 20 02:07	♈ Mar 20 15:27	♊ May 21 01:52	♌ Jul 22 20:43	♎ Sep 23 01:19	♐ Nov 22 08:04
♓ Feb 18 16:20	♉ Apr 20 02:37	♋ Jun 21 09:52	♍ Aug 23 03:45	♏ Oct 23 10:34	♑ Dec 21 21:22

Mercury

Jan 1 26♑	♊ Jun 12 09:15
♒ Jan 2 19:26	♋ Jul 6 00:42
R Jan 16 12♒	♌ Jul 20 09:03
♑ Jan 29 03:46	♍ Aug 5 01:03
D Feb 5 26♑	♎ Aug 26 06:13
♒ Feb 14 18:36	R Sep 11 10♎
♓ Mar 10 18:00	♍ Sep 26 15:23
♈ Mar 28 03:10	D Oct 3 25♍
♉ Apr 11 21:28	♎ Oct 11 06:24
♊ Apr 29 20:14	♏ Oct 30 13:52
R May 12 7♊	♐ Nov 18 03:10
♉ May 28 23:28	♑ Dec 7 14:34
D Jun 5 27♉	R Dec 30 26♑

Venus

Jan 1 1♐	♌ Jun 29 07:21
♑ Jan 10 18:08	♍ Jul 24 01:31
♒ Feb 3 17:16	♎ Aug 18 01:57
♓ Feb 27 17:00	♏ Sep 12 12:22
♈ Mar 23 18:32	♐ Oct 8 15:57
♉ Apr 16 22:53	♑ Nov 5 10:08
♊ May 11 06:30	♒ Dec 10 04:50
♋ Jun 4 17:18	R Dec 29 6♒

Mars

Jan 1 20♈
♉ Jan 19 07:54
♊ Mar 11 08:47
♋ Apr 29 04:43
♌ Jun 16 14:15
♍ Aug 3 13:40
♎ Sep 19 14:42
♏ Nov 4 05:31
♐ Dec 18 05:01

Jupiter

Jan 1 20♉
D Jan 20 26♉
♊ Mar 11 04:34
♋ Jul 31 00:27
R Oct 29 10♋

Saturn

Jan 1 5♑
R Apr 22 13♑
D Sep 11 7♑

Uranus

Jan 1 1♑
R Apr 9 5♑
D Sep 10 1♑

Neptune

Jan 1 9♑
R Apr 13 12♑
D Sep 21 9♑

Pluto

Jan 1 14♏
R Feb 16 15♏
D Jul 23 12♏

1990

Sun

♒ Jan 20 08:01   ♈ Mar 20 21:21   ♊ May 21 07:40   ♌ Jul 23 02:23   ♎ Sep 23 06:58   ♐ Nov 22 13:47
♓ Feb 18 22:14   ♉ Apr 20 08:29   ♋ Jun 21 15:36   ♍ Aug 23 09:22   ♏ Oct 23 16:15   ♑ Dec 22 03:06

Mercury

Jan 1 26♑	♌ Jul 12 00:01		
D Jan 20 10♑	♍ Jul 29 11:15		
♒ Feb 12 01:07	R Aug 25 22♍		
♓ Mar 3 17:11	D Sep 17 9♍		
♈ Mar 20 00:08	♎ Oct 5 17:35		
♉ Apr 4 07:30	♏ Oct 23 01:51		
R Apr 23 16♉	♐ Nov 11 00:00		
D May 17 7♉	♑ Dec 2 00:09		
♊ Jun 12 00:09	R Dec 14 9♑		
♋ Jun 27 20:47	♐ Dec 25 23:07		

Venus

Jan 1 6♒	♋ Jul 20 03:41
♑ Jan 16 15:42	♌ Aug 13 22:05
D Feb 8 20♑	♍ Sep 7 08:20
♒ Mar 3 17:50	♎ Oct 1 12:14
♓ Apr 6 09:10	♏ Oct 25 12:03
♈ May 4 03:53	♐ Nov 18 09:58
♉ May 30 10:15	♑ Dec 12 07:16
♊ Jun 25 00:15	

Mars

Jan 1 9♐
♑ Jan 29 14:14
♒ Mar 11 16:00
♓ Apr 20 22:13
♈ May 31 07:17
♉ Jul 12 14:53
♊ Aug 31 11:10
R Oct 20 14♊
♉ Dec 14 08:40

Jupiter

Jan 1 5♋
D Feb 24 0♋
♌ Aug 18 07:35
R Nov 30 13♌

Saturn

Jan 1 15♑
R May 4 25♑
D Sep 23 18♑

Uranus

Jan 1 5♑
R Apr 13 9♑
D Sep 14 5♑

Neptune

Jan 1 12♑
R Apr 16 14♑
D Sep 23 11♑

Pluto

Jan 1 17♏
R Feb 19 17♏
D Jul 26 14♏

1991

Sun

♒ Jan 20 13:47   ♈ Mar 21 03:01   ♊ May 21 13:23   ♌ Jul 23 08:15   ♎ Sep 23 12:51   ♐ Nov 22 19:37
♓ Feb 19 03:58   ♉ Apr 20 14:10   ♋ Jun 21 21:22   ♍ Aug 23 15:17   ♏ Oct 23 22:07   ♑ Dec 22 08:55

Mercury

Jan 1 24♐	♌ Jul 4 06:04
D Jan 3 24♐	♍ Jul 26 13:04
♑ Jan 14 07:59	R Aug 7 5♍
♒ Feb 5 22:20	♌ Aug 19 21:49
♓ Feb 24 02:33	D Aug 31 23♌
♈ Mar 11 22:29	♍ Sep 10 17:21
R Apr 4 28♈	♎ Sep 28 03:27
D Apr 28 17♈	♏ Oct 15 14:00
♉ May 16 22:17	♐ Nov 4 10:35
♊ Jun 5 02:10	R Nov 28 24♐
♋ Jun 19 05:39	D Dec 18 7♐

Venus

Jan 1 24♑	♍ Jul 11 05:19
♒ Jan 5 05:01	R Aug 1 7♍
♓ Jan 29 04:43	♌ Aug 21 14:49
♈ Feb 22 09:01	D Sep 13 20♌
♉ Mar 18 21:45	♍ Oct 6 21:21
♊ Apr 13 00:10	♎ Nov 9 06:40
♋ May 9 01:32	♏ Dec 6 07:24
♌ Jun 6 01:27	

Mars

Jan 1 27♉
D Jan 1 27♉
♊ Jan 21 01:22
♋ Apr 3 00:58
♌ May 26 12:31
♍ Jul 15 12:44
♎ Sep 1 06:47
♏ Oct 16 19:08
♐ Nov 29 02:24

Jupiter

Jan 1 11♌
D Mar 30 3♌
♍ Sep 12 06:16
R Dec 30 14♍

Saturn

Jan 1 25♑
♒ Feb 6 18:45
R May 17 6♒
D Oct 5 0♒

Uranus

Jan 1 9♑
R Apr 18 13♑
D Sep 19 9♑

Neptune

Jan 1 14♑
R Apr 19 16♑
D Sep 26 13♑

Pluto

Jan 1 19♏
R Feb 22 20♏
D Jul 28 17♏

1992

Sun

♒ Jan 20 19:32	♈ Mar 20 08:46	♊ May 20 19:11	♌ Jul 22 14:11	♎ Sep 22 18:45	♐ Nov 22 01:26
♓ Feb 19 09:43	♉ Apr 19 19:54	♋ Jun 21 03:15	♍ Aug 22 21:12	♏ Oct 23 03:58	♑ Dec 21 14:42

Mercury

Jan 1 18 ♐	♌ Jun 27 05:22
♑ Jan 10 01:37	R Jul 20 18 ♌
♒ Jan 29 21:12	D Aug 13 5 ♌
♓ Feb 16 07:03	♍ Sep 3 08:09
♈ Mar 3 21:34	♎ Sep 19 05:40
R Mar 17 11 ♈	♏ Oct 7 10:15
♓ Apr 4 01:53	♐ Oct 29 17:15
D Apr 9 28 ♓	R Nov 11 8 ♐
♈ Apr 14 17:44	♏ Nov 21 19:43
♉ May 11 04:09	D Dec 1 21 ♏
♊ May 26 21:19	♐ Dec 12 08:10
♋ Jun 9 18:34	

Venus

Jan 1 0 ♐	♌ Jul 13 21:08
♑ Jan 25 07:13	♍ Aug 7 06:27
♒ Feb 18 16:39	♎ Aug 31 16:09
♓ Mar 13 23:57	♏ Sep 25 03:30
♈ Apr 7 07:15	♐ Oct 19 17:43
♉ May 1 15:41	♑ Nov 13 12:45
♊ May 26 01:19	♒ Dec 8 17:47
♋ Jun 19 11:24	

Mars

Jan 1 23 ♐	♉ Jun 14 16:11
♑ Jan 9 09:48	♊ Jul 26 19:12
♒ Feb 18 04:42	♋ Sep 12 06:20
♓ Mar 28 02:06	R Nov 28 27 ♋
♈ May 5 21:45	

Jupiter

Jan 1   14 ♍
D Apr 30 4 ♍
♎ Oct 10 13:36

Saturn

Jan 1   5 ♒
R May 28 18 ♒
D Oct 16 11 ♒

Uranus

Jan 1   13 ♑
R Apr 21 18 ♑
D Sep 22 14 ♑

Neptune

Jan 1   16 ♑
R Apr 20 18 ♑
D Sep 27 16 ♑

Pluto

Jan 1   22 ♏
R Feb 24 22 ♏
D Jul 30 20 ♏

1993

Sun

♒ Jan 20 01:23	♈ Mar 20 14:39	♊ May 21 01:01	♌ Jul 22 19:52	♎ Sep 23 00:25	♐ Nov 22 07:07
♓ Feb 18 15:35	♉ Apr 20 01:47	♋ Jun 21 09:00	♍ Aug 23 02:53	♏ Oct 23 09:39	♑ Dec 21 20:25

Mercury

Jan 1 27 ♐	R Jul 1 28 ♋
♑ Jan 2 14:47	D Jul 25 19 ♋
♒ Jan 21 11:25	♌ Aug 10 05:38
♓ Feb 7 16:13	♍ Aug 26 07:08
R Feb 27 24 ♓	♎ Sep 11 11:20
D Mar 22 11 ♓	♏ Oct 1 02:06
♈ Apr 15 15:08	R Oct 25 21 ♏
♉ May 3 22:03	D Nov 15 6 ♏
♊ May 18 06:53	♐ Dec 7 00:55
♋ Jun 2 03:38	♑ Dec 26 12:46

Venus

Jan 1 26 ♒	♋ Aug 1 22:34
♓ Jan 3 23:55	♌ Aug 27 15:46
♈ Feb 2 12:37	♍ Sep 21 14:22
R Mar 11 20 ♈	♎ Oct 16 00:15
D Apr 22 3 ♈	♏ Nov 9 02:08
♉ Jun 6 10:01	♐ Dec 2 23:54
♊ Jul 6 00:19	♑ Dec 26 20:10

Mars

Jan 1 20 ♋	♍ Jun 23 07:40
D Feb 15 8 ♋	♎ Aug 12 01:10
♌ Apr 27 23:49	♏ Sep 27 02:13
♍ Jun 23 07:40	♐ Nov 9 05:29
	♑ Dec 20 00:31

Jupiter

Jan 1   13 ♎
R Jan 28 14 ♎
D Jun 1   4 ♎
♏ Nov 10 08:09

Saturn

Jan 1   16 ♒
♓ May 21 02:02
R Jun 10 0 ♓
♒ Jun 30 12:24
D Oct 28 23 ♒

Uranus

Jan 1   17 ♑
R Apr 26 22 ♑
D Sep 27 18 ♑

Neptune

Jan 1   18 ♑
R Apr 22 21 ♑
D Sep 30 18 ♑

Pluto

Jan 1   24 ♏
R Feb 26 25 ♏
D Aug 2 22 ♏

1994

Sun

♒ Jan 20 07:07	♈ Mar 20 20:27	♊ May 21 06:46	♌ Jul 23 01:40	♎ Sep 23 06:22	♐ Nov 22 13:08
♓ Feb 18 21:22	♉ Apr 20 07:33	♋ Jun 21 14:45	♍ Aug 23 08:44	♏ Oct 23 15:40	♑ Dec 22 02:25

Mercury

Jan 1 8♑	D Jul 6 29♊
♒ Jan 14 00:17	♋ Jul 10 12:16
♓ Feb 1 10:27	♌ Aug 3 06:10
R Feb 11 7♓	♍ Aug 18 00:40
♒ Feb 21 15:22	♎ Sep 4 05:05
D Mar 5 23♒	♏ Sep 27 08:49
♓ Mar 18 11:58	R Oct 9 5♏
♈ Apr 9 16:27	♎ Oct 19 06:16
♉ Apr 25 18:26	D Oct 30 20♎
♊ May 9 21:16	♏ Nov 10 12:41
♋ May 28 14:52	♐ Nov 30 04:40
R Jun 12 8♋	♑ Dec 19 06:26
♊ Jul 3 01:33	

Venus

Jan 1 6♑	♌ Jun 15 07:25
♒ Jan 19 16:29	♍ Jul 11 06:35
♓ Feb 12 14:04	♎ Aug 7 14:37
♈ Mar 8 14:27	♏ Sep 7 17:11
♉ Apr 1 19:20	R Oct 13 18♏
♊ Apr 26 06:23	D Nov 23 2♏
♋ May 21 01:27	

Mars

Jan 1 9♑	
♒ Jan 28 04:04	
♓ Mar 7 11:00	
♈ Apr 14 18:02	
♉ May 23 22:43	
♊ Jul 3 22:30	
♋ Aug 16 19:25	
♌ Oct 4 16:06	
♍ Dec 12 11:38	

Jupiter

Jan 1 9♏	
R Feb 28 14♏	
D Jul 2 4♏	
♐ Dec 9 10:32	

Saturn

Jan 1 27♒
♓ Jan 28 23:19
R Jun 23 12♓
D Nov 9 5♓

Uranus

Jan 1 21♑
R Apr 30 26♑
D Oct 2 22♑

Neptune

Jan 1 20♑
R Apr 25 23♑
D Oct 2 20♑

Pluto

Jan 1 27♏
R Mar 1 28♏
D Aug 5 25♏

1995

Sun

♒ Jan 20 13:04	♈ Mar 21 02:16	♊ May 21 12:35	♌ Jul 23 07:28	♎ Sep 23 12:14	♐ Nov 22 19:02
♓ Feb 19 03:14	♉ Apr 20 13:23	♋ Jun 21 20:34	♍ Aug 23 14:34	♏ Oct 23 21:32	♑ Dec 22 08:17

Mercury

Jan 1 20♑	♋ Jul 10 17:01
♒ Jan 6 22:19	♌ Jul 25 22:17
R Jan 26 21♒	♍ Aug 10 00:10
D Feb 16 6♒	♎ Aug 29 02:14
♓ Mar 14 21:28	R Sep 22 19♎
♈ Apr 2 07:28	D Oct 14 4♎
♉ Apr 17 07:56	♏ Nov 4 08:51
♊ May 2 15:35	♐ Nov 22 22:44
R May 24 18♊	♑ Dec 12 02:53
D Jun 17 9♊	

Venus

Jan 1 23♏	♋ Jul 5 06:39
♐ Jan 7 12:10	♌ Jul 29 17:32
♑ Feb 4 20:15	♍ Aug 23 00:44
♒ Mar 2 22:13	♎ Sep 16 05:01
♓ Mar 28 05:13	♏ Oct 10 07:49
♈ Apr 22 04:08	♐ Nov 3 10:17
♉ May 16 23:21	♑ Nov 27 13:22
♊ Jun 10 16:17	♒ Dec 21 18:20

Mars

Jan 1 2♍	
R Jan 2 2♍	
♌ Jan 23 00:36	
D Mar 24 13♌	
♍ May 25 16:16	
♎ Jul 21 09:21	
♏ Sep 7 06:54	
♐ Oct 20 21:03	
♑ Nov 30 13:52	

Jupiter

Jan 1 4♐	
R Apr 1 15♐	
D Aug 2 5♐	

Saturn

Jan 1 7♓
R Jul 6 24♓
D Nov 21 17♓

Uranus

Jan 1 25♑
♒ Apr 1 14:23
R May 5 0♒
♑ Jun 9 00:26
D Oct 6 26♑

Neptune

Jan 1 22♑
R Apr 27 25♑
D Oct 5 22♑

Pluto

Jan 1 29♏
♐ Jan 17 12:28
R Mar 4 0♐
♏ Apr 21 00:14
D Aug 8 27♏
♐ Nov 10 21:18

1996

Sun

♒ Jan 20 18:53	♈ Mar 20 08:04	♊ May 20 18:23	♌ Jul 22 13:17	♎ Sep 22 18:00	♐ Nov 22 00:47
♓ Feb 19 09:01	♉ Apr 19 19:10	♋ Jun 21 02:23	♍ Aug 22 20:21	♏ Oct 23 03:18	♑ Dec 21 14:05

Mercury

Jan 1 29♑
♒ Jan 1 17:49
R Jan 9 6♒
♑ Jan 17 09:37
D Jan 30 19♑
♒ Feb 15 02:29
♓ Mar 7 11:55
♈ Mar 24 08:01
♉ Apr 8 03:17
R May 3 28♉
D May 27 18♉
♊ Jun 13 21:31
♋ Jul 2 07:32
♌ Jul 16 09:54
♍ Aug 1 16:16
♎ Aug 26 04:37
R Sep 4 3♎
♍ Sep 12 09:30
D Sep 26 18♍
♎ Oct 9 03:31
♏ Oct 27 00:59
♐ Nov 14 16:36
♑ Dec 4 13:52
R Dec 23 20♑

Venus

Jan 1 12♒
♓ Jan 15 04:29
♈ Feb 9 02:33
♉ Mar 6 02:05
♊ Apr 3 15:30
R May 20 28♊
D Jul 2 11♊
♋ Aug 7 06:13
♌ Sep 7 05:04
♍ Oct 4 03:20
♎ Oct 29 12:00
♏ Nov 23 01:33
♐ Dec 17 05:34

Mars

Jan 1 24♑
♒ Jan 8 10:59
♓ Feb 15 11:49
♈ Mar 24 15:08
♉ May 2 18:15
♊ Jun 12 14:37
♋ Jul 25 18:34
♌ Sep 9 20:07
♍ Oct 30 07:04

Jupiter

Jan 1 29♐
♑ Jan 3 06:38
R May 4 17♑
D Sep 3 7♑

Saturn

Jan 1 19♓
♈ Apr 7 08:18
R Jul 18 7♈
D Dec 3 0♈

Uranus

Jan 1 29♑
♒ Jan 12 08:29
R May 8 4♒
D Oct 10 0♒

Neptune

Jan 1 24♑
R Apr 29 27♑
D Oct 6 24♑

Pluto

Jan 1 1♐
R Mar 5 3♐
D Aug 10 0♐

1997

Sun

♒ Jan 20 00:42	♈ Mar 20 13:53	♊ May 21 00:17	♌ Jul 22 19:12	♎ Sep 22 23:54	♐ Nov 22 06:45
♓ Feb 18 14:51	♉ Apr 20 01:02	♋ Jun 21 08:17	♍ Aug 23 02:15	♏ Oct 23 09:13	♑ Dec 21 20:06

Mercury

Jan 1 13♑
D Jan 12 3♑
♒ Feb 9 05:52
♓ Feb 28 03:55
♈ Mar 16 04:21
♉ Apr 1 13:48
R Apr 15 8♉
♈ May 5 02:58
D May 8 29♈
♉ May 12 10:29
♊ Jun 8 23:45
♋ Jun 23 20:40
♌ Jul 8 05:19
♍ Jul 27 01:09
R Aug 17 15♍
D Sep 10 3♍
♎ Oct 2 05:41
♏ Oct 19 12:08
♐ Nov 7 17:44
♑ Nov 30 18:32
R Dec 7 3♑
♐ Dec 13 18:15
D Dec 27 17♐

Venus

Jan 1 18♐
♑ Jan 10 05:33
♒ Feb 3 04:29
♓ Feb 27 04:02
♈ Mar 23 05:27
♉ Apr 16 09:44
♊ May 10 17:21
♋ Jun 4 04:17
♌ Jun 28 18:38
♍ Jul 23 13:16
♎ Aug 17 14:32
♏ Sep 12 02:15
♐ Oct 8 08:20
♑ Nov 5 08:43
♒ Dec 12 04:31
R Dec 26 3♒

Mars

Jan 1 29♍
♎ Jan 3 08:07
R Feb 6 5♎
♍ Mar 8 19:52
D Apr 27 16♍
♎ Jun 19 08:53
♏ Aug 14 08:38
♐ Sep 28 22:19
♑ Nov 9 05:24
♒ Dec 18 06:31

Jupiter

Jan 1 25♑
♒ Jan 21 14:27
R Jun 10 21♒
D Oct 8 12♒

Saturn

Jan 1 1♈
R Aug 1 20♈
D Dec 16 13♈

Uranus

Jan 1 3♒
R May 13 8♒
D Oct 14 4♒

Neptune

Jan 1 26♑
R May 1 29♑
D Oct 9 27♑

Pluto

Jan 1 4♐
R Mar 8 5♐
D Aug 13 2♐

1998

Sun

♒ Jan 20 06:45   ♈ Mar 20 19:53   ♊ May 21 06:06   ♌ Jul 23 00:55   ♎ Sep 23 05:37   ♐ Nov 22 12:34

♓ Feb 18 20:55   ♉ Apr 20 06:57   ♋ Jun 21 14:04   ♍ Aug 23 07:58   ♏ Oct 23 14:59   ♑ Dec 22 01:54

Mercury

Jan 1 19 ♐
♑ Jan 12 16:30
♒ Feb 2 15:14
♓ Feb 20 10:22
♈ Mar 8 08:32
R Mar 27 21 ♈
D Apr 20 9 ♈
♉ May 15 02:24
♊ Jun 1 08:06
♋ Jun 15 05:29
♌ Jun 30 23:53
R Jul 31 28 ♌
D Aug 23 16 ♌
♍ Sep 8 02:04
♎ Sep 24 10:11
♏ Oct 12 02:53
♐ Nov 1 16:11
R Nov 21 17 ♐
D Dec 11 1 ♐

Venus

Jan 1 3 ♒
♑ Jan 9 21:23
D Feb 5 18 ♑
♒ Mar 4 16:06
♓ Apr 6 05:34
♈ May 3 19:16
♉ May 29 23:34
♊ Jun 24 12:27
♋ Jul 19 15:17
♌ Aug 13 09:19
♍ Sep 6 19:24
♎ Sep 30 23:15
♏ Oct 24 23:08
♐ Nov 17 21:06
♑ Dec 11 18:32

Mars

Jan 1 10 ♒
♓ Jan 25 09:26
♈ Mar 4 16:17
♉ Apr 13 01:07
♊ May 24 03:41
♋ Jul 6 09:00
♌ Aug 20 19:13
♍ Oct 7 12:25
♎ Nov 27 10:19

Jupiter

Jan 1 22 ♒
♓ Feb 4 10:35
R Jul 18 28 ♓
D Nov 13 18 ♓

Saturn

Jan 1 13 ♈
♉ Jun 9 05:19
R Aug 15 3 ♉
♈ Oct 25 20:19
D Dec 29 26 ♈

Uranus

Jan 1 7 ♒
R May 17 12 ♒
D Oct 18 8 ♒

Neptune

Jan 1 28 ♑
♒ Jan 29 00:51
R May 4 2 ♒
♑ Aug 23 04:14
D Oct 11 29 ♑

Pluto

Jan 1 6 ♐
R Mar 11 8 ♐
D Aug 16 5 ♐

1999

Sun

♒ Jan 20 12:37   ♈ Mar 21 01:44   ♊ May 21 11:53   ♌ Jul 23 06:45   ♎ Sep 23 11:34   ♐ Nov 22 18:25

♓ Feb 19 02:45   ♉ Apr 20 12:45   ♋ Jun 21 19:50   ♍ Aug 23 13:52   ♏ Oct 23 20:54   ♑ Dec 22 07:45

Mercury

Jan 1 21 ♐
♑ Jan 7 01:57
♒ Jan 26 09:31
♓ Feb 12 15:26
♈ Mar 2 22:58
R Mar 10 4 ♈
♓ Mar 18 09:29
D Apr 2 20 ♓
♈ Apr 17 21:51
♉ May 8 21:28
♊ May 23 21:22
♋ Jun 6 23:59
♌ Jun 26 15:26
R Jul 12 10 ♌
♋ Jul 31 19:16
D Aug 6 28 ♋
♌ Aug 11 02:40
♍ Aug 31 15:09
♎ Sep 16 12:53
♏ Oct 5 05:15
♐ Oct 30 20:04
R Nov 5 1 ♐
♏ Nov 9 20:41
D Nov 25 14 ♏
♐ Dec 11 02:04

Venus

Jan 1 25 ♑
♒ Jan 4 16:24
♓ Jan 28 16:14
♈ Feb 21 20:47
♉ Mar 18 09:59
♊ Apr 12 13:16
♋ May 8 16:32
♌ Jun 5 21:34
♍ Jul 12 15:14
R Jul 30 5 ♍
♌ Aug 15 14:20
D Sep 11 18 ♌
♍ Oct 7 16:52
♎ Nov 9 02:20
♏ Dec 5 22:44

Mars

Jan 1 18 ♎
♏ Jan 26 12:01
R Mar 18 12 ♏
♎ May 5 21:25
D Jun 4 23 ♎
♏ Jul 5 04:02
♐ Sep 2 19:34
♑ Oct 17 01:34
♒ Nov 26 06:49

Jupiter

Jan 1 21 ♓
♈ Feb 13 01:10
♉ Jun 28 09:39
R Aug 25 4 ♉
♈ Oct 23 05:41
D Dec 20 25 ♈

Saturn

Jan 1 26 ♈
♉ Mar 1 00:09
R Aug 30 17 ♉

Uranus

Jan 1 10 ♒
R May 21 16 ♒
D Oct 23 12 ♒

Neptune

Jan 1 1 ♒
R May 7 4 ♒
D Oct 14 1 ♒

Pluto

Jan 1 9 ♐
R Mar 13 10 ♐
D Aug 19 7 ♐

Astrological Software and Chart Services

ASTROLOGICAL SOFTWARE

Time Cycles Research, 27 Dimmock Road, Waterford, CT 06385
   Voice: (860) 444-6641
   Fax: (203) 442-0625
   1-800-827-2240

CHART SERVICES

Note: The chart services listed below provide a natal chart for $5.00. Send check or money order along with your birth information—Name, Date of Birth, Time of Birth, and Place of Birth (city and state or city and country if outside USA). If you do not have a time of birth, request either a midnight, noon, or sunrise chart.

- Paisley Charts, 26 Four Mile River Road, Old Lyme, CT 06371
- KNS Chart Services, 1315 St. Joseph's Ct., Crownsville, MD 21032
- Llewellyn Chart Services, P.O. Box 64383, St. Paul, MN 55164-0383

Birth Data Sources

Theodore Bundy

Birth data of November 24, 1946, at 10:35 PM EST, is credited to T. Patrick Davis from the birth certificate. The same data appeared in *Mercury Hour*, credited to astrologer Dorothy Hughes.

Grace Kelly

The Circle Book of Charts compiled by Stephen Erlewine #1123 states birth data as November 12, 1929, 5:31 AM EST; Philadelphia, Pennsylvania, from *Astrology Magazine* article by H. Paquette: "from birth certificate."

Mata Hari

T. Patrick Davis quotes birth data from Douglas Lannark of Copenhagen for 12:34 PM.

Theodore Roosevelt

William DeGregorio's book, *The Complete Book of U. S. Presidents*, states on p. 376 that Roosevelt was born on October 27, 1858, at 7:45 PM, at the family brownstone on East 20th Street, New York City. The same data is given on p. 29 in Nathan Miller's book, *Theodore Roosevelt: A Life*.

Bibliography

Bishop, Joseph Bucklin, ed. *Theodore Roosevelt's Letters to His Children.* New York: Charles Scribner's Sons, 1919.

Edwards, Anne. *The Grimaldis of Monaco: The Centuries of Scandal—The Years of Grace.* New York: William Morrow and Company, Inc., 1992.

Lacey, Robert. *Grace.* New York: G.P. Putnam's Sons, 1994.

Michaud, Steven G. and Aynesworth, Hugh. *Ted Bundy: Conversations With a Killer.* New York: Penguin Books, 1989.

Michaud, Steven G. and Aynesworth, Hugh. *The Only Living Witness.* New York: Simon and Schuster, 1984.

Miller, Nathan. *The Roosevelt Chronicles: The Story of a Great American Family.* Garden City, New York: Doubleday and Company, Inc., 1979.

_____. *Theodore Roosevelt: A Life.* New York: William Morrow and Company, Inc., 1992.

Morris, Edmund. *The Rise of Theodore Roosevelt.* New York: G.P. Putnam's Sons, 1979.

Ostrovsky, Erika. *Eye of Dawn: The Rise and Fall of Mata Hari.* New York: Dorset Press, 1978.

Quine, Judith Balaban. *The Bridesmaids.* New York: Grove/Atlantic, Inc., 1989.

Rule, Ann. *The Stranger Beside Me.* New York: W. W. Norton & Co., 1989.

Spada, James. Grace: *The Secret Lives of a Princess*. New York: Doubleday Publishing, 1987.

Wheelwright, Julie. *The Fatal Lover: Mata Hari and the Myth of Women in Espionage*. London: Collins & Brown Ltd., 1992.

ASTROLOGY BOOKS

Adams, Evangeline. *Astrology For Everyone: What It is and How It Works*. New York: Dell Publishing Company, Inc., 1972.

_____. *Astrology: Your Place Among the Stars*. New York: Dell Publishing Company, Inc., 1972.

Escobar, Thyrza. *Essentials of Natal Interpretation: Parts One and Two with Study Guide*. Hollywood, California: Golden Seal Research Headquarters, 1972.

George, Llewellyn. *A to Z Horoscope Maker and Delineator*. St. Paul, Minnesota: Llewellyn Publications, 1973.

Gettings, Fred. *The Arkana Dictionary of Astrology*. London: Arkana, 1990.

McCaffery, Ellen. *Graphic Astrology: The Astrological Home Study Course*. Richmond, Virginia: Macoy Publishing Company, 1952.

Michelsen, Neil F. *The American Ephemeris for the 20th Century 1900 to 2000 at Midnight*. San Diego, California: ACS Publications, Inc., 1988.

_____. *The American Ephemeris for the 21st Century 2000 to 2050 at Midnight*. San Diego, California: ACS Publications, Inc., 1990.

Sakoian, Frances and Acker, Louis S. *The Astrologer's Handbook*. New York: Harper and Row Publishers, Inc., 1973.

Shanks, Thomas G. *The American Atlas: US Latitudes and Longitudes, Time Changes and Time Zones*. San Diego, California: ACS Publications, Inc., 1978.

_____. *The International Atlas: World Latitudes, Longitudes and Time Changes*, San Diego, California: ACS Publications, Inc., 1985.

Skalka, Julia Lupton. *The Instant Horoscope Reader*. St. Paul, Minnesota: Llewellyn Publications, 1995.

BOOKS THAT CONTAIN CHARTS OF FAMOUS PEOPLE

Erlewine, Stephen. *The Circle Book of Charts*. Tempe, Arizona: American Federation of Astrologers, 1980.

Penfield, Marc. *An Astrological Who's Who*. York Harbor, Maine: Arkane Publications, 1962.

Rodden, Lois. *The American Book of Charts*. San Diego California: Astro Computing Services, 1980.

_____. *Astro-Data III*. Tempe, Arizona: American Federation of Astrologers, 1986.

_____. *Astro-Data IV*. Tempe, Arizona: American Federation of Astrologers, 1990.

_____. *Astro-Data V*. Tempe, Arizona: American Federation of Astrologers, 1991.

_____. *Profiles of Women*. Tempe, Arizona: American Federation of Astrologers, 1979.

Endnotes

1. Ann Rule, *The Stranger Beside Me*. (New York: Signet, 1989), 469.

2. Steven G. Michaud and Hugh Aynesworth, *Ted Bundy: Conversations with a Killer*,(New York: NAL, 1989), 12–13.

3. Ibid., 13–14.

4. Ibid., 15.

5. Ibid., 14.

6. Ibid., 24.

7. Rule, *The Stranger Beside Me*, 28.

8. Steven G. Michaud and Hugh Aynesworth, *The Only Living Witness*. (New York: NAL, 1986), 64.

9. Rule, *The Stranger Beside Me*, 19.

10. Ibid., 19.

11. Michaud and Aynesworth, *The Only Living Witness*, 65.

12. Ann Rule, *The Stranger Beside Me*, 34.

13. Ibid., 39.

14. Michaud and Aynesworth, *The Only Living Witness*, 350.

15. Michaud and Aynesworth, *Ted Bundy: Conversations with a Killer*, 149–150.

16. Ibid., 22–23.

17. Michaud and Aynesworth, *The Only Living Witness*, 119.

18. Michaud and Aynesworth, *The Only Living Witness*, 113.

19. Judith Balabine Quine, *The Bridesmaids*. (New York: Weidenfeld & Nicholson, 1989), 337.

20. Robert Lacey, *Grace*. (New York: G. P. Putnam's Sons, 1994), 40.

21. Ibid., 44.

22. James Spada, *Grace: The Secret Lives of a Princess*. (New York: Dell Publishing, 1987), 21.

23. Lacey, *Grace*, 106.

24. Ibid., 149.

25. Ibid., 133.

26. Ibid., 200.

27. Spada, *Grace: The Secret Lives of a Princess*, 117.

28. Lacey, *Grace*, 210.

29. Ibid., 319.

30. Quine, *The Bridesmaids*, 347.

31. Ibid., 339.

32. Spada, *Grace: The Secret Lives of a Princess*, 285.

33. Lacey, *Grace*, 345–346.

34. Quine, *The Bridesmaids*, 444.

35. Spada, *Grace: The Secret Lives of a Princess*, 306.

36. Lacey, *Grace*, 339.

37. Ibid., 341.

38. Spada, *Grace: The Secret Lives of a Princess*, 324–325.

39. Lacey, *Grace*, 341.

40. Ibid., 344.

41. Ibid., 347.

42. Ibid., 363.

43. Quine, *The Bridesmaids*, 450.

44. Erika Ostrovsky, *Eye of Dawn: The Rise and Fall of Mata Hari*. (New York: Dorset Press, 1978), 14–16.

45. Ibid., 24.

46. Ibid., 26.

47. Ibid., 27.

48. Ibid.

49. Ibid., 29.

50. Ibid., 30.

51. Ibid., 34.

52. Julie Wheelwright, *The Fatal Lover: Mata Hari and the Myth of Women in Espionage.* (London: Collins & Brown Ltd., 1992), 12.

53. Ibid., 9.

54. Ibid., 10.

55. Ibid., 11.

56. Ibid.

57. Ibid., 12.

58. Ostrovsky, *Eye of Dawn: The Rise and Fall of Mata Hari*, 66.

59. Ibid., 67.

60. Wheelwright, *The Fatal Lover: Mata Hari and the Myth of Women in Espionage*, 14.

61. Ostrovsky, *Eye of Dawn: The Rise and Fall of Mata Hari*, 69–70.

62. Ibid., 70.

63. Ibid., 73.

64. Wheelwright, *The Fatal Lover: Mata Hari and the Myth of Women in Espionage*, 28.

65. Ostrovsky, *Eye of Dawn: The Rise and Fall of Mata Hari*, 78.

66. Ibid., 101.

67. Ibid., 106.

68. Wheelwright, *The Fatal Lover: Mata Hari and the Myth of Women in Espionage*, 51.

69. Ibid., 55.

70. Ibid., 59.

71. Ibid., 61.

72. Ibid., 66.

73. Ibid., 67.

74. Ibid., 84.

75. Edmund Morris, *The Rise of Theodore Roosevelt.* (New York, Ballantine Books, 1979), 95.

76. Ibid., 142.

77. Ibid., 143.

78. Ibid., 162.

79. Ibid.

80. Ibid., 154.

81. Ibid., 184.

82. Ibid., 199–200.

83. Ibid., 230.

84. Ibid., 230–231.

85. Ibid., 257.

86. Ibid., 319.

87. Ibid., 339.

88. Ibid., 338.

89. Ibid., 372.

90. Ibid., 374.

91. Ibid., 392.

92. Ibid., 392–393.

93. Nathan Miller, *Theodore Roosevelt: A Life.* (New York: William Morrow and Company, Inc., 1992), 205.

94. Morris, *The Rise of Theodore Roosevelt,* 472.

95. Ibid.

96. Ibid., 474.

97. Miller, *Theodore Roosevelt: A Life,* 226.

98. Ibid., 228.

99. Ibid., 229.

100. Miller, *Theodore Roosevelt: A Life*, 230.

101. Ibid., 232–233.

102. Ibid., 251–252.

103. Ibid., 252.

104. Morris, *The Rise of Theodore Roosevelt*, 589–590.

105. Miller, *Theodore Roosevelt: A Life*, 265.

106., Morris, *The Rise of Theodore Roosevelt*, 602.

107. Ibid.

108. Ibid.

109. Ibid., 604.

110. Ibid., 615.

111. Miller, *Theodore Roosevelt: A Life*, 309.

112. Ibid., 322.

113. Morris, *The Rise of Theodore Roosevelt*, 732.

114. Miller, *Theodore Roosevelt: A Life*, 354.

115. Ibid.

116. Ibid., 382.

117. Ibid., 385.

118. Ibid., 399.

118. Ibid., 471–472.

Permissions

Grateful acknowledgment is made to the following for permission to reprint extensive material from copyrighted works:

From *The Stranger Beside Me*, © 1980 by Ann Rule. Published by W. W. Norton & Company, Inc. Reprinted by permission of the publisher.

From *Ted Bundy: Conversations with a Killer*, © 1989 by Stephen G. Michaud and Hugh Aynesworth. Published by Penguin Books. Reprinted by permission of the publisher.

From *The Only Living Witness*, © 1983 by Stephen G. Michaud and Hugh Aynesworth. Published by Simon and Schuster. Reprinted by permission of the publisher.

From *Grace: The Secret Lives of a Princess*, © 1987 by James Spada. Published by Doubleday. Reprinted by permission of the publisher.

From *Grace*, © 1994 by Robert Lacey. Published by G. P. Putnam's Sons. Reprinted by permission of the publisher.

From *The Bridesmaids*, © 1989 by Judith B. Quine. Published by Grove/Atlantic, Inc. Reprinted by permission of the publisher.

From *Eye of Dawn: The Rise and Fall of Mata Hari*, © 1989 by Erika Ostrovsky. Published by Dorset Press. Reprinted by permission of the author.

From *The Rise of Theodore Roosevelt*, © 1979 by Edmund Morris. Published by G. P. Putnam's Sons. Reprinted by permission of the publisher.

☾ LOOK FOR THE CRESCENT MOON

Llewellyn publishes hundreds of books on your favorite subjects! To get these exciting books, including the ones on the following pages, check your local bookstore or order them directly from Llewellyn.

ORDER BY PHONE

- Call toll-free within the U.S. and Canada, 1-800-THE MOON
- In Minnesota, call (612) 291-1970
- We accept VISA, MasterCard, and American Express

ORDER BY MAIL

- Send the full price of your order (MN residents add 7% sales tax) in U.S. funds, plus postage & handling to:

  Llewellyn Worldwide
  P.O. Box 64383, Dept. (K668-8)
  St. Paul, MN 55164–0383, U.S.A.

POSTAGE & HANDLING

(For the U.S., Canada, and Mexico)

- $4.00 for orders $15.00 and under
- $5.00 for orders over $15.00
- No charge for orders over $100.00

We ship UPS in the continental United States. We ship standard mail to P.O. boxes. Orders shipped to Alaska, Hawaii, The Virgin Islands, and Puerto Rico are sent first-class mail. Orders shipped to Canada and Mexico are sent surface mail.

International orders: Airmail—add freight equal to price of each book to the total price of order, plus $5.00 for each non-book item (audio tapes, etc.)

Surface mail—Add $1.00 per item.

Allow 4–6 weeks for delivery on all orders.
Postage and handling rates subject to change.

DISCOUNTS

We offer a 20% discount to group leaders or agents. You must order a minimum of 5 copies of the same book to get our special quantity price.

FREE CATALOG

Get a free copy of our color catalog, *New Worlds of Mind and Spirit*. Subscribe for just $10.00 in the United States and Canada ($30.00 overseas, airmail). Many bookstores carry *New Worlds*—ask for it!

Visit our web site at www.llewellyn.com for more information.

THE INSTANT HOROSCOPE READER
PLANETS BY SIGN, HOUSE AND ASPECT
Julia Lupton Skalka

Find out what was written in the planets at your birth! Almost everyone enjoys reading the popular Sun sign horoscopes in newspapers and magazines; however, there is much more to astrology than knowing what your Sun sign is. How do you interpret your natal chart so that you know what it means to have Gemini on your 8th house cusp? What does astrology say about someone whose Sun is conjoined with natal Jupiter?

The Instant Horoscope Reader was written to answer such questions and to give beginners a fresh, thorough overview of the natal chart. Here you will find the meaning of the placement of the Sun, the Moon and each planet in the horoscope, including aspects between the natal planets, the meaning of the houses in the horoscope and house rulerships. Even if you have not had your chart cast, this book includes simple tables that enable you to locate the approximate planetary and house placements and figure the planetary aspects for your birthdate to give you unique perspectives about yourself and others.

1-56718-669-6, 6 x 9, 272 pp., illus. $14.95

ASTROLOGY FOR WOMEN
ROLES & RELATIONSHIPS
Gloria Star, editor

Despite the far-reaching alterations women have experienced collectively, individual women are still faced with the challenge of becoming themselves. In today's world, a woman's role is not defined so much by society's expectations as by the woman herself. This book is a first look at some of the tasks each woman must embrace or overcome. Ten female astrologers explore the many facets of the soulful process of becoming a whole person:

- Jan Spiller—The Total Woman
- Demetra George—Women's Evolving Needs: The Moon and the Blood Mysteries
- M. Kelley Hunter—The Mother-Daughter Bond
- Carol Garlick—Daughter's and Fathers: The Father's Role in the Development of the Whole Woman
- Barbara Schermer—Psyche's Task: A Path of Initiation for Women
- Gloria G. Star—Creating Healthy Relationships
- Madalyn Hillis-Dineen—On Singleness: Choosing to Be Me
- Ronnie Gale Dreyer—The Impact of Self-Esteem
- Kim Rogers-Gallagher—Who Should I Be When I Grow Up?
- Roxana Muise—The Sacred Sisterhood

1-56718-860-5, 5³⁄₁₆ x 8, 416 pp., charts, softcover $9.95

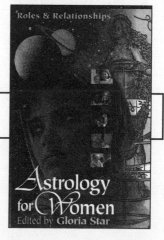

To order call 1-800-THE MOON
Prices subject to change without notice.

THE BOOK OF LOVERS
MEN WHO EXCITE WOMEN, WOMEN WHO EXCITE MEN
Carolyn Reynolds

What are you looking for in a lover or potential mate? If it's money, set your sights on a Pisces/ Taurus. Is exercise and health food your passion? Then a Virgo/Cancer will share it with you.
Where do you find these people? They're all here, in *The Book of Lovers*. Astrologer Carolyn Reynolds introduces a new and accurate way to determine romantic compatibility through the use of Sun and Moon sign combinations. And best of all, you don't have to know a single thing about astrology to use this book!
Here you will find descriptions of every man and woman born between the years 1900 and 2000. To see whether that certain someone could be "the one," simply locate his or her birthdata in the chart and flip to the relevant pages to read about your person's strengths and weaknesses, sex appeal, personality and most importantly, how they will treat you!

0-87542-289-0, 464 pp., 6 x 9, softcover $14.95

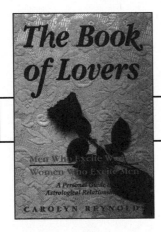

WHEN WILL YOU MARRY?
FIND YOUR SOULMATE THROUGH ASTROLOGY
Rose Murray

Never before has an astrology book so thoroughly focused on timing as a definitive factor in successful marriage relationships. Written in language the beginner can easily follow, When Will You Marry? will engage even the most advanced student of astrology in search of the perfect mate. *When Will You Marry?* guides you through the process of identifying what you need in a marriage partner and the most favorable times to meet that partner based on transits to the natal chart. *When Will You Marry?* then provides clear instruction on comparing your chart with that of a potential mate. This premier match-making method is laid out chapter-by-chapter, with instruction progressing from the basics—like the natal chart and compatible signs—to fine tuning with Sun-Moon midpoints, chart linkups and Arabian parts. By the time the you reach the book's latter parts, you will be able to confirm with great exactness whether or not a particular person is "the one!"

1-56718-479-0, 6 x 9, 240 pp., softbound $12.95

TWELVE FACES OF SATURN
YOUR GUARDIAN ANGEL PLANET
Bil Tierney

Astrological Saturn. It's usually associated with personal limitations, material obstacles, psychological roadblocks and restriction. We observe Saturn's symbolism in our natal chart with uneasiness and anxiety, while intellectually proclaiming its higher purpose as our "wise teacher."

But now it's time to throw out the portrait of the creepy-looking, scythe-wielding Saturn of centuries ago. Bil Tierney offers a refreshing new picture of a this planet as friend, not foe. Saturn is actually key to liberating us from a life handicapped by lack of clear self definition. It is indispensable to psychological maturity and material stability—it is your guardian angel planet.

Explore Saturn from the perspective of your natal sign and house. Uncover another layer of Saturnian themes at work in Saturn's aspects. Look at Saturn through each element and modality, as well as through astronomy, mythology and metaphysics.

1-56718-711-0, 6 x 9, 360 pp. $16.95

MEET YOUR PLANETS
FUN WITH ASTROLOGY
Roy Alexander

Astrology doesn't have to be mind boggling. Now there is a playful way to master this ancient art! In this book, the planets are transformed into an unforgettable lot of characters with very distinctive personalities and idiosyncrasies. Maybe you're the Temple Dancer, a temptress oozing with exotic flair... the Tennis Champion, with his win-at-all-costs attitude ... or maybe the Math Teacher, an unrelenting stickler for proof and accuracy. Furthermore, the twelve signs of the zodiac are turned into 9-to-5 jobs; if a planet doesn't like its job, it will complain, procrastinate, throw a temper tantrum—typical human behavior. Now you can relate to the planets as people you know, work and play with. Finally, astrology doesn't take itself so seriously! You'll be amazed at how easy and fun learning the art of astrology is ... seriously!

1-56718-017-5, 224 pp., 6 x 9, 142 illus., softcover $12.95

To order call 1-800-THE MOON
Prices subject to change without notice.

LLEWELLYN'S ASTROLOGICAL ANNUALS

Llewellyn's MOON SIGN BOOK and Gardening Almanac. Approximately 450 pages of valuable information on gardening, fishing, weather, stock market forecasts, personal horoscopes, good planting dates, and general instructions for finding the best date to do just about anything! Articles by prominent forecasters and writers in the fields of gardening, astrology, economics and cycles. This special almanac, different from any other, has been published annually since 1906. It's fun, informative and has been a great help to millions in their daily planning. 5¼ x 8 format. **$6.95**

Llewellyn's SUN SIGN BOOK: Horoscopes for Everyone! Your personal horoscope for the entire year! All 12 signs are included in one handy book. Also included are forecasts, special feature articles, and an action guide for each sign. Monthly horoscopes are written by Gloria Star, author of Optimum Child, for your personal sun sign and there are articles on a variety of subjects written by well-known astrologers from around the country. Much more than just a horoscope guide! Entertaining and fun the year around. 5¼ x 8 format. **$6.95**

DAILY PLANETARY GUIDE: Llewellyn's Astrology Datebook. Includes all of the major daily aspects plus their exact times in Eastern and Pacific time zones, lunar phases, signs and voids plus their times, planetary motion, a monthly ephemeris, sunrise and sunset tables, special articles on the planets, signs, aspects, planetary hours, rulerships, and much more. Large 5¼ x 8 format for more writing space, spiral bound to lie flat, address and phone listings, time-zone conversion chart and blank horoscope chart. **$9.95**

Llewellyn's Astrological Pocket Planner: Daily Ephemeris & Aspectarian. Designed to slide easily into a purse or briefcase, this planner is jam-packed with those dates and planetary information astrologers need when forecasting future events. Comes with a regular calendar section, a smaller section for projecting dates into the year ahead, a 3-year ephemeris, a listing of planetary aspects, a planetary associations chart, a time-zone chart and retrograde table. 4¼ x 6 format. **$7.95**

Llewellyn's ASTROLOGICAL CALENDAR with Horoscopes for Everyone. Large wall calendar of 48 pages is our top seller. Beautiful full-color paintings. Includes special feature articles by famous astrologers, and complete introductory information on astrology. It also contains a lunar gardening guide, celestial phenomena, a blank horoscope chart, and monthly date pages which include aspects, Moon phases, signs and voids, planetary motion, an ephemeris, personal forecasts, lucky dates, planting and fishing dates, and more. 10 x 13 size. Set in Eastern time, with conversion table for other time zones worldwide. **$12.00**

To order call 1-800-THE MOON
Prices subject to change without notice.